ECONOMICS HANDBOOK SERIES

SEYMOUR E. HARRIS, Editor

National Income Behavior

An Introduction to Algebraic Analysis

ECONOMICS HANDBOOK SERIES

SEYMOUR E. HARRIS, Editor

ADVISORY COMMITTEE: Edward H. Chamberlin, Gottfried Haberler, Alvin H. Hansen, Edward S. Mason, and John H. Williams. *All of Harvard University.*

Hansen · MONETARY THEORY AND FISCAL POLICY
Hoover · THE LOCATION OF ECONOMIC ACTIVITY
Schelling · NATIONAL INCOME BEHAVIOR
Sweezy · SOCIALISM
Wright · CAPITALISM

National Income Behavior

Behavior

An Introduction
to Algebraic Analysis

By

Thomas C. Schelling

Economic Analyst, ECA

FIRST EDITION

New York   Toronto   London
McGRAW-HILL BOOK COMPANY, INC.
1951

NATIONAL INCOME BEHAVIOR

PREFACE

This book has two purposes. One is to develop the algebra of national-income analysis in a manner not requiring of the reader a previous acquaintance with mathematics; the other is to cover, in the development of the analysis, the basic analytical problems in the theory of national-income behavior.

As far as the algebra is concerned the book is intended to be self-contained. The attempt has been to begin at the beginning and omit no steps in the development. But some knowledge of economics—sufficient to permit the reader to judge the plausibility of hypotheses and the importance of problems—is assumed. Emphasis has been related to analytical complexity rather than to economic importance. No empirical justification of hypotheses has been presented, nor is the problem of empirical verification discussed.

If the book has a theme it is that a wide range of theoretical problems in the field of national-income behavior can be analyzed efficiently by the use of some fairly simple mathematics, and that these mathematics provide an orderly technique that permits us to set out the data of a problem unambiguously and deduce their implications in a straightforward fashion.

A large part of the analysis that appears in this book is to be found in the economic literature of the past decade; another large part is, though unpublished, fairly common property among economists. Acknowledgment is generally not given in the text since in most cases only a long history would serve; references have been confined to articles in which the reader may find an extension or alternative formulation of the analysis. Special acknowledgment is due, however, to the work of Professors Paul Samuelson and Lloyd Metzler.

The author has been particularly helped by his association with Professors Arthur Smithies, Wassily Leontief, James Duesenberry, James Tobin, and William Capron, and Mr. Sidney Alexander. The most valuable help was received from Corinne S. Schelling, who contributed continual hard work toward keeping the style readable and the analysis free of error.

Thomas C. Schelling

Washington, D. C.
December, 1950

v

CONTENTS

EDITOR'S INTRODUCTION

For years many teachers of economics and other professional economists have felt the need of a series of books on economic subjects which is not filled by the usual textbook, nor by the highly technical treatise.

This present series, published under the general title, *The Economics Handbook Series*, was planned with these needs in mind. Designed first of all for students, the volumes are useful in the ever-growing field of adult education, and also are of interest to the informed general reader.

The volumes are not long—they give the essentials of the subject matter within the limits of a few hundred pages; they present a distillate of accepted theory and practice, without the detailed approach of the technical treatise. Each volume is a unit, standing on its own.

The authors are scholars, each writing on an economic subject of which he is an authority. In this series the author's first task was not to make important contributions to knowledge—although many of them do—but so to present his subject matter that his work as a scholar will carry its maximum influence outside as well as inside the classroom. The time has come to redress the balance between the energies spent on the creation of new ideas and on their dissemination. Economic ideas are unproductive if they do not spread beyond the world of scholars. Popularizers without technical competence, unqualified textbook writers, and sometimes even charlatans control too large a part of the market for economic ideas.

In the classroom the texts in *The Economics Handbook Series* will serve, it is hoped, as brief surveys in one-semester courses, as supplementary reading in introductory courses, and in other courses in which the subject is related.

In this volume, Mr. Schelling analyzes national income and the related problems of business cycles and fiscal policy. He uses highly effective but relatively simple mathematical techniques; the student requires no previous mathematical training to understand them. Covering the entire range of topics on national income, the author discusses wage-price and other distributive problems, international-income problems, and dynamic problems of investment and inventory behavior. The book serves both as an introductory text in mathematical method and as an analytical survey of national-income behavior. The nature of the economic system as a set of interacting relationships is stressed throughout, and national-income behavior is presented as the resultant of these interacting tendencies.

This is a unique volume in that it develops, in complete fashion, the algebra required for reading the modern literature in the field of national-income behavior.

In the sense that all the required mathematics is developed herein, this is an elementary text. The book, however, is advanced in analytical content; elementary problems are treated in complete fashion, but gradually and effectively the analytical method is extended to cover the most advanced problem. The analytical method is unified throughout, with the result that the reader is gradually and painlessly led from the simple to the complex. In short, Mr. Schelling has written a book in the currently popular field of aggregative or income economics, which will contribute greatly to the clarification of modern economics for students—both beginners and advanced. As far as the editor knows, there is no other volume like it.

Thomas Schelling is a graduate of the University of California (with honors) and has studied and taught at Harvard where he was elected Junior Fellow of the Society of Fellows. He has been an economist with the Bureau of the Budget and with the ECA Mission to Denmark. At present (November, 1950), he is an economist with the Office of the Special Representative in Europe, ECA.

The current volume is the fruit of Schelling's determined efforts to clarify income analysis for his students at Harvard. It is hoped that the publication of this volume will serve a similar purpose for students and teachers of economics everywhere.

SEYMOUR E. HARRIS

PART I

PART I

CHAPTER 1

THE NATIONAL INCOME

The national income has three interpretations. It represents a receipts total, it represents an expenditure total, and it represents a total value of production. This threefold interpretation arises out of the fact that every expenditure is at the same time a receipt; and, if the goods or services bought are valued at their sales prices, we have the threefold identity that the value received equals the value paid equals the value of the goods or services given in exchange.

Defining the national income is a process of enumerating the things which will be added up. We might begin by defining the national income in terms of certain kinds of receipts; we could then match each included receipt against its corresponding expenditure to obtain an expenditure counterpart to the receipts total. Or we could begin by defining an expenditure total and then match it with the sum composed of the corresponding receipts. Or, finally, we could define a production total in terms of the market value of the goods and services produced and sold, and match this total against the corresponding outlays for its purchase and receipts from its sale.

While it is clear that to each sum of receipts there corresponds a matching payments total, it is less obvious that the counterpart to an interesting receipts sum will itself be a significant payments total. The receipts of all red-headed people can be traced to the corresponding set of payments; but there may be no distinguishing characteristic of the payments sum. (It is not, of course, the expenditures of red-headed people that exactly correspond to their receipts; their expenditures may be related to their receipts but are not necessarily identical with them. The matching expenditure sum is composed of payments *to* the red-headed people; this sum is identical with their receipts.) But when we define the national income in terms of the current incomes of all the members of the economy, we do find that the expenditure counterpart, and also the production counterpart, are significant. In fact, if we were to define independently the most plausible value sum to serve as "total production," we should find it to be the production counterpart to the receipts sum which seems best to measure "total incomes." And when we trace out the expenditure counterpart to this same income or production total we find it to be interesting in its own right. It is because there are three significant interpretations of the same total that we use the term "national income" in a generic sense to refer to the national sum of all current incomes, the national total value of current production, or a national expenditure total.

3

It also explains why the term "national product"—descriptively oriented toward the production aspect of the total—is frequently used synonymously with "national income."

We have yet, however, to define the national income; to this we proceed immediately. From what has been said, it is apparent that we have a choice whether to begin by defining a receipts total, an expenditure total, or a production-value total. We shall elect the receipts approach, and define the national income in terms of receipts. Having defined it, we shall observe to what production total the income total corresponds, and deduce the equivalent expenditure total.

In defining such a concept as national income, it is often useful to begin, not by defining it "realistically," but by defining it as it would be if the economic system were less complicated than it actually is. This technique helps to bring out certain salient aspects of the concept; subsequent refinements can be added readily once the general nature of the concept has been made clear. Accordingly we shall begin by discussing an economy in which (a) the government plays no economic role, purchasing nothing, collecting no revenues, carrying on no production of any sort; (b) there is no production of machinery, equipment, plant, or tools of any sort; and, (c), everything that is produced is sold, there is no accumulation of raw materials or finished or semifinished goods within the firms. And we shall take all production as occurring within "firms"; any individual engaged in handicraft or professional fields will be considered to constitute a firm.

We define an individual's "income" as his earnings from the productive process, be they wages, salary, profits, interest, rents, royalties, or any other current claim on the receipts of a firm. And we define the "national income" as the sum of all the incomes of all the persons in the economy.

We shall assume that "wages" and other nonprofit incomes have clear meanings, and proceed only to define "profits" as a residual category. The profits of any firm are defined as the difference between sales receipts and total expenses, such expenses including all wages and other nonprofit incomes paid out as well as payments to other firms for goods and services. If we let S stand for the sales of the firm, W for the wages it pays, O for other income payments (interest, royalties, etc.), and E for expenses to other firms for goods and services, we have profits, P, defined by the equation

(1) $$P = S - W - O - E$$

The total of incomes earned in any given firm is the sum of P, W, and O, which may be written as

(2) $$P + W + O = (S - W - O - E) + W + O$$
$$= S - E$$

Equation (2) simply states that the difference between sales receipts and payments to other firms constitutes the incomes earned in the firm.

It should be noted that profits, wages, sales, etc., are values, not physical quantities, *i.e.*, they are measured in money terms. It must also be noted that each of them can be measured only over a period of time. And the interpretation of equation (2) is that the total of incomes deriving from a given firm during any given period of time is identical in money value with the difference between total sales and total payments to other firms, both measured in value terms, and both measured over that same period of time.

We next perform a summation, adding up all the profits, wages, and other incomes earned throughout the economy. For this purpose we introduce the symbol Σ to indicate summation. (Σ, the Greek letter "sigma," corresponds to S, the initial letter of "sum.") We shall, for example, write ΣP to denote the sum of all the profits earned in all the firms, and ΣS to stand for the sum of all the sales of all firms, etc. Since, for each firm, $P + W + O = S - E$, the sum of $P + W + O$ for all firms equals the sum of all $S - E$, so that we have

$$(3) \qquad \Sigma P + \Sigma W + \Sigma O = \Sigma S - \Sigma E$$

The left-hand side of this equation is now, by definition, the national income, and we shall denote it by the letter Y;

$$(4) \qquad Y = \Sigma S - \Sigma E$$

The next is the crucial step. We divide total sales into two parts: those to consumers, denoted by ΣS_c, and those by one firm to another firm, denoted by ΣS_o. Since all sales are either to consumers or to other firms, $\Sigma S_c + \Sigma S_o = \Sigma S$, and we may split ΣS in equation (4) into its two parts:

$$(5) \qquad Y = \Sigma S_c + \Sigma S_o - \Sigma E$$

Here we can effect a cancellation. ΣS_o is the sum of all receipts of one firm *from* another; ΣE is the sum of all payments of one firm *to* another. They are obviously identical in amount, since they refer to the same transactions. So, striking out $\Sigma S_o - \Sigma E$, whose value is necessarily zero,* we arrive at our final equation,

$$(6) \qquad Y = \Sigma S_c$$

or, letting C stand for total consumer expenditures,

$$(7) \qquad Y = C$$

---

* It is important to note that for a given firm Sc is not equal to So except by coincidence; it is only for the aggregate of all firms taken together that purchases by firms from firms are identical in value with sales by firms to firms.

Here is the expenditure, or production, interpretation of the national income in our simplified economy. National income, the sum of all income receipts throughout the economy, is equal to the total consumption expenditure. Furthermore, we can immediately see the correspondence between the income side and the production side of the economy: in an economy where the end result of all production is sale to consumers, where there is no nonconsumption use of goods other than further fabrication for eventual sale to consumers, where there is no accumulation of stocks, and where there are no incomes earned in government, the total output of consumer goods is indeed a plausible measure of productive activity, and its total value may be taken as the "value of national production."

At this stage we add a complication to our model economy. While not yet introducing the economic activity of government, we shall make allowance for (a) accumulation of stocks of goods, i.e., inventory, and (b) the production and using up of capital goods, i.e., of plant, equipment, tools, etc.

Again we begin by defining profits. It may seem strange to single out profits as the one income category which requires definition. The reason for taking profits as our point of departure is partly that, when account is taken of inventory accumulation and depreciation of plant and equipment, profits are the most difficult income component to identify; they are one income component that requires an accounting statement for its evaluation.* (This is particularly true when we recognize "virtual receipts," i.e., income accrued as distinct from income paid.) But principally the reason for beginning with a residual definition of profits is that such a definition leads us directly to an identity between an exhaustive total of incomes and an important total of sales, i.e., of expenditures.

We need some new symbols at this stage, for we have some new accounting categories. Total sales will be divided three ways: into S_c, sales to consumers; S_k, sales of capital goods (plant, equipment); and S_o, other sales from one firm to another. Expenditures to other firms will be divided into E_k, expenses for capital equipment, and E_o, all other expenses for goods and services. The wear and tear on plant and equipment occurring within the firm during the accounting period will be denoted by D, for "depreciation." And the accumulation of stocks of raw materials and

---

* They are the only income category that requires an accounting statement for the analytical purposes of this book. In other contexts almost any income category may be sufficiently complicated to require careful accounting in its definition. How to compute net rental income on a depreciating house, how to allow in wage income for social insurance premiums or taxes or for business expenses, etc., are questions which require careful analytical answers if analysis is to be refined, since the questionable items may influence expenditure behavior.

finished or semifinished goods within the firm will be denoted by i, for "inventory." This latter item, i, is to be considered a "net" value item within the firm; it is the sum of all increases in stocks minus the sum of all decreases, in the event that some stocks are increased while stocks of other materials are drawn down. If a firm purchases, or hires to be produced, more of some material than it uses during the accounting period, the stock of that material rises during the period; and, vice versa, if it uses up more than it purchases the stock is diminished. If it sells less than its whole final output, its inventory of finished goods rises; if it sells more that inventory falls.

We now define the profits of a firm as

$$(8) \qquad P = S - W - O - E_o - D + i$$

The explanation of this definition is as follows: The profit position of a firm, under circumstances of investment, depreciation, and inventory change, is not adequately given by its cash position. The net receipts available to the firm would be given by the difference between sales, S, and the money outlays, $(W + O + E_k + E_o)$, of the firm. But if some of the outlays were for purchase of machinery or buildings, and at the end of the period the firm has more machinery and greater plant than at the beginning of the period, some allowance must be made for this increase in the "value of the enterprise," $i.e.$, in the assets of the firm. If a firm foresees profits during the year, it may spend an amount equal to anticipated profits on new equipment during the year. Its outlays then equal its receipts; yet the profits are there, ploughed back into the firm. Similarly with an increase in inventories: if outlays were high because the firm stocked up on raw materials, the profits calculation must recognize this fact and include the additional inventory accumulated during the period as part of the profits. Or if the firm stocks up on finished goods by producing more than it sells, its receipts may appear low compared with outlays; but the firm has only been investing its profits in inventory of finished goods.

Accordingly we do not charge as a current cost during the period the entire outlay on equipment; instead we consider as cost the depreciation of equipment actually incurred. If such equipment outlays, E_k, are just equal to the wear and tear on equipment, then D equals E_k and there has occurred no new investment in plant and equipment. If E_k is greater than D, then profits are greater by this difference, $E_k - D$, than if all of E_k were charged as cost; and this difference is exactly the amount by which the value of the fixed assets of the enterprise have expanded. Conversely, if the firm spends less on new equipment than is sufficient to make good the depreciation, then E_k understates the costs; $D - E_k$ is the "disinvestment" in equipment during the period. Thus the correct "cost" of equipment during the period is the depreciation D. It should be noted that the term $-D$ in equation (8) is the equivalent of an alternative formulation, $-E_k + (E_k - D)$ where the E_k terms cancel out leaving only $-D$. The latter expression, $-E_k + (E_k - D)$, would take E_k as a cost and then "adjust" by adding into profits the net increase $E_k - D$ in the value of fixed assets over the period.

It should be noted that the change in inventory, i, may be either positive or negative. If inventories have fallen, outlays are deceptively low compared with receipts; either money outlays were kept down by drawing down stocks of materials, or sales were augmented by selling out of stocks. Either way, the true profit position can be seen only by considering the decline in the tangible value of the enterprise. Thus profits must reflect the change in inventories, which may be either positive or negative.

With the profits definition thus explained, we can proceed to add up total incomes. We begin with the single firm; the total of incomes earned in connection with the production of a single firm, as obtained from equation (8), is given by

$$(9) \qquad\qquad P + W + O = S - E_o - \dot{D} + i$$

and for the economy as a whole we have

$$(10) \qquad Y = \Sigma P + \Sigma W + \Sigma O = \Sigma S - \Sigma E_o - \Sigma D + \Sigma i$$

where Σi is positive or negative depending on whether the increases in inventory do or do not outweigh the decreases, for all firms taken together.

In order to effect a cancellation, we split total sales into the three parts mentioned above, S_c, S_k, and S_o.

$$(11) \qquad\qquad Y = \Sigma S_c + \Sigma S_k + \Sigma S_o - \Sigma E_o - \Sigma D + \Sigma i$$

Here again ΣS_o and ΣE_o are by definition equal to each other, since the interfirm sales included under ΣS_o are the same as those included as costs to purchasing firms under ΣE_o. So these two terms cancel out, and we have

$$(12) \qquad\qquad Y = \Sigma S_c + \Sigma S_k - \Sigma D + \Sigma i$$

The total net increase in the physical assets of firms we shall call the current net investment, denoted by the letter I. This net increase in assets is the sum of the net increase in fixed assets, $\Sigma S_k - \Sigma D$, and the net increase in inventories. We use the term "net" to indicate, in the one case, that the outlays on new plant and equipment, ΣS_k, are offset by the depreciation of plant and equipment, ΣD; and in the other case to indicate that inventory increases are offset by any inventory decreases. Either of these components, $\Sigma S_k - \Sigma D$ or Σi, may be positive or negative.

Again writing C for total consumption, we have

(13) $$Y = C + I$$

Let us look at the production interpretation of this total. We are dealing with an economy whose production is, in a certain sense, devoted exclusively to the production of consumer goods. (This is not a comment on economic motivation, only a technical comment on the apparent fact that machines are produced to help produce consumer goods, or to help produce other machines which help produce consumer goods, etc.) But part of this economic activity is devoted immediately to building up the stock of productive assets if I is positive; or, if I is negative, current production fails to account for the total of current consumption. So the total result of current economic activity is inadequately measured by the current outflow of consumer goods; we must, if we wish to account for all the activity involved or all the resources employed, make allowance for that part of production whose immediate effect is the augmentation of business assets; or, if I is negative, for that element in current consumption not sustained by current productive activity. According to this view, the national income is equal to total current production, since it equals the output of consumer goods plus the rise in inventories plus the excess of new equipment over the wear and tear during the period. (Or minus the reduction in inventories or the deficiency of new equipment relative to depreciation.)

From the point of view of expenditures, a qualification is in order. It is customary to paraphrase equation (13) by saying that national income is equal to the sum of expenditures on consumer goods plus the expenditure on new investment, i.e., outlay on enlarged inventory and augmented plant. We shall generally employ this terminology; but it should be pointed out that some of the expenditures in this total are only virtual expenditures. At the same time we must admit that some of the "receipts" are also only virtual receipts. Take the case of a firm which pays $80 in expenditures for labor, materials, etc., producing 100 units of product, and sells 80 units of product for $1 apiece. The remaining 20 units represent enlarged inventory, which may be valued at $20 (or perhaps something less, since they are not yet sold). In this case the firm has earned $20 profits, without having received the $20 in the form of money. The owners of the firm have "spent" their $20 income on enlarged inventory. Both the receipt and the expenditure are "virtual," so far as money is concerned; it is only a convenient manner of speech to say that income "receipts" included the $20 profits, and investment "expenditures" included the $20 outlay on increased business assets.

As a matter of fact, the whole concept of national income may be taken as independent of actual cash flows. Incomes may be thought of as claims on output, expenditures as the exercise of those claims. The monetary aspect is interesting in its own right; but the flow of cash is not an essential aspect of the national-income *concept*.

It will have been noticed that certain kinds of receipts and expenditures have been left out of account in the foregoing development of the national-income concept. Gifts have been omitted, as have gambling earnings and gambling losses. So have secondhand sales, and sales of real estate. These omissions fall into two categories: those in which no goods or services are given in consideration, and those in which goods are transferred against money. In the first case, such as gambling gains and losses, there is no net earning involved; one person's gain offsets another's loss. Nor is anything involved which ought to be added into the production total. In the second case, where, for example, real estate is sold, there is simply the exchange of one form of asset for another; one exchanges money for goods, another exchanges goods for money. Neither "earns" anything in the transaction; so no "income" is represented.* Nor is there anything involved which ought to be added into the production total. (If the sale is that of a house, the house has, of course, been produced; but it was added into the production total of the period in which it was produced; and the incomes earned in its production were accounted for in the income total of the period in which it was produced.)

It is time now to make allowance for the economic activity of the government; but here we meet a dilemma. Heretofore there has been little difficulty in determining what we meant by a person's income. When we pay attention to taxes, we must decide whether to consider a person's income with or without allowance for the taxes he pays. If we decide to deduct his taxes, do we then content ourselves with adding up only personal incomes after deduction of taxes to arrive at national income, or do we then add the taxes as a sort of "government income" into the national-income total and so get back to where we started? Heretofore we have only considered the income of persons. (Although we spoke of profits as accruing to the firm, they were the income of the firm's owners). Do we now admit the government as a recipient of income?

There are several ways to solve this problem, some of them quite ar-

---

* If one of the parties does "gain" in the transaction, his gain is of one of two sorts. He may have got the better of the other person, in which case the gain is offset by another's loss and we exclude it accordingly. Or he may have made an "agent's commission" on the transaction. In the latter case, we should include his income in the national-income total as he is performing a professional service comparable to other services, such as transportation, entertainment, legal advice, etc., and the value of the service belongs in the production total. But the entire sales value of the house would not be included in the national-income total.

bitrary. One way is to get around it as mentioned above, by treating the government as though it were a person, deducting taxes from individual incomes and letting them reappear as government income; this way leaves the total unaffected by the explicit recognition of taxes. Another is to consider the taxes not as a deduction from individual incomes, but as that part of individuals' incomes which the government simply spends for them, on education, protection, streets, etc. A third way would be to let the production aspect of the national income decide it—to choose that total which best corresponds to total production.

Even here the answer is not clear; for it is similarly controversial just what is the best measure of total production. On the one hand, we may say that the goods and services consumed by government result in services to the population, and hence these services should be added into total production. But it has been maintained that many of the services provided by government are not additional to those consumed directly, but auxiliary to them as a "cost" item. For example, fire and police protection to a cookie factory is not production of services additional to the output of cookies, but is just one of the costs of producing cookies; and an increase in the police force is not an increase in consumable services but only an increased cost of producing the same cookies.

On the other hand, "productive activity" need not be taken solely in "output" terms, but can be interpreted in terms of "inputs" as well. While enlarged government activity (or decreased activity) may not be associated with enlarged (or reduced) output of consumable services, it may nevertheless be associated with increased (or decreased) employment of resources, of manpower and equipment. This consideration may throw the benefit of doubt over to the side of including the services of government in the total, rather than (in effect) canceling them out as we do interfirm sales and purchases.

Further elaboration of this problem could involve us in a volume devoted to the concept, rather than the analysis, of the national income; so we shall stop here and make a decision. The decision will not, however, be irrevocable.*

We shall define the national income as heretofore, i.e., without deduction of taxes, but with the addition of incomes earned directly from the government. We shall define a separate term, known as "disposable income,"

* The inference is not intended that the analysis to be presented in this book can proceed without attention to important conceptual problems; the analysis is useful only if its abstract conclusions have an interesting and valid economic interpretation, and the rudimentary accounting of this chapter does not provide the beginning of a basis for such an interpretation. The purpose of the present chapter is only to develop a minimum necessary accounting basis for certain accounting equations which recur throughout the analysis.

to make allowance for taxes. But disposable income will not be simply the national income minus taxes; there is another aspect of government which is a kind of expenditure counterpart to taxes. This is the category of "transfer payments." Many of the expenses of government are neither purchases of goods, nor wages, nor other payments in consideration of current productive services, but are instead money payments to individuals on other accounts. There are, for example, pensions, old age and unemployment benefits, subsidies, and refunds. These receipts will not be included as "incomes" in adding up to the national-income total, but will be included under the category of "disposable income."

We now introduce such new symbols as we need. S_g will denote sales by firms to government; W_g will denote wages and salaries paid by government; T_x will denote total taxes collected by government; and T_r will denote total transfer payments by government to individuals.*

National income is the same as before except for an additional term, W_g, the wages paid by government, and a new component of total sales, S_g, sales to government. If we revert to equation (12), we may modify that equation by enlarging $\Sigma S_c + \Sigma S_k$ to $\Sigma S_c + \Sigma S_k + \Sigma S_g$ and adding W_g at the end:

$$(14) \qquad Y = \Sigma S_c + \Sigma S_k + \Sigma S_g - \Sigma D + \Sigma i + W_g$$

or

$$(15) \qquad Y = C + I + \Sigma S_g + W_g$$

Let us write G for government expenditures on goods and services; then

$$(16) \qquad Y = C + I + G$$

(Notice that G is not total government expenditures; the transfer payments have been omitted. $G + T_r$ would represent total government expenditures.)

Disposable income, X, being defined as

$$(17) \qquad X = Y - T_x + T_r$$

is accordingly equal to

$$(18) \qquad X = C + I + G - T_x + T_r$$

---

* For convenience we shall ignore any nonwage, nonsalary income payments by government directly to individuals such as interest, royalties, commissions, etc., or else consider such individuals to be firms. (Whether government interest payments represent "income" in the sense of remuneration for current productive services, or transfer payments, is a topic we shall not consider.) Similarly we shall ignore transfer payments to business firms. And we are leaving out the possibility of sales by government to firms or individuals.

(It may be noted that, if the government's total outlays are equal to its total receipts, X is equal to the sum of $C + I$.)

As remarked above, the decision to define the national income as we have defined it does not constitute an irrevocable choice. For if one should prefer to leave out of the national-income total that part of current output absorbed by government, one has only to introduce a new symbol, Z, defined as $Z = Y - G$, and take Z as the national income. Our symbol Y then drops its interpretation as national income, and becomes simply a useful abbreviation for, on the one hand, $\Sigma P + \Sigma W + \Sigma O$, and on the other, by virtue of the accounting of this chapter, $C + I + G$. The analysis of this book is not vitiated by denying Y the status of "national income." Indeed, any variable defined in terms of other variables, as $X = Y - T_x + T_r$, or $Y = \Sigma P + \Sigma W + \Sigma O$, can be dispensed with. For it is only a matter of giving a name to a sum; and if the sum is given no name, we can still refer to it by enumerating its components. Later on, for example, we shall define terms such as "government deficit," equal to $G + T_r - T_x$; but we can always get along without the term deficit and speak instead of $G + T_r - T_x$. Again, we shall speak of the "net export balance," denoted by B, and defined as $B = E - M$. (Balance equals exports minus imports). But such a term is dispensable; its value in the analysis is that of abbreviation. Anything said of B can be said of $E - M$; and when we have learned all we can about E and M, we have learned all we can about their difference, and hence about the special term defined as their difference. So, in summary, it remains true that, whether or not we wish to call Y the national income, Y when defined as $\Sigma P + \Sigma W + \Sigma O$ has been found identical with $C + I + G$.

Finally we must make allowance in our national-income concept for international trade. While much of the analysis of this book will deal with a "closed" economy, *i.e.*, one which has no transactions with other economies, some explicitly international problems will be dealt with. Furthermore, the analytical basis for treating a part of the national economy separately from the rest is similar to that for treating international trade.

We now recognize that firms sell (*a*) to consumers, (*b*) to each other, and (*c*) abroad. Firms purchase (*a*) from each other, and (*b*) from abroad, and pay incomes in the form of wages, interest, etc. Consumers buy (*a*) from domestic firms, and (*b*) directly from abroad. Government (*a*) hires labor, paying wages and salaries, (*b*) purchases goods and services from domestic firms, and (*c*) purchases goods from abroad. (We shall not further complicate the picture by having any residents of the home country earn incomes abroad, either by working there or letting out the use of their property.)

We begin, as usual, by defining the residual category of income in the firm, namely profits.

(19) $P = S_c + S_k + S_o + S_g + S_a - W - O - E_{oh} - E_{oa} - D + i$

where S_c = sales to consumers in the home country
S_g = sales to government
S_k = sales of capital goods in home country
S_o = other sales to other firms in home country
S_a = sales abroad
E_{oh} = purchases, other than capital goods, from other firms in home country
E_{oa} = purchases, other than capital goods, from abroad

The above definition of profits is perfectly comprehensive; all possible sales are represented, as are all costs. Capital-equipment costs are represented in the term D covering depreciation during the period; consequently outlays on capital equipment do not appear as costs. All purchases of materials and services from firms are represented in E_{oh} and E_{oa}. Allowance is made for rise or fall in stocks by the term i, the net change in value of inventories. And wages and other incomes are provided for under W and O.

Total incomes earned in the single firm are, accordingly,

(20) $P + W + O = (S_c + S_k + S_o + S_g + S_a)$

$$- (E_{oh} + E_{oa}) - D + i$$

and the sum of all incomes earned in all firms is

21) $\Sigma P + \Sigma W + \Sigma O = \Sigma S_c + \Sigma S_k + \Sigma S_o + \Sigma S_g$

$$+ \Sigma S_a - \Sigma E_{oh} - \Sigma E_{oa} - \Sigma D + \Sigma i$$

Adding the incomes earned directly in government, W_g , we have

(22) $Y = \Sigma S_c + \Sigma S_k + \Sigma S_o + \Sigma S_g + \Sigma S_a - \Sigma E_{oh}$

$$- \Sigma E_{oa} - \Sigma D + \Sigma i + W_g$$

It is time now to cancel and combine terms. Our aim is to arrive at a simple expression for Y, containing only C, I, G, and a "net foreign balance" term. We can immediately cancel ΣS_o against ΣE_{oh} ; for the first of these denotes sales other than capital goods by one domestic firm to another, and the second purchases other than capital goods by one domestic firm from another. The two are consequently identical. This operation leaves

(23) $Y = \Sigma S_c + \Sigma S_k + \Sigma S_g + \Sigma S_a - \Sigma E_{oa} - \Sigma D + \Sigma i + W_g$

We next introduce the two terms, net current investment denoted by the letter I, and "net foreign balance" denoted by the letter B.   Net current investment is defined by the equation

(24) $$I = \Sigma E_{kh} + \Sigma E_{ka} - \Sigma D + \Sigma i$$

ΣE_{kh} denotes total purchases of capital equipment from other domestic firms, ΣE_{ka} denotes total purchases of capital equipment from abroad, and ΣD represents the using up of capital equipment during the accounting period; these three terms together yield the net increase (or decrease) in the total value of fixed capital. Σi denotes the net increase (or decrease) in inventories.

The definition of the net foreign balance is the following equation:

(25) $$B = \Sigma S_a - \Sigma E_{ka} - \Sigma E_{oa} - E_{ga} - C_a$$

ΣS_a denotes total sales abroad.   Total expenditures abroad are of four kinds: purchases of capital equipment, ΣE_{ka} ; other purchases of domestic firms from abroad for materials, etc., ΣE_{oa} ; government purchases abroad, E_{ga} ; and consumer purchases directly from abroad, C_a .   (We could, but need not, break up ΣS_a into sales to foreign firms, to foreign consumers, and to foreign governments.)

If we revert now to equation (23), we may effect some substitutions. First we note that ΣS_c , sales of domestic firms to consumers, is the difference between total consumption and consumer purchases directly from abroad, so that

(26) $$\Sigma S_c = C - C_a$$

Second we note that ΣS_g , sales of domestic firms to government, plus W_g , wages paid directly by government, are equal to total government outlays on goods and services minus government purchases from abroad, *i.e.*,

(27) $$\Sigma S_g + W_g = G - E_{ga}$$

And, third, we note that the terms $\Sigma S_k - \Sigma D + \Sigma i$ would represent total net current investment if only the purchase of capital equipment from abroad were added, *i.e.*,

(28) $$\Sigma S_k - \Sigma D + \Sigma i = I - \Sigma E_{ka}$$

If, therefore, we group the terms of equation (23) as done below in equation (29), we may beneath it write an equivalent expression in terms of C, I, and G, as follows:

(29) $$Y = \Sigma S_c + (\Sigma S_g + W_g) + (\Sigma S_k - \Sigma D + \Sigma i) + \Sigma S_a - \Sigma E_{oa}$$

(30) $$Y = (C - C_a) + (G - E_{ga}) + (I - \Sigma E_{ka}) + \Sigma S_a - \Sigma E_{oa}$$

Removing parentheses and regrouping terms, we have

(31) $Y = C + G + I + (\Sigma S_a - \Sigma E_{oa} - C_a - E_{ga} - \Sigma E_{ka})$

(32) $Y = C + I + G + B$

The string of terms enclosed in parentheses is precisely what we have identified as the net foreign balance, the excess of total sales abroad over total purchases from abroad, *i.e.*, exports minus imports. This term may, of course, be negative, if sales abroad are less than imports.

Here then is our final, complete definition of the national income. National income is *defined* as the sum of wages, salaries, profits, interest, etc., earned either in private business or within government, throughout the entire economy. It has been found to be identical in value with the sum of (*a*) consumer expenditures during the accounting period, (*b*) net current investment during the accounting period, *i.e.*, the increase, positive or negative, in the value of fixed plant and equipment and inventories, (*c*) the goods and services purchased by government, and (*d*) the difference between sales abroad and purchases from abroad.

Disposable income, X, is again defined as $Y - T_x + T_r$, so that

(33) $X = Y - T_x + T_r = C + I + G + B - T_x + T_r$

(It should be remembered that G is not the total government expenditure, but just expenditures for goods and services; transfer payments must be added to obtain the total government outlay.)

One more adjustment might be mentioned with respect to disposable income. Since much of the total profits earned throughout the economy is earned by corporations, it is frequently useful to distinguish the profits *earned* from the profits *distributed* to the owners. Corporations often distribute less than their total current profits to the stockholders and frequently distribute more. If we wish to consider such undistributed profits as outside the disposition of the stockholders, we may define disposable income as excluding that part of corporate profits not currently distributed to the owners, or as augmented by any excess of current dividends over current corporate earnings. Writing U for undistributed profits, disposable income would then be defined as $X = Y - T_x + T_r - U$, where U may be either positive or negative, according as corporations distribute less or more than current earnings as profits to the owners.

Our definition is now complete. We have developed the national-income concept as far as will be required for the purposes of this book. We have taken as our reference for definition the receipts side of the picture. We have developed an equivalent sum on the expenditures side: the sum of income receipts comprising the national income has been demonstrated to equal the sum of consumer expenditures, outlay on new current investment, government expenditures for goods and services, and the net expenditures of foreign countries in the home country, *i.e.*, the excess of foreign-country purchases over purchases from foreign countries. And similarly we have developed a production aspect of the national income: the sum of the income receipts comprising the national income is, to paraphrase the expenditure interpretation, the sum of the values of the outflow of consumer goods and services, the *net* augmentation of assets, the flow of goods and services to government, and the *net* provision of goods and services to foreign countries.

Before ending this chapter two more points should be stressed. First, we have by no means exhausted the problem of definition and development of the national-income concept. We have gone so far as to make allowance for consumption, investment, government, and foreign trade. There are yet a multitude of adjustments and complications which might receive attention. They are omitted here not because they are trivial, or because some of them are controversial (as many of them are), but because (*a*) to follow them much further would involve us in an entire volume on the subject and prevent our ever getting to the analysis which is the purpose of this book, and (*b*) the analysis we are to perform will not hinge on the treatment of such complicating matters. To provide some notion of what problems are omitted, the following examples are mentioned: what to do with incomes received directly from abroad or paid directly to recipients abroad; whether social security taxes are to be treated as taxes and deducted from disposable income, or treated as private insurance premiums; whether occupiers of their own homes shall be considered to pay to themselves and receive from themselves a rent; how to allow for home-grown home-consumed produce on farms; whether government interest payments are to be considered "in respect of services" and hence an income payment or simply a transfer payment; how to value incomes received in kind where the recipient is not able to elect what goods he shall receive; and what provision to make for capital gains, *i.e.*, appreciation of stocks, bonds, or inventory.*

The second point is that the national income is to be considered a flow over time. Actual accounting always requires the specification of an accounting period. The national income is thus the total of income receipts between two points in time, say the beginning and the end of the year or the

---

* For an excellent discussion of these issues see the article on the national income by S. S. Kuznets in the *Encyclopaedia of the Social Sciences*, vol. 11, p. 205, 1933, reprinted in *Readings in the Theory of Income Distribution*, p. 3, Philadelphia, 1946. For a detailed treatment of national-income accounting, using actual 1947 figures for the United States economy, see R. Ruggles, *An Introduction to National Income and Income Analysis*, New York, 1949.

month or the day.   The same rate of activity would yield twelve times the national income in the course of a year as it does over the period of a month.   The value of the national income thus has what we might call a different "time dimension" from values such as the quantity of money, or the total stock of inventory, or the accumulated value of all past investment.   We can always answer the question: What is the total value of inventories at a given point in time?   However, the question: What is the value of the national income? must be answered as between two points in time.   This difference is the same as that between the stock of water in a lake and the flow of water in a river.

Nevertheless, we can speak of the national income as having a certain *rate* at a given point in time, just as we can speak of the flow of a river as having a certain rate at any point in time.   We may, for example, speak of the national income as being "at the rate of 200 billion dollars per year" by which we mean that the rate of expenditure, or of receipts, or of production is such that, if maintained for 1 year, the national income would amount to 200 billion dollars.   This aspect is clear when we speak of the national income during a given month as "200 billion dollars, annual rate."   The actual national income for the month is one-twelfth of 200 billion; but it is expressed as an annual rate in order to allow ready comparison between say, the month of May, the July–August–September quarter, and the year 1948.

We shall conceive, therefore, of the national income as a continuous flow to be measured as a rate per year, month, or some standard period of time. An *amount* of production, or an *amount* of receipts, is relevant only to a period of time.   But, just as a car can travel 40 miles per hour without necessarily traveling so for an hour, the national income can flow at a rate of 200 billion dollars per year without necessarily maintaining that rate for a year's time.

An important aspect of this time context of the national income is that the value of the national income cannot in any absolute sense be compared with other values which are not similarly time rates.   For example, to compare the national income with the stock of money yields a ratio which depends entirely on the period of time according to which we measure the national income.   If we do biennial accounting, the annual rate of 200 billion is a biennial rate of 400 while its monthly rate is less than 20 billion. Similarly, to compare the rate of current investment with the total stock of productive assets yields a ratio which depends on the arbitrary accounting period by which we measure the current investment rate.   If the total stock of fixed assets is valued at 400 billion dollars, and current investment in fixed assets $(\Sigma S_k - \Sigma D)$ is at a rate of 20 billion per year, the ratio of one to the other is $\frac{1}{20}$.   If this should appear large, we have only to say that current investment is at a rate of 1.67 billion per month, and the ratio becomes $\frac{1}{240}$. Or, if the ratio looks small, we can speak of investment at a rate of 200 billion per decade, and the ratio becomes $\frac{1}{2}$. To avoid this arbitrariness, it is sometimes said that the capital stock equals (in terms of the above figures) 20 years' investment at the current rate. This figure, 20 years, is the same whether we express investment as 20 per year, 200 per decade, or 1.67 per month; for 20 years equals 240 months equals 2 decades. This method of comparison emphasizes the time dimension of such magnitudes as national income, consumption, rate of investment, etc.

CHAPTER 2

EQUATIONS

Algebra has to do with equations. It is the purpose of the present chapter to introduce the various kinds of equations to be encountered in this book.

One kind of equation is called the "identity," or "identical equation." An identity is an equation which defines a variable in terms of other variables, or paraphrases such a definition, or states the combined implications of two or more definitions taken together. It therefore "identifies" a variable, or a sum of variables, in terms of other variables. Such an equation asserts an equality which is true by definition. It is like an accounting statement: whatever the values of the variables involved, the variables are so defined that the two sides of the equation necessarily equal each other.

The definition of the national income, $Y = \Sigma P + \Sigma W + \Sigma O + W_g$, is an identity. It simply tells us what the symbol Y will stand for. Similarly, the definition of the net foreign balance, $B = \Sigma S_a - \Sigma E_{oa} - \Sigma E_{ka} - C_a - E_{ga}$, is an identical equation. There is no question whether B does or does not equal $\Sigma S_a - \Sigma E_{oa} - \Sigma E_{ka} - C_a - E_{ga}$, for "net foreign balance," once we have defined it so, simply *means* that sum of terms.

If we turn these identities about, writing $\Sigma O = Y - \Sigma P - \Sigma W - W_g$, or $\Sigma S_a = \Sigma E_{oa} + \Sigma E_{ka} + C_a + E_{ga} + B$, we obtain identities. For if any symbol be defined as the sum of several terms, any one of those terms is by definition equal to the difference between that sum and the rest of the terms.

Likewise, $\Sigma S_o = \Sigma E_o$ is an identity, for the total sales of firms to each other are defined in such a manner that they are the same as total purchases of firms from each other. A sale is not the same as a purchase; selling is defined differently from purchasing; but the *amount* sold is defined the same as the *amount* purchased. In the same way, wages received equal wages paid. This is so obvious that we did not bother to separate them, as concepts, in the previous chapter. The wage payments, charged as a cost in the equation defining profits, are equal to the wage receipts which add into the national income; thus, although a wage payment is not the same thing as a wage receipt, the amount paid is by definition the same as the amount received. We might call these identities, such as $\Sigma S_o = \Sigma E_o$ and W (received) $= W$ (paid), "balance-sheet identities," to distinguish them from the more obviously definitional identities; but in reality, both types follow from definition, wage costs equal wage receipts only because we have defined them in identical terms.

Combining identities we arrived at further identities in the preceding chapter, identities such as $Y = C + I + G + B$ or $X = C + I + G + B -$

$T_x + T_r - U$. These were not themselves definitions; national income was defined in terms of receipts, not expenditures. But combining the definition of Y with our balance-sheet identities we arrived at an expression for Y in terms of expenditures (or production values) which was identically true, *i.e.*, which followed from the definitions of the terms involved.

Another kind of equation expresses a *relationship* between two or more variables. An example of this kind would be $C = 0.75Y$, the statement that consumption is equal to 0.75 times the national income. This is not an identity; consumption may or may not equal 0.75 times the national income. (It obviously does only if $I + G + B$ equals the remaining 25 per cent.) It is an equation asserting an hypothesis about economic behavior. Another example of an equation expressing a relationship would be $T_x = 0.20Y$, expressing the hypothesis that taxes equal 0.20 times the national income. This equation also describes economic behavior (though perhaps not human behavior, since the relationship is mainly derived from the tax structure; it is the behavior of economic variables which is involved.) Or, again, we might have a relationship between the net foreign balance and the national income, such as $B = 0.05(150 - Y)$, indicating that when Y is less than 150 billion there is a positive net foreign balance equal to 0.05 times the difference, while if Y exceeds 150 billion there is a negative foreign balance equal to 5 per cent of the excess of Y over 150 billion. These equations all assert something about economic behavior; as statements of equality they may or may not be true, having thereby a property not enjoyed by the identities which could be false only by violating definitions.

If we combine two relationship equations we may obtain a third. Suppose, for example, that taxes were related to consumption expenditures and that the only tax were a 20 per cent sales tax. Then $T_x = 0.2C$. If at the same time we maintain the hypothesis that $C = 0.75Y$, these two equations yield an implied relationship between taxes and the national income: $T_x = 0.2C = 0.2 \times 0.75Y = 0.15Y$. This new equation may be called a "derived relationship," or an "implication" of the original two equations.

Again, we may combine an identity with a relationship to obtain a new relationship. Let us write our national-income identity as $Y = C + N$, where N stands for all the "nonconsumption" expenditure, $I + G + B$. If we postulate that $C = 0.75Y$, then it follows that Y must equal four times the value of N, whatever that value may be. (N must equal the other 25 per cent of Y if the hypothesis is to be satisfied.) Furthermore, C is by the same token equal to three times N. If these conclusions are not obvious they will be demonstrated in the next chapter; here the point is simply that *if* the original relationship holds, then necessarily the two derived relationships, $Y = 4N$ and $C = 3N$, must hold as well.

We have thus two types of distinctions to make among our equations, according to whether they are original or derived and according to whether they are identities or relationships. The original, or fundamental, equations are the starting point of the mathematics; the derived equations, the implications, are the end result. If we have a sufficient number of original equations we may obtain, as our implications, not derived relationships among variables but exact specifications of the values of the variables, such as that $Y = 200$, $C = 150$. These may be considered as "limiting cases" of relationships. Occasionally we may have an original equation involving a single variable, such as $N = 50$. While this is not, strictly speaking, a relationship among variables, our mathematics may proceed as though it were and we shall consequently not concern ourselves with naming it.

What should be emphasized is that from the original equations to the derived equations is sheer mathematics. It is a matter of economics to choose the original equations, obtaining them from statistical observation or simply postulating them to test their implications, and it is a matter of economics to interpret the implications and check them against observation; but it is purely mathematics to derive the quantitative implications of the quantitative hypotheses. By saying that it is purely mathematics we mean that the operations are formal, or abstract. If we postulate that $Y = C + N$ and $C = 0.75Y$, then it follows that $N = .0.25Y$ and $N = 0.33C$, regardless of the economic content of the symbols C, N, and Y. If we intend that they refer to consumption, nonconsumption expenditure, and national income respectively, then the hypothesis that consumption equals 0.75 times national income implies that national income equals four times nonconsumption expenditure. But if C, N, and Y denote adults over fourteen, children under fourteen, and total population, then the hypothesis that adults are 0.75 times the population implies that the population equals four times the number of children under fourteen. Or, to take another example in which the payments-receipts analogy appears, we may let C, N, and Y denote gifts given by members of a family to one another, gifts received within the family from outsiders, and total gifts received within the family, no gifts being given by the family to outsiders. Then the hypothesis that members of the family, altogether, give gifts equal in value to 0.75 times the value of all the gifts they receive implies that total gifts received will equal four times the gifts received from outside the family, and that gifts given by the family equal three times the gifts received from outside.

The mathematics are the same whatever the intended content of the variables. The mathematical operations are determined by the economic content only to the extent that, of all the operations we might perform, we choose those leading to the *form* in which we want our implications expressed. But the logic of the operations, the reasoning behind each step, is sheer mathematics.

CHAPTER 3

THE SIMPLEST SYSTEM

Our first economic system will be represented by only two equations. The system rests on the sole hypothesis that consumer expenditure depends on the level of national income. That is, we postulate that to each level of national income there corresponds a particular rate of consumer expenditure. One of the two equations expresses this hypothesis; the other simply identifies the national income.

We shall, for simplicity, assume that the relationship between national income and consumer expenditures is *linear*, that is, that a graph of the relationship would show a straight line. Writing C for consumer expenditure, and Y for national income, our consumption hypothesis is expressed by the equation

$$(1) \qquad\qquad C = a + bY$$

where the letters a and b stand for two (unspecified) numbers.

If the reader were to draw a graph, with income measured along the horizontal axis and consumption along the vertical axis, and plot a line such that its value above any point on the Y axis were equal to some number a plus some number b times the value of Y he would see that the resulting line would be a straight line. Any relationship which, when plotted on a graph, yields a straight line can be written algebraically in the form $C = a + bY$, where a and b stand for two numbers which depend on the position and direction of the line. And, vice versa, any relationship such as $C = a + bY$, where a and b denote any two numbers, yields a straight line when plotted on a graph. The key characteristic of such a "linear" relationship is that C increases or decreases at a fixed rate, relative to Y, as Y increases.

In the equation as written, a and b stand for unspecified numbers. To replace a and b with actual numbers would be to give a particular form to the consumption-income relationship. One such form, for example, would be $C = 40 + 0.6Y$; this particular equation states that C is equal to 0.6 times Y, plus 40. With Y equal to 200, C would equal 160; with Y equal to 100, C would equal 100. In our analysis we deal with the letters a and b rather than with actual numbers. We do this so that our results can be generalized to any such linear relationship, and so that we may see precisely how our results depend on the values of a and b, *i.e.*, on the precise shape of the relationship.

The symbols a and b are called parameters. They are considered to have certain fixed (unspecified) values. In contrast, C and Y are called variables,

23

or unknowns. It is the latter whose values we seek to determine, or between which we seek new relationships.

Our second equation is

(2) $$Y = C + N$$

where N is composed of all the nonconsumption expenditure components of the national income. This equation is an identity, identifying Y in terms of C and N.

It will be noticed that we are not, in this chapter, beginning at the very beginning; we are proceeding on the basis of the "identification" derived in Chap. 1. The plausibility of the consumption hypothesis depends on the identification of Y in terms of incomes, i.e., receipts; while equation (2) in this chapter identifies Y in terms of two expenditure components. It is a jump from the hypothesis that consumer expenditure is related to income to the assertion that it is related to the sum of itself plus another expenditure item; this jump was accomplished in Chap. 1, where Y, defined as the sum of wages, profits, and other income receipts, was deduced to be identical in value with a sum of expenditure items. This identity of expenditure with receipts is crucial; it is what allows us to identify a relationship between an expenditure item, consumption, and a receipts item, national income, as a relationship between an expenditure total and one of its parts.

We now have two equations in the three variables C, Y, and N; and we proceed to solve them simultaneously. But before proceeding to the manipulations which will effect the solution, we must explain what is meant by "solving" them together. Solving them means to discover those values for the three variables which satisfy at the same time both equations, i.e., which make both equations true statements of equality.

To illustrate, we revert to numerical terms. Suppose that the particular form of the consumption-income relationship is

$$C = 20 + 0.7Y$$

and suppose that N has the value 25.

The first equation, the consumption-income relationship, is satisfied by values of 90 and 100 respectively for consumption and income, and also by the values 160 and 200. For it is true that

$$90 = 20 + 0.7 \times 100$$

and

$$160 = 20 + 0.7 \times 200$$

But then the second equation, $Y = C + N$, is not satisfied, for, putting N equal to 25, it is not true that

$$100 = 90 + 25$$

or that

$$200 = 160 + 25$$

On the other hand, the second equation is satisfied by the values, $Y = 100$, $C = 75$; it also holds if $Y = 200$ and $C = 175$,

$$100 = 75 + 25 \qquad \text{and} \qquad 200 = 175 + 25$$

But then the first equation is not satisfied, for it is not true that

$$75 = 20 + 0.7 \times 100$$

or that

$$175 = 20 + 0.7 \times 200$$

And there are, of course, values such as 50 for C and 90 for Y, or 160 for C and 170 for Y, which fail to satisfy either equation.

If, however, we try C equal to 125 and Y equal to 150, both equations are satisfied; for both the following are true:

$$125 = 20 + 0.7 \times 150$$

and

$$150 = 125 + 25$$

"Solving" the two equations simultaneously means finding the values, such as 125 and 150 for C and Y, which satisfy both of the equations. In the present case we quite arbitrarily put N equal to 25. If we take N equal to 10, the values $C = 90$ and $Y = 100$ constitute a "solution." Or if N is put at 40, the solution values are 160 and 200. If each triplet of numbers is called a "solution," we have (25, 125, 150), (10, 90, 100), and (40, 160, 200) as solutions, where the three numbers in each case denote N, C, and Y respectively. We could go on choosing arbitrary values for N; each time there would correspond a unique set of values for C and Y. (This uniqueness will become evident only when we have gone through the formal process of solution.)

These triplets of numbers, which constitute the solutions, all follow a pattern. Part of that pattern was known already; it was given by our equations. We knew from our equations that, of any set of three numbers denoting solution values for N, C, and Y, the first would equal the difference between the second and third, and the second would equal 20 more than seven-tenths of the third. But there is more to the pattern; if the reader inspects the three sets of solution values given in the previous paragraph, or takes any arbitrary values for N and ascertains the corresponding solution values for C and Y, he will find that Y always equals $N + 20$ divided by 0.3, and that C always equals $0.7N + 20$ divided by 0.3. This part of the pattern was not initially obvious.

Thus, from the original two equations, $C = 20 + 0.7Y$ and $Y = C + N$, we deduce that

$$Y = \frac{N + 20}{0.3} \quad \text{and} \quad C = \frac{0.7N + 20}{0.3}$$

These two derived relationships are the implications of the original two; they are necessarily satisfied by any values of C and Y which satisfy the two original equations.

Solving the Equations

It must now be demonstrated how to arrive directly at solutions, and how to deduce that, for any value of N, the two derived equations hold. We proceed to solve the two original equations by the method of "substitution." We drop the particular numerical values for a and b used above, 20 and 0.7, and revert to the literal form. First we repeat the two equations,

(1)　　　　　　　　　　$C = a + bY$

(2)　　　　　　　　　　$Y = C + N$

We reason as follows: *If* the first equation is satisfied, $a + bY$ equals C; and we may replace C, wherever it occurs, by its equivalent, $a + bY$. So we substitute $a + bY$ for C in the second equation. From

$$Y = C + N$$

(3)　　　　　　　　　　$Y = a + bY + N$

Equation (3) expresses Y in terms of itself and N; our aim is to express Y in terms of N alone. The next step is to subtract bY from both sides of the equation:

(4)　　　　　　　$Y - bY = a + bY + N - bY$

(5)　　　　　　　$Y - bY = a + N$

Writing $Y - bY$ as $Y(1 - b)$, that is, as Y multiplied by $1 - b$,

(6)　　　　　　　　$Y(1 - b) = a + N$

Finally, both sides of equation (6) are divided by $(1 - b)$. The $1 - b$ cancels out on the left-hand side, leaving

(7)　　　　　　　　　$Y = \dfrac{a + N}{1 - b}$

Here is the general solution for Y, given in terms of N and the two parameters. The usefulness of such a solution, which still leaves us with a and b as well as N, will be discussed in a moment; let us immediately deduce the solution value of C in similar terms. If $C = a + bY$, then also

$$(8) \qquad C = a + b \left(\frac{a + N}{1 - b} \right)$$

This expression can be simplified as follows:

$$(9) \quad C = a + b \left(\frac{a + N}{1 - b} \right) = a \left(\frac{1 - b}{1 - b} \right) + b \left(\frac{a + N}{1 - b} \right)$$

$$= \frac{a - ab + ab + bN}{1 - b} = \frac{a + bN}{1 - b}$$

This is the relationship between C and N implied in the two original equations. We might pause here to check whether C and N actually do add up to the solution value of Y, that is, whether adding N to the solution value for C yields the solution value of Y.

$$(10) \quad C + N = \frac{a + bN}{1 - b} + N = \frac{a + bN}{1 - b} + \frac{N(1 - b)}{1 - b}$$

$$= \frac{a + bN + N - bN}{1 - b} = \frac{a + N}{1 - b}$$

which is the expression for Y obtained above [equation (7)].

It does not matter in which direction the substitution is made. We chose to substitute in the second equation the expression for C obtained from the first equation, namely, $a + bY$. We could as well have done the reverse; we could have substituted in the first equation the value for Y given in the second, namely, $C + N$. In that case we should have obtained

$$(11) \qquad C = a + b(C + N)$$

$$= a + bC + bN$$

$$(12) \qquad C - bC = a + bN$$

$$(13) \qquad C(1 - b) = a + bN$$

$$(14) \qquad C = \frac{a + bN}{1 - b}$$

just as before.

Adding N to this expression for C, as done above in checking $C + N$

against Y in equation (10), brings us to the solution value for Y as shown in equation (7).

Or, to demonstrate the flexibility of the method, we could proceed in still another way. We could substitute in the second equation the value of Y (rather than, as earlier, the value of C) given by the first. According to equation (1), $C = a + bY$. Deducting a from both sides, we have $C - a = bY$; dividing both sides by b yields $Y = (C - a)/b$. This expression for Y can be substituted in the second equation, leaving

$$(15) \qquad \frac{C - a}{b} = C + N$$

Multiplying both sides by b,

$$(16) \qquad C - a = bC + bN$$

Adding $a - bC$ to both sides,

$$(17) \qquad C - bC = a + bN \qquad \text{or} \qquad C\,(1 - b) = a + bN$$

and finally

$$(18) \qquad C = \frac{a + bN}{1 - b}$$

as before.

Thus, the rule to follow in solving the two equations for C and Y in terms of N is as follows: In either equation substitute for C or Y its equivalent as given in the other equation; this substitution eliminates one variable from the equation in which the substitution takes place. Then manipulate the resulting equation, by adding equal quantities to both sides, or by multiplying or dividing both sides by the same quantity, until C or Y (whichever was not eliminated) stands alone on one side, with an expression involving N on the other. Finally, substitute this solution for C (or Y) in either equation, obtaining one involving Y (or C) and N, and again manipulate until Y (or C) stands alone; at this point one has expressions for both C and Y in terms of N. (Instead of this final step, to obtain the solution for the variable originally eliminated, the first process could be repeated with elimination this time of the other variable.)

Much space has been taken to solve equations (1) and (2) in a variety of ways, partly to show that however one goes about it the same result is obtained, and partly to demonstrate the logical basis of the method. The whole procedure rests on two principles: (a) if both equations are satisfied, then either variable may be replaced at will by its equivalent according to either equation; (b) adding the same quantity to both sides of an equation, or multiplying or dividing both sides by the same quantity, does not vitiate the equality.

Significance of the Solution

It may next be inquired what good it does to have this "solution," where the solution is composed of two derived equations involving N and a pair of unspecified parameters. Unless we are closer to numerical values for C and Y, it may seem that we have only transmuted one pair of equations into a new pair of no greater value. There are as many unspecified parameters in our result as in the original problem—indeed, what was the "problem," if this is the solution?

First, and least significant, is the answer that the algebra provides a model for solving numerical equation systems. Having at hand a technique for orderly solution may eliminate some guessing at solutions when our equations are like $C = 20 + 0.7Y$ and a numerical value is had for N. This answer carries more weight when our equation system is more complicated, as it will be in later chapters. Furthermore, the alternative values of Y corresponding to alternative equations in numerical form can quickly be obtained from the formula giving Y in terms of N, in the event that we wish to compare the implications of several numerical hypotheses.

A more important answer is that our algebra has demonstrated a unique correspondence between the value of Y and the value of N, whatever the exact numerical shape of that correspondence may be—a correspondence which was not immediately obvious in the formulation of the consumption hypothesis. Through the algebra of Chap. 1 we convert a relationship between consumption expenditure and income receipts into a relationship between consumption expenditure and an expenditure total of which consumption is a part; from this it follows that the nonconsumption component of the total must also be related to the total. Thus it is a significant accomplishment to have deduced a correspondence between Y and N.

Finally, even though we do not know the numerical values of the parameters which fix the consumption-income relationship, having a formula for Y in terms of N containing those parameters allows us to see how the (Y,N) relationship depends on the nature of the (C,Y) relationship. And, if we know certain minimal properties of the (C,Y) equation, such as whether b is positive or negative or whether it is greater or less than 1, we may be able to make positive statements about the relation of Y to N. We turn now to a demonstration of this point.

The first question we might ask about the derived relation between Y and N is whether a higher or a lower value of Y is associated with a higher value of N. According to Chap. 1, an increase in N would entail an exactly equivalent increase in Y if the value of C were unaffected. But if we postulate that $C = a + bY$, the value of C is not indifferent to alternative values of Y and hence is not indifferent to alternative values of N. The total effect on Y of a change in the value of N is composed of two parts: the change in N itself, and the associated change in C.

Related Changes in Y and N

Having arrived at equation (7) above, giving Y in terms of N (and a and b), it is an easy matter to derive the change in Y effected by a change in the value of N. We shall assume that N has initially some value denoted by H, and that subsequently·its value increases by the amount h, that is, to the value $H + h$. (H and h, thus, denote fixed numbers, as do a and b; N does not denote a fixed number; it stands for the nonconsumption expenditure component of Y, whatever amount that may be. We fix the value of N by putting $N = H$, or $N = H + h$.) There are two corresponding values of Y, that corresponding to $N = H$ and that corresponding to $N = H + h$. Let us denote by K the first value of Y, and by $K + k$ the second. Thus, when N changes by the amount h, Y changes by the amount k; and it is the comparison of k to h that we seek. According to equation (7) above,

$$(19) \qquad K = \frac{a + H}{1 - b}$$

and

$$(20) \qquad K + k = \frac{a + H + h}{1 - b}$$

To find the value of k, which equals $(K + k) - K$, we deduct the expression for K from that for $K + k$:

$$(21) \qquad k = \frac{a + H + h}{1 - b} - \frac{a + H}{1 - b}$$

$$= \frac{a + H + h - a - H}{1 - b}$$

$$= \frac{h}{1 - b}$$

Here is the relationship between h, the change in the value of N, and k, the change in the value of Y, under the condition that *both our equations, (1) and (2), remain satisfied*.

Letting h stand for any arbitrary difference between two alternative values of N, we conclude that the two corresponding values of Y differ by $1/(1 - b)$ times h. There is only one parameter in this expression, namely b; so, clearly, the relation between h and k depends on the shape of the consumption-income relationship (which depends also on the value of b) as we could have anticipated. Before identifying b any more closely than this, let us see what conclusions we can reach about the relation of k to h.

First we put this relation into ratio form; dividing both sides of equation (21) by h, we have

(22)
$$\frac{k}{h} = \frac{1}{1 - b}$$

Next we ask: do Y and N change in the same direction? If the ratio is positive, they do, for a fraction is positive if both numerator and denominator have the same (plus or minus) sign. If the ratio is negative, numerator and denominator have opposite signs, indicating that when h is positive, k is negative, and vice versa.

Obviously, then, k and h have the same sign or not depending on the value of b. If b is negative, $(-b)$ is positive, $1 - b$ is positive, and the fraction $1/(1 - b)$ is positive. So negative b means that a change in N is accompanied by a change of Y in the same direction.

If, however, b is positive, then the denominator of the ratio (and hence the ratio itself, for the numerator is positive) is positive or negative according as b is less than, or greater than, $+1$. If b is a positive fraction, $1 - b$ is also a positive fraction, so that $1/(1 - b)$ is positive and greater than $+1$. But if b is greater than $+1$, then $(1 - b)$ is negative; so is $1/(1 - b)$, and the changes in Y and N are of opposite sign, i.e., in opposite directions.

Let us next identify the parameter b more precisely in terms of the (C, Y) relationship. Just what characteristic of that relationship is described by the parameter b? To answer this question, we shall repeat for C and Y what we have done for Y and N, namely compare changes. Let K and $K + k$ denote two alternative values of Y; and let J denote the value of C corresponding to K, and let $J + j$ denote that value of C corresponding to $Y = K + k$. Or, phrasing this differently, let k be the (arbitrary) difference between two values of Y, and let j denote the (unknown) difference between the two corresponding values of C. Then the value of j is given by

(23)
$$j = (J + j) - J$$

(24)
$$j = [a + b(K + k)] - (a + bK)$$
$$= a + bK + bk - a - bK$$
$$= bK$$

Thus j, the difference between values of C, is equal to b times the difference between values of Y. In ratio form,

(25) $$\frac{j}{k} = b$$

Thus the parameter b denotes the rate at which C increases relative to Y or decreases relative to Y. Reverting to the graph discussed on the first page of this chapter, the straight line denoting the consumption-income relationship, $C = a + bY$, has the property that as the distance k is traversed horizontally the line climbs the distance bk vertically; i.e., the slope or steepness or gradient of the line is the ratio $j/k = b$. This parameter will generally be referred to as the "marginal consumption–income ratio."

The marginal ratio of Y to N, in the (Y,N) relationship, depends then on the marginal ratio of C to Y in the (C,Y) relationship. If the marginal consumption-income ratio is negative, Y necessarily increases as N does. Also if that marginal ratio is a positive fraction, Y and N necessarily increase or decrease together. If the marginal consumption-income ratio is greater than $+1$, Y and N change in opposite directions—if, we must add, the two equations hold simultaneously; for there may be something in the economic interpretation of our equations that makes certain values of b inconsistent with the satisfaction of our equations. (It will later be shown that the equations should not be expected to hold if b is greater than $+1$.)

Let us concentrate now on the hypothesis that b is a positive fraction, i.e., has a value between zero and $+1$. We can conclude that, so long as b remains between zero and $+1$, the larger b is the greater is the ratio of the change in Y to the change in N. For this ratio is, according to equation (22),

$$\frac{k}{h} = \frac{1}{1 - b}$$

The larger the fraction b, the smaller is the difference $1 - b$; and the smaller the denominator, the larger is the ratio. With numerical examples:

If $b = 0.2$,

$$\frac{1}{1 - b} = \frac{1}{1 - 0.2} = \frac{1}{0.8} = 1.25$$

If $b = 0.5$,

$$\frac{1}{1 - b} = \frac{1}{1 - 0.5} = \frac{1}{0.5} = 2.0$$

If $b = 0.8$,

$$\frac{1}{1 - b} = \frac{1}{1 - 0.8} = \frac{1}{0.2} = 5$$

If $b = 0.9$,

$$\frac{1}{1 - b} = \frac{1}{1 - 0.9} = \frac{1}{0.1} = 10$$

and as b approaches the value 1.0, the ratio $1/(1 - b)$ increases without bound. If $b = 0$ (*i.e.*, if $C = a$), there is no change in C, and the change in Y is exactly equal to the change in the N component as indicated by

$$\frac{h}{k} = \frac{1}{1 - b} = \frac{1}{1 - 0} = 1$$

To summarize what has been accomplished so far: we have demonstrated that a relationship between consumption expenditure and national income implies a relationship between national income and the nonconsumption expenditure component of the national income; we have derived the algebraic equation, or formula, which relates the value of Y to that of N; and we have related the shape, or characteristics, of the (Y,N) relationship to the shape of the (C,Y) relationship by analyzing the influence of the parameter b in the derived relationship.

It may next be asked where the parameter a enters in the description of the (Y,N) relationship, and how its presence is interpreted. We have already seen that the *marginal* (Y,N) ratio depends on b alone, just as the marginal (C,Y) ratio was represented by the value of b. Looking at the formula for Y in terms of N [equation (7)] we find

$$Y = \frac{a + N}{1 - b}$$

If we rearrange this formula it will look like any linear equation:

$$(26) \qquad Y = \frac{a}{1 - b} + \frac{N}{1 - b}$$

$$= \left(\frac{a}{1 - b}\right) + \left(\frac{1}{1 - b}\right) N$$

This is an ordinary linear equation between Y and N, with the two parameters $a/(1 - b)$ and $1/(1 - b)$. If we define the letters c and d to stand for them,

$$(27) \qquad c = \frac{a}{1 - b}$$

$$(28) \qquad d = \frac{1}{1 - b}$$

then we have, simply,

$$(29) \qquad Y = c + dN$$

an equation of exactly the same form as $C = a + bY$. The marginal (Y,N) ratio, denoted by d, is related to b in the form shown by equation (28); while C, the "constant" in the equation, is related to both a and b, as shown in equation (27). Thus the "constant" part of the (C,Y) relationship affects only the constant part of the (Y,N) equation, while the marginal parameter, the coefficient of Y in the (C,Y) equation, enters both the constant and the coefficient in the (Y,N) relationship.

Diagrammatic Solution of the Equations

A diagrammatic illustration may help to clarify these relationships. There is a perfect correspondence between the algebraic methods of this book and the alternative methods of geometry. The geometric technique is extremely difficult once we progress beyond a single pair of equations; but for this two-equation case, geometry can be applied easily. The frequency with which one encounters geometric analysis of this subject adds to the advisability of appreciating the correspondence between algebra and geometry.

We draw a two-dimensional diagram; but we have three variables in our system, C, Y, and N. In order to reduce our system to two variables, we must suppress one by giving it a fixed value. This we do to N. We take the value of N as given, and proceed to solve the two equations geometrically for the solution values of C and Y corresponding to this arbitrary value of N. In drawing the diagram we have a choice of several methods of procedure, just as earlier we had a choice of several directions in which substitution could proceed to a solution of equations. We shall present the method which seems most clearly to illustrate the correspondence between linear equations and lines on a graph.

We label the two axes C and Y, with Y measured horizontally and C measured vertically. We first plot the line representing the consumption equation, $C = a + bY$. Taking any arbitrary values for a and b, we plot the line such that its height above the horizontal axis is equal to the parameter a plus b times Y. Next we plot the second equation, $Y = C + N$. First we rearrange this equation to read $C = Y - N$, and then give an arbitrary value to N, equal to the distance from 0 to N_1 on the diagram. We then plot this line, which has the characteristic that the height is equal to the horizontal distance measured from N_1 ; this line makes a 45-degree angle with the axis, since C increases at the same rate as Y along this line.

The intersection of these two lines occurs at values for C and Y such that, simultaneously, $C = a + bY$ and $C = Y - N$; that is, these values satisfy the equations and are the solution values for C and Y corresponding to the assumed value of N. By giving any other value to N and drawing the new 45-degree line (such as from N_2), we obtain the solution values for

C and Y corresponding to the new value of N. If the reader experiments with various values of N, recording the various related values of Y, and plots the line on a graph of Y and N, he will find that the line is a straight line, cutting the vertical axis at a numerical value equal to $a/(1 - b)$ and rising to the right at the rate $1/(1 - b)$.

We can deduce geometrically the relation between a change in N and the associated change in solution value of Y. Since the two 45-degree lines from N_1 and N_2 are parallel, the segment r is equal to the change in N. The segment $r + q$ denotes the change in Y, for the solution values of Y are Y_1

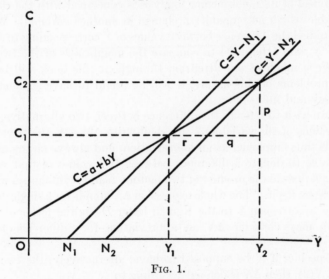

FIG. 1.

and Y_2. Furthermore, $p = q$ by construction of the 45-degree line. The ratio of the change in Y to the change in N is given by

$$\frac{r + q}{r} = \frac{1}{\dfrac{r}{r + q}} = \frac{1}{\dfrac{r + q - q}{r + q}}$$

$$= \frac{1}{\dfrac{r + q}{r + q} - \dfrac{q}{r + q}} = \frac{1}{1 - \dfrac{q}{r + q}} = \frac{1}{1 - \dfrac{p}{r + q}}$$

But b is the marginal ratio of C to Y according to the equation $C = a + bY$; it is therefore equal to the ratio of p, the rise in C, to $q + r$, the rise in Y. So, identifying $p/r + q$ as equal to b, we have

$$\frac{r + q}{r} = \frac{1}{1 - [p/(r + q)]} = \frac{1}{1 - b}$$

The two methods therefore agree; the ratio of a change in Y to the associated change in N is equal to the reciprocal of 1 minus the marginal consumption-income ratio.

The reader may experiment with negative values of b, or values greater than 1, to check geometrically the derived relationship of the marginal (Y,N) ratio to the marginal (C,Y) ratio.

Increments and Incremental Ratios: Some Terminology and Notation

A good deal of national-income analysis is concerned with the change in one variable which accompanies a change in another variable. We have already studied the difference between values of Y corresponding to different values of N, and attempted to compare the magnitudes of the two differences. Since much of our attention throughout this book will be taken up with problems of this nature, it will be useful to have some standard terminology and notation.

When we wish to refer to the difference between two alternative, or successive, values of the variable N, we shall write ΔN. Δ, the Greek letter "delta," is thus employed as an abbreviation, and always occurs attached to a variable to denote a difference between two values of that variable. ΔN does not denote the product of two factors, Δ and N; in fact, Δ will have no meaning by itself. The whole expression ΔN stands for a single quantity and, since Δ corresponds to the Roman letter D—initial letter of "difference"—we may consider ΔN an abbreviation for "difference between N's."

To be specific: if N be supposed to have, alternatively, the two values $N(1)$ and $N(2)$, then ΔN is defined according to

$$(30) \qquad\qquad \Delta N = N(2) - N(1)$$

Similarly, ΔY shall denote the difference between two alternative or successive values of Y. It does not matter which of the two values of N, $N(1)$ or $N(2)$, is subtracted from the other in arriving at ΔN, i.e., which is taken as the "first" value; but we must be careful to define $Y(2)$ as corresponding to $N(2)$, and $Y(1)$ as corresponding to $N(1)$. The ratio of ΔY to ΔN is the same, whichever pair of values is taken as the first, for

$$(31) \qquad \frac{\Delta Y}{\Delta N} = \frac{Y(2) - Y(1)}{N(2) - N(1)} = \frac{-[Y(2) - Y(1)]}{-[N(2) - N(1)]} = \frac{Y(1) - Y(2)}{N(1) - N(2)}$$

Multiplying numerator and denominator of a ratio by -1 does not change the sign of the ratio. In most cases we shall speak of a "first" value and a "second" value for N and for Y; this will be a manner of speech only, to help keep discussion orderly. Usually it will be better to think of $Y(1)$

and $Y(2)$ as alternative, rather than successive, values, and the differences are to be thought of as comparisons rather than changes over time.

The quantities denoted by ΔN, ΔY, ΔC, etc., we shall call "increments." The term increment implies an addition to some original value, suggesting perhaps that there is an original, "first," value, followed by a second. What was said in the preceding paragraph applies here; "increment" will usually refer to the difference between alternative, rather than chronologically successive, values. And we shall not understand increments to be necessarily positive, *i.e.*, additions, but as either positive or negative. (We shall speak of "negative increments" rather than of decrements.)

The ratio of the increments of two variables will be termed an "incremental ratio."* Thus the incremental ratio of Y to N is

$$(32) \qquad \frac{\Delta Y}{\Delta N} = \frac{Y(2) - Y(1)}{N(2) - N(1)}$$

Certain of the incremental ratios we shall refer to as "multipliers." In general, we shall call multipliers those incremental ratios whose values can be derived only from two or more of the original equations taken together; furthermore the term "multiplier" will for the time being be restricted to those incremental ratios whose denominators denote differences between alternative values of "independent" components of the national income or of disposable income. By "independent" we mean here a component whose behavior is not described by one of the original relationships. Thus the ratio $\Delta Y/\Delta N$ is a multiplier; it can be derived only from both equations, (1) and (2), taken together. The ratio $\Delta Y/\Delta C$ is not a multiplier because C does not denote an "independent" component of the national income, its behavior being subject to the equation $C = a + bY$. And the ratio $\Delta C/\Delta Y$ is not called a multiplier because its value is derived from the single relationship between C and Y and only constitutes part of the description of an original relationship.†

The Increment in Consumption

We shall apply at once to the increment in consumption the notation introduced above. From equation (1) it follows that $\Delta C/\Delta Y$ is equal to

---

* We shall use the term "marginal ratio" to refer to an incremental ratio derived from one of the original postulated relationships taken by itself; a "marginal ratio" is thus an elementary type of incremental ratio.

† The distinction between what is and what is not a multiplier is stressed here mainly to emphasize the conceptual distinction between incremental ratios which depend on simultaneous solution of two or more equations and those which describe the structure of a single relationship. It is not intended here to be strict about how the word should be used and, as a matter of fact, we shall not adhere closely to the definition given in the text.

b; to obtain the incremental ratio $\Delta C/\Delta N$ we may accordingly write

$$(33) \qquad \frac{\Delta C}{\Delta N} = \left(\frac{\Delta C}{\Delta Y}\right)\left(\frac{\Delta Y}{\Delta N}\right) = b\left(\frac{1}{1-b}\right) = \frac{b}{1-b}$$

The same result may be obtained by operating on equation (9) which gives C in terms of N. We let N and $N + \Delta N$ denote the two alternative values of N, and C and $C + \Delta C$ the two corresponding values of consumption.

$$(34) \qquad\qquad\qquad C = \frac{a + bN}{1 - b}$$

$$(35) \qquad C + \Delta C = \frac{a + b\,(N + \Delta N)}{1 - b} = \frac{a + bN + b\,\Delta N}{1 - b}$$

Subtracting the former from the latter,

$$(36) \qquad \Delta C = (C + \Delta C) - C = \left(\frac{b}{1 - b}\right)\Delta N$$

In ratio form,

$$(37) \qquad\qquad\qquad \frac{\Delta C}{\Delta N} = \frac{b}{1 - b}$$

An alternative algebraic form of (37) is obtained as follows:

$$(38) \qquad \frac{\Delta C}{\Delta N} = \frac{b}{1-b} = \frac{1 + b - 1}{1 - b} = \frac{1}{1-b} + \frac{b-1}{1-b} = \frac{1}{1-b} - 1$$

Using this form we can check our results against equation (2). According to that equation, $\Delta Y = \Delta C + \Delta N$, or $\Delta C = \Delta Y - \Delta N$. Consequently,

$$(39) \qquad\qquad \frac{\Delta C}{\Delta N} = \frac{\Delta Y}{\Delta N} - 1 = \frac{1}{1 - b} - 1$$

which is identical with the expression obtained in (38).

In summary, since one of the two increments whose sum is ΔY is equal to $b\Delta Y$, the other increment, ΔN, must be equal to the remainder of ΔY, namely, $(1 - b)\Delta Y$; and the increments in the two components are in the ratio $\Delta C/\Delta N = b/(1 - b)$, and the ratio of the increment in the sum to the increment in ΔN is equal to $\Delta Y/\Delta N = 1/(1 - b)$.

The Aggregative Nature of the Equation System

The equation system treated in this chapter has two significant characteristics: (a) it deals with "aggregates," i.e., the equations are "aggregative," and (b) the system is "static." We shall take up these two characteristics in turn.

The analysis of this chapter is called "aggregative" because it deals, not with the individual units of behavior in the economic system—the "family," or the "household," or the "firm"—but with the aggregate of all families or all households or all firms. The individual decision with respect to consumption expenditure is made at the household level; and a detailed hypothesis that consumption expenditure is determined by income would have to contain an equation for each family, relating the consumption of each family to its family income. (Or, if each family's consumption is considered to be partly determined by the consumption, or income, of other families, the equations would have to relate each family's consumption to many variables, each denoting the income or consumption of another family whose behavior influenced the consumption of the family in question.) And somehow each family's income would have to be related to the national income. Then, taking together all the equations relating family incomes to national income, and family consumption to family income, we could finally add up the total consumption corresponding to each level of national income and so derive a relationship between aggregate consumption and national income. This process of relating individual behavior to our aggregative relationships is passed over here; we begin directly on the aggregative level. Thus our relationships, such as $C = a + bY$, where C denotes aggregate consumption and Y national income, must be taken as the net over-all resultant of a myriad of individual relationships.

The Static Nature of the Equation System

The equation system of this chapter and the analysis of this chapter have been "static." By this we mean that the adjustment processes whereby variables proceed from one set of solution values to another have been ignored. When we discussed the implications of a rise in the value of N, we did not look into the timing of the response of C, or the rate at which C rose or fell to its new solution value; we simply let C take its new solution value and then compared the new value with the old.

Now in "real life" the rate of consumption does not jump instantaneously from one solution value to another upon a change in N (supposing for the moment that "real life" can be represented by the two-equation system of this chapter). Economic behavior is involved, economic decisions have to be made; and there is no prearranged schedule whereby all firms and individuals shift their behavior in unison to a new level. Even allowing a sudden jump in government or investment expenditure, consumer expenditures rise in response to, not simultaneously with, the change in the level of income. And anticipating the rise in income would not be simple, since income rises not only by the increase in nonconsumption expenditure but also by the rise in consumption expenditure itself. Thus the change in the value of N is accompanied, with greater or lesser time lag, by repercussions on consumption; and however long or short it may be, or however little we may interest ourselves in the process of adjustment per se, there is an adjustment. The fact of that adjustment is important to recognize for it means that there are implicit dynamics even in our static equation system.

The reason why it is important to recognize the presence of an adjustment process, i.e., the presence of "implicit dynamics" in the equation system, is that there may be something in those dynamics which invalidates our analysis, which makes irrelevant the solution of our equations. On page 32 we suggested that certain values of the parameter b—in particular, values of $+1$ or greater—were somehow inconsistent with the satisfaction of the equation system. There is nothing in the static analysis of this chapter to put large values of b in a different category from fractional values; only by attending to the implicit dynamics of the equation system can we make this discrimination. To that problem we turn in the following chapter.

CHAPTER 4

THE COMPATIBILITY OF BEHAVIOR EQUATIONS

The purpose of this chapter is to follow up the question raised at the end of the last, to look into the implicit dynamics of the equation system and study the dynamic compatibility of the equations. We shall precede the study of dynamic compatibility, however, with a brief discussion of static compatibility.

The Static Compatibility of Equations

A set of equations will be described as "statically incompatible" if there is no solution or if the solution values of any of the variables are inadmissible. The occurrence of "no solution" arises in the equation system of the preceding chapter if the value of the parameter b equals $+1$. In that case we have, according to equation (7) of Chap. 3,

$$(1) \qquad Y = \frac{a + N}{1 - b} = \frac{a + N}{0}$$

Now the operation of division by zero is impossible; to divide by zero means (in the present case) to find a number such that its product, upon multiplication by zero, equals $a + N$. Unless the value of $a + N$ happens to be zero there can be no such number; and if $a + N$ does equal zero, any number will do. If, then, b equals $+1$ and $1 - b$ is consequently zero, we conclude either that there is no value of Y which satisfies the two equations, or, in the case of $a + N = 0$, that any value of Y will satisfy them.

The occurrence of "inadmissible" solution values is illustrated by supposing that $a + N$ is negative while $1 - b$ is positive. In that case the solution value for Y is negative. Since "negative national income" has no meaning, we must reject this solution. And to reject the solution is to reject one or more of the behavior equations (in the case of Chap. 3 we had only one). The equation system cannot be considered to describe economic behavior if the behavior implied is impossible.

Again, an inadmissible solution is reached if $a + N$ is positive but a itself is negative and large enough to make negative the solution value for C. Unless all variables have economically meaningful solution values, the whole set of solution values is to be rejected, for one or more of the behavior equations cannot be a valid description of economic behavior.

And even if the solution values are economically meaningful, they may lie outside certain numerical limits which we impose. In dealing with numerical parameters, based on empirical observation, we may wish to impose limits on the values of the variables to represent either physical limits within the economic system or to represent the limits outside which we have no confidence in the relationships. Such things as labor force, plant capacity, etc., may put upper limits on the values which the variables may actually attain. Or we may consider that at very low levels of income consumption ceases to be directly influenced by the level of income, or at least ceases to be influenced in the particular manner indicated by the consumption equation we use. These limits, imposed for empirical rather than logical reasons, also lead to the rejection of the behavior relationships when they lead to rejection of the solution values.

Finally, however, it should be remarked that rejecting the behavior relationships because they lead to ridiculous or empirically inadmissible solution values does not necessarily imply that they have no meaning. The rejected behavior equations may still have a certain more narrow validity; what they lack is *adequacy* to describe the economic system. It may be that consumers, or investors, or government fiscal units tend to behave or try to behave in the manner described by the behavior equations, but that physical or other limits imposed keep them from satisfying their intentions. Their intentions are frustrated, but the equations may still be valid representations of behavior tendencies. If the solution value of national income exceeds some physical limit, we must reject both the solution and the assumption that the equations describe the results of economic behavior; we cannot from those same equations, without supplementary hypotheses, deduce what value of Y actually will obtain. But the original behavior equations may still form part of the basis for the new or enlarged set of hypotheses which must supplant the original set if economic behavior is to be described. What may be needed is a set of supplementary hypotheses, based on the original equations, which indicate how the economy behaves when decisions are frustrated, when fundamental behavior patterns throughout the economy are incompatible with each other. (This step usually involves explicitly dynamic analysis.)

The Dynamic Compatibility of Equations

Let us suppose next that the solution value for national income, as obtained in the preceding chapter, is positive, and that the solution value for consumption is also positive, but that the denominator in the solution, $1 - b$, is negative. (This is possible if the numerator is also negative; for the time being we have no particular reason to insist that $a + N$ be positive.) As was deduced in Chap. 3, a rise in N will in this case be accompanied by a fall in the value of C; for, from

(2) $$C = \frac{a + bN}{1 - b}$$ [Equation (9), Chap. 3]

it follows that

(3) $$\frac{\Delta C}{\Delta N} = \frac{b}{1 - b}$$ [Equation (37), Chap. 3]

This ratio is negative when numerator and denominator are of opposite sign. This condition is met when and only when b exceeds $+1$, making numerator positive and denominator negative.

Furthermore, in the event that $1 - b$ is negative, the decrease in C which accompanies an increase in N more than outweighs the increase in N, and Y itself decreases; for the change in Y is given by

(4) $$\frac{\Delta Y}{\Delta N} = \frac{1}{1 - b}$$ [Equation (22), Chap. 3]

And yet, when we think it through without the mathematics, it seems that C and Y ought to increase. The increase in N initially increases Y by the same amount; C then should increase, in accordance with $C = a + bY$, for b is positive; and the increase in C, by constituting at the same time a further increase in Y, should only lead to further upward adjustments. How, then, can a rise in N lead to lower consumption and a lower level of national income? The answer is that it does not. The multiplier only says that consumption, and income, must fall *if the equations are to be satisfied*. The multiplier does not say that the equations will be satisfied.

There is no quarrel with the multiplier when it is properly interpreted. It only tells us that if the equations were satisfied and then N were to rise, the only values of C and Y which would again satisfy the equations would be lower values. It tells us that if, when N increased, C fell in the ratio shown in (3), consumption would accord with its behavior equation and the equation would be satisfied.

The moment we said that "initially" the rise in N raises income, leaving consumption in the position of having to adjust upward, we stepped over into the field of dynamics.* It suddenly became of crucial importance just how the response in C occurred. It was by taking things in a kind of chronological sequence that we discovered the inconsistency between the *adjustment* behavior of C and the change in its solution value.

---

* Although we have used the word "initially" before we have not used it in a chronological sense. The "initial" value of a variable was only one of two *alternative* values which for convenience of speech was referred to as the initial, or first, of the two.

Here is a case, then, in which dynamic considerations make us discard a solution which on static grounds is perfectly admissible. We find that there is a solution, that there is a set of values for C, Y, and N which satisfies all the behavior equations; yet the values of the variables do not assume those solution values—on the contrary, they move away from them. What values they actually do ultimately assume we do not know from the equations, or even whether they ever do settle down to new solution values or keep forever adjusting. But we do know that there is little sense in concentrating on the solution of the equations and analyzing related changes in C, Y, and N on the assumption that the equations hold, if the adjustment behavior of the variables is inconsistent with their attainment of solution values. The equations are an invalid representation of the way consumption and income behave.

Although we should prefer to leave dynamic analysis for the last section of this book, we obviously cannot. We must immediately go sufficiently into the subject to develop criteria for the acceptance or rejection of the solution of a set of equations. We must consequently make explicit the adjustment process which is implicit in the behavior equations.

The Adjustment Process

Inherent in the notion of an adjustment process, or in the concept of dynamic compatibility of equations, is the recognition that the equations are not satisfied at all moments in time. In other words, when we write as our consumption equation that $C = a + bY$ we do not mean to assert as our consumption hypothesis that consumption does at all times equal $a + bY$; we mean that consumption *tends toward*, or adjusts toward, the value of $a + bY$. More specifically, the full interpretation of the equation

$$(5) \qquad\qquad C = a + bY$$

is this: When C is less than $a + bY$, C increases; when C is greater than $a + bY$, C decreases; when C equals $a + bY$, C is stationary.

This interpretation is at once narrower and broader than the flat statement that C equals $a + bY$; it is narrower in that it weakens the statement, it is more cautious; it is broader in that it allows the equation (5) to retain some relevance and validity even though it is dynamically incompatible with the identity $Y = C + N$, or with other behavior equations of the system.

Let us next identify three different "C" concepts. First, there is the actual value of consumption expenditure, denoted by the letter C. Second, there is the solution value of C, obtained by solution of all the equations, denoted by $\bar{C}$. Third, there is what we may call the "equation value" of consumption, namely $a + bY$, which we shall denote by C'. The solution value is unique, so long as a given value for N obtains; it is one of the particular values which the variable C may have. C', however, is not unique; it may run the entire gamut of values. To every value of Y there corresponds a value of C' which may be computed from equation (5). Of course, to every value of Y there also corresponds a particular value of C, so long as N is constant, namely $C = Y - N$; for to fix a value to N, and then to assume an arbitrary value for Y, fixes implicitly a value for C since Y is necessarily equal to the sum of C and N. But the value of C' and the value of C are not necessarily equal. As a matter of fact, they are equal only when $C = \bar{C}$, that is, when the actual value of C is its solution value.

Now the criterion for dynamic compatibility of the equations is that when C exceeds $\bar{C}$, C' is less than C; when C is less than $\bar{C}$, C' is greater than C.

For when C has a value greater than its solution value, dynamic compatibility requires that the value of C adjust downward; but since C adjusts toward C', C adjusts downward only when C' is less than C, that is, when $a + bY$ is less than C. And when the value of C is less than its solution value, C must adjust upward if it is to approach its solution value, and it will adjust upward only if $a + bY$ is greater than C itself.

Let us now restate this criterion in terms of the parameter b. The solution value of C, denoted by $\bar{C}$, is

$$(6) \qquad \bar{C} = \frac{a + bN}{1 - b}$$

And the solution value for Y, denoted by $\bar{Y}$, is

$$(7) \qquad \bar{Y} = \bar{C} + N = \frac{a + bN}{1 - b} + N = \frac{a + N}{1 - b}$$

Let us suppose that C has an actual value which differs from its solution value by the amount h.

$$(8) \qquad C = \bar{C} + h$$

And Y, consequently, has the value

$$(9) \qquad Y = C + N = \bar{C} + h + N$$

If, now, we compute the value of C', that is, the value of $a + bY$, in order to deduce in which direction the value of C will move, we find

$$(10) \qquad C' = a + bY = a + b(\bar{Y} + h)$$
$$= a + b\bar{Y} + bh$$

But according to the definitions of $\bar{C}$ and $\bar{Y}$, the solution value for C can be written as

(11) $$\bar{C} = a + b\bar{Y}$$

So we may rewrite (10) as

(12) $$C' = a + b\bar{Y} + bh$$
$$= \bar{C} + bh$$

We now apply our criterion. If h is positive, that is, if C exceeds $\bar{C}$, is C' less than C? Since $C = \bar{C} + h$, while $C' = \bar{C} + bh$, the answer hinges on whether b is greater or less than $+1$. If b is less than $+1$, C' is less than C, so that C adjusts *downward*, which is in the direction of its solution value. If b exceeds $+1$, bh exceeds h and C' is greater than C; C adjusts *upward*, away from its solution value. Finally, if b equals $+1$, C shows no tendency to adjust in either direction; this is the case in which (if there is a solution) any value is a solution, discussed a few pages ago under static incompatibility. If we take h to be negative, so that C is less than $\bar{C}$, the criterion still holds that b must be less than $+1$; for C' is less than or greater than C according as b is greater or less than $+1$; and C adjusts therefore away from or toward its higher solution value according as b is greater than or less than $+1$.

It is important to notice that as C adjusts, its equation value, denoted by C', also changes. If N is constant, a given rise or fall in the value of C changes the value of Y by an amount equal to the change in C; it changes, consequently, the value of C' by an amount equal to b times the change in C, that is, $\Delta C' = b \, \Delta C$. We may say, then, that C does or does not adjust toward its solution value depending on whether a change in the value of C causes a lesser or greater change in the value of C'. If, for a given change in the value of C, its equation value C' changes by a greater amount in the same direction, C is farther away than before from its equation value and cannot, by its process of adjustment toward C', reach C'. Accordingly we may say that the equation system is or is not dynamically compatible according as adjustment of C toward its equation value leaves C closer to or farther from its equation value after an adjustment.

The multiplier can be deduced directly from this adjustment process. If the values of the variables once satisfy the equations, and then the value of N is considered to change by the amount h, C must increase by an amount such that it reaches C'. Since C' increases by b times any change in Y, it initially increases by bh and it subsequently increases by $b \, \Delta C$. In the original situation, $C = C'$, and in the new solution $C = C'$. Thus $\Delta C = \Delta C'$, while $\Delta C' = bh + b \, \Delta C$. It follows that $\Delta C = bh + b \, \Delta C$ or, subtracting $b \, \Delta C$ from both sides of this equation, that $\Delta C(1 - b) = bh$, and finally, dividing both sides of the latter equation by $1 - b$, that $\Delta C = bh/(1 - b)$. And ΔY is obtained by adding ΔN and ΔC, *i.e.*, by adding h and $bh/(1 - b)$, which has been seen in the previous chapter to yield $h/(1 - b)$.

The analysis above is the kind that must accompany any solution of a static set of equations. It represents the minimum necessary dynamics which must underlie every static system of equations we use. In this particular case, in which reference is to the elementary equation system of Chap. 3, we do not need to take account of the *speed* of adjustment of C toward C'; it is sufficient to concentrate on the direction. The speed is irrelevant because there is only one adjusting variable. In other cases which we shall analyze there will be more than one adjusting variable, and in some cases the equations will be dynamically compatible or incompatible depending on the relative speeds of adjustment of certain variables, at least for certain values of the parameters.

The question to which we have addressed ourselves in this chapter is sometimes called the question of "stability of equilibrium," or "stability of a solution." A solution is "stable," or the equilibrium it represents is "stable," if deviations of the variables from their solution values lead to adjustment back to those solution values. (The deviation may be caused either by the random or arbitrary deviation of some dependent variable such as C, or by a change in the value of an independent variable, such as N, which entails a new solution value and thus leaves C out of line.) A solution or equilibrium is unstable if variables, when they have other values than their solution values, move away from their solution values.

But the terms "stability" and "instability" understate the case. Instability, or dynamic incompatibility, as we have called it in this book, does not simply mean that the solution is precarious; it really means that the solution is irrelevant. For not only must deviations, especially of the sort represented by changes in the independent variables, be considered an essential part of the economic system, and not only would most of our analysis have to be discarded because it deals explicitly with "deviations," but there would moreover be no reason why the variables would have had their solution values in the first place. If the solution is unstable, then only by coincidence would the variables be initially in conformity with the equations. Thus, although the terms stability and instability aptly describe the issue, they may be taken as synonymous with relevance or irrelevance of the solution of the static equations, and adequacy or inadequacy of the given static equation system to describe economic behavior.

What has been said does not mean that the equations themselves are irrelevant to the description of economic behavior, only that their solution is irrelevant. The equations themselves may become relevant to an explicitly dynamic analysis in which we study the process of adjustment; in that case, adjustment away from solution values is probably just as interesting as adjustment toward them.

It should be noted that the question of dynamic compatibility of equations refers only to the system of equations taken together. A single equation in isolation is taken to be stable. That is to say, the equation $C = a + bY$ is taken to mean that C adjusts toward $a + bY$, not away from it. We deal in static analysis only with systems of equations in which the individual equations, taken by themselves, are considered to be stable. The reason is that if a single equation were unstable, the particular variable showing such unstable behavior would not attain its equation value anyway and there would be no sense in analyzing the behavior of all variables on the assumption that it did.*

Alternative Formulation of the Adjustment Process

The preceding discussion of the adjustment process treated consumption as lagging behind its equation value. A rise in N, or a fall in N, raises or lowers income initially by the same amount; consumption then begins its adjustment and remains in a process of adjustment until it reaches its solution value. In other words, the lag between the initial change in N and the attainment by the variables of their solution values is an expenditure lag, i.e., a lag in expenditure behavior. There is an alternative conceptual framework for analyzing the adjustment process; we may view the lag as occurring not in expenditure behavior but in production behavior.

When a rise occurs in national income, via an increase in nonconsumption expenditure, we may consider the recipients of the new income to react almost instantly. There may be a lag; but it certainly need not be appreciable. It could conceivably be a negative lag, i.e., a "lead," where-

---

* It may be that a single unstable equation becomes stable when decomposed into more elementary equations and combined with other equations, i.e., that although considered in isolation the variable in question does not adjust toward its equation value, the behavior of other variables of the system is such that the unstable variable does assume its equation value. Examples of this case will appear in later chapters. Just as an unstable *system* of equations may become stable with the addition of new equations (as will be demonstrated by the modification of the present stability condition in the chapters to come), so may an unstable equation in isolation be considered an unstable *solution* of more elementary equations, and the addition of new equations to that unstable system may make it stable. This footnote is not intended to dispose of the subject but only to anticipate the further elaboration which will be provided by later chapters.

by consumption expenditure rose in anticipation of the subsequent rise in income. An enlargement of investment outlays or government expenditure may be anticipated; people hired today to go to work next Monday may begin at once to spend for consumption at a rate geared to the income level which they expect to reach next week. Where an appreciable lag may occur is on the production side; production of consumer goods may not rise as quickly as sales of consumer goods.

If production lags behind sales, there is selling out of inventory. There may be reduction in inventory of finished goods in the hands of retailers or manufacturers; and there may be reduction in inventory of semifinished goods as they are rushed to completion in response to the increased level of sales. The full production response to the increased level of consumer sales may take some time; and until it does occur the secondary rise in income, resulting from the increased consumer outlay, is postponed or partly postponed.

On the other hand, the income identity derived in Chap. 1 indicates that both an increase in N and an increase in C cannot occur without Y rising by the sum of these increases. How do we allow, in the accounting statement represented by our income identity, for the production lag?

What we must do is identify, within the nonconsumption-expenditure category, N, a component representing accumulation or disaccumulation of inventory. In other words, the initial rise in N is accompanied both by a rise in C and an equal secondary fall in N, the latter due to the decrease in the inventory-accumulation component of N as a result of the increased rate of consumer purchases. (If inventory accumulation was zero, it now becomes negative, indicating that production of, and incomes earned in production of, consumer goods are less than the value of sales to consumers.)

We revert, then, to equation (12) of Chap. 1 and isolate the inventory-accumulation component of nonconsumption expenditure, re-writing our income identity as

$$(13) \qquad\qquad Y = C + i + N$$

where N now excludes inventory accumulation which was previously treated (or ignored) as a component of N. N, then, is nonconsumption outlay exclusive of investment in inventory.

Production of consumption goods and services we shall denote by C_p; and sales of consumption goods and services we shall denote by C_s. The difference between C_p and C_s is the rate of inventory accumulation,

$$(14) \qquad\qquad i = C_p - C_s$$

Our adjustment hypothesis will be this: production tends to equal sales, i.e., production adjusts toward equality with sales. When C_p exceeds C_s

(when i is positive) the rate of production decreases; when C_p is less than C_s (when i is negative) the rate of production increases. Thus our static behavior equations are two,

(15) $$C_s = a + bY$$

(16) $$C_p = C_s$$

The latter may be put in the alternative form*

(17) $$i = 0$$

The solution of these equations is clearly

(18) $$C_p = C_s = \frac{a + bN}{1 - b}$$

(19) $$i = 0$$

(20) $$Y = \frac{a + N}{1 - b}$$

For if equation (16) is satisfied, the value of i is zero in the solution, and we may solve for Y and $C_s = C_p$ just as in Chap. 3.

Let us now denote the solution values of Y, C_s, and C_p, by $\bar{Y}$, $\bar{C}_s$, and $\bar{C}_p$, and suppose that the actual value of C_p differs from its solution value by the *positive* amount h, that is,

(21) $$C_p = \bar{C}_p + h$$

---

* It should be noted that the present formulation of the adjustment process ignores the level of inventories; it assumes that production responds so as to avoid either positive or negative accumulation of inventories. This is not quite the same as assuming that producers so adjust production as to keep inventories constant; for we have made no allowance for the compensation of losses or gains of inventory during intervals of inequality of C_p and C_s. This formulation may be a satisfactory approximation to production behavior if it can be assumed that inequalities between production and sales are short-lived, *i.e.*, that adjustment is so rapid that accumulation or disaccumulation during the interval of adjustment is negligible. If, however, adjustment is not that rapid, then the omission of compensatory behavior is significant. From an initial position of equality of sales and production, and "normal" inventory, suppose sales suddenly to jump. Production must not only adjust upward until it reaches sales but it must—if inventory is to be brought to its original level— for some time exceed sales to compensate for loss of inventory during the interval between the initial jump in sales and the time production caught up. Furthermore, it may be supposed that what inventory is "normal" depends on the level of sales itself. Thus equation (16) or (17) is an exceedingly rough approximation to a description of inventory behavior; allowance for more complicated behavior will be made in part IV of this book.

Putting equations (13) and (14) together we have also

(22) $$Y = C_p + N = \bar{C}_p + N + h$$

Whether production falls toward its solution value or rises away from it depends on whether consumption sales are less than or greater than production. We derive the value of consumption sales as follows:

(23) $$\begin{aligned} C_s &= a + bY \\ &= a + b(\bar{C}_p + N + h) \\ &= a + b\bar{Y} + bh \\ &= \bar{C}_s + bh \\ &= \bar{C}_p + bh \end{aligned}$$

Equation (23) makes it clear that whether C_s is less than or greater than C_p depends on whether bh is less or greater than h, i.e., whether b is less than or greater than $+1$. If b is less than $+1$, C_s is less than C_p, and the adjustment of C_p toward C_s constitutes adjustment toward $\bar{C}_p$. If b exceeds $+1$, C_s is greater than C_p and adjustment of C_p toward C_s constitutes adjustment away from $\bar{C}_p$. C_p will consequently approach or diverge from its solution value, and so at the same time will C_s and Y, according as b is less or greater than 1. (If b is exactly equal to $+1$ the values of C_s and C_p are equal and no adjustment occurs; but we have already seen that there are solution values in this case only if $a + N$ happens to equal zero, and in that case any value of C_p is a solution value.)*

In conclusion, we are led to the same single condition for dynamic compatibility of the equation system of Chap. 3 whether we assume the adjustment lag to occur on the side of consumption demand or on the side of production. The condition involves the value of one of the parameters of the system.

In the chapters to come we shall always be concerned with the dynamic compatibility of the equation systems under investigation; by and large the conditions are derived by a process similar to that developed in the present chapter. In some cases we shall deal with two adjusting variables, rather than one, and in some of those cases the relative speeds of adjustment will be crucial to dynamic compatibility. In some cases there will be a choice among several alternative formulations of the dynamic adjustment problem, just as there were at least two alternative formulations in the case just treated. Sometimes the particular compatibility conditions

---

* Cf. the discussion of static compatibility of equations earlier in the present chapter.

derived will depend on the particular dynamic formulation chosen for the adjustment analysis. It must not be anticipated that to each system of equations there corresponds a unique formulation of the stability problem nor a unique set of conditions in terms of parameter values. Just as, in future chapters, we shall have a choice among several static representations of any given problem, and a choice of the degree of complexity we are willing to allow in the analysis, so will there always be a choice among the systems of dynamic equations to represent the underlying adjustment processes, and a choice of the degree of complexity to be allowed in the dynamic validation of the static analysis.

CHAPTER 5

THE NUMBER OF EQUATIONS IN A SYSTEM

In Chap. 3 we studied a system of two linear* equations involving three variables, C, Y, and N. Simultaneous solution of the two equations yielded two new equations, expressing relationships implicit in the original two equations. That is to say, solution of the equations led to new equations expressing C and Y in terms of N.

It is a general property of systems of linear equations that the nature of the solution depends on a comparison of the number of original equations with the number of variables. When there is one less equation than the number of variables in the system, solution of the system gives each variable in terms of one other variable.† If on the other hand there are as many equations as variables, solution leads to a unique set of values for all the variables; that is to say, the values of all the variables are in this case completely determined by the equations.

---

* Although only the linearity of $C = a + bY$ was discussed, the other equation of Chap. 3, $Y = C + N$, is also to be considered linear. For our purpose the following definition of linearity will suffice: an equation is linear if it represents, or can be made by manipulation to represent, one variable in terms of the others in the general form $Y = a + bX_1 + cX_2 + dX_3 + \cdots$ where the X's denote the several other variables involved in the equation and the letters a, b, c, $\ldots$ denote parameters or expressions involving parameters. Each of the variables in terms of which the one variable is expressed enters additively into the equation, being multiplied by a coefficient which involves only parameters. (Minus signs are not excluded by the above formulation, of course, since the coefficients may be positive or negative.) The particular equation $Y = C + N$ may be considered a particular case of the general equation $Y = a + bC + cN$ where $a = 0$ and $b = c = 1$. This definition is equivalent, though we shall not prove the equivalence, to the following: an equation in any number of variables is linear if the relation between *any* two of the variables is linear (in the two-dimensional straight-line sense) when the values of all other variables are held constant, whatever those constant values may be. One of the most significant characteristics of a linear equation is that if all but two variables be held constant, the ratio of the changes in the two, $\Delta Y/\Delta X_n$ (where X_n is any variable other than Y), is constant regardless of the values of any of the variables or the absolute sizes of ΔY and ΔX_n. Thus, in the general equation given in the definition of linearity above, the incremental ratio of, say, Y to X_2 is given by $\Delta Y/\Delta X_2 = c$, irrespective of the values of X_1, X_3, or the alternative values of Y and X_2 of which ΔY and ΔX_2 are the differences. And that same general equation can be manipulated to yield X_1 in terms of Y, X_2, X_3, $\ldots$ with incremental ratios according to $\Delta X_1/\Delta Y = 1/b$, $\Delta X_2/\Delta X_3 = -d/c$, etc.

† Generally, we say that the solution of the equations of Chap. 3 gives Y in terms of N, or C in terms of N. This way of describing the solution indicates our point of view as economists; from a purely formal or mathematical point of view we may just as well say that it gives N in terms of Y. Whether we write $Y = (a + N)/(1 - b)$,

This principle may be restated as follows: if there are as many linear equations as variables, there is only one set of values for all the variables which satisfies the equations; if there is one equation less than there are variables, fixing the value of any one variable leaves completely determined the values of the other variables; if there are two equations less than there are variables, fixing the values of two leaves the rest completely determined. And so forth, for any number fewer equations than variables.

To illustrate this point let us restate the results of Chap. 3 and investigate the effect of adding a third and fourth equation to the original two. Our original two equations were

(1) $$C = a + bY$$

(2) $$Y = C + N$$

Our conclusion in Chap. 3 was that, if these equations held,

(3) $$Y = \frac{a + N}{1 - b}$$

and

(4) $$C = \frac{a + bN}{1 - b}$$

Suppose we add a third equation to the first two, a relationship between N and Y similar to that between C and Y:

(5) $$N = d + eY$$

The solution is obtained by substitution; substituting in equation (2) the expressions for C and N obtained from equations (1) and (5) we have

(6) $$Y = C + N$$
$$= (a + bY) + (d + eY)$$
$$= (a + d) + (b + e)Y$$

(7) $$Y - (b + e)Y = a + d$$

(8) $$Y(1 - b - e) = a + d$$

(9) $$Y = \frac{a + d}{1 - b - e}$$

or $N = (1 - b)Y - a$, or the completely indiscriminate $(1 - b)Y - N = a$ or $N - (1 - b)Y + a = 0$, is not dictated by the mathematics. We may be interested in having Y given in terms of N, because we consider the value of N to be somehow independently determined and that of Y to follow along in accord with the relationship; when discussing the pure mathematics of the system we may say that we obtain either variable in terms of the other.

Equation (9) is the solution for Y in terms of parameters alone; given the shapes of the two relationships, *i.e.*, given the particular values of a, b, d, and e, there is a unique value of Y which satisfies all three equations. The values of C and N which satisfy the equations can next be obtained as follows:

$$(10) \qquad C = a + b\left(\frac{a+d}{1-b-e}\right) = \frac{a(1-b-e)+b(a+d)}{1-b-e}$$

$$= \frac{a - ab - ae + ab + bd}{1-b-e}$$

$$= \frac{a(1-e)+bd}{1-b-e}$$

$$(11) \qquad N = Y - C = \frac{a+d}{1-b-e} - \frac{a - ae + bd}{1-b-e}$$

$$= \frac{a+d-a+ae-bd}{1-b-e}$$

$$= \frac{d(1-b)+ae}{1-b-e}$$

(We could have computed N from $N = d + eY$; instead, we subtracted C from Y to derive it. Or, since equations (1) and (5) are symmetrical in structure, we could have just reversed the positions of a and d, and of b and e in (10) to arrive at the solution for N.)

What is important for the moment is not that, if we knew the values of the parameters (*i.e.*, the exact shapes of the relationships) we could compute numerical values for all three variables from the solution, nor that without knowing parameter values we can see how the different parameters enter into or influence the solution values; what is significant at this point is that, having imposed three separate conditions on the three variables, *i.e.*, having postulated three equations to be satisfied by the values of the three variables, there is a unique set of values for Y, C, and N which satisfies those equations. We cannot this time inquire into the effect on the solution for Y of a change in the value of N; the value of N cannot change from its unique solution value without violating one or more of the original equations.

Let us revert, now, to the two-equation system but add a new variable. We shall suppose consumption to be related not to national income but to national income minus taxes (to disposable income). The letter T will stand for rate of taxation ("rate" in the sense of rate of collection over time, not "rate" in the sense of a ratio or percentage). The consumption equation becomes

(12) $$C = a + b(Y - T)$$
$$= a + bY - bT$$

Substituting this expression for C in equation (2),

(13) $$Y = N + a + bY - bT$$

(14) $$Y(1 - b) = N + a - bT$$

(15) $$Y = \frac{N + a - bT}{1 - b}$$

Equation (15) gives us Y in terms of the two variables, N and T. Substituting this expression for Y in equation (12) would yield an expression for C in terms of N and T, which we shall proceed to obtain in the following chapter. What is to be noticed here is that, having four variables and two equations, solution leads to expressions for Y and C in terms of the four minus two variables, T and N.*

The question next arises: What are the implications of having more equations than variables? The answer is simple: except by coincidence they cannot all be satisfied. If to the three equations solved above [equations (1), (2), and (5)] we add a fourth equation, such as $C = rN$, or $C - N = p + qY$, or some such relationship, we could not expect this new one to hold along with the rest. For the values of Y, C, and N were already completely determined by the original three equations; their values either do or do not satisfy the fourth equation as well. If they do, it is coincidence, and if they do not they can only do so by changing their values, violating one or more of the original three equations.

We have illustrated, but have not proved, this relationship between the number of variables appearing in the solution and the number of equations

---

* Cf. last footnote. Here again it may be most useful to have Y expressed in terms of N and T, but from a purely mathematical point of view this formulation has no priority over the expression of T, say, in terms of Y and N, which the reader may by manipulation of (15) find to be $T = [N + a - (1 - b)Y]/b$, or the expression of N in terms of Y and T, $N = Y(1 - b) + bT - a$. In other words, we may paraphrase equation (15) by saying that if N and Y have any two given values, the value of T will be that indicated by the equation shown in the previous sentence if the equations are all satisfied. From an economic point of view we may wish to consider N and T the "independent" variables, and Y the one whose value is "determined" by the particular values assumed by N and T. Sometimes, however, even from the point of view of our particular analytical purpose, the T formulation is intuitively more useful: we may wish to see what value of T must obtain if, with a given value of N, a particular value of Y is to be possible in accordance with the original equations.

and variables in the system. The reason for this relationship may be suggested by considering the process of solution by substitution. We begin with an original set of equations involving some number of variables. Any one equation gives, or can be made to give after manipulation, one variable in terms of other variables. In the other equations, then, we substitute for that one variable, wherever it occurs, the equivalent expression in terms of other variables obtained in the first equation. Having thus "used" one equation we have a remaining set of equations, one less in number, in which the eliminated variable does not appear, having been replaced by an expression involving only some or all of the other variables. Next we take any one of the remaining equations, arrange it if necessary so that it gives one variable in terms of other variables, and replace that one variable everywhere it occurs in the remaining equations by its equivalent expression in terms of other variables. Having thus "used" a second equation we have also eliminated, from the remaining equations, another variable. When there remains but one equation, we have performed one less substitution than the number of original equations, and have eliminated a number of variables equal to one less than the original number of equations. If, then, there were p equations originally, involving q (greater than or equal to p) variables, we have in our final equation the difference between q and $p - 1$ variables left, or $q - p + 1$ variables. Arranging this to give any one in terms of the others, we have any one variable given in terms of $q - p$ other variables. Since we can perform this substitution in any direction we please, to eliminate whichever variables we please, we can so arrange the solution as to give any one variable in terms of any other $q - p$ variables. If $q = p$, if, that is, there are originally as many equations as variables, the last equation contains but one variable which is consequently expressed solely in terms of the parameters of the various equations, and we may so arrange our solution as to have whichever variable we please in that situation.

Before leaving this subject, several qualifications must be attached. First, no two equations must be inconsistent if solution is to be possible, *i.e.*, if all equations are to be satisfied. If two of the equations should be $C = a + bY$ and $C = d + bY$, they can both be satisfied only if a is equal to d. Either, then, a equals d and both equations represent the same relationship, *i.e.*, do not constitute two separate equations, and one should not be counted, or else a does not equal d and not both of them can be satisfied by any value of Y. In that case they are called "inconsistent."

Second, it is important not to count as two equations two forms of the same equation. $Y = C + N$ and $Y - N = C$ are to be considered the same equation, since they both impose the same conditions on the values of the variables; any values of Y, N, and C which satisfy one, necessarily satisfy the other.   Similarly, $C = a + bY$ and $C - a = bY$ and $Y - C = Y(1 - b) - a$ are to be considered but different forms of the same equation; either one implies the others; values of Y and C which satisfy any one necessarily satisfy the others.

Third, it may happen that one or more of the variables can, in the solution, be expressed in terms of a lesser number of variables than the difference between number of variables and number of equations; in particular it may be that with fewer equations than variables one or more of the variables are completely determined.   If, for example, in a system of five equations and seven variables, three of the equations involve only the same three variables, those three equations are sufficient to determine completely the values of those three variables.   As a matter of fact the example given for "static incompatibility" of equations in Chap. 4 involved a case of this sort.   If we have two equations, $C = a + bY$ and $Y = C + N$, in the three variables, C, Y, and N, and then give to the parameter b the particular value $+1$, the first of those two equations becomes $C = a + Y$. Thus we have two equations, $C = a + Y$ and $C = Y - N$, which together are sufficient to determine completely the value of the variable N, namely $N = -a$.   No other value of N can satisfy both equations.   If N has any other value than that of $-a$, not both equations can be satisfied by any values of C and Y.

Fourth, the generalizations given in this chapter must be qualified to refer to linear equations, i.e., equations whose graphs are straight lines. If other forms of relationships are allowed, such as $C = a + bY + cY^2$, or $C = a/Y$, or $N = CY$, there would occur the possibility of multiple solutions, i.e., a finite number of sets of values rather than a unique set in the case of an equal number of equations and variables, or several values of C corresponding to any given values of Y and T, say, when there are two fewer equations than variables.   (The reason is analogous to the possibility of curved lines intersecting more than once.)   As we shall generally deal with linear equations the possibility of multiple solutions will seldom be a consideration.

CHAPTER 6

ENLARGEMENT OF THE SYSTEM—I

In this chapter we shall enlarge our equation system by recognizing the economic role of government. We shall also postulate a relationship between investment and national income similar to the one already introduced for consumption behavior.

Part of the national product represents consumption, *i.e.*, the production of goods and services for household consumption; another part represents addition to the stock of plant, equipment, and inventory; a third part represents goods and services produced by firms for sale to government and services performed directly for the government against payment of wages and salaries. Again ignoring in this chapter any international transactions, we may represent the national income as in the following equation which was derived in Chap. 1:

$$(1) \qquad Y = C + I + G$$

where C = consumption

I = net current investment

G = government purchases of goods and services.

The symbol N of Chap. 3 has been divided here into the two components I and G.

The government also collects taxes and distributes transfer payments. These two activities directly affect the disposable income of consumers; and it is disposable income to which we shall consider consumer expenditure related. Denoting disposable income by the letter X, this variable is defined by the identity

$$(2) \qquad X = Y - T_x + T_r$$

where T_x and T_r denote taxes and transfer payments respectively.

We have two hypotheses, one with respect to consumption behavior and one regarding investment behavior. The hypothesis about consumption behavior is expressed by the relationship

$$(3) \qquad C = a + bX$$

where X, disposable income, occupies the place of Y in the preceding chapter. Investment is considered related to the national income according to the equation

$$(4) \qquad I = u + vY$$

where u and v are parameters whose values depend on the shape of the linear relationship between I and Y.

This system consists of four equations, two of which are identities and two of which express relationships, and seven variables, Y, C, I, G, T_x, T_r, and X. Assuming, as usual, that the variables take such values as satisfy our equations, we solve by the method of substitution for such additional relationships as are implicit in the equation system.

The first substitution will convert the relationship between C and X into one between C and Y, T_x, and T_r. In equation (3) we substitute for X its equivalent as given by equation (2),

$$(3) \qquad C = a + bX$$
$$= a + b(Y - T_x + T_r)$$
$$(5) \qquad C = a + bY - bT_x + bT_r$$

Next we substitute in equation (1) the equivalent values of C and I as given by equations (4) and (5),

$$(1) \qquad Y = C + I + G$$
$$= (a + bY - bT_x + bT_r) + (u + vY) + G$$
$$(6) \qquad Y = (a + u) + (b + v)Y + (G - bT_x + bT_r)$$

In equation (6) we have grouped together the terms in Y [bY and vY, written as $(b + v)Y$], the two parameters a and u, and the three terms involving the variables G, T_x, and T_r. To solve equation (6) for Y in terms of G, T_x, and T_r, we deduct $(b + v)Y$ from both sides of the equation, obtaining

$$(7) \qquad Y - bY - vY = (a + u) + (G - bT_x + bT_r)$$
$$(8) \qquad Y(1 - b - v) = (a + u) + (G - bT_x + bT_r)$$

and finally, dividing both sides by $1 - b - v$,

$$(9) \qquad Y = \frac{a + u + G - bT_x + bT_r}{1 - b - v}$$

This is the "solution" for Y; it is a relationship between Y and the three independent variables G, T_x, and T_r. If the values of these three independent variables be specified, the value of Y is fixed. The relationship between Y and G, T_x, and T_r involves the same parameters as described the relationships between C and X and between I and Y. It will be noted that Y is given in terms of three variables, and that three is the difference between the number of variables (seven) and the number of original equations (four).

Since C and I are uniquely related to Y, their values are also determined by the values of the three independent variables. The value of C can be obtained from equation (5) now that we have Y in terms of G, T_x, and T_r. Substituting the solution for Y in equation (5) we obtain

$$(10) \qquad C = a + b \left(\frac{G - bT_x + bT_r + a + u}{1 - b - v} \right) - bT_x + bT_r$$

The structure of the dependence of C on the three independent variables will appear more clearly if the terms of equation (10) are regrouped as

$$(11) \quad C = b \left(\frac{1}{1 - b - v} \right) G - b \left(1 + \frac{b}{1 - b - v} \right) T_x$$

$$+ b \left(1 + \frac{b}{1 - b - v} \right) T_r + \left(1 + \frac{b}{1 - b - v} \right) a + \left(\frac{b}{1 - b - v} \right) u$$

Or, since $1 + \dfrac{b}{1 - b - v}$ is equal to $\dfrac{1 - b - v + b}{1 - b - v}$ or $\dfrac{1 - v}{1 - b - v}$, equation (11) may be further simplified in the form

$$(12) \qquad C = \frac{b[G - (1 - v)T_x + (1 - v)T_r] + (1 - v)a + bu}{1 - b - v}$$

This expression is still too long, perhaps, to permit apprehension at a glance. Its interpretation will become clearer when marginal relationships are derived between C and G, T_x, and T_r. Meanwhile let us obtain a similar expression for I by substituting the solution value for Y in equation (4),

$$(13) \qquad I = u + v \left(\frac{G - bT_x + bT_r + a + u}{1 - b - v} \right)$$

Putting everything over a common denominator and regrouping terms,

$$(14) \qquad I = \frac{v(G - bT_x + bT_r) + (1 - b)u + va}{1 - b - v}$$

As an exercise the reader may add the values of C and I as given by equations (12) and (14), and add G to confirm that the resulting sum is the solution for Y of equation (9).

Conditions for the Dynamic Compatibility of the Equations

Again in the present chapter we must verify that the implicit dynamics of the equation system are such as to validate an analysis based on the assumption that the equations hold; that is, we must assure ourselves that the adjustment behavior of the variables is such as to lead them toward their solution values. Or, if for certain values of certain parameters they do adjust toward their solution values, while for other parameter values they adjust away from the solution values, we must determine for which values of parameters the solution is stable. Only for parameter values consistent with adjustment toward solution values is an analysis valid which assumes satisfaction of the equations.

The present equation system differs in two respects from the system previously analyzed; it involves a new relationship, that between I and Y, and it involves three new variables, X, T_x, and T_r. Only the former difference is essential to stability analysis, since we assume the values of G, T_x, and T_r to be given, i.e., not to depend on the values of Y, C, or I, and since the variable X clearly drops out of the analysis once we have used it to convert the (C, X) relationship and the definition of X in terms of Y, T_x, and T_r into a relationship between C and Y, T_x, and T_r. In other words, all the terms in the numerator of the solution for Y, equation (9), can be taken as given by the parameters of the system and the assumed (fixed) values of G, T_x, and T_r; the basic difference is in the denominator which involves the two marginal ratios, that of C to Y and that of I to Y.

To focus on this problem, let us rewrite equation (9),

$$(15) \qquad \bar{Y} = \frac{H}{1 - b - v}$$

where H stands for the sum of terms composing the numerator of (9), corresponding to given values of G, T_x, and T_r, and where $\bar{Y}$ is used to emphasize the fact that the equation is the solution for Y. Let us next suppose that the actual values of C and I exceed their solution values by *positive* amounts equal to h and k respectively, i.e.,

$$(16) \qquad\qquad C = \bar{C} + h$$

$$(17) \qquad\qquad I = \bar{I} + k$$

The actual value of Y is then given by

$$(18) \qquad Y = \bar{C} + h + \bar{I} + k + G = \bar{Y} + h + k$$

Assuming that C adjusts toward the value given by the right-hand side of the consumption equation (5) and I adjusts toward the value given by the right-hand side of the investment equation (4), adjustment for C and Y will be in the direction of $\bar{C}$ and $\bar{I}$ only if these equation values lie below the actual values of C and I. Taking first the case of C, its equation value is given by

$$(19) \quad a + bY - bT_x + bT_r = a + b\bar{Y} + b(h + k) - bT_x + bT_r$$

$$= \bar{C} + b(h + k)$$

and for investment,

$$(20) \qquad u + vY = u + v\bar{Y} + v(h + k)$$
$$= \bar{I} + v(h + k)$$

C will adjust *upward* (away from its solution value) if it is less than its equation value, *i.e.*, if

$$(21) \qquad \bar{C} + h < \bar{C} + b(h + k)$$

That is, if

$$(22) \qquad h < b(h + k)$$
$$h(1 - b) < bk$$

And I will adjust *upward* (away from its solution value) if

$$(23) \qquad k < v(h + k)$$
$$k(1 - v) < vh$$

The difficulty in the present problem lies in the fact that C and I may adjust in opposite directions relative to their solution values. If, for example, b is positive and v less than $+1$, we can choose a value for k large enough to satisfy inequality (22) at the same time that it contradicts inequality (23); while if v is positive and b is less than $+1$ we can choose a value for h large enough to satisfy inequality (23) and contradict inequality (22). We cannot, then, assume in our analysis that both variables adjust in the same direction relative to their solution values.

We must consequently converge on our conclusions step by step, there being several cases to consider. First we may make one clear, positive statement: if both v and b exceed $+1$, both C and I will adjust upward for *any* positive values of k and h; and since h and k remain positive as long as adjustment is upward, adjustment from initial positive values of k and h can never approach $\bar{C}$ and $\bar{I}$. By the same reasoning, on the assumption of negative h and k, we arrive at the conclusion that from any initial negative values of h and k adjustment can never be upward toward $\bar{C}$ and $\bar{I}$. Consequently we must consider the equations dynamically incompatible if *both* b and v are as great as $+1$. (If v and b are exactly equal to $+1$, both variables obviously adjust upward from any positive initial values of h and k.)*

* We have not considered the case of h and k of opposite sign and b and v both greater than 1; it is not necessary. We would not accept as valid an analysis based on the assumed satisfaction of a set of equations which required, for their eventual satisfaction, that any divergence of one variable from its solution value be accompanied simultaneously by a specified type of divergence of another variable, in the absence of any explicit relationship to that effect in the original set of equations.

Second, if either b or v exceeds $+1$ and both are positive, either C or I will adjust always upward for any initial positive values of h and k. Let b exceed $+1$; then, according to (22), C will immediately adjust upward since h is less than bh and certainly less than $bh + k$. C could adjust downward only if k became negative; that, however, is impossible according to the postulated adjustment behavior of I, since to become negative, k would first have to become zero* at which point, with h still positive, I would rise. Thus I cannot go below its solution value so long as h is positive, and h remains positive so long as I does not become less than $\overline{I}$. The same argument with C and I reversed indicates that v may not exceed $+1$ or else I will adjust ever upward away from $\overline{I}$. Since analysis based on the assumed satisfaction of equations is invalid unless all variables approach their solution values from any other original values, a requirement for compatibility is that neither b nor v be as great as $+1$. (Again, if either b or v exactly equals $+1$, C or I will adjust upward for any positive divergence of the other, and the latter's divergence could not become negative if originally positive.)

Third, since from an initial positive value k cannot become negative unless h does, nor h unless k does, any approach of C and I toward their solution values must be an approach from above if the initial divergences were positive. In order that both C and I be capable of decreasing while both exceed their solution values, the left-hand sides of (22) and (23) must be capable of exceeding the right-hand sides for *some* positive values of h and k. Consequently the product of the two right-hand sides must be less than the product of the two left-hand sides for some positive values of h and k (except in the event that one of the right-hand sides is negative, an event already ruled out in the preceding paragraphs). Thus stability requires that, for some positive h and k,

$$(24) \qquad\qquad (bk)(vh) < h(1 - b)k(1 - v)$$

Since hk is positive we may divide through by hk,

$$(25) \qquad\qquad bv < 1 - b - v + bv$$

$$0 < 1 - b - v$$

In other words, $1 - b - v$ must be positive in order that C and I be capable of approaching their solution values from *any* initial values greater

---

* It will be noted that, for convenience, we are treating h and k as *variables* in the exposition of adjustment. Thus h and k are used to denote new variables defined according to

$$h = C - \overline{C}$$

$$k = I - \overline{I}$$

than those solution values. By reversing values we obtain the same condition for approach from values below the solution values. We need not (though the reader may wish to) prove this condition for approach from divergences in opposite directions from $\bar{C}$ and $\bar{I}$; we cannot base our analysis on the assumption that divergences will always occur in opposite directions for the two variables.

It may be observed that this condition, that $b + v$ be less than $+1$, is the same as would be obtained by considering C and I together. Combining equations (4) and (5) we have

$$(26) \qquad (C + I) = (a + u) + b(T_r - T_x) + (b + v)Y$$

$$= A + BY$$

where A and B are new parameters defined entirely in terms of the original parameters and the fixed values of T_x and T_r. Taking C and I together in this fashion, we could apply the stability analysis of Chap. 4, since there is but one adjusting variable when the separate identities of C and I are ignored. That analysis would yield the requirement $B < 1$, for stability; and since B can be identified in (26) as equal to $b + v$, we have the same condition as derived above.

In a general problem involving two adjusting variables we cannot combine those two variables for stability analysis. In the present case we can because we have considered only positive values of b and v. Since the sum of b and v cannot be as great as $+1$, and since both are taken to be positive, it follows that neither alone can be as great as $+1$. But in the general case we should have to consider the possibility of negative b or v, in which case the positive parameter could exceed $+1$ while the negative parameter kept their sum under $+1$. And when we let either b or v be negative, while the other exceeds $+1$, the relative adjustment speeds of the two variables are crucial to dynamic stability. This point can be illustrated by an extreme case; suppose that $b = 1.1$ while $v = -0.2$, so that $b + v = 0.9$. Using equation (26) we should decide that the sole stability condition is that $b + v$ must be less than $+1$, hence the system shows dynamic compatibility. But if investment adjusts at a negligible rate of speed, I may be considered constant for purposes of stability analysis and the stability criterion is that b must be less than $+1$ which it is not.

The Derivation of Incremental Ratios

It seems plausible that both taxes and transfer payments should be related to the national income, at least in the short run during which the tax and social security structures are fixed. Taxes tend to vary with personal incomes, with sales receipts, with business incomes, etc.; and transfer payments may be related either directly to the national income or indirectly via the relation of employment to national income. It will be interesting, therefore, to postulate such relationships and see what form the solution takes then. That step will be taken in the succeeding chapter; the rest of the present chapter will be devoted to the exploitation of the system already presented. In particular we shall derive the incremental ratios based on the independence of T_x and T_r.

If we suppose G, T_x, and T_r to have a certain initial set of values, and subsequently to assume a second set of values different from the first, the set of solution values for Y, C, and I will also change, for their values depend on those of the three independent variables. Writing ΔG, ΔT_x, and ΔT_r for the differences between the second and the first values of G, T_x, and T_r, and ΔY, ΔC, and ΔI for the increments in the dependent variables, we can denote the first set of values by the usual symbols, Y, I, C, G, T_x, and T_r and the second set of values by $Y + \Delta Y$, $I + \Delta I$, $T_x + \Delta T_x$, etc.*

Accordingly the two different values of the national income are given by

$$(9) \qquad Y = \frac{a + u + G - bT_x + bT_r}{1 - b - v}$$

$$(27) \quad Y + \Delta Y = \frac{a + u + (G + \Delta G) - b(T_x + \Delta T_x) + b(T_r + \Delta T_r)}{1 - b - v}$$

Removing parentheses and separating the new terms, this second equation (27) can be written as

$$(28) \quad Y + \Delta Y = \frac{a + u + G - bT_x + bT_r}{1 - b - v} + \frac{\Delta G - b\,\Delta T_x + b\,\Delta T_r}{1 - b - v}$$

The first term on the right-hand side is the same expression as appears in equation (9); deducting Y from $Y + \Delta Y$ thus gives us

$$(29) \qquad \Delta Y = [(Y + \Delta Y) - Y] = \frac{\Delta G - b\,\Delta T_x + b\,\Delta T_r}{1 - b - v}$$

* Again it should be stressed that the chronological sequence between the "first" and the "second" set of values is of no significance It is intended that they should be considered as alternative sets of values; the "first" and "second" terminology is used only for expository convenience. "Changes" in values should be interpreted as "differences between alternative values." If the two sets of values be thought of in chronological sequence, it must be kept in mind that it may take time for the dependent variables to assume their solution values; it is the changes in *solution values* which are under analysis when we derive incremental ratios. In neither interpretation, however, is there involved any discrimination between the "first" and the "second" sets of values; it is a matter of indifference which set is considered "initial."

Equation (29) shows how the value of Y changes when the values of G, T_x, and T_r change.*

If, to separate out their individual effects on Y, we suppose that only G changes, while T_x and T_r maintain constant values, then

$$(30) \qquad \Delta Y = \left(\frac{1}{1 - b - v}\right) \Delta G \quad (\text{when } \Delta T_x = 0 = \Delta T_r)$$

Writing the above result in the form of an incremental ratio,

$$(31) \qquad \frac{\Delta Y}{\Delta G} = \frac{1}{1 - b - v} \quad (\text{when } \Delta T_x = 0 = \Delta T_r)$$

If, on the other hand, T_x changes while both G and T_r retain fixed values, then ΔG and ΔT_r are zero and ΔY is

$$(32) \qquad \Delta Y = \left(\frac{-b}{1 - b - v}\right) \Delta T_x \quad (\text{when } \Delta G = 0 = \Delta T_r)$$

In ratio form,

$$(33) \qquad \frac{\Delta Y}{\Delta T_x} = \frac{-b}{1 - b - v} \quad (\text{when } \Delta G = 0 = \Delta T_r)$$

And similarly, when only T_r changes,

$$(34) \qquad \frac{\Delta Y}{\Delta T_r} = \frac{+b}{1 - b - v} \quad (\text{when } \Delta G = 0 = \Delta T_x)$$

These ratios may be called "multipliers," although T_x and T_r are not expenditure components of the national income, but are rather components of disposable income. We shall call them multipliers, but we have to exercise care in using this term; first of all because there are three different multipliers for Y alone (and we can derive three more apiece for C and I), and second because each is valid only if two of the independent variables are assumed unchanged in value. Thus the qualifying phrase, "when T_x and T_r are constant," is an integral part of the multiplier expression; otherwise the ratio of ΔY to ΔG may have any value whatever depending on how the values of T_x and T_r change, and the same may be said for the ratios of ΔY to ΔT_x and ΔY to ΔT_r. In order to avoid confusion we should always denote such a multiplier by the full expression

$$(35) \qquad \frac{\Delta Y}{\Delta G} (\Delta T_x = 0 = \Delta T_r) = \frac{1}{1 - b - v}$$

* Cf. R. A. Musgrave, "Alternative Budget Policies for Full Employment," *American Economic Review*, vol. 35, p. 387. For a diagrammatic treatment of the subject see A. H. Hansen, "Three Methods of Expansion through Fiscal Policy," *American Economic Review*, vol. 35, p. 382; R. L. Bishop, "Alternative Expansionist Fiscal Policies: a Diagrammatic Analysis," in *Income, Employment and Public Policy, Essays in Honor of Alvin H. Hansen*, p. 317, New York, 1948.

where the expression in parentheses indicates what is assumed to happen simultaneously to the rest of the independent variables.

It should also be clear that the multiplier depends on the whole system of equations, so that even (35) identifies the multiplier only within the context of the present chapter; if we had not postulated an investment-income relationship, or if we had had more than two original relationships, $\Delta Y/\Delta G$ would be given by some different expression, even for $\Delta T_x = 0 = \Delta T_r$.

Let us look now at the general form of the three multipliers we have derived. They have a common denominator equal to $1 - b - v$. In Chap. 3 the denominator was $1 - b$; in that chapter there was no postulated relationship between I and Y. If we rewrite the present denominator as $1 - (b + v)$ it is apparent that $b + v$ occupies the place occupied by b alone in Chap. 3. In that chapter a marginal consumption-income ratio equal to 0.5 yielded a multiplier equal to $1/(1 - 0.5)$, or 2. It now appears that the same marginal consumption-income ratio, when accompanied by a marginal investment-income ratio of, say, 0.1, yields a multiplier of $1/(1 - 0.6)$, or 2.5. Thus when two expenditure components of the national income are related to the national income, the denominator of the multiplier for Y shows both the marginal ratios subtracted from 1.

Next we look at the numerators. The multipliers appropriate to changes in T_x and T_r have the same absolute value but opposite signs. The difference in sign comes obviously from the fact that a rise in transfer payments raises disposable income while a rise in taxes lowers disposable income. If we take b to have a value between zero and $+1$, $\Delta Y/\Delta G$ is greater in absolute value than either $\Delta Y/\Delta T_x$ or $\Delta Y/\Delta T_r$ (assuming in each case that the other two variables do not change). Thus the following relationships hold among the multipliers:

$$(36) \qquad \frac{\Delta Y}{\Delta T_r} (\Delta G = 0 = \Delta T_x) = b \frac{\Delta Y}{\Delta G} (\Delta T_x = 0 = \Delta T_r)$$

$$= -\frac{\Delta Y}{\Delta T_x} (\Delta G = 0 = \Delta T_r)$$

We can go on to derive composite multipliers, letting two of the independent variables change together in some prescribed fashion. Let us suppose that G and T_x change together by exactly the same amount, with no change in T_r. Thus the net surplus or deficit in the government budget is not affected; expenditures and receipts of government change by the same amount. In this case ΔY is given by*

$$(37) \qquad \Delta Y = \frac{\Delta G - b \, \Delta T_x}{1 - b - v}$$

* Cf. T. Haavelmo, "Multiplier Effects of a Balanced Budget," *Econometrica,*

or, since $\Delta T_x = \Delta G$,

$$(38) \qquad \Delta Y = \frac{\Delta G - b\,\Delta G}{1 - b - v} = \left(\frac{1 - b}{1 - b - v}\right)\Delta G$$

An alternative form for the equation just derived is obtained as follows:

$$(39) \qquad \frac{1 - b}{1 - b - v} = \frac{1 - b - v + v}{1 - b - v} = \frac{1 - b - v}{1 - b - v}$$
$$+ \frac{v}{1 - b - v} = 1 + \frac{v}{1 - b - v}$$

so that

$$(40) \qquad \Delta Y = \left(1 + \frac{v}{1 - b - v}\right)\Delta G$$

Having derived incremental ratios to show how changes in the values of G, T_x, and T_r affect the value of Y, we may derive similarly those showing the related changes in C and I. For this purpose we may revert to equations (12) and (14) and operate on them as we did on the solution for Y, or we may alternatively derive from equations (4) and (5) the incremental equations

$$(41) \qquad \Delta C = b\,\Delta Y - b\,\Delta T_x + b\,\Delta T_r$$

$$(42) \qquad \Delta I = v\,\Delta Y$$

and insert into them the incremental values for Y already obtained. If we choose the former method we obtain, for example for I,

$$(43) \qquad \Delta I = \frac{v\,\Delta G - vb\,\Delta T_x + vb\,\Delta T_r}{1 - b - v}$$

From (43) we obtain directly

$$(44) \qquad \frac{\Delta I}{\Delta T_x} = \frac{-vb}{1 - b - v} \qquad (\Delta G = 0 = \Delta T_r)$$

And from (42), using the relation of ΔY to ΔT_x already obtained,

$$(45) \qquad \frac{\Delta I}{\Delta T_x} = v\left(\frac{\Delta Y}{\Delta T_x}\right) = v\left(\frac{-b}{1 - b - v}\right) \qquad (\Delta G = 0 = \Delta T_r)$$

which is identical. The same technique can be applied to all the ratios.

The incremental ratios which we have derived so far in the present section are of the kind called "multipliers"; they relate changes in the

vol. 13, p. 311, and the discussion by R. Goodwin, T. Haavelmo, G. Haberler, and E. Hagen under the same title, *Econometrica*, vol. 14, p. 150*ff*.

values of dependent variables to changes in the values of independent variables. (By "independent variables" we mean G, T_x, and T_r whose values are not assumed to depend on the values of other variables in the system.) We may identify yet another class of incremental ratio, represented in the present system of equations by $\Delta C/\Delta I$ or $\Delta I/\Delta C$. This ratio is not a multiplier, since both variables are dependent. But it is a ratio whose value can be derived in terms of parameters only by the simultaneous solution of two or more equations. It is thus in a different class from both the multiplier ratios and the elementary ratios represented by the parameters which are derived from single equations in isolation.

It should be noticed that $\Delta C/\Delta I$ is not a unique ratio; for C and I can change only when one or more of the independent variables change, and the changes in C and I then depend on the precise manner in which those three variables, G, T_x, and T_r, change together. If, for simplicity, we assume only G to change, while ΔT_x and ΔT_r are equal to zero, then we have

$$(46) \qquad \Delta C = \left(\frac{b}{1 - b - v}\right) \Delta G$$

and

$$(47) \qquad \Delta I = \left(\frac{v}{1 - b - v}\right) \Delta G$$

The ratio of ΔC to ΔI, when $\Delta T_x = 0 = \Delta T_r$, is thus

$$(48) \qquad \frac{\Delta C}{\Delta I} (\Delta T_x = 0 = \Delta T_r) = \frac{\left(\dfrac{b}{1 - b - v}\right) \Delta G}{\left(\dfrac{v}{1 - b - v}\right) \Delta G} = \frac{b}{v}$$

This result could have been obtained from equations (3) and (4) alone. For if T_x and T_r remain fixed, $\Delta C = b \, \Delta Y$, whatever the size of ΔY, and $\Delta I = v \, \Delta Y$, whatever the value of ΔY. So without paying any attention to ΔY, we may say that if T_x and T_r have constant values, any changes in C and I are equal to $b \, \Delta Y$ and $v \, \Delta Y$ respectively, and so are in the ratio b/v.

If, on the other hand, T_r is assumed to change while G and T_x remain fixed, we have, from equations (12) and (14),

$$(49) \qquad \Delta C = \left(\frac{b(1 - v)}{1 - b - v}\right) \Delta T_r$$

$$(50) \qquad \Delta I = \left(\frac{vb}{1 - b - v}\right) \Delta T_r$$

And the ratio of ΔC to ΔI, corresponding to a change in the value of T_r while T_x and G remain fixed, is

$$(51) \qquad \frac{\Delta C}{\Delta I} (\Delta G = 0 = \Delta T_x) = \frac{b(1 - v)}{bv} = \frac{1 - v}{v}$$

This result can also be obtained directly from equations (1) and (4) taken together, without regard to the consumption equation. With $\Delta G = 0$, any change in Y is composed of two parts, ΔC and ΔI. The latter, according to equation (4), is equal to $v \Delta Y$ whatever the size of ΔY. The former, ΔC, must then equal $(1 - v)\Delta Y$ since it constitutes the remainder of the change in Y. Their ratio, then, is $(1 - v)/v$. For an increase in T_x the same ratio is valid; both ΔC and ΔI are in that case negative; their ratio is the same as for a change in T_r.

Similarly we may derive the incremental ratios of C to Y under alternative assumptions about the values of ΔG, ΔT_x, and ΔT_r. If only the value of G changes, then equation (5) gives us $\Delta C = b \Delta Y$, with the incremental ratio equal to b. If G is constant, and T_x is constant, while T_r undergoes a change in value, the incremental ratio of C to Y will have a different value. The latter ratio may be obtained by comparing the values of $\Delta Y/\Delta T_r$ and $\Delta C/\Delta T_r$, or it may more simply be obtained as in the preceding paragraph, namely by noting that ΔC must equal $(1 - v)\Delta Y$ if the investment equation holds.

We can now revert to the comparison of multipliers given in the series of equations (36) above and see why $\Delta Y/\Delta G$ should exceed $\Delta Y/\Delta T_r$. Let us consider $v = 0$, so that the investment-income relationship is set aside; in that case the effect on C is the same whether it is G or T_r which changes. From (41),

$$(52) \qquad \Delta C = b \Delta Y + b \Delta T_r$$

when T_x is constant. If it is G which changes, we have

$$(53) \qquad \Delta C = b \left(\frac{1}{1 - b} \right) \Delta G + 0 = \left(\frac{b}{1 - b} \right) \Delta G$$

When it is T_r which changes,

$$(54) \qquad \Delta C = b \left(\frac{b}{1 - b} \right) \Delta T_r + b \Delta T_r = b \left(1 + \frac{b}{1 - b} \right) \Delta T_r$$

$$= b \left(\frac{1 - b + b}{1 - b} \right) \Delta T_r = b \left(\frac{1}{1 - b} \right) \Delta T_r = \left(\frac{b}{1 - b} \right) \Delta T_r$$

Thus the change in C is indifferent between equal alternative changes in G or in T_r. The only difference, then, in the value of ΔY is (since ΔI

is assumed zero) that it includes ΔG but does not include ΔT_r, the latter being included in *disposable* income but not in national income. In the one case there is production of goods and services for government, whose value goes into the national-income total; in the other case there is no production of goods and services for government and the only change in the national income is that represented by the change in consumption. (When v is not zero, there occurs also a rise in I and the increase in C is correspondingly greater.)

The Separation of Influences

In the present chapter there were added two new aspects of the economic system; one was the economic role of the government, the other was the investment-income relationship. Adding these two new aspects together may tend to confuse their separate influences on the solutions and derived ratios. It is tedious, however, to add each new aspect one at a time when both may conveniently be added in a single step. It is important, therefore, to know how to single out of the conclusions those new results which are attributable to the one new aspect and those which are attributable to the other.

In the present chapter it is a simple matter to eliminate from any equation either of the two new parts of the system. To eliminate the influence of the investment-income relationship it is only necessary to put v equal to zero; wherever v occurs additively in an equation it may be dropped, wherever v multiplies another factor, their product may be dropped. If investment is, then, to be treated as an independent variable, the parameter u from the investment equation can be identified as I, for the equation $I = u + vY$ becomes simple $I = u$ when the influence of Y on I is dropped. And any influence of government may similarly be eliminated by putting T_x and T_r equal to zero wherever they occur, and letting $G + u$ equal the variable N of Chap. 3.

CHAPTER 7

ENLARGEMENT OF THE SYSTEM—II

In the preceding chapter the variables G, T_x, and T_r were considered independent; that is, their behavior was not described by any of the original equations. In the present chapter explicit allowance will be made for relationships between T_x and Y and between T_r and Y, and several forms of behavior of G will be investigated. The present chapter will also make allowance for certain refinements in the equations describing the behavior of C and I.

Taxes and Transfer Payments as Dependent Variables

We shall now enlarge the equation system of the preceding chapter by adding two new relationships. We shall consider taxes and transfer payments to be linearly related to the national income. Altogether then we shall have six equations with seven variables; they are numbered and listed immediately below.*

(1)	$Y = C + I + G$
(2)	$X = Y - T_x + T_r$
(3)	$C = a + bX$
(4)	$I = u + vY$
(5)	$T_x = s + tY$
(6)	$T_r = p + rY$

Comparing the number of equations with the number of variables we see that solution should give us each variable in terms of one other. That is, specifying the numerical value of one variable should leave the values of the rest completely determined.†

---

* See the three articles by A. Smithies, J. Mosak, and S. M. Livingston, "Forecasting Postwar Demand," *Econometrica*, vol. 13, pp. 1ff., for a similar system involving numerical parameters based on statistical observation.

† Although the variable G will be the only one considered "independent" in the present system, the statement applies to any pair of variables. Not only is the value of, say, C fixed when the particular value of G is specified, but so is the value of, for example, I. Since there is an implicit linear relation between C and G, and also such a relation between I and G, there is consequently a relation between C and I. If the value of C be specified, then there is one value of I which satisfies the equations, since there is a unique value of G to which that particular value of C corresponds and to that value of G there corresponds a particular value of I. We may, then, solve our equations for C in terms of I just as well as for C in terms of G, even though G is the only variable considered independent.

The first substitution occurs in equation (2); we shall express C in terms of Y alone. Substituting in equation (2) the equivalents of T_x and T_r as given by equations (5) and (6),

$$(7) \qquad X = Y - (s + tY) + (p + rY)$$
$$= (p - s) + (1 - t + r)Y$$

Next we substitute this expression for X in equation (3).

$$(8) \qquad C = a + b[(p - s) + (1 - t + r)Y]$$
$$= (a - bs + bp) + b(1 - t + r)Y$$
$$= A + b(1 - t + r)Y$$

where A is substituted as an abbreviation for $a - bs + bp$ which is composed only of parameters none of which measure marginal ratios. Equation (8) is the derived relationship between C and Y. The incremental ratio of C to Y is $b(1 - t + r)$, the product of the incremental ratio of C to X and the incremental ratio of X to Y.

Solution for Y then follows the usual pattern. The values of C and I in terms of Y are taken from equations (8) and (4) and substituted into equation (1),

$$(9) \qquad Y = A + b(1 - t + r)Y + u + vY + G$$
$$= \frac{A + u + G}{1 - [b(1 - t + r) + v]}$$

This is the solution for Y, given in terms of G alone.* There is one independent variable, G, and a change in G equal to ΔG will be accompanied by a change in Y according to

$$(10) \qquad \frac{\Delta Y}{\Delta G} = \left(\frac{1}{1 - b(1 - t + r) - v} \right) \Delta G$$

Stability analysis modeled after that of the preceding chapter demonstrates that the denominator of this multiplier, and hence the multiplier itself, must be positive. The multiplier follows the general pattern of such incremental ratios; subtracted from 1 in the denominator is the sum of the marginal consumption-income ratio, $b(1 - t + r)$, and the marginal investment-income ratio. The only difference between the present multiplier and the one derived in the preceding section is that the marginal consumption-income ratio is the product of two factors, b, the marginal ratio of consumption to disposable income, and $1 - t + r$, the marginal ratio of disposable income to national income.

---

* For diagrammatic treatment of the subject see T. C. Schelling, "Income Determination: a Graphic Solution," *Review of Economics and Statistics*, vol. 30, p. 227.

The other incremental ratios follow at once. ΔT_x is equal to $t\,\Delta Y$, ΔT_r is equal to $r\,\Delta Y$, and ΔX is equal to $\Delta Y - \Delta T_x + \Delta T_r$ which equals $\Delta Y(1 - t + r)$. ΔC is equal to $b(1 - t + r)\Delta Y$, and ΔI is equal to $v\,\Delta Y$. Taking ΔY as given by (10) the reader may add up the three components, $\Delta C + \Delta I + \Delta G$, to check whether their sum is equal to the right-hand side of (10). Other incremental ratios in which we may be interested are $\Delta C/\Delta I$ which is equal to $b(1 - t + r)/v$, or $\Delta I/\Delta T_x$ which equals v/t. This latter ratio, $\Delta I/\Delta T_x$, is interesting in that it illustrates the kind of linear relation which may obtain between two variables neither of which is immediately related to the other.

A Problem in Criteria: the Government Budget

As a special problem suggested by the present system of equations we may introduce the new variable B, denoting here the government budgetary balance, defined according to

(11) $$B = G + T_r - T_x$$

and inquire whether it is possible for this variable to assume a smaller value when the value of G is increased. If, of course, T_x and T_r were fixed, any increase in G would be reflected in an equivalent increase in the value of B, i.e., would increase any government deficit or decrease any government surplus by an equal amount. But since T_x and T_r in the present context are not independent of changes in Y, they are not independent of changes in G and we cannot assume them invariant while we investigate changes in G. Hence arises the question whether the increase in Y which accompanies an increase in G may so increase the tax yield as to reduce the value of B, that is, reduce a government deficit or increase a revenue surplus.

Regardless of the economic significance of this question, its investigation will illustrate some interesting and important complexities in the use of the knowledge derived from stability analysis.

To see whether B may actually be decreased by a rise in G we might substitute for T_x and T_r, in the definition of B, their solution values expressed in terms of G, and derive the incremental ratio of B to G. Alternatively we may convert (11) to incremental form and use only the incremental ratios of T_x and T_r to Y, and of Y to G:

(12) $$\Delta B = \Delta G - (t - r)\Delta Y$$
$$= \Delta G[1 - M(t - r)]$$

where M stands for the multiplier, the incremental ratio of $\Delta Y/\Delta G$ obtained in equation (10). The question can now be put in terms of the value of the multiplier: can $(t - r)$ times the multiplier exceed $+1$? If so, the incremental ratio $\Delta B/\Delta G$ can actually be negative, a rise in government expenditure being associated with a greater rise in revenues. There are two requirements to be met: first, t must exceed r, else any rise in G is accompanied by a greater rise in transfer payments than in taxes and the condition certainly is not met; second, the multiplier must be large. It is the second condition that is most interesting; is there anything in the stability condition which prevents $M(t - r)$ from exceeding $+1$?*

As the multiplier stands, there is no such restriction. Looking at the denominator of (10), we can see that for *any* values of t and r such that t exceeds r, values of b and v can be found to meet the stability condition; starting with any such values of b and v we can increase the value of v until the value of the multiplier is as high as we please, higher in particular than $1/(t - r)$. To be exact, the condition for $t - r$ to exceed the denominator of the multiplier [so that $M(t - r)$ exceeds 1] is

$$(13) \qquad t - r > 1 - b + b(t - r) - v$$

$$(t - r)(1 - b) > 1 - b - v$$

If b is less than $+1$, while $b + v$ exceeds $+1$, the right-hand side of this inequality is negative and the left-hand side is positive—assuming that t exceeds r—and the condition is necessarily met. That is to say, if the values of b and v are such that the system would be unstable in the absence of the tax-income and transfer payments–income equations, but stable with those equations, then necessarily $\Delta B/\Delta G$ is negative. This is an example—of which there will be several throughout this book—of a "paradox" being explained by the "potential instability" of an equation system.† By "potential instability" we mean the characteristic that, if certain dependent variables were to be treated as independent, the system would be unstable. Values for b and v consistent with the paradox of negative $\Delta B/\Delta G$ would be dynamically incompatible without the T_x and T_r equations, *i.e.*, if T_x and T_r were independent of the other variables of the system, as they were in the preceding sections.

What has been said is not meant to imply that $b + v$ greater than 1 is a *necessary* condition for negative $\Delta B/\Delta G$. It is a *sufficient* condition, *i.e.*,

* Nothing has been said about the algebraic sign of the parameter r. If transfer payments tend to vary directly with unemployment, and employment directly with national income (as would appear to be the general rule), they will vary inversely with Y, and r should be considered negative. In that case $t - r$ exceeds t and the increment in taxes net of transfer payments which accompanies an increment in Y is greater than the increment in taxes alone.

† At least, a paradox is so explained in the present case if the reader finds it a paradox that a rise in government expenditure leads to a greater government budgetary surplus or smaller deficit. Other such paradoxes will be observed in the chapters on income distribution and international trade.

whenever $b + v$ exceeds 1 while b is less than 1, $\Delta B/\Delta G$ will be negative; but the ratio of ΔB to ΔG may be negative even though $b + v$ is less than 1. In particular, if $t - r$ exceeds 1, the condition is met so long as v is positive, for then $(t - r)(1 - b)$ exceeds $1 - b$ and certainly exceeds $(1 - b) - v$, for the latter is still smaller. This condition, $t - r$ greater than 1, however, is itself a very special condition; it implies that the marginal tax-income ratio (figured net of transfer payments) exceeds 100 per cent. It also implies that C varies inversely with Y, for with $t - r$ greater than 1, X varies inversely with Y. Finally, however, it may also be observed that the condition may be met with both $b + v$ and $t - r$ less than 1, namely when

$$(14) \qquad\qquad 1 > t - r > 1 - \frac{v}{1 - b} > 0$$

If $b + v$ is less than $+1$ (and if b is less than $+1$ which it then is so long as v is positive) the third element of (14) is positive and less than $+1$, so that there is a positive value of $t - r$ less than 1 which satisfies the condition.

Several other possible cases may be considered. If v is zero, that is, if I is fixed, $\Delta B/\Delta G$ will be negative with b greater than 1 and $t - r$ less than 1, or with b less than 1 and $t - r$ greater than 1. With v equal to zero there is no middle ground, one of these special cases must obtain. The inequality (13) could be met with negative $t - r$, if $1 - b$ is negative at the same time; that case is ruled out, however, because the stability condition is not met if the denominator of (10) is negative.

An especially interesting case occurs if b exceeds $+1$ and v is positive. First we note that if $t - r$ is less than 1, inequality (13) holds and $\Delta B/\Delta G$ is negative. For we may divide both sides of (13) by the negative $1 - b$, thus reversing the inequality sign, and the condition becomes

$$(15) \qquad\qquad t - r < 1 + \frac{v}{b - 1}$$

With $t - r$ less than 1 the inequality necessarily holds.* If $t - r$ exceeds $+1$ by more than the amount $v/(b - 1)$, the inequality is not met. Here is an interesting case in which a higher marginal tax-income ratio reduces the incremental tax yield. The rationale would seem to be that the higher value of $t - r$ has such a depressing effect on the national income that the product of $t - r$ and ΔY is less than it would be for a smaller value of $t - r$.

This point may be made more clear by reference again to the incre-

---

* It should be recalled that, with v positive, stability requires $b(1 - t + r)$ to be less than $+1$. With b greater than $+1$, this condition imposes the lower limit $(b - 1)/b$ on the value of $t - r$ since any lower value makes $b(1 - t + r)$ greater than $+1$ and the equations unstable.

mental equation relating $\Delta(T_x - T_r)$ to ΔG; for convenience we shall use t' in place of $t - r$ and refer to the marginal tax-income ratio net of transfer payments.

(16) $$\frac{\Delta(T_x - T_r)}{\Delta G} = t'\left(\frac{\Delta Y}{\Delta G}\right) = \frac{t'}{1 - b + bt' - v} = \frac{t'}{bt' + k}$$

where $k = 1 - b - v$. With positive k, any increase in the value of t' raises the value of this ratio, raising the value of $\Delta(T_x - T_r)$ which accompanies any given increment in G. For if we add the positive amount h to the value of t',

(17) $$\frac{t' + h}{bt' + bh + k} > \frac{t'}{bt' + k}$$

That inequality (17) necessarily holds may be seen by multiplying both sides by $bt' + k$ and dividing both sides by t', that is, by cross multiplying, which we may do without violating the inequality since all terms are positive.

(18) $$(t' + h)(bt' + k) > t'(bt' + bh + k)$$
$$bt'^2 + t'k + bht' + hk > bt'^2 + bht' + kt'$$
$$hk > 0$$

Thus if k is positive, that is, if $1 - b - v$ is positive, any increase in the value of t' raises the ratio $\Delta(T_x - T_r)/\Delta G$. If, however, k is negative, inequality (18) does not hold; the left-hand side is negative and cannot exceed zero; adding any positive amount h to the value of t' reduces the incremental ratio $\Delta(T_x - T_r)/\Delta G$.

In conclusion: when $b + v$ is less than $+1$, the direct effect of a higher marginal tax-income ratio outweighs the indirect effect (via depression of ΔY) on the incremental tax yield; but when $b + v$ is greater than $+1$ or equal to $+1$, as it may be consistently with stability in the present system, the direct effect of an increase in the marginal tax yield on the incremental ratio of $T_x - T_r$ to G is less than the indirect adverse effect via the reduced value of ΔY, and the higher value of t' is associated with a lower ratio of $\Delta(T_x - T_r)$ to ΔG.

Equation (16) also confirms our previous conclusions. When k is negative but b itself is less than 1, the ratio in (16) is greater than $+1$ for any positive value of t', and $\Delta B/\Delta G$ is negative as we earlier deduced. But when b exceeds 1 and k is negative (as it then is if v is positive), the ratio of $\Delta(T_x - T_r)$ to ΔG as shown in (16) is equal to 1 when $t' = bt' + k$ and is less than 1 for higher values of t'. And when $t' = bt' + k$, $t' = k/(1 - b) = 1 + v/(b - 1)$ which is exactly the criterion in (15).

This question of the effect on B of a change in G which has been investigated at such length illustrates certain principles regarding the use of stability criteria.   In general, the possibility of a certain ratio's being of one sign or the other, or of one increment's exceeding another, hinges on the use of stability criteria.   Certain possibilities can be excluded on the grounds that the necessary parameter values are inconsistent with the dynamic compatibility of the relationships.   On the other hand, possibilities excluded in the context of one equation system may be reinstated when the system is enlarged by the addition of new relationships, because the new relationships modify the original stability criteria.   In particular, when variables originally treated as independent are treated as dependent on the values of other variables, the stability criteria may be so modified as to make admissible certain paradoxical results which had been discarded as inadmissible in the former context.

Government Expenditure as Dependent Variable

As a next step we shall consider G itself to be related to some other variable or variables.   If we retain the original six equations, a new relationship involving G brings the number of equations up to seven, the number of variables (unless we add new variables in the equation for G), leaving completely determined in terms of parameters the values of all the variables. To illustrate such a system, we add the equation

$$(19) \qquad\qquad G = e + gY$$

to the other six original equations.   Reverting to equation (9) we replace G with its equivalent according to the new equation

$$(20) \qquad Y = A + b(1 - t + r)Y + u + vY + e + gY$$

$$= \frac{A + u + e}{1 - [b(1 - t + r) + v + g]}$$

In this case the solution for Y contains only parameters.   None of the usual multipliers can be derived; there are no independent variables.   None of the variables can change its value without violating some of the original equations.   The form of the solution is, however, perfectly familiar; in the denominator the incremental ratios of C to Y, of I to Y, and of G to Y are all subtracted from 1.   The form suggests that if we had allowed a fourth component of national income in addition to C, I, and G (such as some independent part of one of these three variables), in the national-income identity there would have been a multiplier of the usual form with the parameter g joining v and $b(1 - t + r)$ in the denominator.

Although there is in this case no independent variable whose value may change, and there are consequently no incremental ratios to derive, there is still a kind of change we may investigate. We may let one of the original equations change. That is, we may allow for a shift in one of the relationships, such as by allowing the equation $I = u + vY$ to be replaced by the alternative equation $I = (u + k) + vY$, and investigate the effect on the solution values of the variables of this shift in the investment equation. To that subject we shall turn in the following chapter.

As a special case of an equation representing government expenditure we may impose the condition that $G + T_r - T_x = 0$, i.e., that the government budget should balance within the framework of given tax and transfer-payments relationships.*

$$(21) \qquad G = T_x - T_r = (s - p) + (t - r)Y$$

In order to leave ourselves room for variation, let us at the same time return to I its independent status, omitting equation (4) from the system. We have, then,

$$(22) \quad Y = \frac{a + (s - p)(1 - b) + I}{1 - b - (t - r)(1 - b)} = \frac{a + (s - p)(1 - b) + I}{(1 - b)(1 - t + r)}$$

Assuming $t - r$ less than $+1$, stability analysis modeled after that of earlier chapters leads to the condition that b must be less than $+1$ and the denominator of (22) consequently positive.

The incremental ratio $\Delta Y / \Delta I$ can be represented as the product of $1/(1 - b)$ and $1/(1 - t + r)$; it is thus $1/(1 - t + r)$ times as great as it would be if government expenditure, taxes, and transfer payments were fixed. It is interesting to note that if the denominator of (22) is written as $1 - [b(1 - t + r) + (t - r)]$ the bracketed terms may be interpreted as representing a weighted average of b and $+1$, those being respectively the marginal ratios of expenditure to disposable income of the two groups, consumers with disposable income equal to $Y - T_x + T_r$, and government with "disposable income" consisting of taxes net of transfer payments, $T_x - T_r$. The weights used in the weighted average are the relative marginal shares of private incomes and government "incomes" in the economy equal to $1 - t + r$ and $t - r$, whose sum is $1 - t + r + t - r = 1$.

A variation on the above system would be the consideration of two separate government units, representing perhaps national government on the one hand, and state and local government on the other. Two separate tax equations would be used, one for $T_x(N)$ and one for $T_x(SL)$ where the symbols represent national-government taxes and state- and local-government taxes respectively. National-government expenditure, $G(N)$, might

---

* Again we make explicit allowance for transfer payments; the algebra may be simplified by omitting T_r and the parameters p and r, corresponding to the T_r equation, and dealing with taxes net.

then be taken as an independent variable while state- and local-government expenditure could be put equal to state and local taxes, $G(SL) = T_x(SL)$, and the system solved accordingly. Or the system could be further elaborated to let $G(SL) = A + BT_x(SL)$ where A is positive, B less than $+1$, to allow budgetary deficits at low levels of revenue, budgetary surpluses at high levels of revenue.

Refinement of the Investment Equation

One aspect of the relationships postulated so far, which has contributed to their algebraic simplicity, is that all variables have been related directly or indirectly to the national income, or else considered independent. Consumption in the present chapter has been related directly to disposable income, but since the latter is related via taxes and transfer payments to the national income, straightforward substitution has provided the desired relationship between C and Y. Similarly, in the government-expenditures case treated at the end of the last section, G was not directly related to Y but was related to T_x which was itself related to Y, and we could obtain by ordinary substitution the direct relation of G to Y.

In later chapters we shall deal with systems in which straightforward substitution does not put everything into direct relationship with Y; the interrelationships will be more ramified. To demonstrate such a system, and to introduce a way of handling it, we shall take up immediately the case of an equation relating investment separately to C, I, and G.

We replace equation (4) with the new relationship

$$(23) \qquad I = u + vC + wI + qG$$

This equation is intended to state the hypothesis that investment activity is geared not directly to total production but separately to the three components of production, C, I, and G. According to this hypothesis, investment in industries producing consumption goods and services depends on the level of consumption, investment in industries producing goods and services for government use depends on the level of government expenditure for goods and services, and investment in industries producing investment goods and services depends on the level of total investment. (We ignore the inventory component of investment.) If all three parameters, w, v, and q, were equal we could replace the three separate terms by vY and have the original investment equation.

The first step in solution is to remove I from the right-hand side of this equation.

$$(24) \qquad I - wI = u + vC + qG$$

$$(25) \qquad I = \frac{u + vC + qG}{1 - w}$$

Next we substitute for C in equation (25) its equivalent in terms of Y obtained from equation (8), first rewriting that equation for convenience as $C = A + BY$, where $A = a + bp - bs$ and $B = b(1 - t + r)$,

$$(26) \qquad I = \frac{u + vA + vBY + qG}{1 - w}$$

Finally we substitute in the national-income identity the values of C and I obtained from (8) and (26) respectively, again utilizing the abbreviations A and B.

$$(27) \quad Y = A + BY + \frac{u}{1 - w} + \left(\frac{v}{1 - w}\right)(A + BY) + \left(\frac{q}{1 - w}\right)G + G$$

$$= \frac{A\left(1 + \dfrac{v}{1 - w}\right) + \dfrac{u}{1 - w} + \left(1 + \dfrac{q}{1 - w}\right)G}{1 - B\left(1 + \dfrac{v}{1 - w}\right)}$$

Equation (27) is the solution for Y in terms of G. Its form may be more clear when it is rewritten as

$$(28) \qquad Y = \frac{A(1 + v - w) + u + (1 + q - w)G}{1 - w - B(1 + v - w)}$$

Analysis of this solution is facilitated if we deduce at once the value of the incremental ratio $\Delta Y/\Delta G$ as follows:

$$(29) \quad \frac{\Delta Y}{\Delta G} = \frac{1 + q - w}{1 - w - B(1 + v - w)} = \frac{1 + q - w}{1 - B(1 + v) - w(1 - B)}$$

First it may be noted that, if $w = v = q$, this ratio degenerates into the simpler multiplier deduced already in equation (10), namely the reciprocal of $1 - B - v$, since $q - w$ and $v - w$ are then zero. The effect of the expression in parentheses in the denominator is to augment the denominator in accordance with any excess of v over w (or the contrary if w exceeds v), and in the numerator the addition of $q - w$ serves to correct for the difference between q and w. The effect of $q - w$ in the multiplier is to raise the multiplier in proportion to $q - w$, while the influence of $v - w$ depends on the value of B. In either case, for a given value of w, the multiplier is the larger, the larger is the excess of q or v over w. Or, as a matter of fact, we may say that the value of the multiplier varies directly with the values of B, w, q, and v. That an increase in w raises the value of the multiplier may not be evident from (29) since the numerator is lower, the higher is the value of w. From (27), however, it is clear that the larger value of w implies the larger value for the multiplier. In the numerator, the larger is w the smaller is $1 - w$ and the larger is $q/(1 - w)$; in the denominator the larger is w the smaller is $1 - w$ and the larger is $Bv/(1 - w)$, hence the smaller the whole denominator and the larger the multiplier.

The Stability Criteria

Again we must verify whether the equations, on whose solution we base our analysis, are dynamically compatible. The stability analysis presented in the preceding chapter cannot directly be applied because the structure of the relationships is different in the present case. Earlier there were two adjusting variables each of which adjusted toward a value which depended on the national income; in the present case there are two adjusting variables, C and I, but the value of I cannot be described as adjusting toward a value depending on Y. As a matter of fact it seems necessary, in the present case, to identify three separate components of I, namely that part of investment related to the value of C, that part related to the value of G, and that part related to the value of I itself. Let us denote them by Ic, Ig, and Ii respectively.*

First let us consider Ig. This variable has a solution value which may be represented as $\overline{I}g = u' + qG$, where u' is some constant whose value need not concern us. (We shall suppose that the investment equation represents the summation of three separate equations, $Ic = u''' + vC$, $Ii = u'' + wI$, and $Ig = u' + qG$, so that $u' + u'' + u''' = u$.) Since the value of G is independent of the values of any other variables, the value of $u' + qG$ is fixed for any given value of G, and so long as Ig tends to adjust toward $u' + qG$ it adjusts toward $\overline{I}g$ and there is no stability problem with respect to Ig. The question of dynamic compatibility of the equations is thus independent of the value of q.

Having disposed of the parameter q, we are left with three crucial parameters whose values are pertinent to the stability question, B, v, and w, where B stands for $b(1 - t + r)$. (We are considering T_x and T_r to be instantaneously adjusted in accordance with the value of Y; thus disposable income is in the constant relation to national income, $X = Y(1 - t + r) + (p - s)$. We consequently treat the single coefficient $b(1 - t + r)$ as the relevant parameter for adjustment of C.) In order to deduce the conditions which must be met in order that stability be present, we shall begin by supposing that C, Ic, and Ii exceed their solution values by the positive amounts h, d, and k, respectively. The value of Ig we assume equal to

---

*This is not a necessary treatment of investment, it is rather one particular way of considering the adjustment of I. There is no "necessary" interpretation of the investment equation for purposes of adjustment analysis. The treatment in the text relies on what seems to be a plausible structure of adjustment behavior to impute to I; the reader may experiment with alternative patterns of behavior adjustment and will generally find that the stability conditions are not significantly different from those to be derived.

$\bar{I}g$. And we consider what is necessary in order that C, Ic, and Ii approach their solution values.

First we observe toward what values the three variables are in *immediate* adjustment. C adjusts toward the value of $\bar{C} + B(h + d + k)$ since the value of Y is equal to $\bar{Y} + h + d + k$. Ic adjusts toward the value of $\bar{I}c + vh$ since C exceeds $\bar{C}$ by the amount h. And Ii adjusts toward the value of $\bar{I}i + w(d + k)$ since I exceeds $\bar{I}$ by the amount $d + k$. It should be particularly noted that since h, d, and k are all positive, each of these values toward which the variables are in immediate adjustment exceeds the corresponding solution value. From this we deduce that *the process of adjustment takes no variable beneath its solution value*, i.e., adjustment eventually, if not at once, is *toward the solution values from above* for each of the three adjusting variables. (We say eventually, if not at once, to make allowance for the possibility that one of the variables initially tends to adjust upward; *e.g.*, Ic will adjust immediately upward, even though it exceeds its solution value, if d is less than vh, a possibility we do not exclude. If, however, C approaches its solution value, vh will eventually approach zero and will thus eventually be less than the value of d, so that Ic will eventually adjust downward if the equations are stable.) The truth of this assertion is clear if we consider what its contradiction implies; in order that a variable, say Ic, should go below its solution value in its process of adjustment, it must first pass through that solution value, *i.e.*, equal it for an instant. At the instant when it does equal its solution value it must be adjusting toward vh which is positive; it must thus be rising, not falling, and cannot therefore be crossing $\bar{I}c$ to go below $\bar{I}c$. The value of vh could be negative only if C had previously crossed the value of $\bar{C}$ and gone beneath it which it cannot do unless $B(h + d + k)$ has become negative, which it cannot unless d or k has become negative. Thus no one of the three variables can be the *first* to become less than its solution value; or, considering h, d, and k to be variables, we may say that no one of h, d, or k may be the first to become negative. (If they all became negative simultaneously they would all have their solution values simultaneously and would stop adjusting.)

Thus we may assume that adjustment toward solution values from any initial values greater than the solution values constitutes, ultimately, adjustment downward from above. There are two possible patterns to be investigated; adjustment may be ultimately simultaneous downward adjustment for all three variables, or it may be an oscillatory type of adjustment with the variables reversing direction in the course of adjustment and never more than two variables moving in the same direction, and with none of the variables ever going beneath its solution value.

We consider first the possibility of simultaneous downward adjustment for all three variables, noting that if all three variables ever show simultaneous downward adjustment they will necessarily continue to adjust simultaneously downward, for no variable can be the first to reverse its direction. This is apparent from the fact that h, for example, cannot turn upward in its course unless $B(h + d + k)$ rises, for h cannot otherwise adjust downward toward $B(h + d + k)$ and arrive beneath it. Thus h can turn up only if d or k is already rising; similarly d cannot turn upward unless h is already rising, nor can k turn up unless d or k is already rising (so that $d + k$ may be rising). Thus if all three once adjust simultaneously downward, none can be the first to turn upward.

The possibility of simultaneous downward adjustment from values above the solution values implies that, for *some* values of h, d, and k*

$$(30) \qquad\qquad B(h + d + k) < h$$

$$(31) \qquad\qquad vh < d$$

$$(32) \qquad\qquad w(d + k) < k$$

These must hold, since, for example, $C = \bar{C} + h$ and adjusts toward the value of $\bar{C} + B(h + d + k)$ which is less if adjustment is downward; and similarly for the other two inequalities.

Rewriting (30) and (32) as

$$(33) \qquad\qquad B(d + k) < h(1 - B)$$

$$(34) \qquad\qquad wd < k(1 - w)$$

it appears as a necessary condition for stability that B and w each be less than $+1$, else the right-hand side of (33) or (34) would be negative and could not exceed the left which is necessarily positive. (We are not considering negative values for B or w). It may be noted that there is no similar restriction evident from the inequalities regarding the value of v.

Next we add the left-hand sides of (31) and (32) and assert that this sum is less than the sum of the right-hand sides of the same two inequalities, the justification for which is evident.

$$(35) \qquad\qquad vh + w(d + k) < d + k$$

From this it follows that

$$(36) \qquad\qquad vh < (d + k)(1 - w)$$

Finally we multiply the left-hand sides of (33) and (36) and assert that this

---

* Even if one of the three variables adjusts very rapidly relatively to the other two, it does not reach its solution value ahead of the others, but rather reaches the value given by its own equation, namely $\bar{C} + B(h + d + k)$ for C, etc. Thus eventually all three are adjusting downward from above.

product is less than the product of the right-hand sides, which is permissible since the left-hand sides are necessarily positive by assumption, the right-hand sides necessarily positive if those inequalities hold, and consequently both products are products of positive factors.

$$(37) \qquad Bv(d + k)h < h(d + k)(1 - w)(1 - B)$$

Since $(d + k)h$ is positive it may be canceled without violating the inequality

$$(38) \qquad Bv < 1 - w - B + Bw$$

$$0 < (1 - w) - B(1 - w + v)$$

Since $1 - w$ has already been inferred to be necessarily positive, we may divide through by $1 - w$ and obtain, as our final condition,

$$(39) \qquad 1 - B\left(\frac{1 - w + v}{1 - w}\right) = 1 - B\left(1 + \frac{v}{1 - w}\right) > 0$$

This is a most useful stability condition, for it indicates that the denominator of the solution for Y, and similarly the denominator of the multiplier for $\Delta Y / \Delta G$, is necessarily positive if the equations are dynamically compatible.

We have considered so far, however, only the case of simultaneous downward adjustment for the three variables. There remains the possibility that, although the three variables never move simultaneously in the same direction, they do approach their solution values by a process of downward oscillation. This possibility must be considered. First let us make some observations, however.

It should be noted that the analysis given above may be reversed to show that simultaneous upward adjustment, away from solution values, requires the reverse of the inequalities deduced above for stability. Also, if the variables ever attain simultaneous adjustment away from solution values, they remain in simultaneous adjustment away from solution values from then on according to the same kind of argument given above for the converse proposition.

It should also be noted that the necessity to look into the oscillation case would be eliminated if we could prove that stability or instability were independent of the initial set of values of h, d, and k, that is, if we could prove that stability depends only on the values of the parameters of the equations; for we have already proved that if (33), (34), and (39) hold, the equations are stable for some values of h, d, and k, and that if they do not hold, the equations are unstable for some values of h, d, and k.

We proceed now to the case of oscillatory adjustment, *i.e.*, of adjustment during which the three variables never move in the same direction, upward or downward.   First it may be noted that if any of the variables oscillates, k must oscillate; for if k moved steadily downward, d could turn down only while vh was descending; and the turning down of d would yield simultaneous downward movement for all three variables.   We shall concentrate, then, on k and show that if inequality (39) holds, the successive peak values of k are in descending order, while if inequality (39) does not hold, the successive trough values of k are in ascending order.

Let k_0 denote the value of k on some occasion when k is just turning downward, *i.e.*, a peak value of k.   Then, with d_0 denoting the value of d on that occasion, the equation must hold

$$(40) \qquad\qquad w(d_0 + k_0) = k$$

Since the value of d must be decreasing in order that k be turning downward, and since the value of h must be increasing in order that k's turning not yield simultaneous downward movement for all three,

$$(41) \qquad\qquad d_0 > vh_0$$

$$(42) \qquad\qquad h_0 < B(h_0 + d_0 + k_0)$$

If the next succeeding peak value of k is greater than k_0, there must have been an intermediate point when $k = k_0$ and k was increasing, that is, when

$$(43) \qquad\qquad k = k_0$$

$$(44) \qquad\qquad k < w(d + k_0)$$

$$k < \left(\frac{w}{1 - w}\right) d$$

Equations (40), (43), and (44) imply that d is greater than d_0.   Since d_0 was a descending value of d, d would have had to turn upward; the value of d could not then go above the greatest value attained by vh during the interval.

Nor could h have exceeded the greatest value of $B(h + d + k)$ attained during the interval.   Let us denote by h', d', and k' the greatest values attained by these variables during the interval; then

$$(45) \qquad\qquad k' = k$$

$$(46) \qquad\qquad d' \leqslant vh'$$

$$(47) \qquad\qquad h' \leqslant B(h' + d' + k')$$

These, together with (44), imply

$$(48) \qquad\qquad h' < Bh' + Bvh' + Bvh'\left(\frac{w}{1 - w}\right)$$

Canceling h' which is positive, (48) becomes

$$(49) \qquad\qquad 1 < B\left(1 + \frac{v}{1 - w}\right)$$

Inequality (49) is precisely the contradiction of (39); so as long as (39) holds, the successive peak values of k will descend.

It is left to the reader to restate the argument in terms of trough values of k to show that unless (39) holds the trough values of k will ascend, i.e., to show that the trough values can descend only if (39) holds.

This concludes the stability analysis of the present equation system. The present line of reasoning will provide a model for the analysis of similar three-variable cases in subsequent chapters. Again we have considered only the case of positive values of the variables, on the grounds that unless the equations are stable for positive deviations from solution values they are of little relevance. The entire argument can be restated for the case of negative deviations. It is left to the reader to deduce the validity of these stability conditions for the case of mixed deviations, some positive and some negative.

The Implicit Investment-income Relationship

Although we have used an equation relating I separately to C, G, and I, we can derive the implicit relationship between I and Y. That there is such an implicit relationship is evident from the fact that G is the sole independent variable; to each value of G there corresponds a certain value of Y and, since C is related to Y, a certain value of C. Subtracting from this value of Y the values of G and C leaves us with a unique value of I; thus there corresponds a particular value of I to each value of Y. We shall derive the incremental relationship only; the complete relationship is of the form $I = U + VY$, where V is the incremental ratio $\Delta I/\Delta Y$, which we are about to derive, and U is some constant which could be determined by a process of substitution in the solution for Y.

From equation (25) it follows that

$$(50) \qquad \frac{\Delta I}{\Delta Y} = \frac{v(\Delta C/\Delta Y) + q(\Delta G/\Delta Y)}{1 - w} = \frac{vB + (qD/N)}{1 - w}$$

where N and D stand respectively for the numerator and denominator of (29); qD/N is, of course, equal to $q\,\Delta G/\Delta Y$, since $\Delta G/\Delta Y$ is the reciprocal of $\Delta Y/\Delta G$ which is equal to N/D, the multiplier.

Since $\Delta C = B\,\Delta Y$, and since ΔG is of the same sign as ΔY, it ought to follow that ΔI is less than $(1 - B)\Delta Y$ for any stable values of v, w, and q. If $\Delta I/\Delta Y$ were greater than $1 - B$, the increments in C and I would more than exhaust any increment in Y so that ΔG would have to be negative in order that the national-income identity hold, that is, in order that $\Delta Y = \Delta C + \Delta I + \Delta G$. Since we know that ΔG and ΔY are of same sign from the stability condition, it must follow that $\Delta I/\Delta Y$ is less than $1 - B$ for stable values of the parameters.

Yet we earlier determined that stability was independent of the value of q; it must follow that the expression on the right-hand side of (50) cannot exceed $1 - B$ for any positive value of q if the stability condition holds. To demonstrate the validity of this deduction let us put the right-hand side of (50) less than $1 - B$ and attempt to prove the inequality. Multiplying through by $1 - w$, which is positive if the equations are stable, we have

$$(51) \qquad vB + q\left(\frac{D}{N}\right) < (1 - w)(1 - B)$$

$$q\left(\frac{D}{N}\right) < 1 - w(1 - B) - B(1 + v)$$

$$\frac{q}{(1 - w) + q} < 1$$

$$0 < 1 - w$$

In the next to last step we divided through by D, known to be positive, and since the right-hand side was identical with the denominator of (29), we were left with $+1$ on that side. Since the last inequality, $1 - w$ greater than 0, is a necessary condition for stability, it follows that so long as the stability conditions earlier derived are met, there is no positive value of q so great as to raise the value of $\Delta I/\Delta Y$ above $1 - B$. The rationale, of course, is that although a large value of q makes large the value of $\Delta I/\Delta G$, it affects similarly the value of $\Delta Y/\Delta G$, keeping the ratio of ΔI to ΔY within the limiting value $1 - B$.

Refinement of the Consumption Equation

Another refinement of a behavior equation which is worth investigating is the distinction among the effects on consumption of alternative increases in disposable income occurring via (a) an increase in the national income, (b) a decrease in the rate of taxation, or (c) an increase in the rate of transfer payments. The impact of taxes is selective; individuals do not necessarily share tax increments in the same proportions as they share general rises in income, nor are transfer payments generally shared proportionately to marginal income shares. The distribution of disposable income, in other words, is not indifferent to the alternative increments, ΔY, $-\Delta T_x$, or ΔT_r.

To make allowance for these distinctions we revise the consumption equation to read as follows:

$$(52) \qquad\qquad C = a + bY - cT_x + dT_r$$

Thus the marginal consumption–income ratio for the economy as a whole is equal to b; it is to be considered a weighted average of each group's (or of each individual's) marginal consumption–income ratio, the weights being their marginal shares in a general rise in the national income.   The marginal consumption-taxation ratio is equal to c, and corresponds to such a weighted average with weights equal to each group's or each individual's marginal share in tax payments.   And similarly with the parameter d which represents the average marginal consumption–income ratio when the weights are equal to marginal shares in the receipt of transfer payments.   It is generally considered that $d > b > c$, this order corresponding inversely with the supposed average income levels to which the three categories correspond, taxes being considered to fall proportionately more on the higher incomes and transfer payments being considered to benefit more the lower incomes in the marginal sense.   (This order of size among the three parameters will not be essential to the analysis which follows.)

If we retain equations (5) and (6), relating T_x and T_r to Y, this consumption hypothesis yields a fairly elaborate relationship between C and Y; substituting (5) and (6) into equation (52),

$$(53) \qquad\quad C = a + bY - c(s + tY) + d(p + rY)$$
$$= (a - cs + dp) + (b - ct + dr)Y$$

This new marginal ratio between C and Y contains five parameters; and the solution for Y is affected accordingly, its denominator becoming $1 - [(b - ct + dr) + v]$ with the investment equation retained in its simplest form.

This refinement in the consumption equation is more pertinent to the case in which T_x and T_r are considered independent; otherwise the separate marginal ratios combine into what is essentially just a weighted average in which the weights take account of the marginal shares in disposable income under given tax and transfer structures.   Equation (53) is useful in showing just how the general marginal ratio of C to Y is constructed of the elementary marginal ratios; but unless T_x and T_r are considered capable of independent variation the separate parameters c and d are only two of the many separate marginal ratios which might be combined from many separate income categories into a composite, weighted by marginal income shares.

With T_x and T_r considered independent, we solve equations (1), (2), (3), and (4) to obtain

$$(54) \qquad Y = \frac{a + u + G - cT_x + dT_r}{1 - b - v}$$

The multipliers pertinent to Y become

$$(55) \qquad \frac{\Delta Y}{\Delta T_x} = \frac{-c}{1 - b - v}$$

$$(56) \qquad \frac{\Delta Y}{\Delta T_r} = \frac{d}{1 - b - v}$$

A specific application of this hypothesis may be made to the case of increased government expenditure accompanied by an equal increase in taxation. To facilitate comparison with previous results let us drop the investment-income relation, putting $v = 0$; then, with T_r fixed and G and T_x increasing or decreasing by equal amounts,

$$(57) \qquad \frac{\Delta Y}{\Delta G} (\Delta T_x = \Delta G, \Delta T_r = 0) = \frac{1 - c}{1 - b}$$

Our previous result for this case [equation (40), Chap. 6] was that $\Delta Y / \Delta G = 1$ when $\Delta G = \Delta T_x$, $\Delta T_r = 0$, and $v = 0$. In that case there was no change in consumption; the only change in the value of Y was that corresponding directly to the change in G. In the present case, if we suppose $b > c$ so that $1 - c > 1 - b$, the increase in Y exceeds the increase in G, the difference being increased consumption. In both cases the "direct" effect on disposable income of the change in the government budget is zero, increased taxes offsetting increased expenditure. But the shift in the distribution of income, resulting from the differential impact of taxes and incomes earned in production for government use, affects consumption expenditure. The amount by which the rate of consumption rises is seen when the multiplier is dissected:

$$(58) \qquad \frac{1 - c}{1 - b} = \frac{1 - c + b - b}{1 - b} = \frac{1 - b}{1 - b} + \frac{b - c}{1 - b} = 1 + \frac{b - c}{1 - b}$$

The increase in consumption, then, is equal to $(b - c)/(1 - b)$ times the balanced increase in the government budget. If $c > b$ the consumption effect is opposite to the change in the government budget, a rise in G and T_x is accompanied by a fall in consumption which keeps ΔY less than ΔG.

Supposing that c exceeds b we may inquire whether the adverse impact on income of the redistribution involved can entirely offset the increase in government expenditure, leaving ΔY negative in company with positive ΔG. Since the stability condition is that b be less than $+1$ (or, allowing for the investment relationship, that $b + v$ be less than $+1$) negative $\Delta Y / \Delta G$ requires that the numerator of (57) be negative, that is, that c exceed $+1$.

Whether c may exceed $+1$ is purely an empirical question in the present context, since the value of c is irrelevant to the question of dynamic compatibility when T_x is considered independent; a marginal consumption–income ratio in excess of 1, however, is frequently considered extreme, since it implies a lower rate of saving at a higher level of income. Final appeal, of course, is to empirical observation.

Again we may consider a pure shift in the distribution of income unaccompanied by any change in government expenditure, effected by equal increases in T_x and T_r. The effect on national income is given by

$$(59) \qquad \frac{\Delta Y}{\Delta T_x}\,(\Delta T_x = \Delta T_r,\, \Delta G = 0) = \frac{d - c}{1 - b}$$

in the absence of the investment relationship. Thus the effect on income is equal to the difference between the marginal consumption–income ratio of the receiving group and that of the tax-paying group, multiplied by the amount of transfer and multiplied by the ordinary multiplier. In the absence of the investment-income relationship the entire increase in Y is equal to the increase in consumption; if the investment relation is reinstated, ΔI is given by

$$(60) \qquad \Delta I = v\,\Delta Y = v\left(\frac{d - c}{1 - b - v}\right)\Delta T_x$$

and the increase in consumption is consequently equal to

$$(61) \qquad \Delta C = \Delta Y - \Delta I = \left[\frac{(1 - v)\,(d - c)}{1 - b - v}\right]\Delta T_x$$

Another refinement which may be made in the consumption equation is the recognition that the distribution of disposable income might be significantly affected by changes in the composition of the national income as among C, I, and G. We have quite generally introduced "independent" changes in I and G and assumed (tacitly) that the consumption equation was invariant with respect to the composition of Y. In general, if the composition of Y is pertinent to the form of the consumption-income relationship, but the components of Y remain in a fixed linear relation to Y itself, we may suppose the consumption equation already to reflect the pattern of composition, just as when T_x and T_r are related to Y we can skip over the explicit comparison of b, c, and d and assume them reflected in the parameters of the simpler consumption equation, a and b. If, however, part of our analysis involves the explicit manipulation of the composition of Y, such as is involved when either G or I may change independently, we cannot assume the consumption equation to be invariant unless we assume equal marginal consumption–income ratios for the incomes earned in the production of consumption goods and services, for the incomes earned in the production of investment goods and services, and for the incomes earned in producing goods and services for the government.

In Chap. 9 we shall deal explicitly with this problem in income distribution.

Some Algebraic Patterns

It frequently happens that certain algebraic results appear in an unfamiliar form which, by a few manipulations, can be converted to a familiar one. We have already had occasion to make several such conversions, *e.g.*, in equations (27), (28), and (29) of this chapter. It is useful to be able to recognize alternative patterns of the same expression, not only for the identification of one's results but so that advantage may be taken of certain simpler or more convenient forms.

To illustrate this point and to introduce a family of alternative forms, we shall introduce an arbitrary equation,

$$(62) \qquad Y = a + bY + cY + G$$

This equation is comparable to equation (9), (20), or (27) of the present chapter, with the parameters simplified. The usual solution has been in the form

$$(63) \qquad Y = \frac{a + G}{1 - b - c}$$

$$(64) \qquad \frac{\Delta Y}{\Delta G} = \frac{1}{1 - b - c}$$

If, however, we subtract bY from both sides of (62) we may obtain the alternative form

$$(65) \qquad Y = \frac{a + cY + G}{1 - b}$$

$$(66) \qquad \frac{\Delta Y}{\Delta G} = \frac{1}{1 - b} + \left(\frac{c}{1 - b}\right)\frac{\Delta Y}{\Delta G}$$

Solving (66) for $\Delta Y/\Delta G$ we may subtract $[c/(1 - b)]\Delta Y/\Delta G$ from both sides, divide both sides by $1 - c/(1 - b)$ and obtain

$$(67) \qquad \frac{\Delta Y}{\Delta G} = \frac{1/(1 - b)}{1 - (c/1 - b)} = \frac{1}{(1 - b)\,[1 - (c/1 - b)]}$$

We have also had occasion to make use of the identity

$$(68) \qquad \frac{1}{1 - b - c} = \frac{1 - b - c + b + c}{1 - b - c} = 1 + \frac{b + c}{1 - b - c}$$

These do not exhaust the possibilities; (68) for example may readily be converted to

$$(69) \qquad 1 + \frac{b + c}{1 - b - c} = 1 + \frac{1}{(1/b + c) - 1}$$

Finally we may set up a still more general equation of the form

$$(70) \quad Y = a_1 + a_2 + a_3 + \cdots + a_n + b_1Y + b_2Y + b_3Y + \cdots + b_rY$$

$$= \sum_1^n a_i + \sum_1^r (b_jY)$$

$$(71) \qquad Y = \frac{\sum_1^n a}{1 - \sum_1^r b}$$

Any system of equations, then, which can be put into the form of equation (70), with Y equal to a sum of constants plus a series of multiples or fractions of Y itself, can be put into the form shown in equation (71).

The Interpretation of Equations

An equation of the form $C = a + bY$ is frequently described as showing C equal to the sum of two parts, a "constant" part equal to a, and a "variable" part equal to v times Y. The parameter a is often referred to as the "constant" in the equation. This separation of the two parts should be thought of as a purely mathematical operation; it has no economic counterpart. In particular, we do not mean to imply that consumption expenditures can be divided into two identifiable components, one of which is dependent on, the other of which is independent of, the national income.

If we investigate the effect on the several variables of a system of a shift in the consumption relationship, we often represent that shift as an increase or decrease in the value of the parameter a. This manipulation of the value of a should not be interpreted as the hypothesis that an increase occurs in some "constant" or independent component of consumption; it represents only an upward or downward shift of the line on a graph portraying the relation of C to Y.* Geometrically, the parameter a is only a reference point in the drawing of a line. When, in Chap. 12, we discuss the relaxation of the linearity assumption, it will become even more clear that the two parts, a and bY, cannot be separated, since the value of a

---

* Even if the two parts were considered economically separable, adding the amount h to the parameter a would affect the equation exactly as would the addition of the same amount to the part bY. One way we have $(a + h) + bY$, the other way, $a + (bY + h)$; both equal $a + h + bY$.

depends on which particular region of a curved line is being approximately represented by a linear equation.

In the case of some equations there may be an economically meaningful separation of the two parts. In the tax equation $T_x = s + tY$ we might attempt to identify the parameter t with an average rate of income taxation, and the parameter s with the sum of taxes independent of the national income. If the only taxes were an income tax of constant rate and head taxes independent of income this identification would be entirely justifiable; even when the tax structure is not capable of description in such simple terms we may consider s and t as approximations to certain identifiable parts of the tax structure. If, however, the tax-income relationship is not really considered to be linear, but is thought to be more closely represented by an equation of the form $T_x = s + tY + t'Y^2$, which allows the line to show curvature, we should have difficulty in identifying any category of taxation which can be economically identified as dependent on the square of the national income.

In some cases, then, we may be able to identify particular economic magnitudes, such as particular tax rates, whose values are represented by parameters of the system; but those are to be considered special cases. In general we consider the linear equation to portray the shape of a relationship between two variables; and the values of the separate parameters are not expected to correspond to identifiable economic categories.

The question arises whether it is preferable to consider all parameters to have positive values, and use minus signs to denote negative relationships, or to link all terms by plus signs and let negative parameter values denote negative relationships. In the transfer equation, for example, we had $T_r = p + rY$ where it seemed likely that the value of r was negative. Could we not as well or better rewrite that equation as $T_r = p - rY$, imputing to r a positive value?

This question involves only mathematical convenience. When the signs of all parameters are known or stipulated in the original formulation of the relationships, it is probably helpful to use parameters of positive value and insert minus signs to denote negative relationships, the minus signs serving to remind us which values in the solutions are negative. When, however, it is intended that certain parameters may be either positive or negative, or when we prefer not to commit ourselves on the sign of a parameter but simply use a parameter of unknown sign to allow for a relationship whose form is not sufficiently known to be identified as direct or inverse, it is preferable to use plus signs in the original equations, letting negative parameter values denote negative relationships. A mixture of the two practices is confusing; one has to remember in precisely which original equations one used minus signs for negative relationships, and in which one used plus signs with negatively valued parameters.

A final word is necessary on the investment equation used in Chaps. 6 and 7. This investment–national income relationship should not be identified with the relationship often referred to as the "principle of acceleration"; that relationship is conceptually distinct from the one analyzed so far. The principle of acceleration relates not a change in the value of I to a change in the value of Y, but the value of I itself to a change in the value of Y. That is to say, it is not a relationship of I to Y which is involved in the acceleration principle, it is a relationship of I to ΔY; and in that relationship ΔY is specifically interpreted as a change in the value of Y over time. That is, there exists an essential chronology in the analysis of the acceleration principle; Y is the difference between two successive, not two alternative, values of Y. In Part IV of this book, "Dynamics," the acceleration principle will be analyzed.

Some Remarks about Purpose

So much pure algebra has been undergone in these chapters that a few further words are in order about the purpose of the analysis. In particular, the reader may question why we can call a "solution" an expression for, say, Y, which contains as many parameters as originally there were variables in the system. To throw into an equation a handful of parameters which masquerade as "knowns" while other "unknowns" are eliminated may appear to be the substitution of one kind of ignorance for another. What have we accomplished in solving equations and deriving incremental ratios?

First, we have developed a technique for the solution of equations in which the parameters are actual numbers obtained by statistical observation. When parameter values are known, or known within limits, solution values and values of incremental ratios are known or known within limits.

Second, we have made explicit the implications of certain original hypotheses. We have deduced what other relationships necessarily hold among economic variables when certain postulated relationships hold.

Third, we have seen how the form or shape of the implied relationships depends on the shapes of the original, postulated relationships. We have seen, for example, whether an implied incremental ratio is the greater or the smaller, the greater is some particular incremental ratio of an original relationship.

Fourth, although we may not be able to specify numerical values for the parameters, we may be able to attach certain limits to their values, such as that they must be positive or negative or should not be expected to exceed

$+1$. In that case we can often deduce the necessary algebraic signs of certain derived incremental ratios.

Fifth, we have seen how to attach limits to the values of certain parameters on the grounds that, if those limits were not observed, the postulated relationships would be dynamically incompatible with each other and their implied relationships not a valid basis for analysis.

Finally, there is a statistical interpretation of the second point. We might observe statistically that there is, say, a close relationship between investment and the rate of taxation, and be led to conclude that the rate of taxation is a principal determinant of the rate of investment. If, however, we hold that consumption is related to disposable income, and that taxes are related to the national income, we know that there is an implicit relationship of investment to taxes (in the absence of variation in government expenditure) which necessarily holds so long as the other relationships hold. And if variations in I are large relative to variations in G, even variations in the latter will not greatly disturb this implied relationship. Or we may take the simple case studied in Chap. 3. If there is a relationship between consumption expenditure and national income, then there is necessarily another relationship between the national income and the sum of all the other components of the national income; and we can be on our guard against counting as two independent relationships what are really only two aspects of the same. And knowing whether a given relationship is "original" or "derived" is necessary if we expect another relationship to break down and cease to operate; $I = u + vY$ may remain valid while $C = a + bY$ changes its form or ceases to hold; $I = (1 - b)Y - G - a$ will break down if $C = a + bY$ ceases to operate.*

* For an excellent discussion of "original" and "derived" relationships see the article by J. S. Duesenberry, "Income Consumption Relations and Their Implications," in *Income, Employment and Public Policy, Essays in Honor of Alvin H. Hansen*, p. 54, New York, 1948. Cf. also the interesting controversy between L. Klein and M. Ezekiel in *Econometrica*, vol. 12, pp. 89 and 91, in articles entitled "The Statistical Determination of the Investment Schedule"; also L. Klein, "Pitfalls in the Statistical Determination of the Investment Schedule," *Econometrica*, vol. 11, p. 246.

CHAPTER 8

SHIFTS IN THE RELATIONSHIPS

In the analysis of the preceding chapters, variation in the values of variables has been of two kinds: arbitrary variation in the values of independent variables—variation in the value of N in Chap. 3, variation in the values of G, T_x, T_r, or I in Chaps. 6 and 7—or induced variation in the values of dependent variables in accordance with their relationships to other variables—variation in Y or C or, when they were dependent variables, in I, T_x, or T_r.

We shall now introduce a third kind of variation. This will be a kind of superimposed variation; dependent variables will be allowed to diverge, in specified fashion, from their relationships to other variables. Or, to be more exact, the relationships themselves will be subjected to shifts. To illustrate this type of variation, let us suppose that all equations hold, all variables having their solution values, and that one of the equations expresses a relationship between T_x and Y. Now let the tax relationship change in such fashion that taxes will be greater by some fixed amount, at any given level of income, than they would have been according to the tax-income relationship.

This shift in the tax relationship may be represented algebraically as follows: Taxes initially are determined according to the equation $T_x = s + tY$; they are now to exceed by the amount h what they would have been at any particular level of income according to that equation. Taxes are therefore now to equal $(s + tY) + h$ for any given level of income. Since the tax-income relationship has in effect been lifted upward by the amount h, there has actually been a substitution of the new equation $T_x = (s + h) + tY$ for the original equation; and a new set of solution values emerges for all the variables.

It is the determination of the associated changes in the values of all the variables which constitutes the problem now to be analyzed. It should in particular be noted that a new solution value for T_x occurs, and the new solution value will not differ from the original by the amount h, which has been added to taxes at any given level of income, for with the resulting change in the value of Y there occurs a change in the value of tY, and the net effect on the value of T_x depends on all the parameters of the system which determine the related change in the value of Y. We cannot, consequently, identify h as ΔT_x; ΔT_x will equal the difference between $s + tY$ for the original solution value of Y and $s + h + tY$ for the new solution value of Y; thus ΔT_x will be given by the expression $h + t \, \Delta Y$.

Shift in the Tax Relationship

To determine the effect on the solution values of all the variables of a shift in the tax relationship of the type described above, let us assume the equation system of Chap. 7 [equations (1) to (6)] and rewrite the solution for Y

$$(1) \quad Y = \frac{a + bp - bs + u + G}{1 - [b(1 - t + r) + v]} = M(a + bp - bs + u + G)$$

where M (multiplier) stands for the reciprocal of the denominator.

In order to determine the effect of a shift in the tax equation on the solution value of Y we could replace equation (5) of Chap. 7, $T_x = s + tY$, by the new equation $T_x = s + tY + h$, and again solve the entire set of equations. It is not necessary, however, to solve the equations again, since the only effect of the shift in the tax equation is the substitution of $s + h$ for s in that equation. We may consequently operate directly on the solution for Y, replacing s with $s + h$ and observing the effect on Y in (1). Writing ΔY for the difference between the solution value of Y when $T_x = s + h + tY$ and the solution value of Y when $T_x = s + tY$,

$$(2) \quad \Delta Y = M[a + bp - b(s + h) + u + G] - M(a + bp - bs + u + G)$$

$$= -Mbh$$

$$(3) \quad \frac{\Delta Y}{h} = -Mb$$

If the reader compares this incremental ratio, $\Delta Y/h$, with the expression for $\Delta Y/\Delta T_x$ of Chap. 6 [equation (33)] he will see that the numerator is the same but that the denominator differs in the present case by the inclusion of the factor $1 - t + r$. Equation (33) of Chap. 6 was derived on the assumption that T_x was an independent variable; in the present case the denominator, by involving t, indicates that the marginal tax-income ratio affects the result. The influence of this marginal tax-income ratio can be demonstrated by solving for ΔT_x.

$$(4) \quad \Delta T_x = [(s + h) + t(Y + \Delta Y)] - (s + tY)$$

$$= h + t \, \Delta Y$$

$$= h \, (1 - Mbt)$$

For an upward shift in the tax equation (positive h), ΔT_x is less than h on the assumption of positive b and t, since M is positive if the equations are dynamically stable. ΔT_x is less than h because the change in Y is downward, and $t \, \Delta Y$ therefore negative; that $\Delta Y/h$ is necessarily negative is apparent from (3) unless we consider b negative, that is, consider consumption inversely related to national income.

The question arises whether ΔT_x can be negative with h positive, that is, whether the downward effect on income can so reduce the value of tY that taxes actually fall with a rise in the tax-income relationship. Writing out the full expression for ΔT_x,

$$(5) \quad \frac{\Delta T_x}{h} = 1 - \frac{bt}{1 - b + bt - br - v} = \frac{1 - b + bt - br - v - bt}{1 - b + bt - br - v}$$

$$= \frac{1 - b(1 + r) - v}{1 - b(1 - t + r) - v}$$

The only restriction imposed on the parameters by the condition of dynamic stability is that the denominator should be positive. With b and t positive, this condition allows the numerator to be negative; and ΔT_x may consequently be of opposite sign to h as far as dynamic stability is concerned.

If the numerator of (5) is negative, so that $\Delta T_x/h$ is negative, $\Delta Y/\Delta T_x$ is positive, and the change in the solution value of national income is in the same direction as the change in the value of taxes. It is interesting to observe that the condition for $\Delta T_x/h$ negative, or $\Delta Y/\Delta T_x$ positive, is that the parameters should have such values that the equations would be dynamically unstable in the absence of the tax-income relationship. For the numerator of (5) is what the denominator of the solution for Y would be if T_x were an independent variable; and with $b(1 + r) + v$ greater than $+1$ the equations would be unstable with T_x independent. Thus the apparent paradox of a positive incremental relationship between Y and T_x is explained by the "partial instability" of the equation system; removing the tax-income equation would leave the system unstable when $\Delta Y/\Delta T_x$ is positive.

This point becomes more clear if we deduce at once the value of $\Delta Y/\Delta T_x$.

$$(6) \quad \frac{\Delta Y}{\Delta T_x} = \frac{-Mbh}{(1 - Mbt)h} = \frac{-b}{1 - b(1 + r) - v}$$

This ratio is precisely what would be obtained for $\Delta Y/\Delta T_x$ if T_x were considered an independent variable. (It is identical with equation (33) of Chap. 6 except for the presence of r in the denominator which follows from the inclusion of the (T_r, Y) relationship in the present system.) If we omitted the tax equation from the present system, treating T_x as independent, and derived the incremental ratio (6) from the reduced system, we should be obliged to discard the possibility that this ratio might be positive on the grounds that a negative denominator would not be consistent with the dynamic compatibility of the equations. It is the presence of the tax-income relationship which allows the equations to be stable in the event $b(1 + r) + v$ exceeds $+1$. In either case equation (6) expresses the ratio of ΔY to ΔT_x on the condition that the equations are satisfied; but without the tax-income equation the equations would not be satisfied with $[b(1 + r) + v]$ greater than 1.

As a special point it may be noted that if $\Delta Y/\Delta T_x$ is positive, that is, if $\Delta T_x/h$ is negative, the ratio of ΔY to ΔT_x cannot be less than $1/t$. For if the denominator of (6) is to be negative, while the denominator of (1) is to be positive for stability, the denominator of (6) must become positive with the addition of $+bt$; the absolute value of that denominator must then be less than bt and the ratio of $-b$ to the denominator must be greater than $b/bt = 1/t$. Thus any value of $\Delta Y/\Delta T_x$ is possible, consistent with stability, except a value between zero and $+1/t$. The reason for this restriction becomes more apparent when (6) is inverted to read

$$(7) \qquad \frac{\Delta T_x}{\Delta Y} = \frac{h + t\,\Delta Y}{\Delta Y} = t + \frac{h}{\Delta Y}$$

We know from equation (3) that $h/\Delta Y$ is negative, therefore $t + h/\Delta Y$ is not greater than t; $\Delta Y/\Delta T_x$ is consequently not less, if positive, than $1/t$.

[If $1 - b(1 + r) - v$ exactly equals zero, the denominator of (6) is zero and the ratio cannot be formed. In that case we may invert the ratio and write it as $\Delta T_x/\Delta Y = 0$. This is the case dividing positive and negative values of $\Delta T_x/h$; no change occurs in the value of T_x with a shift in the tax-income equation. The effect on Y, however, is still in accordance with equation (3). The value of ΔY in that case is equal to $-h/t$ as is seen from equation (7), or from equation (3) when the denominator of the latter is put equal to $+bt$.]

A most important point in the above analysis is the conclusion that, for a shift in the tax equation, $\Delta Y/\Delta T_x$ has the same value as it would have if T_x were independent (except that the range of admissible values is extended to cover positive values when the tax-income relationship is present). This point can be generalized to shifts in any of the other relationships. Before presenting a verbal rationale of this principle we shall perform the same operation on the investment equation.

A shift in the investment equation $I = u + vY$ may similarly be represented by the addition of the arbitrary amount k (the amount of the shift) to the parameter u. Changing u to $u + k$ in equation (1) changes the solution value of Y to $Y + Mk$ as may be seen by repeating for u what has been done for s; consequently $\Delta Y = Mk$. The amount k is not, however, the entire change in the value of I, unless the parameter v is equal to zero. The change in I is given by

(8)
$$\Delta I = [u + k + v(Y + \Delta Y)] - (u + vY)$$
$$= k + v \Delta Y$$
$$= k + vMk = k(1 + Mv)$$

The ratio of ΔY to ΔI is then given by

(9)
$$\frac{\Delta Y}{\Delta I} = \frac{M}{1 + Mv} = \frac{1}{v + (1/M)} = \frac{1}{v + 1 - b(1 - t + r) - v}$$
$$= \frac{1}{1 - b(1 - t + r)}$$

Thus the ratio $\Delta Y/\Delta I$ is the same as it would have been had we dropped the investment-income relationship and considered I an independent variable.

The rationale of this principle may be made clear by the following considerations: if G and T_x are both independent variables, and the equation system is as it has been here assumed except for the absence of the tax-income equation, there corresponds a particular set of values of Y, C, I, and T_r to each pair of values for G and T_x. If G remains constant, there is a particular set of solution values for Y, C, I, and T_r corresponding to each value of T_x. Any change in the value of T_x is associated with changes in the solution values of Y, C, I, and T_r which depend solely on the parameters b, v, and r and on the size and direction of change in T_x. One of the particular values which T_x may have is the value which would be its solution value if the tax-income equation were used with the other equations. If T_x moves away from that particular value (which we may call its "solution value" even though we do not solve for T_x when T_x is independent) by any given amount, the solution values of Y, C, I, and T_r will change by amounts depending on the amount by which T_x changes. How the change in T_x is determined does not affect the relationships of ΔY, ΔC, ΔI, and ΔT_r to ΔT_x. The fact that variation in T_x is constrained by some relationship to Y only determines how the particular value of ΔT_x is related to the value of h; it does not affect the ratios of ΔY, ΔC, etc., to the change in T_x which emerges. So long as none of the other relationships shifts (and so long as G is constant) the ratios of ΔY, etc., to ΔT_x remain fixed; the shape of the tax-income relationship and the size of its shift, together with the other relationships, determine the *absolute size* of ΔT_x and consequently the *absolute sizes* of ΔY, etc.; but the *ratio* of ΔY to ΔT_x is independent of how the particular change in the value of T_x was determined.

The same analysis may be applied to a shift in the consumption equation;

application of the principle developed above suggests that, when the consumption relationship shifts, changing a to $a + h$, the change in the solution value of Y is Mk but in relation to ΔC is simply

$$(10) \qquad \Delta Y = \frac{\Delta C}{1 - v}$$

This change, which may be written in ratio form as $\Delta Y/\Delta C = 1/1 - v$, is obtained by putting b equal to zero in the denominator of (1) and applying the resulting multiplier expression to the change in the value of C This particular ratio could alternatively be arrived at by the following reasoning: so long as G is constant, $\Delta Y = \Delta C + \Delta I$; so long as the investment equation does not change, $\Delta I = v \Delta Y$; of any change in the value of $Y = C + I + G$, $v \Delta Y$ denotes the change in I and the remainder, $(1 - v)\Delta Y$, must denote the change in C. Thus $\Delta C/\Delta Y = 1 - v$ or $\Delta Y/\Delta C = 1/(1 - v)$.

Variable Parameters

In this chapter we have elevated parameters practically to the status of variables. We have referred to shifts in the relationships, denoted by the addition of some fixed amount (such as h) to the right-hand side of an equation (such as $s + tY$) and have characterized this addition as an upward (if h is positive) shift in the whole relationship.* We may just as well refer to the shift as an addition, h, to the value of s, or as an addition, k, to the value of u. We may then replace h by Δs and k by Δu. Our ratios then appear as $\Delta Y/\Delta s$, $\Delta Y/\Delta u$, $\Delta C/\Delta s$, etc. Thus the parameters which are subject to change—whose changes constitute the shifts in the relationships—are treated much as independent variables are treated in so far as the mathematics are concerned.

There remains this distinction, however: variables denote identifiable economic magnitudes, quantities which have meaning quite aside from any relationships among them. Parameters have, in general, only mathematical definitions; they denote numbers which describe the relationships among variables. In general, the amount h or Δs by which a relationship shifts upward is not intended to denote the addition to T_x of some new identifiable tax which yields the revenue denoted by $h = \Delta s$; nor does the upward shift equal to $k = \Delta u$ in the investment relationship generally imply the occurrence of some new identifiable element, equal to k in magnitude, in the rate of investment expenditure. As it was remarked in Chap. 7, the parameters are mathematical reference points in the de-

---

* A downward shift is involved if h is negative; the analysis applies to positive or negative values of h, k, etc.; in ratio form the discrimination between positive and negative shifts cancels out, since the sign of the ratio $\Delta Y/h$ is the same whether ΔY is positive with h negative, or ΔY is negative with h positive.

scription of a relationship; an addition to the "constant" parameter of some arbitrary amount such as h or k is generally to be interpreted as a change in the whole relationship between the variables involved, T_x and Y or I and Y, as the case may be.

We are not limited, however, to that interpretation of the shift in the relationship. We may, for example, wish to investigate the implications of some identifiable addition to consumption expenditure, or of some identifiable new element of investment expenditure at the rate denoted by k, or of some new element of taxation. The annual rate (or rate during the accounting period over which we measure our variables) of this new element may be added to T_x, I, C, or whatever the category is in which we wish to include it. In that case, h or k (or Δs or Δu) does represent some identifiable economic magnitude; and h or k is then properly considered an independent variable. Logically, in that case, we should not denote h by Δs_x or k by Δu since it does not denote a general upward shift in a previously existing relationship but the appearance of a new variable in the system. Or it may be that h does not represent an entirely new element in taxation or investment but an increase in some *independent component* of T_x or of I. Thus, we may distinguish two elements of taxation whose magnitudes are denoted by $T_x{}'$ and $T_x{}''$, with $T_x{}'$ fixed in value and $T_x{}''$ variable with the level of income; $T_x{}'$ is equal to s', $T_x{}''$ equal to $s'' + tY$. Total taxes are then denoted by $T_x{}' + T_x{}'' = s' + s'' + tY = s + tY$ (where s denotes the sum of s' and s''). An independent change in $T_x{}'$ is denoted by $\Delta T_x{}'$; this change can be absorbed into the over-all tax-income relationship by adding $\Delta T_x{}' = h$ to $s + tY$; the total resulting change in T_x would be the sum of $\Delta T_x{}' = h$ and $\Delta T_x{}'' = t\,\Delta Y$.

The mathematical technique developed in this chapter, however, lends itself to either interpretation. A shift in the tax or investment equation may be expressed algebraically as a change in the value of the appropriate parameter, Δs or Δu; we may then interpret this shift either as a general upward or downward shift in the whole relationship between two (or among more than two) variables, or alternatively as an independent addition to some identifiable component of the dependent variable. The technique is the same, the interpretation alone differs; whether s is a parameter, or stands for the sum of some parameter plus an independent variable, it is our privilege to specify.

PART II

CHAPTER 9

INCOME DISTRIBUTION

We shall undertake in this chapter an analysis of two problems involving the distribution of income. Our purpose in one case will be to determine the effect on national income, and on component shares of the national income, of an independent shift in the distribution of income. In the other case our purpose will be to introduce greater precision into the analysis by breaking down some of the aggregates into smaller parts. In the one case we shall distinguish between wage income and profit income, in the other case we shall distinguish among incomes earned in consumer-goods industries, incomes earned in investment-goods industries, and incomes earned in government or in industries producing for government.

Distribution between Profits and Wages

We take up first the profits-wages problem.* We distinguish two kinds of income, profits and wages, and consider them to be so defined as to include all incomes, *i.e.*,

$$(1) \qquad\qquad W + P = Y$$

where W and P stand for wages and profits respectively. Any other income shares than wages or profits will be considered allocated to the W category or to the P category.

We must also distinguish between taxes paid (or transfer payments received) by the two groups separately. These we shall denote by T_w and T_p respectively; and each will be considered net of transfer payments, that is, T_w denotes taxes paid by wage earners minus transfer payments received by wage earners, and similarly for T_p. (Considering taxes net of transfer payments is not necessary, but is convenient unless we particularly want to consider taxes and transfer payments separately.) Each of these, T_w and T_p, is considered to be related to its respective income component† according to the equations

$$(2) \qquad\qquad T_w = r + sW$$

$$(3) \qquad\qquad T_p = \rho + \sigma P$$

---

* Cf. L. A. Metzler, "Effects of Income Redistribution," *Review of Economic Statistics*, vol. 25, p. 49, and T. C. Schelling, "Raise Profits by Raising Wages?" *Econometrica*, vol. 14, p. 227. The former article illustrates the present problem with numerical parameters. The latter treats a similar problem by the use of some elementary calculus.

† Without increasing the number of variables in the system we could elaborate the tax relationships by letting, *e.g.*, T_w be linearly related both to wage income and to

107

Next we adopt two equations expressing the relationships between consumption of wage earners and disposable wage income, and between consumption of profit earners and disposable profit income,

(4) $$C_w = a + b(W - T_w)$$

(5) $$C_p = \alpha + \beta(P - T_p)$$

where C_w and C_p denote the consumption of wage and profit earners, respectively.

It should be remarked at the outset that there is no purpose in this distinction between wage income and profit income unless the incremental ratios s and σ, or the incremental ratios b and β, are expected to differ from each other; so we explicitly intend that they may be different.

We adopt again the investment-income relationship

(6) $$I = u + vY$$

and we necessarily have as one of our equations the identity

(7) $$Y = C_w + C_p + I + G$$

where the value of G, government expenditure for goods and services, will be considered an independent variable.

Since G is to be the only independent variable, the system should be soluble for all variables in terms of G alone. We have, however, nine variables including G, but only seven equations. What we lack are relationships between W, P, and Y. We consequently adopt the following:

(8) $$W = h + wY$$

(9) $$P = k + pY$$

With these two relationships for W and P, however, we have too many. Nine equations, nine variables; the values of all variables are then determined in terms of parameters. Yet we specifically intend G to be independent; the value of G is supposed to be unrestricted. If all nine equa-

---

consumption of wage earners, supposing that certain types of taxes such as excise and sales taxes tend to be related to aggregate consumption. Since, however, consumption is to be considered related to disposable income, the eventual form of the consumption-income equation will not be greatly affected by the choice to relate taxes explicitly only to income. If, for example, we let the wages-tax equation be $T_w = r + sW + tC_w$, where C_w denotes consumption by wage earners, while $C_w = a + b(W - T_w)$, we have $C_w = a + bW - br - bsW - btC_w = [(a - br) + b(1 - s)W]/(1 - bt)$. This latter equation is a linear equation in C_w and W which can be rewritten as $C_w = A + BW$ with the values of A and B depending only on the values of the original parameters.

tions hold, the value of G would appear to be restricted; there would seem to be only one solution value for G which allows satisfaction of all nine equations.

Perhaps we can eliminate one equation, and so return G's flexibility. If we take equations (1) and (8) together, we have, substituting (8) in (1).

$$(10) \qquad\qquad h + wY + P = Y$$

$$(11) \qquad\qquad P = Y - h - wY$$

$$(12) \qquad\qquad P = -h + (1 - w)Y$$

Now equation (12), which is a necessary implication of equations (1) and (8), is either identical with (9) or incompatible with it. That is to say, equations (1) and (8) are sufficient to give P in terms of Y; equation (9) is consequently identical and superfluous, or distinct and inconsistent.* So we drop equation (9). [We could as well retain (9) and drop (8); either one along with (1) determines both W and P in relation to Y.]

Now we have eight equations in nine variables, G being the independent variable.

Solution for Y follows the usual pattern. Equations (2), (4), and (8) give us the relationship between C_w and Y.

$$
\begin{aligned}
(13) \qquad C_w &= a + b(W - r - sW) \\
&= a - br + b(1 - s)W \\
&= a - br + b(1 - s)(h + wY)
\end{aligned}
$$

$$(14) \qquad C_w = [a - br + b(1 - s)h] + b(1 - s)wY$$

And equations (1), (3), and (5) gives us C_p in terms of Y:

$$
\begin{aligned}
(15) \qquad C_p &= \alpha + \beta(P - \rho - \sigma P) \\
&= \alpha - \beta\rho + \beta(1 - \sigma)(Y - W) \\
&= \alpha - \beta\rho + \beta(1 - \sigma)Y - \beta(1 - \sigma)(h + wY) \\
&= [\alpha - \beta\rho - \beta(1 - \sigma)h] + \beta(1 - \sigma)Y - \beta(1 - \sigma)wY
\end{aligned}
$$

$$(16) \qquad C_p = [\alpha - \beta\rho - \beta(1 - \sigma)h] + \beta(1 - \sigma)(1 - w)Y$$

* Equations (9) and (12) are inconsistent (unless they are identical) in the sense that they cannot both hold *for all values of Y*. They are, however, consistent in the sense that, considered apart from the other equations, there is a set of values for Y, W, and P to be found by solving equations (1), (8), and (9) simultaneously which satisfies those three equations. But if we accept this solution, the level of income is already determined by those three equations alone, without regard to the other equations of the system, and those other equations are either inconsistent with the solution of (1), (8), and (9) or else consistent by coincidence but superfluous to the determination of Y.

For algebraic convenience we shall adopt the following abbreviations:

(17) $b' = b(1 - s)$

(18) $\beta' = \beta(1 - \sigma)$

(19) $H = [a - br + b(1 - s)h]$ [from equation (14)]

(20) $K = [\alpha - \beta\rho - \beta(1 - \sigma)h]$ [from equation (16)]

We now substitute into equation (7),

(7) $Y = C_w + C_p + I + G$
$= H + b'wY + K + \beta'(1 - w)Y + u + vY + G$
$= (H + K + u + G) + [b'w + \beta'(1 - w) + v]Y$

(21) $Y = \dfrac{H + K + u + G}{1 - [b'w + \beta'(1 - w) + v]}$

This solution for Y is structurally similar to those obtained earlier. The denominator is the interesting part. It shows, subtracted from 1, a weighted average of b' and β' added to v. In earlier chapters we encountered the denominator form $1 - b' - v$. Here we find the two distinct incremental ratio parameters b' and β', weighted respectively by the marginal wages-income ratio w, and the marginal profits-income ratio $1 - w$. We may characterize it as a weighted average, since the two coefficients w and $1 - w$ add up to 1. And here again the denominator must be positive if the equations are to be dynamically compatible.*

The multiplier relating ΔY to ΔG is apparent and need not be written down here. The incremental ratios of ΔW and ΔP to ΔG are simply $w \Delta Y/\Delta G$ and $(1 - w)\Delta Y/\Delta G$, respectively. If we shift either of the tax relationships, the effects are determinate,

(22) $\dfrac{\Delta Y}{\Delta r} = \dfrac{-b}{1 - [b'w + \beta'(1 - w) + v]}$

as is seen by looking inside H and K for the occurrence of r, which we find represented in H[equation (19)] in the form $-br$. And similarly for the rest of such shifts, which may be deduced in the usual fashion.

What we wish to investigate, now that our solution is obtained, is the effect on Y, W, and P of a shift in the distribution of income against profits in favor of wages, or vice versa. There are two forms in which such a shift may occur, according as the impact is on wages and profits or on disposable wage income and disposable profit income. If the shift is from, say, profits to wages, it is represented by an addition to the parame-

* The derivation of this condition follows the method developed in Chap. 6. It should be noted that in the present "weighted average" the weights are fixed in terms of parameters, not variable with the level of income as in the case studied on p. 88.

ter h (and a subtraction, therefore, from the corresponding profits parameter $-h$). If the shift is via taxes, or transfer payments, it is represented by an addition to the parameter ρ in equation (3) and an equal reduction in the parameter r in equation (2).

Notice that in the case of either of these shifts, the over-all effect on wages, profits, disposable wage income, or disposable profit income is not equal to the amount of the "initial" or "original" shift, *i.e.*, not equal to the amount added to or subtracted from the parameters. Changing the parameters puts the original solution values out of line with the relationships, repercussions occur on all the variables, and a new set of solution values emerges. Shifting an amount d from wages to profits means in this context to shift the wage and profits equations so that, *at any level of income*, wages are lower and profits higher by the amount d than they would have been at the same level of income in the absence of the shift. If the level of income is affected, as it will be unless the wage and profit parameters happen to have identical values, both wages and profits will undergo increases or decreases additional to the amount of shift in the parameters.

We shall illustrate this point by inquiring what happens to profits, wages, and national income when a shift occurs such that at any level of income wages are higher, profits lower, by the amount d than they would have been without the shift; which is to say that equation (8) is adjusted so that

$$(23) \qquad W = h + wY + d$$

and, as a consequence,

$$(24) \qquad \begin{aligned} P &= Y - h - wY - d \\ &= -h - d + (1 - w)Y \end{aligned}$$

The effect on Y can be analyzed in terms of equation (21). We have only to raise h to $h + d$ [which automatically lowers $(-h)$ to $-h - d$ wherever h occurs in that solution] and compare the new solution value for Y with the original solution. Since h does not occur in the denominator, the effect on Y will equal the change in the numerator multiplied by the reciprocal of the denominator of (21). Now, as (21) is written, h does not explicitly appear; but the two abbreviatory parameters H and K must be looked into. According to equations (19) and (20), defining H and K, h occurs in both H and K. Increasing h by the amount d raises the sum of H and K from

$$(25) \qquad H + K = a - br + b(1 - s)h + \alpha - \beta\rho - \beta(1 - \sigma)h$$

to

$$(26) \qquad \begin{aligned} &H + K + \Delta(H + K) \\ &= a - br + b(1 - s)(h + d) + \alpha - \beta\rho - \beta(1 - \sigma)(h + d) \end{aligned}$$

The difference is given by

(27) $\Delta(H + K) = b(1 - s)d - \beta(1 - \sigma)d = (b' - \beta')d$

Consequently, ΔY is given by

(28) $\Delta Y = M(b' - \beta')d$

where M (multiplier) stands for the reciprocal of the denominator of equation (21).

Writing $d = \Delta h$ we have, then,

(29) $$\frac{\Delta Y}{\Delta h} = M(b' - \beta')$$

The effect on Y is thus proportional to the difference between b' and β'. If b', the marginal ratio of C_w to W, exceeds β', the marginal ratio of C_p to P, the national income rises with a shift against profits in favor of wages. If the reverse is true the national income falls with such a shift or rises with the opposite shift. Note that b' equals the product of b and $1 - s$, β' equals the product of β and $1 - \sigma$; equal marginal ratios of consumption to disposable income can yield different marginal ratios of consumption to income (profits or wages) if the marginal tax-income ratios differ.

The ratios $\Delta W/\Delta h$ and $\Delta P/\Delta h$ may be derived next. These are given by

(30) $$\frac{\Delta W}{\Delta h} = 1 + w\left(\frac{\Delta Y}{\Delta h}\right)$$

(31) $$\frac{\Delta P}{\Delta h} = -1 + (1 - w)\left(\frac{\Delta Y}{\Delta h}\right)$$

[These are readily deduced from equations (1), (8), and (21).] If $\Delta Y/\Delta h$ is positive, $\Delta W/\Delta h$ exceeds $+1$ and the effect on W is greater than the amount of the "shift," Δh; similarly, $-\Delta P$ is less than the "initial loss," Δh. If $b' - \beta'$ is negative, $\Delta Y/\Delta h$ is negative and $\Delta W < \Delta h$, $-\Delta P > \Delta h$.

Two interesting questions arise: (a) can ΔY be so great that ΔP is actually positive, that is, can the "income effect," $(1 - w)\Delta Y$, offset the "shift effect," $-\Delta h$; and (b) if income falls (that is, if b' is less than β') can the adverse income effect on wages, $w \Delta Y$, offset the "shift effect," Δh, so that wages actually fall?

There is nothing in either equation (30) or (31) to indicate the answers to these questions; we must look to some fuller expression for ΔW and ΔP to see whether limitations are present which prevent the income effects from completely offsetting or more than offsetting the shift effects.

The first of the above questions is whether $\Delta P/\Delta h$ can be positive. To see what a positive value of $\Delta P/\Delta h$ implies, let us rewrite equation (31) as

$$(32) \quad \frac{\Delta P}{\Delta h} = -1 + (1 - w)\left[\frac{b' - \beta'}{1 - b'w - \beta'(1 - w) - v}\right]$$

$$= \frac{-1 + b'w + \beta'(1 - w) + v + (1 - w)b' - (1 - w)\beta'}{1 - b'w - \beta'(1 - w) - v}$$

Canceling terms in the numerator,

$$(33) \quad \frac{\Delta P}{\Delta h} = \frac{-(1 - b' - v)}{1 - b'w - \beta'(1 - w) - v}$$

The denominator is positive if the equations are dynamically compatible; $\Delta P/\Delta h$ can therefore be positive only if the numerator is positive, that is, if $b' + v$ is greater than $+1$. In other words, a high marginal ratio of C_w to W, or a high marginal ratio of I to Y, is necessary for the condition to be met. As a matter of fact, the values of b' and v must be so high that, if β' were equal to b', the equations would be dynamically unstable. If there is no investment-income relationship, that is, if $v = 0$, the condition is that b' must exceed $+1$ [which means a value of b greater than $1/(1 - s)$]. A relatively large multiplier is an implication of this condition, since the multiplier is the greater, the greater are the values of b' and v.

The reader can now follow a similar procedure to answer the second question posed above. He will find a symmetrical answer; a shift in favor of wages can cause a net reduction in wages via the income effect only if $\beta' + v$ exceeds $+1$. (In that case, of course, b' must be less than β', both to make $\Delta Y/\Delta h$ negative and to allow the equations to be dynamically stable.)

Returning again to the beginning of the income-shift problem, we may inquire how the national income changes if taxes are shifted from wages to profits (or vice versa). Such a shift involves adding an amount d to the parameter ρ and subtracting the same amount from the parameter r in equations (2) and (3) (or subtracting it from ρ and adding it to r). The net result on the solution value for Y can be obtained from equation (21) when the full expressions for H and K are written out. Replacing ρ wherever it occurs with $\rho + d$ and r with $r - d$ changes the numerator of (21) by $bd - \beta d$ or $(b - \beta)d$. The ratios of the increment in Y to the increments in ρ and r are given by

$$(34) \quad \frac{\Delta Y}{\Delta \rho} = -\frac{\Delta Y}{\Delta r} = M(b - \beta)$$

where M again stands for the reciprocal of the denominator of (21). This result is similar to that of equation (26) except that the ratio here is proportional to the difference between marginal ratios of consumption to disposable wage and profit income, b and β, instead of the marginal ratios, b' and β', of C_w and C_p to wages and profits gross of taxes.

Whether $b - \beta$ is greater or less than $b' - \beta'$, that is, whether the income effect of a shift in income distribution is greater when accomplished through a tax shift than when done through a pure 'income transfer, is the next question. If tax rates (in the marginal tax-income sense) are equal for the two groups, so that $1 - s = 1 - \sigma$, then the effect on Y is greater when the transfer is via taxes; that is, $b - \beta$ is greater than $b' - \beta'$, for the latter is equal to $(1 - s)(b - \beta)$ and $1 - s$ is a positive fraction if s is, as we may probably assume.

The general criterion according to which $b - \beta$ or $b' - \beta'$ is the greater is

(35)
$$b(1 - s) - \beta(1 - \sigma) > b - \beta$$
$$b(1 - s) > b - \beta + \beta(1 - \sigma)$$
$$1 - s > 1 - \frac{\beta}{b} + \frac{\beta}{b} - \left(\frac{\beta}{b}\right)\sigma$$
$$-s > -\left(\frac{\beta}{b}\right)\sigma$$

(36)
$$\frac{s}{\sigma} < \frac{\beta}{b} \quad \text{or} \quad bs < \beta\sigma$$

(The last step involved reversing the inequality because signs were switched from minus to plus. Reversing signs on both sides of an inequality reverses the direction of the inequality as well. This may be seen by taking it in two steps: First, exchange both sides of the inequality; this reverses the signs. Second, turn the whole expression around; this reverses the direction of the inequality sign and puts both parts back on the sides they started from.)

Verbal paraphrase is complicated, but we may express (35) in words as follows: the effect on Y of an *income* transfer exceeds that of a *disposable-income* transfer if the ratio of the recipient group's marginal tax-income ratio to the other group's is less than the ratio of the latter group's marginal consumption–disposable income ratio to the former group's. It should be noted that if both sides of (35) are negative, the larger algebraic value of the left-hand side is the smaller absolute value. It may also be noted that if σ is greater than s, $b - \beta$ can be negative while $b(1 - s) - \beta(1 - \sigma)$ is positive.

What happens to total taxes when taxes are shifted from the one group to the other is determined from the following equation.

(37)
$$\Delta T = \Delta T_w + \Delta T_p$$
$$= \Delta r + s\,\Delta W + \Delta\rho + \sigma\,\Delta P$$
$$= sw\,\Delta Y + \sigma(1 - w)\Delta Y$$
$$= M[sw + \sigma(1 - w)](b - \beta)\Delta\rho$$

where again we have used M to denote the reciprocal of the denominator of (21). Since $\Delta\rho$ and Δr cancel each other in the total, the direction of change of total taxes is the same as the direction of change of national income, assuming that T_w and T_p vary directly, not inversely, with W and P. The bracketed expression, $sw + \sigma(1 - w)$, may be considered a weighted average of marginal tax-income ratios, the weights being the marginal-income shares of W and P.

As a further exercise we may suppose that the tax authorities determine to keep the level of total taxes constant throughout the shift in the distribution of taxes. If the shift is in the direction which raises income, this determination requires that r and ρ be further reduced, i.e., reduced in addition to the changes represented by the shift. There are several ways in which r and ρ might be manipulated in order to keep $T_w + T_p$ constant; the simplest is probably to let T_w and T_p retain their original solution values except for the equal opposite changes, $\Delta r = -\Delta\rho$, representing the shift. In that case the effect is the same as though T_w and T_p were independent variables, with values equal to those obtained by the original solution of equations; the effect on national income of the shift in taxation is given by

$$(38) \qquad \frac{\Delta Y}{\Delta T_p} = -\frac{\Delta Y}{\Delta T_w} = \frac{b - \beta}{1 - [bw + \beta(1 - w) + v]}$$

as the reader may verify by dropping equations (2) and (3) and treating T_w and T_p as independent variables.

Throughout the above analysis we have referred to the two income categories as "wages" and "profits." This characterization is not essential to the analysis; W and P could have referred to any two categories of income (so long as the two categories were exhaustive of the national income) which varied with the level of income. The problem can be generalized to allow for another income category, or other income categories, in addition to the two between which the shift in distribution occurs. If the reader cares to allow for some third income category, Z, he need only specify a consumption relationship between C_z and $Z - T_z$, a tax relationship between T_z and Z, and an income-share relationship of the form $Z = x + zY$. He must then revise the two identities (1) and (7) so that $Y = W + P + Z$ and $Y = C_w + C_p + C_z + I + G$. The incremental ratio of P to Y becomes, in this case, $1 - w - z$; the solution is structurally similar to equation (21) but the denominator shows the three marginal consumption–income ratios weighted by their respective marginal-income shares.

Income Distribution by Production Categories

The second problem in income distribution will distinguish among incomes earned in consumer-goods industries, incomes earned in investment-goods industries, and incomes earned in producing for government. For simplicity, we shall ignore the fact that some investment may be in the form of consumer-goods inventories, and that the income corresponding to such investment is really earned in consumer-goods industries; *i.e.*, we shall let investment-industries income be identical with investment expenditure. We shall similarly ignore the important distinction between incomes earned (principally wages and salaries) within government itself, and incomes earned in industries producing goods for sale to government.

The reason for making such a distinction among three kinds of income sources is that there may be significantly different marginal ratios of consumption to disposable income, or significantly different marginal tax-income ratios, among the three types of income; and added precision is obtainable through the distinction. If the question is raised, why we concentrate on this particular three-way breakdown among C, I, and G incomes, rather than on another, perhaps more significant, breakdown (significant in terms of more disparate parameter values for consumption and taxes), the answer is that these are the particular three categories of income whose variations we are analyzing on the expenditure side, and that I and G are two particular income sources whose variation we often consider independent in our analysis. In other words, our analysis specifically considers separate variations in C, I, and G; any differences in consumption or tax behavior among these three groups therefore require explicit recognition. Other income divisions, such as the wages-profits division of the preceding section, are relevant if a deliberate shift in income distribution is under investigation; in this section we analyze only those shifts in income distribution which are necessarily involved in any analysis of variations in C, I, and G.

Why we might expect significantly different marginal consumption or tax ratios among the three categories of income recognized here is not susceptible of any categorical answer. Geographical or sociological factors might contribute to the difference; investment-goods industries generally show some sort of geographical concentration. Differences in average family-income sizes, as between durable-goods and nondurable-goods industries, could be a factor both on the consumption side and on the tax side. Different distributions of income between wage-salary income and property incomes might account for a difference. The reader can undoubtedly think of other factors which would tend to keep consumption or tax behavior from averaging out equal among the three categories of income recipients.

Proceeding to the analysis, we shall adopt some simplifications to keep the algebra neat. We shall not explicitly allow for the effect of taxation, but shall let our consumption equations express both the direct consumption–disposable income relationship and tax-income relationship. We shall initially treat I as an independent variable. Accordingly we have the following consumption equations:*

(1') $C_c = a + bC$

(2') $C_i = \alpha + \beta I$

(3') $C_g = \text{A} + \text{B}G$

where C_c, C_i, and C_g denote the consumption of those whose incomes derive respectively from consumption expenditure, from investment expenditure, and from government purchase of goods and services.
We have also the two identities

(4') $Y = C + I + G$

(5') $C = C_c + C_i + C_g$

There are five equations, seven variables, and we should expect to be able to solve for Y, C, C_c, C_i, and C_g in terms of the two independent variables I and G. It should be noticed that in this case, as distinct from the previous problem in income distribution, we do not require specific income-share equations, such as $W = h + wY$; the expenditure behavior, as expressed in equations (1') (2'), and (3'), serves at the same time to relate C to Y both in the expenditure-category sense and in the income-category sense.

Proceeding to the solution, we meet some trouble if we follow our previous pattern. If we substitute (1'), (2'), and (3') into (4') and then (4') into (5') we obtain

(6') $Y = a + bC + \alpha + \beta I + \text{A} + \text{B}G + I + G$

which leaves C on the right-hand side. Substituting in (6') the value for C given in (5') leaves us with

(7') $Y = a + b(C_c + C_i + C_g) + \alpha + \beta I + \text{A} + \text{B}G + I + G$

Substituting again from (1'), (2'), and (3') yields

(8') $Y = a + b(a + bC) + b(\alpha + \beta I) + b(A + BG)$
$$+ \alpha + \beta I + \text{A} + \text{B}G + I + G$$

and we still have C on the right-hand side. If we again substitute for C in (8') its value as given in (5') we must once more substitute from (1'), (2'), and (3') and we get a longer and longer expression, always with C reappearing on the right-hand side.

*Equations are numbered with primes so that we may begin again with number 1 without confusion.

In order to eliminate C, and eventually express Y in terms of I and G alone, we must go back a step and work with equations (1'), (2'), and (3') before attempting substitution in (4'). Let us begin by substituting in (5') from (1'), (2'), and (3').

$$(9') \qquad C = C_c + C_i + C_g$$
$$= a + bC + \alpha + \beta I + \text{A} + \text{B}G$$

Now we can eliminate C from the right-hand side, and express C in terms of I and G,*

$$(10') \qquad C(1 - b) = a + \alpha + \beta I + \text{A} + \text{B}G$$

$$(11') \qquad C = \frac{a + \alpha + \beta I + \text{A} + \text{B}G}{1 - b}$$

Now we can substitute (11') into (4'),

$$(12') \quad Y = \frac{a + \alpha + \beta I + \text{A} + \text{B}G}{1 - b} + I + G$$

$$= \frac{a + \alpha + \text{A}}{1 - b} + I\left(1 + \frac{\beta}{1 - b}\right) + G\left(1 + \frac{\text{B}}{1 - b}\right)$$

$$(13') \quad Y = \frac{a + \alpha + \text{A}}{1 - b} + I\left(\frac{1 + (\beta - b)}{1 - b}\right) + G\left(\frac{1 + (\text{B} - b)}{1 - b}\right)$$

Equation (13') is the solution for Y in terms of I and G. The reader can quickly verify that if $b = \beta = \text{B}$, that is, if we ignore differences in marginal consumption–income ratios, (13') degenerates into the familiar

$$(14') \qquad Y = \frac{H + I + G}{1 - b}$$

where we have gathered a, α, and A into the single parameter H.

The multipliers pertinent to I and G are

$$(15') \qquad \frac{\Delta Y}{\Delta I} = \frac{1}{1 - b} + \frac{\beta - b}{1 - b}$$

$$(16') \qquad \frac{\Delta Y}{\Delta G} = \frac{1}{1 - b} + \frac{\text{B} - b}{1 - b}$$

The incremental ratio in (16') differs from that derived in Chap. 6 [equation (35)] by the addition of the second term $(\text{B} - b)/(1 - b)$. (To make the comparison with Chap. 6 we must drop the parameter v from

* This treatment of C is similar to that accorded to I in Chap. 7, equations (24) and (25), where I was given in terms of C, I, and G.

the latter to make it comparable.)   The reason for this difference becomes clear if we divide the increment in Y into its component parts,

$$(17') \qquad \Delta Y = \Delta C_c + \Delta C_i + \Delta C_g + \Delta I + \Delta G$$

In the case where I varies and G remains constant, $i.e.$, the case pertinent to multiplier (15'), equation (17') becomes

$$(18') \qquad \Delta Y = \Delta C_c + \Delta C_i + \Delta I$$

since ΔG is zero and, according to equation (3'), when ΔG is zero so is ΔC_g.   Now if I undergoes change in the amount h, so that $\Delta I = h$, then

$$(19') \qquad \Delta Y = \Delta C_c + \beta h + h$$

Since ΔY is equal to ΔI multiplied by the expression of (15'), we can obtain ΔC_c in either of two ways,

$$(20') \qquad \Delta C_c = \Delta Y - h(1 + \beta)$$

$$= \left(\frac{1}{1 - b} + \frac{\beta - b}{1 - b} \right) h - h(1 + \beta)$$

$$= h \left(\frac{1 + \beta - b - (1 + \beta)(1 - b)}{1 - b} \right)$$

$$(21') \qquad \Delta C_c = h \left(\frac{b\beta}{1 - b} \right)$$

(as may be seen by multiplying out $(1 + \beta)(1 - b)$ and canceling terms). Or, by combining equations (1') and (11'),

$$(22') \qquad \Delta C_c = b \, \Delta C$$

$$= b \left(\frac{\beta \, \Delta I}{1 - b} \right)$$

$$= \left(\frac{b\beta}{1 - b} \right) h$$

Thus the increment in Y is made up of the increment in I, ΔI; the increment in C_i, equal to $\beta \, \Delta I$; and the increment in C_c, equal to $(b/1 - b)\Delta C_i$ or $(b\beta/1 - b)\Delta I$. We may think of these as the primary, secondary, and tertiary effects of the additional investment outlay: the primary effect on income is the direct income receipt of the investment outlay proceeds; the secondary effect is the effect on incomes in consumer-goods industries of the consumption, $\beta \, \Delta I$, of those whose incomes were immediately affected by the additional investment; and the tertiary effect is the further effect on incomes in consumer-goods industries resulting from the additional consumption undertaken by those in consumer-goods industries themselves. The tertiary effect shows the multiplier, since additional consumption of those in consumer-goods industries raises the income of the same group, and their consumption expenditures continue to rise, raising their incomes, until their consumption bears the postulated relationship to their income.

The same considerations apply to a rise (or fall) in G.

The stability condition in the present case involves only the value of b, that is, the marginal ratio of C_c to C. Since I and G are independent, C_i and C_g adjust toward $\alpha + \beta I$ and $\textsc{a} + \textsc{b}G$, neither of which values are affected by the adjustments of C_c, C_i, or C_g. Thus in any adjustment analysis C_i and C_g may be taken to equal $\alpha + \beta I$ and $\textsc{a} + \textsc{b}G$, that is, to equal $\bar{C}_i$ and $\bar{C}_g$. Letting $C_c = \bar{C}_c + h$, C_c adjusts toward or away from $\bar{C}_c$ according as $\bar{C}_c + h$ is greater or less than $a + b\bar{Y} + bh = \bar{C}_c + bh$; that is, depending on whether bh is less than or greater than h. Thus $b < +1$ is the condition.

Again, as in Chap. 7, there is a consistency problem involved in the dependence of stability only on the parameter b. Before we distinguished the separate parts of C, namely C_c, C_i, and C_g, with their separate marginal ratios, b, β, and $\textsc{b}$, we developed the condition that the over-all marginal ratio applicable to all consumption should be less than $+1$. May not very high values of β and $\textsc{b}$ raise the aggregate marginal ratio above $+1$ yet leave the parameter b less than $+1$? Which condition is correct? Is the system stable or unstable?

The answer is that, regardless of the values of β and $\textsc{b}$, the aggregate marginal ratio is less than or greater than $+1$ according as the single parameter b is less or greater than $+1$. The aggregate marginal ratio is a weighted average of b, β, and $\textsc{b}$; but the weights are not independent parameters, they depend themselves on the values of b, β, and $\textsc{b}$. It is the variability of the weights in the average with any variation in the values of the parameters that assures the consistency. This may be seen as follows: The multiplier may be written as

$$(23') \qquad \frac{\Delta Y}{\Delta I} = \frac{1}{1 - bs - \beta\sigma}$$

where s and σ are the marginal-income shares of the two groups whose consumption expenditures are denoted by C_c and C_i. The parameter, $\textsc{b}$, does not figure in the multiplier since $\Delta G = 0$ and C_g is therefore constant. Now the value of σ is given by

$$(24') \qquad \sigma = \frac{\Delta I}{\Delta Y} = \frac{1 - b}{1 - b + \beta}$$

according to equation (15'). The value of $s = \Delta C/\Delta Y$ is given by

(25′) $$s = \frac{\Delta C}{\Delta Y} = \frac{\Delta Y - \Delta I}{\Delta Y} = 1 - \frac{\Delta I}{\Delta Y} = \frac{\beta}{1 - b + \beta}$$

Then

(26′) $$\frac{\Delta Y}{\Delta I} = \frac{1}{1 - b\left(\dfrac{\beta}{1 - b + \beta}\right) - \beta\left(\dfrac{1 - b}{1 - b + \beta}\right)}$$

$$= \frac{1}{\dfrac{1 - b + \beta - b\beta - \beta(1 - b)}{1 - b + \beta}} = \frac{1 - b + \beta}{1 - b}$$

Thus we have derived (15′) and demonstrated the consistency of the two approaches. However large the value of β, the multiplier remains positive if b is less than $+1$. The rationale is that when β is very large, $\Delta Y/\Delta I$ is very large and, ΔI being given, the relative share of income accruing in consumer-goods industries is also large and keeps the weighted average of b and β less than $+1$.

Next let us eschew simplicity and put into our system the investment equation $I = u + vY$ which we have used before. This insertion reduces the number of independent variables to one, and will complicate the multiplier expression.

We can proceed to solution on the basis of work already done in arriving at equation (11′). Taking together that equation, equation (4′), and the new equation

(27′) $$I = u + vY$$

we can substitute to get

(28′) $Y = C + I + G$

$$= \frac{a + \alpha + \beta I + \text{A} + \text{B}G}{1 - b} + u + vY + G$$

$$= \frac{a + \alpha + \text{A} + \beta(u + vY) + \text{B}G}{1 - b} + u + vY + G$$

$$= \left(\frac{a + \alpha + \text{A} + \beta u}{1 - b} + u\right) + \left(\frac{\beta v}{1 - b} + v\right) Y$$

$$+ \left(\frac{\text{B}}{1 - b} + 1\right) G$$

$$Y = \frac{K + G\left(1 + \dfrac{\text{B}}{1 - b}\right)}{1 - v\left(1 + \dfrac{\beta}{1 - b}\right)}$$

where

(29')
$$K = \frac{a + \alpha + \text{A} + \beta u}{1 - b} + u$$

with a multiplier

(30')
$$\frac{\Delta Y}{\Delta G} = \frac{1 + \dfrac{\text{B}}{1 - b}}{1 - v\left(1 + \dfrac{\beta}{1 - b}\right)}$$

This is a highly complicated multiplier; and yet we know that, except for the differences between b, β, and B, it must reduce to the familiar simple expression $1/(1 - b - v)$. Let us convince ourselves that it does. Putting $\text{B} = \beta = b$ we have

(31')
$$\frac{\Delta Y}{\Delta G} = \frac{\dfrac{1 - b + b}{1 - b}}{1 - v\left(\dfrac{1 - b + b}{1 - b}\right)} = \frac{\dfrac{1}{1 - b}}{1 - \dfrac{v}{1 - b}} = \frac{1}{1 - b - v}$$

If we look back now at the multiplier (30') we may take it apart in this fashion. First, the numerator itself is what the multiplier would be if v were equal to zero. For if v were zero, the denominator would become $+1$; furthermore, if v were zero, the numerator would be exactly the same as (16'), except for grouping of terms. Thus the effect of the denominator is to make allowance for the rise in investment which accompanies the rise in income. This consideration would suggest a denominator of $1 - v$, except that the rise which occurs in investment induces a rise in consumption, both in consumption of those in investment-goods industries and a further rise in consumption of those in consumer-goods industries, consequent to the rise in their incomes resulting from the additional consumption of those in investment-goods industries. So the denominator shows v augmented by the consumption which is consequent to a rise in I.

One final adjustment may yet be made in (30') to make it fit our scheme of things. If we perform the following manipulations,

(32')
$$\frac{\Delta Y}{\Delta G} = \frac{\dfrac{1 + \text{B} - b}{1 - b}}{1 - v - \dfrac{v\beta}{1 - b}} = \frac{1 + (\text{B} - b)}{1 - b - v + bv - \beta v}$$
$$= \frac{1 + (\text{B} - b)}{1 - b - v[1 + (\beta - b)]}$$

we get what is an ordinary multiplier with two specific adjustments for the differences between B and β and b.

Complete stability analysis in the present case requires the study of three simultaneously adjusting variables, C_c, C_i, and I. We shall not develop that analysis here; one example of stability analysis with three adjusting variables has already been presented in Chap. 7 and another example will be given in Chap. 14. The reader may rightly suppose that stability requires $\Delta Y/\Delta G$ positive, since any rise in G tends only to raise C_g, and hence to raise C, causing C_c to rise; this further raises C, and at the same time I tends to rise as Y rises, and so in consequence does C_i. Thus it appears impossible for a rise in G to lead to lower values for C or I, since their initial tendency is to rise and since the higher either value rises, the more they both tend to continue to rise.

CHAPTER 10

IMPOSING OUTSIDE CONDITIONS ON THE VARIABLES

Much of the analysis performed in the preceding chapters has been concerned with the derivation of incremental ratios between two variables. Another use may be made of the equation systems, which is illustrated by the following problem.

Referring to the equation system of Chap. 7, equations (1) to (6), we may inquire for what value of G the government budget will be in balance, balance of the government budget being represented by the equation

$$(1) \qquad G + T_r = T_x$$

Since the system of equations contains but one independent variable, G, the values of both T_x and T_r are given when the value of G is specified; and to any given value of G there corresponds a unique pair of solution values for T_x and T_r. We may substitute in (1) the solution values of T_x and T_r in terms of G, obtaining a single equation in G. The value of G which satisfies (1) is thereby obtained in terms of parameters alone. If we wish to know what level of income will accompany the value of G at which the government budget is balanced, we have only to substitute this value of G in the solution value for Y, equation (9) of Chap. 7, obtaining thereby an expression for Y involving only parameters.

The particular problem outlined above is one of a general type of problem which essentially involves the addition of a new equation, or some new equations, to the system. These new equations have a different status from the relationships comprising the original equation system; they represent not the postulation of new economic relationships but the imposition of certain outside conditions. The original relationships represent conditions imposed on the variables; but they are conditions imposed, or assumed to be imposed, by patterns of economic behavior; the conditions imposed by the new equations are essentially conditions imposed by the analyst. Or we may say that the new equations added in this fashion ask the question: What values must certain independent variables have if—in addition to the economic relationships assumed in the analysis—certain other conditions are to be satisfied?

Another example of this type of problem is suggested by the equation system of Chap. 6, in which G, T_x, and T_r were considered independent variables. There it was deduced that the solution value for Y could be represented as

$$(2) \qquad Y = \frac{a + u + G - bT_x + bT_r}{1 - b - v}.$$

Let us impose the condition that Y have some particular value, for example, the value denoted by F which represents a "full-employment" level of income.   The condition is that $Y = F$; and this condition is imposed by substituting the fixed value F for Y in equation (2).   Since F represents a fixed value, equation (2) becomes an equation in three variables only, G, T_x, and T_r, and may be arranged to express any one of these in terms of the other two.   For example, T_x may be expressed as

$$(3) \qquad T_x = \frac{1}{b}\,[a + u + G + bT_r - F(1 - b - v)]$$

Given any pair of values for G and T_r, there is a unique value of T_x, given by (3), which makes $Y = F$.   Deriving the incremental relationships implicit in (3) we obtain

$$(4) \qquad \Delta T_x = \Delta T_r + \frac{1}{b}\,\Delta G$$

For any given changes in the values of T_r and G there is some particular change in the value of T_x which keeps (3) satisfied, $i.e.$, which keeps Y equal to F.   If G is constant, $\Delta T_x = \Delta T_r$; taxes must change in the same direction and by the same amount as transfer payments if the value of Y is to remain fixed; and, similarly, $\Delta T_x = \Delta G/b$ if T_r is constant.   Equation (4) may be rewritten as $\Delta G + b\,\Delta T_r - b\Delta T_x = 0$ to remove any asymmetry in the treatment of variables; essentially (4) or (3) is a condition imposed on three variables and no one of the three is more to be singled out than another.   It should especially be noticed that the incremental relationship (4) does not involve the parameter F.   Since all equations are linear, incremental ratios are constant, and the related changes in values of dependent variables which leave the value of Y unchanged are the same at every level of Y, that is, they are the same whatever the values of those independent variables (and independent, as well, of the absolute sizes of the increments).

A variant of the problem just treated is the following: let there be an initial solution value of Y (according to the equation system of Chap. 6); suppose that a change in this solution value is to be effected by manipulation in that solution of the values of certain independent variables; what combination of changes in the values of G, T_x, and T_r will effect a change in Y equal to h?   To phrase this question algebraically we return to equation (29) of Chap. 6 and substitute h for ΔY,

$$(5) \qquad \Delta Y = h = \frac{\Delta G - b\,\Delta T_x + b\,\Delta T_r}{1 - b - v}$$

Again we may solve for the increment in, say, ΔG.

$$(6) \qquad \Delta G = (1 - b - v)h + b(\Delta T_x - \Delta T_r)$$

For any given changes in T_x and T_r there is a unique value of ΔG which makes $\Delta Y = h$. As a matter of fact we do not need to introduce h at all in the analysis; ΔY may replace h in (6). In that case, however, we consider ΔY an independent variable.

As a further step we may impose both the conditions $G + T_r = T_x$ and $Y = F$ on the variables, considering G, T_x, and T_r independent. Or, as a variant of that problem, we may impose the two conditions $\Delta G + \Delta T_r = \Delta T_x$ and $\Delta Y = \cdot h$, so that the desired change in the level of income shall be effected by budgetary manipulation which leaves unaffected the original budget balance, *i.e.*, makes no change in the surplus or deficit of the government budget.

Since the original equation system (that of Chap. 6) contained three independent variables and we now impose two new conditions, we have but one fewer equation than variables. We should thus expect to be able to express all variables in terms of any one, or, more pertinently in the present case, to express the increments in all variables in terms of the increment in any one. (The two amount to the same thing; if all variables can be expressed in terms of any one, the differences between alternative values of any two depend on the difference between the alternative values of the one to which they correspond.) Thus, from equation (6) and the incremental equation $\Delta G + \Delta T_r = \Delta T_x$, we obtain

$$\Delta T_x - \Delta T_r = (1 - b - v)h + b(\Delta T_x - \Delta T_r)$$

(7)
$$= \left(\frac{1 - b - v}{1 - b}\right) h = h\left(1 - \frac{v}{1 - b}\right)$$

Alternatively,

(8)
$$\Delta T_x = \left(1 - \frac{v}{1 - b}\right) h + \Delta T_r$$

Thus, to any value of ΔT_r there corresponds a particular value of ΔT_x which, together with the implied value of ΔG raises ΔY by the amount h, and leaves the budget balance as it was initially. In the case of $v = 0$, ΔT_x must exceed ΔT_r by the same amount, h, as income is intended to change. Since $\Delta T_x - \Delta T_r = \Delta G$ as well, the implied value of ΔG is

$$h(1 - b - v)/(1 - b)$$

If T_r remains fixed, ΔG and ΔT_x are of course equal, and both equal h when v is zero and are less than h when v is positive, as was seen in Chap. 6.

It follows from what was said in Chap. 5 that we cannot impose more arbitrary conditions than there are independent variables in the solution of the original equation system. For each condition imposed constitutes a new equation, and the variables cannot satisfy more conditions (equations) than there are variables. We may, however, permit parameter adjustment to meet new conditions.

In that case we may add more than enough equations to bring the number into equality with the number of "variables," but only in the sense that we have failed to recognize parameters as variables.

For example, the equation system of Chap. 7 comprises six equations in seven variables. As we have seen, there is a unique value of G which satisfies $G + T_r = T_x$. There is also a unique value of G which makes $Y = F$. But, except by coincidence, G cannot satisfy both conditions. We may, however, inquire what *shift* in the consumption equation would allow both $Y = F$ and $G + T_r = T_x$. If the value of the parameter a is allowed to vary, the system becomes sufficiently flexible to satisfy both conditions. In this case we must count a among our variables. The reader should have no difficulty in deriving the expression for the value of a which, together with the six equations of Chap. 7 and equation (1) of this chapter, makes Y equal to the (fixed) value of F.

The corresponding incremental problem would be to determine what values of Δa and ΔG would, at the same time, make $\Delta G + \Delta T_r$ equal ΔT_x, and ΔY equal h, and satisfy the original equations of the system. According to the tax and transfer relationships,

$$(9) \qquad \Delta G = \Delta T_x - \Delta T_r = t\,\Delta Y - r\,\Delta Y = (t - r)h$$

According to the solution for Y [equation (9), Chap. 7],

$$(10) \qquad \Delta Y = M\,\Delta a + M\,\Delta G = h$$

$$(11) \qquad \Delta a = \frac{h}{M} - \Delta G$$

$$= [1 - b(1 - t + r) - v]h - (t - r)h$$

$$= [1 - b - v - (t - r)(1 - b)]h$$

Thus Δa is the smaller, the greater are b and v (with $t - r < 1$), as is clear from the usual multiplier considerations. It is also the smaller, the greater is $t - r$, so long as b is less than 1. This follows from the consideration discussed in Chap. 6, equations (37) to (40), that balanced increases in G and T_x raise the level of income. As a matter of fact, the rise in Y which can be attributed to the balanced rise in G, T_x, and T_r is equal to

$$(12) \qquad \Delta Y = \left(\frac{1 - b}{1 - b - v}\right)(t - r)h$$

according to equation (38) of Chap. 6. If, however, the increase in a did not occur, while G did increase by the amount $(t - r)h$, the rise in national income would be given by

$$(13) \qquad \Delta Y = M \ \Delta G = \frac{1}{1 - b(1 - t + r) - v} \ (t - r)h$$

Equation (12) takes for granted $\Delta T_x - \Delta T_r = \Delta G$; equation (13) assumes $\Delta G = (t - r)h$ but leaves $\Delta T_x + \Delta T_r$ equal to $(t - r) \ \Delta Y$; since Δa does not increase in this case, ΔY does not equal h and the condition $\Delta G = \Delta T_x - \Delta T_r$ is not met. It should be noted that (13) ordinarily gives a greater value for ΔY than does (12), the "ordinary" case referring to parameter values such that the T_x and T_r equations cause $\Delta G + \Delta T_r - \Delta T_x$ to increase with a rise in G in the absence of any change in a. If the reader derives the condition under which (13) yields a lower value for ΔY, he will find it to be the same one which was derived in Chap. 7, inequality (13). It may be noticed that the expression in brackets in (11) is identical with the denominator of (22) of Chap. 7 (except that v was considered zero in the latter and was consequently absent).

In any event, however, the required rise in the value of a, that is, the required upward shift in the consumption-income relationship, is the smaller, *the greater the marginal net tax-income ratio*, as seen above. The same holds for a rise in Y equal to h brought about by a shift in the investment equation in company with a balanced rise in the government budget: the greater the marginal tax-income ratio (net of transfer payments), the smaller the upward shift in the (I,Y) relationship needs to be. If Δu, the shift in that relationship, is interpreted as an independent addition to the rate of investment, it need be smaller, the greater $t - r$ in the present case.

This result seems at first paradoxical, namely that a high marginal net tax-income ratio makes necessary a smaller independent rise in investment or consumption; the catch is, of course, that by requiring $\Delta G = \Delta T_x - \Delta T_r$ we have made tax increases a factor for expansion of income, since they automatically raise government expenditure by an equal amount if our budgetary restriction holds. The point is illustrated by equations (21) and (22) of Chap. 7, in which government expenditure is assumed to follow the relationship $G = T_x + T_r = (s - p) + (t - r)Y$. The income multiplier corresponding to a change in I or in the parameter a is the greater, the greater is $t - r$, so long as b is less than 1 which it must be in that case for stability.

As was remarked above, we cannot impose so many outside conditions on the variables as to make the total number of equations greater than the total number of variables (including any variable "parameters" which we may recognize for the purpose). For example, in the system containing a consumption–disposable income relationship and a (net) tax–national income relationship, and with both I and G independent variables, our solution for Y is given by

$$(14) \qquad Y = \frac{a - bs + I + G}{1 - b(1 - t)}$$

Suppose we wish to impose three new conditions, namely, that there be some specified level of income (equal to F), that there be some specified rate of investment, and that $G = T_x$. We cannot; we can have any two of the three conditions, but not all three at once. Corresponding to $Y = F$ there is a particular level of taxes, equal to $s + tF$; with G equal to $s + tF$ the budget would be balanced with $Y = F$ but only by coincidence would $Y = F$ with $G = s + tF$ (unless the tax structure had been deliberately geared to the level of income in question, in which case s or t or both are implicitly variables). Thus to obtain $Y = F$ with $G = s + tF = T_x$ we must let I take whatever value satisfies this condition and drop the particular condition we wished to impose on I. Or we may give I the value or the relationship we please, but then G is the only remaining independent variable and cannot satisfy both $Y = F$ and $G = T_x$ at once.*

From what has been said it must not be inferred that the independent variables can necessarily satisfy a number of new conditions equal to the excess of variables over original equations. That, rather, is the maximum number of outside conditions which they may satisfy. It is obvious, for example, that however many independent variables remain in the solution for Y, if one of the relationships is $T_x = s + tY$ we cannot have both $Y = F$ and at the same time $T_x = kY$, except by coincidence. For these two equations, $T_x = s + tY$ and $T_x = kY$, are sufficient by themselves to determine the value of Y, equal to $s/(k - t)$, and the value of Y is then free to meet no other condition.

An excellent example of this point arises in the consideration of imports and exports. We are generally reserving consideration of foreign trade for Part III of this book, but an elementary problem in that field may be taken up here. According to the accounting of Chap. 1, the national in-

---

* The suggestion is not intended that the rate of investment, or even the rate of government expenditure or the rate of taxation, is subject to manipulation of the type described; we are discussing only the mathematical operation of manipulating variables. Nevertheless, the economic question is as valid as the purely mathematical question, namely, whether all three conditions can be satisfied in the context of the relationships assumed and, if so, what the values are in terms of parameters for which they will be satisfied (or, to put it differently, what other relationships are implied by the conditions under investigation).

come is represented as follows when imports and exports are allowed [equation (32), Chap. 1].

(15)
$$Y = C + I + G + E - M$$

where E and M denote exports and imports respectively. We shall consider only two relationships, one between C and $Y - T_x$ of the usual form, and one between imports and national income in the form*

(16)
$$M = n + mY$$

The solution value of the national income is represented by

(17)
$$Y = \frac{a - bT_x + I + G + E - n}{1 - b + m}$$

There are, in the solution (17), four independent variables. Let us consider the value of E to be fixed and consider what values of G, I, and T_x will meet certain additional conditions. We can readily ascertain values for which $Y = F$, $G = T_x$, and $I = kY$, or $T_x = hY$; any three of these conditions can be satisfied by some values of G, T_x, and I in company with any given value of E. We can similarly find values for G, T_x, and I which make $M = E$. In order that $M = E$ it is necessary that

(18)
$$M = n + mY = E$$

(19)
$$Y = \frac{E - n}{m}$$

Substituting this value for Y in equation (17),

(20)
$$\frac{E - n}{m} = \frac{a - bT_x + I + G + E - n}{1 - b + m}$$

Solving (20) for E,

(21)
$$E = \frac{m(a - bT_x + I + G) + (1 - b)n}{1 - b}$$

The condition (21) can be met by any number of combinations of values of I, G, and T_x; in fact, the values of any two may be specified arbitrarily and the third can assume a value which satisfies the equation.† We can,

---

* We shall not at this point discuss either the merits or the implications of the import equation; the subject will be considered in detail in Part III.

† We may, however, obtain inadmissible values, such as negative taxes, etc. Any limits to the admissible values of certain variables limit as well the values which others may take and yet satisfy certain conditions or allow the relationships to hold. The general considerations of Chap. 4 apply here.

for example, satisfy at the same time another condition such as $G = T_x$ or $C = kY$.*

But we cannot have $Y = F$. For so long as equation (18) holds, *i.e.*, so long as $M = E$, equation (19) holds and $Y = (E - n)/m$. No values of G, I, and T_x can satisfy the original relationships and the extra condition of $M = E$ where E is fixed in value, and leave any freedom to the value of Y. Thus the initial set involved three equations, the consumption equation, the import equation, and the national-income identity, and seven variables, C, I, G, Y, T_x, M, and E; it should therefore be possible to satisfy three more conditions while still treating E as independent. But three additional equations represent only a maximum; not *any* three additional equations can necessarily be satisfied. Treating E as a parameter, the two equations $M = n + mY$ and $M = E$ serve completely to determine the value of Y, and no further equations inconsistent with this value can be satisfied.

It should be emphasized that the foregoing conclusion depends on the identification of E as essentially a parameter. If we consider E capable of variation, it is in no different category from G, I, or T_x; and a value of E can be found which allows both $M = E$ and $Y = F$. It is, in fact, the value $E = n + mF$. And if E be considered a dependent variable, subject to the *relationship* $E = M = n + mY$, then the two final terms of the national-income identity (15) may be dropped (through substitution from these two relationships) and the system reduces to the one used in the earlier analysis. [If the reader substitutes $n + mY$ for E in the numerator of (17), he can rearrange the resulting equation so that the denominator becomes $1 - b$ and neither E nor n remains in the numerator. This result accords with the elimination of E and M in (15) when $E = M$ for all values of M.]

* Again the reservation of footnote 7 applies; if T_x must be positive, C cannot exceed $a + bY$.

CHAPTER 11

REAL VALUES VERSUS MONEY VALUES

So far we have made no reference to prices in our analysis. If the question were asked whether income, consumption, wages, etc., in all the foregoing analyses were meant to be money income or real income, money consumption or real consumption, money wages or real wages, the answer would have to be that the equation systems assumed constant prices and there was consequently no difference. Only an assumption of constant prices could allow us to speak of these economic magnitudes without specifying whether real or money values were intended.

The assumption of constant prices may validate the work we have done, but it does not relieve us of the obligation to investigate the effect on our results of a change in the price level. To pursue this question we must meet the issue of whether the economic relationships expressed by our equations are relationships between real magnitudes or between money values. Is real consumption related to real income, or is money consumption related to money income? (Or, to venture onto more complicated ground, do both the real and the money values of income affect consumption; *i.e.*, does the price level itself have an influence on behavior?) If we wish to relax the assumption of constant prices, or see to what extent our results would be affected by a change in price level, these questions must be met.

There is one possible case in which the real vs. money problem can be avoided, namely, the case in which all relationships are *proportional* relationships. If, for example, consumption were always 80 per cent of national income in money terms, it would also be 80 per cent in real terms. Algebraically, if $C = bY$ (that is, if, in $C = a + bY$, $a = 0$), so that C is just the fraction b times income, then deflating income and consumption by division by a price index, P, would yield $C/P = bY/P$. Writing C' and Y' for deflated consumption and income, we obtain as the real relationship $C' = bY'$ which is identical with the $C = bY$ money relationship. But if consumption is not proportional to income, if a is not equal to zero in the equation $C = a + bY$, the price level does make a difference. Here deflation by a price index P yields the real relationship $C/P = a/P + bY/P$, so that $C' = a/P + bY'$. This equation is affected by the value of P; the "constant" term in the consumption equation is now inversely proportional to the price level. We conclude that, unless our consumption-income relationship is one of proportionality, the price level does matter; a given real relationship yields different money relationships depending on the price levels, and, conversely, a given relationship between money

132

values would yield different relationships in real terms depending on the price levels.*

We can illustrate the possibility of price influence by taking a simple system of equations which makes explicit allowance for the price level. We shall not use an equation relating the price level to any other variables, but shall treat it as independently determined; and we shall experiment with our solution by changing the assumed price level.

First we may dismiss a trivial case. If all our relationships are real relationships, then although the money values in our solution depend on the price level, the real values do not. That is to say, in all the systems we have hitherto studied, if the reader interprets all equations as relating to real values of the variables, then the results may validly be interpreted as giving the real values in the solutions regardless of the price level. In each case, money values can be obtained by multiplying everything by a price level, whatever that level may be. And, conversely, if we consider all our equations to refer to money magnitudes—if, that is, our economic hypotheses all relate to money values—then our results may validly be interpreted as correct solutions in money terms; and real values may be obtained by division throughout by a price index.

The problem arises when some of the equations refer to money values, others to real values, or if some equations contain as variables both real and money values, or when they explicitly contain the price level as a variable. If our hypothesis about consumption is that consumption in real terms bears a linear relationship to real income, while we consider taxes to be geared to the level of money income, then we have a set of relationships involving both real and money variables and our solution will not be free from dependence on the price level.

Real and Money Relationships Combined

Our system for illustration will be this: consumption is related to income in real terms; taxes are related to income in money terms. We shall use C, Y, I, G, and T to denote money magnitudes, *i.e.*, magnitudes expressed in current dollar values. Real income is then represented by Y/P, where P is the price index used for deflation. Real consumption is C/P, real investment is I/P, etc. (In this simple example we use the same price index to deflate all compononts of total expenditure.)

---

* Even proportionality in all our relationships would still leave us the price problem if we considered more than one price index. If we determined real consumption, real investment, real wages, real government expenditure, etc., by deflating each money magnitude by its own appropriate price index, then proportionality of all relationships such as $C = bY$, $W = wY$, $I = vY$, etc., would not save us from having to make explicit allowance for the price level. This question will be raised again in the last section of the present chapter.

The consumption hypothesis is accordingly expressed as

(1)
$$\frac{C}{P} = a + b\left(\frac{Y - T_x}{P}\right)$$

and the tax structure is described by

(2)
$$T_x = s + tY$$

We shall assume that government expenditure and private investment are constant in real terms; that is, we treat real investment and real government expenditure as given. Using G' and I' to denote real government and private investment expenditures respectively, we express the money magnitudes as

$$G = PG' \quad \text{and} \quad I = PI'$$

To solve the equations, we begin by rearranging the consumption equation. Multiplying both sides of (1) by P,

(3)
$$C = Pa + b(Y - T_x)$$

Substituting (2) in (3),

(4)
$$C = Pa + bY - bs - btY = (Pa - bs) + b(1 - t)Y$$

Substituting (4) in the national-income identity,

(5)
$$Y = (pa - bs) + I + G + b(1 - t)Y$$
$$= \frac{(Pa - bs) + I + G}{1 - b(1 - t)} = \frac{P(a + I' + G') - bs}{1 - b(1 - t)}$$

Putting our variables into real terms again by dividing through by P, we obtain the expression for real income

(6)
$$\frac{Y}{P} = \frac{a - bs/P + I' + G'}{1 - b(1 - t)} = \frac{a + I' + G'}{1 - b(1 + t)} - \left(\frac{1}{P}\right)\left[\frac{bs}{1 - b(1 - t)}\right]$$

It is clear that, given a relationship between real consumption and real income and a relationship between the money value of taxes and the money value of national income, and given the real values of investment and government expenditure, we cannot solve for Y unless the price level is known, since the price-index variable appears explicitly in the formula for Y. It is also clear that the influence of the price level comes in via the tax relationship, since the only term containing P in the formula for Y is the term containing s, a parameter in the tax equation. Whether real income is higher or lower, the higher the price level, depends on whether s is positive or negative. If s is positive, a higher price level means a higher level of income, since the term bs/P would be smaller, and this term is subtracted from the numerator. With s negative, the higher the price level the lower would be the level of real income; for in that case $-bs/P$ is positive and varies inversely with P.

Whether the income level indicated by the equation system is directly or inversely related to the price level may be said to depend on whether the marginal tax-income ratio is less than or greater than the average tax-income ratio. For the average tax-income ratio is given by

$$(7) \qquad \frac{T_x}{Y} = \frac{s + tY}{Y} = t + \frac{s}{Y}$$

This ratio depends on the value of Y, but whatever the value of Y it is greater or less than the marginal tax-income ratio $\Delta T_x/\Delta Y = t$, according as s is positive or negative. It is also clear from (7) that if s is positive, the ratio of T_x to Y is the lower, the higher the level of money income. It is this aspect of the ratio which explains the relation of the price-level effect to the sign of s. At a higher price level, taxes are proportionately less in relation to any given level of real income if s is positive. And blowing up money income, by raising the value of P corresponding to a given value of real income, makes the real value of taxes smaller. In other words, taxes rise with a rise in income in lesser proportion than income if s is positive. This is not to say that real taxes are less, the higher the value of Y, but that real taxes are less, the higher the money value of any given real income. That taxes rise in lesser proportion than money income is seen from the fact that, for any given rise in income denoted by ΔY, the proportionate rise in taxes is given by

$$(8) \qquad \frac{\Delta T_x}{T_x} = \frac{t\, \Delta Y}{s + tY}$$

If s is zero, $\Delta T_x/T_x = \Delta Y/Y$ and the proportionate changes are equal; if s is positive the denominator of (8) is greater than tY and the ratio of ΔT_x to T_x is consequently less than that of ΔY to Y.

If s is negative, taxes are the greater in relation to income, the greater the value of Y, and blowing up the money value of a given real income raises taxes relatively to Y, raising thereby the real value of taxes; while Y rises in the proportion that P rises, T_x rises in greater proportion and T_x/P is increased.

It should be observed that a system of income taxes at a fixed percentage rate with exemption of a part of income is represented by a negative value for s. The effect of a general rise in the price level is to reduce the real value of the exemption. "Progressivity" generally in the tax structure tends to make the marginal tax-income ratio greater than the average tax-income ratio for the economy as a whole, i.e., is represented by a negative value of s, and makes the value of Y obtained by solution of the present system of equations the greater, the lower the general price level.

An interesting question arises: do taxes in real terms rise or fall with the change in price level? In the event, for example, that s is positive, real income rises with an increase in P; that is, money income rises in greater proportion than the price level. Money taxes also rise with an increase in P; but they rise in lesser proportion than does money income. Can they rise, nevertheless, in greater proportion than the price level?

In order that taxes rise in real terms, the rise in money taxes must be proportionately greater than the rise in the price level; *i.e.*, in order that T_x/P increase the following inequality must hold when ΔP is positive:*

$$(9) \qquad \frac{T_x + \Delta T_x}{P + \Delta P} > \frac{T_x}{P}$$

$$PT_x + P\,\Delta T_x > PT_x + T_x\,\Delta P$$

$$P\,\Delta T_x > T_x\,\Delta P$$

$$\frac{\Delta T_x}{T_x} > \frac{\Delta P}{P}$$

We know from equation (2) that

$$(10) \qquad \Delta T_x = t\,\Delta Y$$

and it follows from (5) that

$$(11) \qquad \Delta Y = \left[\frac{a + I' + G'}{1 - b(1 - t)}\right]\Delta P = \left(\frac{N}{D}\right)\Delta P$$

where N and D will stand for numerator and denominator of (11) henceforth. Thus,

$$(12) \qquad \Delta T_x = t\left(\frac{N}{D}\right)\Delta P$$

and, also,

$$(13) \qquad T_x = s + tY = s + t\left(\frac{PN - bs}{D}\right)$$

Now we may rewrite (9) as

$$(14) \qquad \left(\frac{tN\,\Delta P}{D}\right)\left(\frac{D}{Ds + tPN - tbs}\right) > \frac{\Delta P}{P}$$

$$tPN > Ds + tPN - tbs$$

$$0 > Ds - tbs$$

---

* For a fall in the price level, that is, ΔP negative, inequality (9) is expressed in reverse to indicate greater proportionate change in T_x than in P.

One step more will bring us to the condition we are seeking. Obviously the s can be canceled to arrive at a condition in terms of b and t, since the abbreviation D involves only the two parameters b and t. But the exact condition depends on whether s is positive or negative; if s is negative, the inequality is reversed by the cancellation. Consider first the case of positive s. We have already seen that, with s positive, real income rises; we have also seen that, with s positive, taxes rise in lesser proportion than income, so that the ratio of taxes to income (in both money and real terms) falls. The condition for a rise in the real value of taxes, $i.e.$, for a proportional (percentage) increase in taxes greater than the proportional rise in the price level, is

$$(15) \qquad 0 > D - tb$$
$$0 > 1 - b(1 - t) - tb$$
$$0 > 1 - b$$

Thus real taxes will rise only if b exceeds $+1$, that is to say, only if the marginal consumption–income ratio is sufficiently great that in the absence of the tax-income relationship the system would be unstable. This condition is consistent with the conclusion reached earlier without reference to the price level; a lowering of the tax-income schedule, represented by a decrease in the (positive) value of s, actually raises taxes through its expansionary effect on national income if b exceeds $+1$. The price-level rise may be interpreted as a decrease in the real value of s; and whether real taxes rise depends then on the same criterion as was reached in Chap. 8.

Next consider s negative, the case of "income progressivity" in the aggregate tax structure. Dividing through (14) by the negative value of s yields the condition

$$(16) \qquad 0 < D - tb$$
$$0 < 1 - b$$

Thus, in this case in which a rise in P leads to lower real income, the real value of taxes rises with the increase in P $unless$ b exceeds $+1$. This condition is also consistent with the earlier analysis; a decrease in the absolute value of s in the ordinary case of constant prices is an upward shift in the tax-income relationship when s is negative. And since the increase in P may be interpreted according to equation (6) as a decrease in the $absolute$ value of (negative) s in so far as the effect on real income is concerned, the fall in income is the result of the upward shift in the tax structure, and the effect on taxes of that upward shift is offset by the downward income effect on taxes only if the equation system would be unstable in the absence of the marginal tax-income relationship.

It should be observed that, in the case of negative s, the rise in the real value of taxes which accompanies a rise in the price level cannot carry real taxes above the limiting value of tN/D; but they may fall to zero with a fall in the price level.* Similarly, with s positive, a rising price level can lower the real value of taxes only to the lower limit, $T_x = tN/D$; while a falling price level can raise them without limit so long as the linear tax-income relationship continues to hold.

All of these considerations can be derived directly from the solution value of T_x/P which appears as

$$\frac{T_x}{P} = \frac{s}{P} + \frac{tY}{P} = \frac{s}{P} + \left(\frac{t}{P}\right)\left(\frac{PN - bs}{D}\right)$$

$$= t\left(\frac{N}{D}\right) + \left(\frac{s}{P}\right)\left(\frac{1 - b}{1 - b(1 - t)}\right)$$

Prices and Income Distribution

Prices may enter the equation system through their implications for the distribution of income between wages and profits. This section will investigate those implications, and will pay particular attention to the question of price flexibility.

Let us denote *real* income by Y and the price level by P, so that money income is represented by PY. Let us consider money wage rates fixed and consider employment proportional to real income, so that aggregate money wages, W, are given by

$$(18) \qquad\qquad\qquad W = wY$$

Aggregate money profits, then, denoted by Π, are given by

$$(19) \qquad\qquad \Pi = PY - W = PY - wY = (P - w)Y$$

The real consumption of wage earners and of profit earners follows the relationships

$$(20) \qquad\qquad\qquad C_w = a + b\left(\frac{W}{P}\right)$$

$$(21) \qquad\qquad\qquad C_\pi = \alpha + \beta\left(\frac{\Pi}{P}\right)$$

Nonconsumption real expenditure is considered independent and fixed in real terms, equal to K, so that the money value of nonconsumption ex-

---

* Their falling to zero with a sufficient drop in the price level requires our considering the linear relation to hold for levels of income as low as make $s + tY = 0$, that is, as low as $Y = -s/t$. The prototype of such a tax structure is the fixed-rate income tax with exemptions; a sufficiently low price level could, at any level of real income, make money incomes so low that everyone's income would fall within his exemption.

penditure equals PK and is proportional to the price level. (We assume one general price level applicable to consumption and nonconsumption goods and services.)

The national income in money terms, PY, then follows the usual accounting identity as developed in Chap. 1,

$$(22) \qquad PY = PK + PC_w + PC_\pi$$

$$PY = PK + Pa + P\alpha + Pb\left(\frac{W}{P}\right) + P\beta\left(\frac{\Pi}{P}\right)$$

$$= PH + bW + \beta\Pi$$

$$= PH + bwY + \beta(P - w)Y$$

$$(23) \qquad Y = H + b\left(\frac{w}{P}\right)Y - \beta\left(\frac{w}{P}\right)Y + \beta Y$$

$$= \frac{H}{1 - b(w/P) - \beta[1 - (w/P)]}$$

The solution for Y, equation (23), contains nothing that was not derived in Chap. 9, since w/P is clearly the marginal (as well as average) share of wages in the national income, and $1 - (w/P)$ is the marginal (and average) share of profits. What is more interesting is to solve equation (22) for P rather than for Y. Since to any value of P there corresponds a different value of Y according to (23), it is also then true that to each value of Y there corresponds a particular value of P. We may thus inquire what price level is consistent with any given value of Y. Solving (22) for P,

$$(24) \qquad P(Y - H - \beta Y) = (b - \beta)wY$$

$$(25) \qquad P = \left[\frac{(b - \beta)w}{Y - H - \beta Y}\right]Y$$

Another form for (25) is

$$(26) \qquad \frac{w}{P} = \frac{Y - H - \beta Y}{(b - \beta)Y}$$

Equation (26) accentuates the fact that it is the *relative* shares of wages and profits for which we have actually solved the equations. In other words, with any given parameters, b, β, K, a, and α, there is a unique distribution of income between wages and profits consistent with any given value of Y.*

Since only positive values of w and P are meaningful, the numerator and

* But if $b = \beta$, the denominator becomes zero and there is no solution, *i.e.*, no distribution of income which will yield the required value of Y, unless $H = (1 - b)Y$ so that the numerator is zero, in which case any values of w and P will do.

denominator of (26) must be of the same sign. To understand this restriction it is useful to introduce the concept of "derived demand." By "derived demand" we shall mean the value of $K + C_w + C_\pi$ implied by equations (18), (19), (20), and (21) corresponding to any given value of Y. That is to say, the "derived demand" is what the total consumption and nonconsumption demand for goods and services is which corresponds to a given level of income. The accounting of Chap. 1 has demonstrated that, by the very definition of national income in terms of wages and profits, the actual values of K, C_w, and C_π add up to the actual value of $\Pi/P + W/P$, whether or not the relationships (18) through (21) hold. Nevertheless the *concept* of derived demand is meaningful, and it helps to understand the construction of equation (26).

The numerator of (26) can be identified as the given value of Y minus the derived demand corresponding to that given value of Y when $w = 0$, that is, when $\Pi = PY$ and all income is profits. If that numerator is positive the derived demand with $w = 0$ would be less than the given value of Y. Now it should be observed that the satisfaction of all the equations implies that "derived demand" equals national income, for the right-hand side of the first line of (23) represents derived demand and if (23) holds, the right-hand side equals the left which is Y itself. Thus in order that a *given* value of Y may represent the solution of the equation system, the parameters and independent variables must have such values that the derived demand equals Y.

If, then, the numerator of (26) is positive, derived demand with $w = 0$ is *smaller* than the necessary value of derived demand for the given value of Y. The derived demand can be changed by changing the value of w from zero to some positive value, *i.e.*, by allowing some income to accrue as wages. If b exceeds β, the income shift from profits to wages will raise derived demand, if b is less than β the shift will lower it. Derived demand can then be made equal to Y only if b exceeds β, and the given value of Y can consequently be consistent with the equations only if b exceeds β.

Conversely, if the numerator of (26) is negative, derived demand must be less if the given value of Y is to obtain. With wages at zero they can only increase. Thus the lower derived demand necessary for the satisfaction of the equations by the given value of Y can be obtained only if b is less than β so that the income shift lowers the derived demand.

The necessity for (26) to show numerator and denominator of the same sign is thus explained.

Next let us look into the condition for $w/P = 1$, that is, for $w = P$. If the parameter values in conjunction with the particular value chosen for Y yield $w/P = 1$, the numerator and the denominator on the right-hand side of (26) must be equal, so that

$$(27) \qquad\qquad Y = H + \beta Y + bY - \beta Y$$
$$= H + bY$$

In other words, the given value of Y is consistent with an income distribution involving wages equal to total income and profits equal to zero if the derived demand corresponding to that level of income would equal that level of income with all income going into wages.

Let us denote by D_w the derived demand corresponding to the chosen value of Y when $w = P$, and by D_π the derived demand corresponding to that chosen level of income when $w = 0$. Then the denominator of (26) is identified as the difference between D_w and D_π,

$$(28) \qquad D_w - D_\pi = (H + bY) - (H + \beta Y) = (b - \beta)Y$$

The process of finding the solution value of w/P corresponding to a given value of Y may then be described as a process of finding that distribution of income, between $W = 0$ and $W = PY$, which yields a derived demand equal to the given level of income. Starting with $w = 0$ we have a certain (suppose positive) value of $Y - H - \beta Y = Y - D_\pi$; if we shift all the way to $w = P$ we have a certain (suppose negative) value of $Y - H - bY = Y - D_w$. The difference is equal to $(b - \beta)Y$ and we need to shift a fraction of the way from $w = 0$ to $w = P$, the fraction being the ratio of $Y - D_\pi$ to $D_w - D_\pi$. This ratio is exactly what is shown by the right-hand side of (26). The wage fraction of total income needs, in order to be consistent with a given level of income, to be the ratio of the required increase in derived demand above D_π, to the total possible increase, $D_w - D_\pi$.

The same conclusion may be reached from the other side. The profits share in total income consistent with a given level of income is represented, using equation (26), by

$$(29) \qquad \frac{\Pi}{PY} = \frac{PY - W}{PY} = \frac{P - w}{P} = 1 - \frac{w}{P} = 1 - \frac{Y - H - \beta Y}{(b - \beta)Y}$$
$$= \frac{bY - \beta Y - Y + H + \beta Y}{(b - \beta)Y} = \frac{Y - H - bY}{(\beta - b)Y} = \frac{Y - D_w}{D_\pi - D_w}$$

The two shares $\dfrac{\Pi}{PY}$ and $\dfrac{W}{PY}$ add up to $+ 1$.

$$(30) \qquad \frac{Y - D_\pi}{D_w - D_\pi} + \frac{Y - D_w}{D_\pi - D_w} = \frac{Y - D_\pi}{D_w - D_\pi} - \frac{Y - D_w}{D_w - D_\pi} = \frac{D_w - D_\pi}{D_w - D_\pi}$$

It should be noted that D_w and D_π represent the limits on the value of derived demand; any distribution of income between $w = 0$ and $w = P$ yields a derived demand between D_w and D_π; a given level of income is not consistent with any distribution of income unless it lies within the range of values between the corresponding D_w and D_π.

Finally let us consider the stability of a system of equations such as the system now under investigation under conditions of price flexibility. By "price flexibility" we mean the tendency of prices to rise when the level of income exceeds the "full-employment" level and their tendency to fall when income is below that level. We shall not here define "full employment" any more definitely than as that level of income about which prices are flexible. (The following paragraphs refer to real income.)

When prices rise, money wage rates being fixed, the distribution of income shifts in favor of profits. If β exceeds b, this shift raises the level of income; if b exceeds β, this shift lowers the level of income. Consequently a system of flexible prices is *stable* about the full-employment level if β is less than b; for then a level of income greater than the full-employment level is associated with rising prices, a shift toward profits, and hence falling income; and a level of income below the full-employment level is associated with falling prices, a shift in favor of wages, and rising income. Since income above full employment tends to fall, while income below tends to rise, income may be said to be stable about full employment when prices are flexible and β is less than b.

If, however, β exceeds b, then income above full employment is associated with rising prices, a shift in favor of profits, and rising income; income below full employment is associated with falling prices, a shift toward wages, and falling income. In this case, i.e., when β exceeds b, price flexibility implies the instability of income.

Alternatively we may consider wage-rate flexibility and price fixity. In this case wage rates rise when employment is overfull, fall when employment is less than full. Income above the full-employment level is associated with rising wage rates, a shift toward wages, and rising income if b exceeds β, falling income if β exceeds b. With income below full employment, wage rates fall, income shifts toward profits, and income falls if b exceeds β, rises if β exceeds b. Thus income is stable about full employment when wage rates are flexible only if b is less than β.

Finally we may consider the mixed case, in which both prices and wage rates rise when income is above, fall when income is below, the full employment level. The effect on income distribution depends on which rise relatively at the greater rate; if prices rise proportionately more rapidly, w/P declines, if prices rise relatively more slowly than wage rates, w/P increases. Thus if prices are the relatively more flexible, $\beta < b$ is the stability condition; if wage rates are the relatively more flexible, $b < \beta$ is the stability condition.

In any case there exists the limitation that neither w nor $P - w$ may go below zero (or below any other limit which may be relevant). The effective flexibility may in either case, consequently, not be sufficient to yield stability. With income above full employment, rising prices cannot return income below the value at which $D_\pi = Y$ since any possibility of shift in income distribution is exhausted at that point. Similarly with income below full employment, income can rise only to the point where $D_w = Y$ since further increase due to the shift in favor of wages is exhausted at that point.

In the event that there is a physical limit to income above the full employment level, the analysis may be rephrased in terms of derived demand; income presses the upper limit when at that upper limit derived demand is greater. The shift in distribution then may still be considered to occur.

Relative Prices in the System

This section will deal with the influence on certain variables of shifts in the different price levels relating to different commodity groups. The particular commodity-group distinction will be that between consumption goods and services and the goods and services devoted to investment or government use.*

Before we take up the analysis it is interesting to note a qualification, relevant at this point, to the algebraic accounting of Chap. 1. If we wish to compare real incomes in two different periods of time in which the general price levels differ, we may adopt the expedient of reducing (or enlarging) one of the national-income figures in the ratio by which price levels differ; this process of statistical "deflation" or "inflation" allows us to speak of the "real" national income as the production of goods and services in either period valued at the particular prices prevailing in one of the periods (or, perhaps, in some third period if both figures have been adjusted to the price level of a third period). The several additive components of the national income, on both the receipts side and the expenditure side, may similarly be deflated and, if a single price-level index is used in deflation, they still add up after deflation to the deflated national-income totals.

But suppose different segments of the totals are deflated by different price-level ratios; do the accounting identities continue to hold? It is important to be careful in this regard. Consider first the expenditure sum of $C + I + G$. To deflate this money-value sum we may divide each of C, I, and G by the ratio of price levels of consumption goods and services,

* The preceding section, involving as it did the relative prices of labor and finished commodities, may also be considered to involve a distinction between relative price levels.

investment goods and services, and goods and services sold to government, respectively, to the price levels of some base period. We then have, using Y_r to denote "real" national income,

$$(31) \qquad Y_r = R_cC + R_iI + R_gG$$

where R_c, R_i, and R_g are the deflation ratios, i.e., reciprocals of the ratios of present respective price levels to those in the base period. On the receipts side we have, for money income,

$$(32) \qquad Y = W + P$$

if we distinguish only two income categories. With which deflation ratios do we deflate W and P to arrive at deflated income receipts, Y'_r, (denoted with a prime to show that Y'_r may not equal Y_r)? If we deflate both W and P by an "average" price index, choosing the average properly, we may make $Y'_r = Y_r$; that is to say, Y'_r will equal Y_r if we deflate W and P by multiplying each by Y_r/Y which is a weighted average of R_c, R_i, and R_g formed according to

$$(33) \qquad \frac{Y_r}{Y} = \left(\frac{C}{Y}\right)R_c + \left(\frac{I}{Y}\right)R_i + \left(\frac{G}{Y}\right)R_g$$

If, however, we consider appropriate the price level of consumption goods only—and what is appropriate depends on the particular analytical use we wish to make of the deflated sum of W and P—we have

$$(34) \qquad Y'_r = R_cW + R_cP \neq Y_r$$

except in the special case when $R_c = R_i = R_g$ or when the divergences of R_i and R_g from R_c cancel each other in the average.

Other interesting accounting identities disappear when we use selective deflation. For example, we may for one purpose deflate government expenditure by an appropriate ratio of price levels, R_g. For another purpose we may deflate taxes by the ratio of consumption-goods price levels, to denote the "real" tax burden to consumers. The net balance of the government budget, expressed in money terms as $G - T_x$ (ignoring transfer payments), becomes, in real terms, $R_gG - R_cT_x$, which may be of opposite sign to $G - T_x$ if divergences in price levels are significant.

Similarly, we may define the current rate of saving as the excess of disposable income over consumption, so that (using S for the rate of saving),

$$(35) \qquad S = Y - T_x - C = (C + I + G) - T_x - C$$
$$= I + G - T_x$$

If we deflate the rate of saving by a consumption-goods price deflator, investment by an investment-goods deflator, and G and T_x by, say, the deflator R_g, the identity will hold only by coincidence.

Numerous other examples can be found in which identities contain variables which, for valid analytical reasons, are deflated by different price level ratios; the deflated variables satisfy the identities only by coincidence. The separate price levels relevant to imports and to exports are interesting examples which may affect differently the "real" production calculation and the "real" disposable-income calculation.

Turning now to the analysis, we shall consider real consumption related to real disposable income, meaning by the latter the money rate of disposable income divided by the price index of consumption goods and services. It should be especially noted that this basic hypothesis considers consumption independent of the price level of investment goods and services or of the price level of goods and services purchased by government. We shall denote "real" variables by C, I, and G and the pertinent price level indexes by P_c, P_i, and P_g, so that

$$(36) \qquad Y = P_c C + P_i I + P_g G$$

where Y denotes money income. Using the tax-income relationship of equation (2) we have disposable income in money terms, X, given by

$$(37) \qquad X = Y - T_x = Y - s - tY = Y(1 - t) - s$$

The consumption hypothesis, then, is

$$(38) \qquad C = a + b \left[\frac{Y(1 - t) - s}{P_c} \right]$$

Equation (38) may be rewritten in terms of the money rate of consumption by multiplying through by P_c,

$$(39) \qquad P_c C = P_c a + bY(1 - t) - bs$$

Substituting (39) in (36) yields

$$(40) \qquad Y = P_c a - bs + bY(1 - t) + P_i I + P_g G$$
$$= \frac{P_c a + P_i I + P_g G - bs}{1 - b(1 - t)}$$

Equation (40) differs from equation (5) in its differentiation among P_c, P_i, and P_g. Let us experiment now with independent changes in only one of the three price levels. First suppose that the general price level of investment goods and services undergoes a change equal to ΔP_i. Undoubtedly we should consider at once the possibility of a directly related change in the real rate of investment, I; but in order to isolate the different factors let us suppose no change in the value of I. What change in the solution value for Y is indicated?

When P_i rises (or falls) to $(P_i + \Delta P_i)$, the value of $P_i I$ in the numerator changes by $I \Delta P_i$, so that

$$(41) \qquad \Delta Y = MI \, \Delta P_i$$

where M ("multiplier") is the reciprocal of $1 - b(1 - t)$.

The related change in C may be obtained from equation (39) which shows that

$$(42) \qquad \Delta(P_c C) = b(1 - t)\Delta Y = \frac{b(1 - t)}{1 - b(1 - t)} I\Delta P_i$$

Since no change is assumed to occur in the value of P_c, the change in real consumption is proportionate to the change in money consumption. If we measure real national income as money national income valued at the original price levels, the change in real national income is equal to $\Delta(P_c C)$.

It is interesting to notice that, so far as the money or real rate of consumption is concerned, only the money rate of investment or the money rate of government expenditure is significant. If, for example, P_i changed in the ratio R, while I changed in the inverse of that ratio, $1/R$, the money value of $P_i I$ would still be equal to $RP_i I/R = P_i I$ and no related change would be indicated in the real or money rate of consumption.

Let us next suppose that it is P_c which undergoes a change. The change in Y is equal to $\Delta Y = Ma \, \Delta P_c$ according to (40). In order to see what happens to C, let us drop from the equation system the variable T_x and its relationship to Y, considering real consumption equal to $a + (bY/P)$ and the solution for Y, consequently, as $M(P_c a + P_i I + P_g G)$. The reader may reinstate taxes in his own work.

The change in C is then given by

$$
\begin{aligned}
(43) \qquad \Delta C &= b \, \Delta\!\left(\frac{Y}{P}\right) \\
&= b\left(\frac{Y + \Delta Y}{P_c + \Delta P_c} - \frac{Y}{P_c}\right) \\
&= b\left[\frac{P_c Y + P_c \, \Delta Y - P_c Y - Y \, \Delta P_c}{P_c(P_c + \Delta P_c)}\right] \\
&= \left[\frac{b}{P_c(P_c + \Delta P_c)}\right](P_c \, \Delta Y - Y \, \Delta P_c) \\
&= \left[\frac{b}{P_c(P_c + \Delta P_c)}\right](P_c Ma \, \Delta P_c - Y \, \Delta P_c) \\
&= \left[\frac{b}{P_c(P_c + \Delta P_c)}\right](P_c Ma - Y)\Delta P_c
\end{aligned}
$$

The bracketed factor is necessarily positive if b is positive.   Thus $\Delta C/\Delta P_c$ is positive or negative according as P_cMa is greater or less than Y.   Since the solution value for Y is equal to $P_cMa + P_iI + P_gG$, the latter exceeds P_cMa (unless a negative value for I occurs which makes $P_iI + P_gG$ negative).   Thus real consumption falls with a rise in the price level of consumption goods.

This result, however, we could have anticipated for, with the tax consideration absent, only relative price levels matter, and a rise in P_c is equivalent to a fall of the same proportion in P_i and P_g.   That only relative prices matter in the absence of the tax effect, according to the present consumption hypothesis, is clear from the fact that multiplication of P_c, P_i, and P_g by any common ratio, R, makes the value of Y equal to $M(RP_ca + RP_iI + RP_gG) = RMY$; real consumption is then equal to $a + (bRY/RP_c) = a + (bY/P_c)$ as before.

Finally we may investigate the effects on consumption, real income, etc., of a change in P_i associated with a change in I.   We may suppose that the rate of investment depends in some fashion on the ratio of the price level of consumption goods and services to the price level of investment goods and services.   With any fixed level of consumption prices, I is assumed to vary inversely with the level of P_i; or, what is the same thing, I is assumed to vary inversely with the ratio of P_i to P_c.   We shall denote by k the ratio of the proportionate change in I to the proportionate change in P_i with which it is associated, that is to say, k is defined according to

$$(44) \qquad - k = \frac{\Delta I/I}{\Delta P_i/P_i} = \left(\frac{P_i}{I}\right)\left(\frac{\Delta I}{\Delta P_i}\right)$$

The parameter k is positive since a positive ΔP is associated with a negative ΔI.

The first step is to derive the change in the money rate of investment, P_iI, associated with the change in P_i and related change in I, in terms of the parameter k:

$$(45) \qquad \begin{aligned} \Delta(P_iI) &= (P_i + \Delta P_i)(I + \Delta I) - P_iI \\ &= P_i\,\Delta I + I\,\Delta P_i + \Delta P_i\,\Delta I \\ &= -kI\,\Delta P_i + I\,\Delta P_i + \Delta P_i\,\Delta I \\ &= [I(1 - k) + \Delta I]\Delta P_i \end{aligned}$$

Next we derive the changes in Y and C:

$$(46) \qquad \Delta Y = M\,\Delta(P_iI) = M[I(1 - k) + \Delta I]\Delta P_i$$

$$(47) \qquad \Delta(P_cC) = b\,\Delta Y = bM[I(1 - k) + \Delta I]\Delta P_i$$

Real income will be defined as the sum of the values of C, I, and G when multiplied by their respective *initial* price levels, *i.e.*,

(48) $$Y_r = P_cC + P_iI + P_gG$$

(49) $$\Delta Y_r = P_c\,\Delta C + P_i\,\Delta I + P_g\,\Delta G$$
$$= \Delta(P_cC) + P_i\,\Delta I$$

since G, P_g, and P_c are assumed constant.

Substituting from (47) and (44) into (49),

(50) $$\Delta Y_r = bM[I(1 - k) + \Delta I]\Delta P_i - kI\,\Delta P_i$$
$$= I\,\Delta P_i\left[\left(\frac{b}{1-b}\right)(1-k) - k + \left(\frac{b}{1-b}\right)\frac{\Delta I}{I}\right]$$

In order that a *rise* in P_i be associated with a *rise* in real income, the expression in brackets must be positive;

(51) $$k\left(1 + \frac{b}{1-b}\right) = \frac{k}{1-b} < \left(\frac{b}{1-b}\right)\left(1 + \frac{\Delta I}{I}\right)$$
$$k < b\left(1 + \frac{\Delta I}{I}\right)$$

where

(52) $$1 > b > b\left(1 + \frac{\Delta I}{I}\right) < 1 + \frac{\Delta I}{I} < 1$$

This condition is plausible. Real income rises only if real consumption rises, since real investment falls with the increase in P_i; real consumption rises only if money investment rises; and money investment rises only if k is less than $1 + (\Delta I/I)$ which itself is less than 1. But it is not sufficient that the change in money income be of positive sign, it must be a large enough increase to induce a sufficient rise in consumption to offset the fall in real investment; consequently k must be even less than $1 + (\Delta I/I)$ by an amount depending on the value of b. The greater is b, the less is the rise in money investment required to induce a given increase in consumption.

If the changes in P_i and I are relatively small, $1 + (\Delta I/I)$ is approximately equal to $+1$ and the condition (51) is approximately that k should be less than b.

Conversely, a fall in P_i will raise real income only if the reverse of the inequality holds, that is, if k exceeds $b[1 + (\Delta I/I)]$. In this case ΔI is positive and k must therefore exceed b. Money investment need not rise; even with constant money investment there occurs a rise in real investment and so a rise in real income. Some decrease may occur in money investment, and so in consumption, and yet allow real income to rise. The allowable decrease in money investment depends on the size of b; if b is large, a relatively large decrease in real consumption accompanies a small decrease in money investment and only a relatively small decrease in money investment may occur if the rise in real investment is to offset the fall in consumption.

If we call k the "elasticity of investment demand with respect to relative investment-goods prices" the condition may be rephrased as follows: a fall in the relative prices of investment goods (or rise in the relative prices of consumption goods) is associated with a rise in real income if investment demand is relatively elastic with respect to prices; and vice versa if demand is relatively inelastic. The critical elasticity is approximately equal to the value of the marginal consumption-income ratio.

It is important to notice a property of the elasticity as we have defined it, however. The property is this: the elasticity as defined above depends on the absolute sizes of ΔP_i and ΔI. A numerical example will make this point clear. Suppose that $\Delta P_i/P_i = +20$ per cent; $\Delta I/I = -10$ per cent; then $(P_i + \Delta P_i)(I + \Delta I) = 1.20 P_i \times 0.9 I = 1.08 \times P_i I$. Again let P_i and I change by $+20$ per cent and minus 10 per cent, respectively; P_i becomes equal to $1.2 \times 1.2 = 1.44$ times its initial value; I becomes equal to $0.9 \times 0.9 = 0.81$ times its initial value; their product becomes equal to $1.44 \times 0.81 = 1.1664$ times its initial value. Taking the two changes together, P_i increased by 44 per cent of its initial value and I decreased by 19 per cent of its initial value. Computing k for either of the two steps of the change yields a value of $-10\!/\!20 = -0.5$; computing k for the sums of the changes yields $-19\!/\!44 \neq -0.5$. In other words, the proportional changes are compounded, not added, and the ratio of the absolute changes varies with the successive application of the ratio k. The distinction is similar to that between simple interest and compound interest.

This ambiguity in the definition of k could be removed by defining it not as the ratio of the actual proportional changes $\Delta I/I$ and $\Delta P_i/P_i$, but as the value, say, of the percentage change in I which, compounded with a 1 per cent (or 0.1 per cent or 10 per cent) change in P_i, would lead to the actual proportional changes $\Delta I/I$ and $\Delta P_i/P_i$. Or the concepts of the calculus could be introduced to remove the arbitrary element in that technique. Since there is little reason to suppose that the demand would have a fixed elasticity at all price levels by any definition, and since the general nature of the results is already clear from the foregoing analysis, further refinement will be omitted here.

CHAPTER 12

THE LINEARITY OF RELATIONSHIPS

All the equation systems studied have been linear; that is to say, all relationships have been assumed to be of such form that when plotted on a graph they would appear as straight lines. We have assumed relationships to be linear because simultaneous solution is much easier when equations are linear than when they represent curvilinear forms, and because incremental ratios are unambiguous when they correspond to relationships which are perfectly linear.

But we cannot assume a priori that economic relationships actually do conform to straight lines. Even statistically derived relationships which appear to be linear often appear so for one of two reasons. (a) Frequently the statistically derived relationship is linear because the statistician has set himself the task of discovering the straight line which best represents the actual relationship; and if one sets out to discover a "best fitting" straight line the result is predestined to linearity. (b) Frequently the apparent relationship contained in the statistical data has such slight curvature that, over a limited range of values, it may sensibly be represented by a straight line. One may, that is, work with a straight line which approximates the curved line. (The particular straight line chosen will in that case often depend on what part of the curve, i.e., what range of values of the variables, one wishes to consider.)

These two reasons are related, in that the second is often the justification for the method mentioned in the first. Unless substantial curvature is apparent, the statistician may limit himself to fitting a straight line to the data, on the grounds that the algebraic simplicity of the straight line is preferred to the greater fidelity of the curve.

The algebraic technique of economic analysis which has been presented here rests in general on the assumption that, within the range of values of the variables which we study, the relationships do not depart from linearity to so great an extent that we cannot ignore the error involved in working with linear approximations. If we intend to consider only relatively small ranges of values, that is, if the increments to which the incremental ratios relate are intended small, the method is valid even though substantial curvature is present in the relationships. The logic of the method is valid, even if curvature cannot be ignored, if we interpret parameters as measuring the average slopes of the curves over the intervals covered by the increments.

In general, if we substitute for a curve some corresponding straight line, the particular straight line chosen depends on the segment of the curve considered relevant to the analysis. The graph in Figure 2 illustrates this point.   Disposable income, X, is measured along the horizontal scale; consumption is measured along the vertical scale.   The relationship is clearly curved, according to the particular line which has been drawn to represent the hypothetical relationship.   Two different straight lines have been fitted to the curve; one is a close approximation to the curve in the neighborhood of $X = 50$; the other is a good fit in the neighborhood of $X = 100$.   Neither straight line is a convincing approximation in the interval to which the other corresponds.*

The value of C corresponding to any value of X in the region about $X = 100$ can be measured quite accurately with reference to the straight

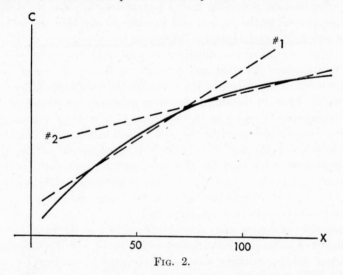

Fig. 2.

line numbered 2; and the difference between two values of C corresponding to two alternative values of X in that neighborhood can be measured on the straight line with results that do not differ seriously from what would be obtained from the curve.

The question arises, how we can solve an equation system for the values of the variables which satisfy the appropriate linear relationships, if we do not know which of the linear relationships is appropriate until we have

---

* The two straight lines shown in the graph have actually been fitted by the simple expedient of marking two points close to and equidistant from $X = 50$ or $X = 100$ and joining the two points in each case with a straight line.   More appropriate methods could be used; for our present purpose this method is adequate.   Note that we are not engaged here in the very complicated process of determining an empirical relationship from statistical data; that task is presumed to have been accomplished satisfactorily in the derivation of the curve.   We are engaged only in the conversion of a curved relationship into a choice of straight lines which may be expressed algebraically in linear equations.

already determined the solution values of the variables. How, referring to the graph, do we know whether to use line 1 or line 2 in solving for C and X, unless we already know beforehand whether the solution value for X is going to be close to 50 or close to 100?

The answer to that question depends on whether our analysis is empirical or purely theoretical. If we are dealing with empirically derived numerical relationships, the answer is that there is a method of successive approximations which leads us out of the dilemma. That method will be described in detail later in this chapter.

If our analysis is purely theoretical—if, that is, we postulate an abstract system of equations involving literal parameters in order to deduce the general properties of the system and in order to see how the incremental ratios of the derived relationships depend on the parameters of the original relationships—we make the dilemma disappear by assuming the (curvilinear) relationships satisfied and considering the linear equations to be those pertinent to the shapes of the curves in the neighborhood of the solution values. Thus, in the simplest system analyzed in Chap. 3, we simply let the parameters a and b in the equation $C = a + bY$ represent those particular values which describe the (C,Y) relationship in the neighborhood of the solution value for Y. Then b is interpreted as the slope of the straight line which best fits the curve around that value of Y; or, if large increments in the values of C, Y, and N are under study, we interpret b as the slope of the straight line between the two points on the curve corresponding to the two alternative values of Y.

It is possible, of course, that there is no solution of the curvilinear equations, no set of values of the variables which satisfy all the curvilinear relationships. This possibility was equally present in the linear case, however, especially if unstable solutions, meaningless solutions, and solutions involving values outside reasonable limits are classed as "no solution." Thus there is no begging of the question in assuming a solution; we have only adopted the relationships in the first place on the grounds that they were pertinent to the economic system, and if they are pertinent it is because they are capable of satisfaction.

In conclusion of this point: the parameters of our linear equations are interpreted as those relevant to the solution values of the variables; the parameters denoting incremental ratios (such as b, v, t, etc., in the foregoing chapters) are interpreted as the slopes of the straight lines which represent the curves within the intervals of values under study; and shifts in the parameters denoting "constants" (a, s, u, etc.) are interpreted as upward shifts in the curves which carry equally upward the relevant straight-line approximations.

The following section will outline the technique of solution of numerical

curvilinear relationships by the use of alternative straight-line approximations.   It is suggested that the reader who has no intention of meeting this
empirical problem read the section anyway; seeing how the problem could
be dealt with makes the logical basis of the abstract theory more tangible.

The Solution of Numerical Relationships

We suppose the numerical forms of two relationships to be known, a relationship between consumption and disposable income and a relationship
between taxes and national income.   (Disposable income refers here to
national income minus taxes.)   Each of the two relationships will be sup-

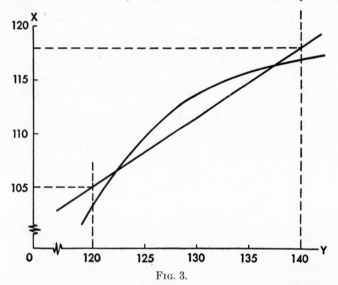

Fig. 3.

posed plotted as a graph.   By deducting from any value of national income
the corresponding value of the tax level, we obtain the corresponding value
of disposable income.   The tax-income relationship can thus be converted
to a graph relating disposable income to national income.

We mark off on the horizontal scale of each graph three intervals which
cover the entire range of values within which we might expect the eventual
solution values to lie.   (If this involves a bad guess we can extend the range
on a second trial.)   Within each of these intervals on each graph we fit a
straight line to the curve, fitting the straight line so that it represents a
reasonable approximation to the curve throughout the interval.

This has been done for the disposable income–national income relationship in Figure 3.   Only one interval—that between $Y = 120$ and $Y = 140$
—is shown.   The end points of the fitted line do not touch the curve; if
they did the line would depart farther from the curve in the middle of the

range. The line shown is a fairly good approximation to the curve for values of Y between 120 and 140.

It would be of convenience, in the present case, to make the intervals of the one graph correspond to the intervals of the other. This is accomplished by marking off, on the consumption–disposable income graph, an interval from $X = 105$ to $X = 118$, the values of X corresponding to the ends of the interval shown for the disposable income–national income relationship. Note that the three successive straight lines corresponding to any one curve may, but need not, coincide at the ends of the intervals; it is of no particular convenience that they should and the lines should be chosen for the fit within the interval rather than for continuity with the lines of the adjacent intervals.

When this has been done, each straight line is represented by the corresponding linear equation, the "constant" being the value of the point on the vertical scale where an extension of the straight line would intersect it (the value of the "intercept"), and the incremental-ratio parameter being the ratio of ΔX to ΔY between any two points on the line, as measured directly from the graph. We thus have three pairs of equations,

$$(1) \quad C = a_1 + b_1 X; \qquad (1') \quad X = c_1 + d_1 Y$$

$$(2) \quad C = a_2 + b_2 X; \qquad (2') \quad X = c_2 + d_2 Y$$

$$(3) \quad C = a_3 + b_3 X; \qquad (3') \quad X = c_3 + d_3 Y$$

Equations (1) and (1') apply to values of Y between 100 and 120 and the corresponding interval of X values; equations (2) and (2') apply to values of Y between 120 and 140 and values of X between 105 and 118; etc.

We assume some fixed (numerical) value for N and solve the equation system composed of (1) and (1'), (2) and (2'), or (3) and (3'), together with the identity $Y = C + N$. Let us begin with equations (2) and (2'). If solution of these equations yields a value for Y between 120 and 140 (that is, within the interval to which the system which we have solved corresponds) we may stop; we have our solution. We can, if we wish, improve the accuracy of our solution by breaking up the interval from 120 to 140 into three (or some other number of) new subintervals and repeating the process.

If solution with equations (2) and (2') yields a value outside the corresponding interval, we drop the result and solve the set of equations corresponding to the interval containing the solution value so obtained. If, for example, the solution value of Y for equations (2) and (2') is 150, we proceed to solve equations (3) and (3'). We shall probably obtain a different value, but one within the interval; the new solution value is the correct one and differs from 150 because a different set of equations has been used.

In either event further subdivision and repetition improves the accuracy of the solution.   If the curve itself is considered only a rough statistical approximation, successive refinements of the fit to the curve are not profitable.

It is possible that solution of equations (2) and (2′) yields a value of Y above 140, while solution of (3) and (3′) yields a value below 140.   Both figures will be close to 140 and this result only indicates that the actual solution of the curved relationship lies near the end points of two adjacent intervals where neither line fits as closely as it does elsewhere in the interval. In this case a new line may be fitted to the interval from 130 to 150 and similarly for the (C,X) relationship; and the new pair will yield the solution.

This basic method can be applied to a system of more than two relationships.   Each relationship is broken into linear segments, with a rough attempt to make end points correspond.   Solution may yield values for some variables within the range of the particular linear relations used, and outside the corresponding range for other variables; in particular this is likely to happen if end points have not been aligned.   In that case the particular equations whose variables were indicated to be outside the range of the equations used are replaced by the set appropriate to those values. Successive approximations will converge on values lying within the intervals of the final set of equations selected.

PART III

PART III.

CHAPTER 13

INTERNATIONAL INCOME ANALYSIS—I

In this and the succeeding chapters of Part III we take up the case of two countries trading with each other and linked together by a common currency or by separate currencies exchangeable at a fixed exchange rate. We shall assume that the central bank of either country is willing to accumulate unlimited balances or liabilities in the currency of the other country. We also assume constant prices. Finally, we assume a closed system, *i.e.*, neither country trades with any third country. (Either country may be considered the "rest of the world" from the point of view of the other country.)

We shall start the analysis from the point of view of one country, treating its exports as independent of its own activity. According to the accounting of Chap. 1, this country's national income, denoted by Y, can be represented as in the following equation when international trade is explicitly recognized:

$$(1) \qquad Y = C + I + G + E - M$$

where E and M denote exports and imports. Because simplicity will become increasingly important as we bring in the second country, we shall reduce our usual system of relationships to the following two:

$$(2) \qquad (C + I + G) = a + bY$$

$$(3) \qquad M = n + m(C + I + G + E)$$

Equation (2) replaces the usual set of equations relating, for example, C to $Y - T_x$, T_x to Y, I to Y, etc.; the parameter, b, may be thought of as equivalent to the composite parameter $b(1 - t) + v$ of earlier chapters. We shall not in the present context treat separately C, I, and G, but shall rather concentrate attention only on their sum. That is to say, we treat $C + I + G$ as a single variable in the present analysis.

Equation (3) indicates that the level of imports is dependent on the levels of consumption, investment, government expenditure for goods and services, and production for export. There is involved some loss of detail in letting a single parameter* represent the incremental ratio of M to C, to I, to G, and to E. We should expect that any change in the level of consumption, or in the rate of investment activity, or in production for export, or even in production of goods and services for government, would affect

---

* It should be noticed that equation (3) can also be written as $M = n + mC + mI + mG + mE$ with $\Delta M/\Delta C = \Delta M/\Delta I = \Delta M/\Delta G = \Delta M/\Delta E = m$.

the level of imports both of finished goods for consumption and finished investment goods, and of raw or semifinished materials for use in production. But we should not expect a rise in consumption to have the same quantitative effect on imports as an equal rise in investment, or in government purchase of goods and services, or in production for export. Greater accuracy in our results could be obtained by relating imports to each of these four variables separately as in $M = n + m_1C + m_2I + m_3G + m_4E$, where the different m's may be supposed to have different values. Algebraic convenience is our only excuse for the loss in detail; the reader may replace equation (3) with the more detailed expression mentioned above and obtain more detail in his results.*

Before proceeding to solve and analyze the equations, we may consider an alternative form of the import equation. Could we not equally well let M be related to Y, especially since we have already foregone any improvement in detail which we might have obtained by treating separately the components of national income? As a matter of fact, we not only could, but we already have an implicit relation between M and Y. For if we operate on equation (3) in conjunction with the identity expressed in equation (1) we have

$$(4) \qquad M = n + m(C + I + G + E) = n + m(Y + M)$$

$$= \frac{n + mY}{1 - m} = n' + m'Y$$

where the new parameters n' and m' stand for $n/(1 - m)$ and $m/(1 - m)$ respectively. Conversely, if we began with the original equation

$$(5) \qquad\qquad\qquad M = n' + m'Y$$

we could substitute to obtain

$$(6) \quad M = n' + m'(C + I + G + E - M)$$

$$= \frac{n' + m'(C + I + G + E)}{1 + m'} = n'' + m''(C + I + G + E)$$

---

* If he does so, however, he must also discard the simplicity of equation (2) which suppresses the individual identities of C, I, and G, and treat those variables separately either as independent or as related to Y or to other variables of the system. As a compromise we could replace equation (3) with $M = n + m_1(C + I + G) + m_2E$. This equation would treat m_1 as an average of the separate m's relating M incrementally to C, I, and G, the average being valid if the increments in C, I, and G can be considered proportional to each other. The equation would then single out only E—which is already separated in the analysis—for an individual marginal import parameter.

where n'' and m'' denote, respectively, $n'/(1 + m')$ and $m'/(1 + m')$. Either way the result is the same, for $n'' = n$ and $m'' = m$, as is demonstrated by

$$(7) \qquad m'' = \frac{m'}{1 + m'} = \frac{m/(1 - m)}{1 + m/(1 - m)} = \frac{m}{1 - m + m} = m$$

Thus equations (3) and (5) appear to be equivalent alternatives. There are, however, two advantages of equation (3) over equation (5). First, equation (3) would seem better to indicate the nature of the direct empirical relationship between imports and other economic magnitudes, imports being more plausibly associated with the production of goods and services for consumption, for investment, for government, and for export; equation (5) is a derived form requiring for its validity the use of equation (1). Second, the stability analysis which must accompany the static analysis of the equation system is affected by the substitution of (5) for (3) if the first advantage holds. For there are two possible interpretations of a negative value for m' in equation (5). If we look into the relation of m to m' we see that a negative value of m' may occur in conjunction with either a negative value of m or a positive value of m greater than $+1$. Either occurrence of negative m' may be considered "peculiar" on empirical grounds, but each represents a different kind of peculiarity. Using the short cut $M = n' + m'Y$ to obtain some algebraic convenience may suppress an important criterion of the dynamic validity of our results, as will be seen below.

We turn now to the solution of the equations, considering E to be an independent variable. The three equations yield

$$(8) \qquad Y = (a + bY + E)(1 - m) - n$$
$$= \frac{(1 - m)(a + E) - n}{1 - b(1 - m)}$$

This solution is not very different from those already familiar. The only new element is the occurrence of $1 - m$ in both numerator and denominator. In the numerator the presence of $1 - m$ is explained as follows: any increment in production for export is directly associated with an increment in imports equal to $m \, \Delta E$, so that $(1 - m)\Delta E$ is the direct impact on national income of the increment in E; similarly with respect to an increment in the parameter a. The explanation of $1 - m$ in the denominator is as follows: any rise in national income equal to ΔY is associated with an increase in $C + I + G$ equal to $b \, \Delta Y$ and consequently with an increment in imports equal to $m \, \Delta(C + I + G)$, leaving as the net impact on income of this increment in $C + I + G$ only the reduced value $(1 - m) \, \Delta(C + I + G) =$

$b(1 - m)\Delta Y$.   (If m is negative the effect is to augment, rather than cushion, the impact on national income.)*

The Dynamic-stability Conditions

Before deriving multipliers we should consider which values of the parameters are consistent with the dynamic compatibility of the equations. Eventually, in the succeeding chapters, the problem of dynamic compatibility will become difficult; here we shall find it simple if we make one assumption. The assumption amounts to this: $C + I + G$ is the sole adjusting variable. The only other candidate for the role of adjusting variable is M. We shall dispose of M by supposing that imports adjust simultaneously with $C + I + G + E$, that is, we suppose the relationship expressed in equation (3) always to hold, never to lag. The apparent rigidity of this assumption could be softened by allowing some inventory flexibility: we might let our assumption be that the *use* of imported goods or materials always follows without lag the relation of equation (3). Thus, even though actual imports may lag behind changes in $C + I + G + E$, the lag is compensated by use or sale of inventory so that the impact on income is the same as if imports adjusted instantaneously in accordance with equation (3).†

Letting M be an instantaneously adjusting variable, our condition for the dynamic compatibility of the equations is that when $C + I + G$ differs from its solution value, $\bar{C} + \bar{I} + \bar{G}$, it shall adjust toward that solution value. And the dynamic interpretation of equation (2) is that $C + I + G$ adjusts toward the value of $a + bY$. Suppose now that $C + I + G$ differs from its solution value (which depends, of course, on the particular given value of E) by the amount d.

$$(9) \qquad (C + I + G) = (\bar{C} + \bar{I} + \bar{G}) + d$$

Then imports are given by‡

$$(10) \qquad\qquad M = \overline{M} + md$$

---

* If the reader follows the suggestion of the footnote on p. 160, replacing the import equation with $M = n + m_1(C + I + G) + m_2E$, the solution will appear as

$$Y = \frac{(1 - m_1)\, a + (1 - m_2)E - n}{1 - b(1 - m_1)}$$

which is consistent with the explanation of $1 - m$ in the text.

† We shall not prove the equivalence of the "inventory-adjustment" assumption with the "import-adjustment" assumption. If the assertion is not sufficiently plausible intuitively—and intuition is seldom to be trusted in stability analysis—the reader may follow the example of Chap. 4 and set up the problem explicitly to demonstrate the equivalence.

‡ It must be understood that our assumption of instantaneous import adjustment keeps imports equal to $n + m(C + I + G + E)$, not equal to $\overline{M}$.

And Y is given by

(11) $$Y = \bar{Y} + d - md = \bar{Y} + d(1 - m)$$

The value toward which $C + I + G$ adjusts is the value of

(12) $$a + bY = (\bar{C} + \bar{I} + \bar{G}) + b(Y - \bar{Y})$$
$$= (\bar{C} + \bar{I} + \bar{G}) + b(1 - m)d$$

Adjustment toward $a + bY$ constitutes adjustment toward $\bar{C} + \bar{I} + \bar{G}$ only if, when d is positive, $b(1 - m)d$ is less than d, and when d is negative, $b(1 - m)d$ is greater than d. In other words, $b(1 - m)$ must not be as great as $+1$. This is our stability condition; it is similar to that of earlier analyses. The marginal ratio of $C + I + G$ to Y, when multiplied by 1 minus the marginal ratio of imports to expenditure, must be less than $+1$. Otherwise the variables adjust away from, rather than toward, their solution values. (It must be stressed that, as usual, these conditions are valid only for the particular context under study; in particular, the present criterion is correct only when exports are considered independent.)

Referring back to the comparison of the alternative equations (3) and (5), we can now see why those two forms are not perfect substitutes for each other. A negative value of m' in equation (5) may denote either negative m, or a positive value of $+1$ or greater for m. If m is equal to or greater than $+1$, the system of equations is necessarily stable, as is clear from equation (12), since $b(1 - m)d$ is then negative or zero and necessarily less than any positive value d. But if m' is negative because m is negative, $b(1 - m)$ is greater than b and the prospects for stability are jeopardized.

Incremental Ratios

We turn now to the derivation of incremental ratios. Since the parameter a and the independent variable E enter symmetrically into the solution for Y, a change in either has the same effect on the value of the national income.

(13) $$\frac{\Delta Y}{\Delta E} = \frac{\Delta Y}{\Delta a} = \frac{1 - m}{1 - b(1 - m)}$$

as is seen directly from the solution for Y, equation (8). The occurrence of $1 - m$ in this multiplier has already been discussed in connection with that solution. It may be noted that if we had let I be related to Y, C to X, and had let T_x equal $s + tY$ to obtain $X = Y(1 - t) - s$, the denominator would have been of the more elaborate form $1 - [b(1 - s) + v](1 - m)$, still supposing that the single parameter m applies to both C and I or denotes an average, and letting G be independent.

It should be observed that the incremental ratios, (13), are positive unless

m exceeds $+1$, in which case they are negative, the numerator being negative and the denominator positive.

Generally our multipliers relating increments in national income to increments in independent expenditure components have been greater than $+1$, *i.e.*, the rise in income exceeds the rise in independent expenditure. In the present case income will rise by more than ΔE only if

$$(14) \qquad\qquad 1 - m > 1 - b + bm$$

$$0 > -b + m + bm$$

$$b > m(1 + b)$$

$$\frac{b}{1 + b} > m$$

That is to say, unless the marginal ratio of imports to expenditure is less than $b/1 + b$, the increment in income will be a fraction, not a multiple, of any increment in exports. The same applies to a rise in the value of a, that is, to an upward shift in the expenditure relationship, since E and a enter the solution for Y symmetrically. Thus if G or I be considered an independent component of $C + I + G$, a change in the value of G or I will be represented by a change in the value of a, and the multiplier will exceed 1 only if m is less than $b/1 + b$. Assuming that b is positive, the condition for m less than $b/1 + b$ necessarily implies m less than b. If, for example, b is equal to 0.8, m must be less than 0.44; if b is equal to 0.5, m must be less than 0.33 if the multiplier is to exceed $+1$.

The plausibility of this result may be enhanced by considering the alternative case in which M is related not to expenditure but to national income. Replacing equation (3) with the alternative, $M = n' + m'Y$ [equation (5)], yields a multiplier

$$(15) \qquad\qquad \frac{\Delta Y}{\Delta E} = \frac{\Delta Y}{\Delta a} = \frac{1}{1 - b + m'}$$

which is greater than 1 only if $1 - b + m'$ is less than 1, that is, if m' is less than b. This condition is identical with that reached in the preceding paragraph, for it has already been shown that m and m' must be related according to the equation $m' = m/1 - m$, so that

$$(16) \qquad\qquad m' = \frac{m}{1 - m} < b$$

$$m < b - bm$$

$$m(1 + b) < b$$

which leads immediately to the condition reached in (14).

We next turn to the effect on imports of a change in E. Since no shift in the import relationship is under consideration, the value of M is that which accompanies any change in the value of $C + I + G + E$. If we first derive the value of $\Delta(C + I + G)$, which equals $b \Delta Y$, we can then add this increment to the increment in exports and multiply by m to obtain the increment in imports. Alternatively we can obtain the change in imports from

(17) $\quad \Delta M = m \Delta(C + I + G + E) = m \Delta(Y + M) = m \Delta Y + m \Delta M$

$$= \frac{m}{1 - m}\left[\frac{1 - m}{1 - b(1 - m)}\right]\Delta E = \left[\frac{m}{1 - b(1 - m)}\right]\Delta E$$

which yields the same result. The method of (17) is based on the identification of $Y + M$ with $C + I + G + E$.

Inspecting (17) it appears, first of all, that ΔM is of the same sign as ΔE if m is positive, the denominator being positive if the solution is dynamically valid. We observe, second, that ΔM will exceed ΔE if the parameter b exceeds $+1$. For the condition that ΔM exceed ΔE is that

(18) $\qquad\qquad\qquad m > 1 - b + bm$

$$0 > 1 - b - m + bm$$

$$0 > (1 - b)(1 - m)$$

Thus if either b or m should exceed $+1$, ΔM will exceed ΔE. (If both b and m should exceed $+1$ the equations are necessarily stable and ΔM is necessarily less than ΔE.) We shall not, in the present chapter, consider values of m greater than $+1$.

We find, then, that not only does inclusion of imports in our analysis allow us to admit values of b in excess of $+1$, but it allows as well the consequences of such values, namely that $\Delta M/\Delta E$ may exceed $+1$ as well. This particular result is quite readily seen to be a natural consequence of letting b exceed $+1$; for in that case any rise in income is accompanied by a greater rise in $C + I + G$ so that the sum of the increments in E and $-M$ must be negative, that is, M must increase more than E if equations (1) and (2) are to be satisfied.

It is interesting to observe that, although the value of $\Delta M/\Delta E$ depends on the value of the parameter m, whether ΔM exceeds ΔE or not is independent of the value of m. That is, the algebraic sign of the change in the trade balance consequent upon a change in export demand is independent of the import relationship—subject only to the qualification that m must have a value consistent with dynamic stability of the equations.

This latter qualification may amount to a substantial restriction on the values of m which are consistent with b greater than $+1$ and dynamic stability. In order that the equations be dynamically compatible, $1 - b + bm$ must be positive, which is equivalent to the inequality $m > (b - 1)/b$. We may state the case in this way: in order that ΔM exceed ΔE, the value of b must be large; a large value of b is ordinarily associated with a large multiplier; but a large value of b must be associated with not too small a value of m or the equations will be dynamically inconsistent. And a large value of m reduces the multiplier, both lowering numerator and raising denominator.

We shall finally inquire into the consequences of a shift in the import relationship. Letting the entire import relationship shift upward is to raise the value of n in equation (3). The effect on income, as shown by equation (8), is

$$(19) \qquad \frac{\Delta Y}{\Delta n} = \frac{-1}{1 - b(1 - m)}$$

The total change in imports, M, as distinct from the amount of shift in the relationship, Δn, is given by

$$(20) \qquad \Delta M = \Delta n + m\,\Delta(C + I + G + E) = \Delta n + m\,\Delta(Y + M)$$

$$= \frac{\Delta n + m\,\Delta Y}{1 - m} = \left(\frac{1}{1 - m}\right)\left[1 - \frac{m}{1 - b(1 - m)}\right]\Delta n$$

$$= \left[\frac{1 - b}{1 - b(1 - m)}\right]\Delta n$$

If b and m are positive fractions, ΔM is of the same sign as, but smaller than, Δn; for in that case both numerator and denominator are positive and the denominator exceeds the numerator by $+bm$ which is positive. If, however, b exceeds $+1$, the change in M is of opposite sign to the change in n; that is, a rise in the import-expenditure relationship actually serves to lower imports. The fall in expenditure, in that case, is so great as to make the "induced fall" in imports outweigh the "initial rise." The same result may be arrived at by comparing m times the change in $C + I + G$ with Δn. (E is constant and need not be considered.) If we set the condition that

$$(21) \qquad -m\,\Delta(C + I + G) > \Delta n$$

we have

$$(22) \qquad -mb\,\Delta Y > \Delta n$$

$$\frac{+mb}{1 - b + bm} > 1$$

$$+mb > 1 - b + bm$$

$$0 > 1 - b$$

which is the same condition as contained in (20).

Finally, to finish with (20), if m is negative ΔM is greater than Δn; in that case, b must be less than $+1$ for the stability condition to be met, and the denominator is smaller by $-mb$ than the numerator.   Here the fall in income which accompanies a rise in n leads to lower expenditure which is associated with higher imports, the induced change in imports thus also being positive and the total change in M exceeding Δn.

If we wish to know the ratio of the increment in income to the entire increment in imports, not just to the increment in the parameter n, we may compare $\Delta Y/\Delta n$ with $\Delta M/\Delta n$,

$$(23) \quad \frac{\Delta Y}{\Delta M} = \frac{\Delta Y/\Delta n}{\Delta M/\Delta n} = \frac{-1}{[1 - b(1 - m)]} \times \frac{[1 - b(1 - m)]}{(1 - b)} = \frac{-1}{(1 - b)}$$

where we have formed the ratio by inverting $\Delta M/\Delta n$ and multiplying. The result corresponds to the conclusion reached in Chap. 8, namely, that the ratio of the increment in Y to the entire increment in the variable whose relationship shifts is the same as would obtain if the latter were considered independent.   In other words, the fact that M remains related to $C + I + G + E$ influences the size of the increment in M resulting from a change in n, but does not affect the ratio of the change in Y to the change in M.

As a check on our results, and as a convenient catalogue of conclusions, we may decompose the change in Y as follows: According to the identity expressed in equation (1), any change in Y can be expressed as the sum

$$(24) \qquad \Delta Y = \Delta(C + I + G) + \Delta E - \Delta M$$

If E is independent and assumed not to change, the increment in Y can be decomposed into two parts, the change in $C + I + G$ and the change in M, the former to be added, the latter to be subtracted.   Putting all our results together, we have, for the case of a change in n,

$$(25) \qquad \frac{-1}{1 - b(1 - m)} = \frac{-b}{1 - b(1 - m)} - \frac{1 - b}{1 - b(1 - m)}$$

where the three fractions denote, respectively, the change in Y (on the left), the change in $C + I + G$, and the change in M, all expressed as ratios to Δn.*

* For a careful exposition of the subject of this chapter see Fritz Machlup, "International Trade and the National Income Multiplier," Philadelphia, 1943.

CHAPTER 14

INTERNATIONAL INCOME ANALYSIS—II

In Chap. 13 we took only a short step in the direction of two-country analysis, not paying explicit attention to the second country and treating exports as an independent variable. There must have been a second country since exports and imports were involved, but the second country was entirely passive as far as our analysis was concerned. In this chapter we shall take a second step in the direction of complete and explicit two-country analysis. The new element in this chapter will be the treatment of exports as a dependent, rather than an independent, variable.*

The analysis of Chap. 13 is a valid approximation to national-income behavior only if the country is small in relation to its partner country or if the partner country's own imports are independent of its national income or production. Otherwise the level of the country's exports would be affected by its own activity. If neither of these conditions is assumed to hold, we must relate the country's exports to some variable of the system. The most plausible relationship seems to be between the country's exports and its imports, for the only connecting link between the economies of the two countries (in terms of the variables under analysis) is their trade with each other. And if we suppose that the partner country's own imports are determined in the same way as the first country's, *i.e.*, via a relation of imports to the C, I, G, and E of that country, the impact of any change in economic activity in the first country on the activity of the second is transmitted via the former's imports.

We consequently add to our system the new equation,

$$(1) \qquad\qquad E = d + eM$$

The exact connection between E and M we shall not make explicit yet, and for the moment we shall take the point of view of one country only. Any change in exports, other than a change resulting from a shift in the export-import relationship, will be a consequence of a change in imports.

The system now consists of four equations, equation (1) and the first three equations of the preceding chapter, and the four variables, Y, E, M, and $C + I + G$. Solution will therefore render each variable in terms of parameters; and variation from the solution values will occur only with the shift in one or another of the relationships.

* Regarding the advantages or disadvantages of different degrees of detail in analysis of this subject, see J. J. Polak, "The Foreign Trade Multiplier," *American Economic Review*, vol. 37, p. 889, and the comment by G. Haberler in the same volume; also the restatement by Polak and Professor Haberler, *ibid.*

Of the various substitution processes by which we might arrive at the solution, the shortest is perhaps the following:

$$\begin{aligned}
(2) \qquad M &= n + m(C + I + G) + mE \\
&= n + ma + mbY + md + meM \\
&= \frac{n + ma + md}{1 - em} + \left(\frac{mb}{1 - em}\right)Y
\end{aligned}$$

Having expressed M in terms of Y, we substitute into the national-income identity

$$\begin{aligned}
(3) \qquad Y &= (C + I + G) + E - M \\
&= a + bY + d - (1 - e)M \\
&= \frac{a + d - (1 - e)\left(\dfrac{n + ma + md}{1 - em}\right)}{1 - b + mb\left(\dfrac{1 - e}{1 - em}\right)} \\
&= \frac{(1 - em)(a + d) - (1 - e)(n + ma + md)}{(1 - b)(1 - em) + mb(1 - e)}
\end{aligned}$$

Multiplying out and collecting terms we arrive at the following final expression for the solution:

$$(4) \qquad Y = \frac{(a + d)(1 - m) - n(1 - e)}{1 - [b(1 - m) + em]}$$

Since the best way to study the structure of a solution is to decompose it into incremental ratios, we shall proceed at once to the derivation of multipliers, leaving aside for the moment the question of dynamic stability. First let us derive the value of $\Delta Y/\Delta a$.

$$(5) \qquad \frac{\Delta Y}{\Delta a} = \frac{1 - m}{1 - [b(1 - m) + em]}$$

If this expression is compared with the corresponding expression of the preceding chapter [equation (13), Chap. 13], the only difference appears in the subtraction of em from the denominator in the present instance. Supposing both e and m to be positive, then, the effect of the dependence of exports on imports is to increase the multiplier, just as we should expect since a rise in domestic expenditure is now accompanied not only by rising imports but as well by rising exports.

We can approach equation (5) from another angle. Whatever the increase in total expenditure, $C + I + G + E$, imports will increase by m times this amount, and the difference, $1 - m$ times $\Delta(C + I + G + E)$, will represent the increase in national income, according to the national-income identity and the import relationship taken together. Since, therefore, $\Delta Y = (1 - m) \Delta(C + I + G + E)$, it must follow from (5) that

$$(6) \qquad \frac{\Delta(C + I + G + E)}{\Delta a} = \frac{1}{1 - b(1 - m) - em}$$

This deduction yields a plausible result. Here we are concerned with expenditure, not income, and the significance of imports is that they divert some part of the impact of expenditure from income, which would induce further expenditure in the ratio b, to abroad where it induces a further expenditure in the ratio e.* Thus, the denominator may be recognized as 1 minus a weighted average of b and e.

Let us now add up the several components of the income change. This summation will serve as a check on the reasoning which led to equation (6). There are four parts: the increment in a, that is, the initial upward shift of the expenditure relationship; the induced change in $C + I + G$, that is, the remainder of the change in $C + I + G$ after separation of the component Δa; the change in M; and the change in E. The first two parts are given by

$$(7) \qquad \Delta(C + I + G) = \Delta a + b\, \Delta Y$$

$$= \left[1 + \frac{b(1 - m)}{D} \right]\Delta a = \left(\frac{1 - em}{D} \right)\Delta a$$

where D stands for the denominator in equations (4) through (6), and $D + b(1 - m)$ equals $1 - em$. Next we derive the change in imports, using equation (2) for this purpose.

$$(8) \qquad \Delta M = \left(\frac{m}{1 - em} \right)\Delta a + \left(\frac{mb}{1 - em} \right)\left(\frac{1 - m}{D} \right)\Delta a$$

$$= \left(\frac{m}{1 - em} \right)\left[\frac{D + b(1 - m)}{D} \right]\Delta a$$

$$= \left(\frac{m}{1 - em} \right)\left(\frac{1 - em}{D} \right)\Delta a = \left(\frac{m}{D} \right)\Delta a$$

Next we obtain ΔE from

$$(9) \qquad\qquad \Delta E = e\, \Delta M$$

$$= \left(\frac{em}{D} \right)\Delta a$$

* The total expenditure abroad is not, of course, denoted by em; here we count as expenditure only the expenditure felt by the country whose national income is under investigation. The total expenditure abroad includes all of the C, I, and G of the partner country, as well as the first country's imports. That expenditure will be our concern in the following chapter.

Combining these we have, from the national-income identity,

$$(10) \qquad \Delta Y = \Delta(C + I + G) + \Delta E - \Delta M$$

$$= \left(\frac{1 - em + em - m}{D}\right) \Delta a = \left(\frac{1 - m}{D}\right) \Delta a$$

exactly as in equation (5).

If we compare ΔE with ΔM, we find that the ratio of the former to the latter is equal to e, as it must be unless the export-import relationship shifts. The question naturally arises whether ΔE may exceed ΔM; for the moment we have no criterion for placing restrictions on the value of the parameter e; if we follow the suggestion of the previous chapter, however, we may suppose that e, the ratio of the partner country's imports to its own exports, may exceed $+1$ if in that country the counterpart to our parameter b is greater than $+1$. (It must be kept in mind that the ratio of ΔE to ΔM is equal to e only so long as the parameter change to which it corresponds is other than in the parameter d of the export-import relationship.)

The Dynamic-stability Conditions

Analysis of the dynamic-stability conditions for the present system of equations is more difficult than for the system of the preceding chapter, for in this case there are three variables each of which ought properly to be considered an "adjusting variable," *i.e.*, a variable capable of diverging from its equation value and whose process of adjustment is pertinent to the dynamic compatibility of the relationships. In the preceding chapter there were only two, and that number was reduced to one by the rather plausible assumption that, although actual imports did not necessarily respond instantaneously to the level of production, the use of imports did remain simultaneously geared to the sum of C, I, G, and E, and we could consequently take the national income to equal $(C + I + G + E)(1 - m) - n$ at all times.

In the present case, even though we consider that assumption still valid, it does not suffice to remove the problem of the actual pattern of adjustment of imports. For exports are probably best considered related not to the rate of use of imports but to the actual rate of importation; exports, which are the partner country's (or countries') imports, should be considered related to the level of production of that partner country, not to the use of imports by the home country. And the level of production abroad reflects the actual production there of goods for export (*i.e.*, production of the goods and services denoted by the variable M). Consequently, even though for the calculation of the current value of Y we may take M to be instantaneously equal to $n + m(C + I + G + E)$, that is, although we allow for an inventory adjustment offsetting any divergence of M from its equation value, nevertheless we must study the adjustment of exports and therefore the adjustment of the actual rate of imports.

Explicit and complete analysis of the stability question, then, is complicated. We shall approach the problem by steps. First we shall limit our parameters to certain values and derive stability conditions, then we shall admit other parameter values and observe how the nature of the stability conditions is affected.

Let us take the value of m to be a positive fraction, and the value of e to be positive. And let us suppose the three variables $C + I + G$, M, and E to diverge initially from their solution values by the positive amounts h, k, and d, respectively. That is,

$$(11) \qquad (C + I + G) = (\bar{C} + \bar{I} + \bar{G}) + h$$

$$(12) \qquad M = \bar{M} + k$$

$$(13) \qquad E = \bar{E} + d$$

To assume the use of imports to be instantaneously geared to the level of production according to the import equation is to assume an inventory-accumulation component of the national income whose value is instantaneously given by

$$(14) \qquad i = M - n - m(C + I + G + E)$$

And the national income is given by

$$
\begin{aligned}
(15) \quad Y &= C + I + G + E - M + i \\
&= (C + I + G + E)(1 - m) - n \\
&= (\bar{C} + \bar{I} + \bar{G} + \bar{E})(1 - m) - n + (h + d)(1 - m) \\
&= \bar{Y} + (1 - m)(h + d)
\end{aligned}
$$

The analysis here will be patterned after that of Chap. 7, where a three-variable case was also involved. We have three "divergence" variables, h, d, and k, adjusting as follows:

h adjusts toward the value of $b(1 - m)(h + d)$

d adjusts toward the value of ek

k adjusts toward the value of $m(h + d)$

According to the reasoning given in Chap. 7, adjustment from any initial set of positive values for h, d, and k will lead them only to other positive values; no single value can be the first to become negative; none can therefore become negative through a process of adjustment. Ultimate adjustment toward solution values is consequently either simultaneous adjustment downward for the three variables, or an oscillatory type of adjustment with all three variables oscillating, all three never moving in the same direction, and never becoming negative in their oscillation toward solution values. We first consider the case of simultaneous adjustment downward. Such adjustment requires

(16) $$h > b(1 - m)(h + d)$$

(17) $$d > ek$$

(18) $$k > m(h + d)$$

Since the values of b, e, m, and $1 - m$ are considered positive, the following operations may be performed to obtain the implied inequalities which constitute the stability conditions.

Multiply the left-hand sides of (17) and (18) and put the product greater than the product of the right-hand sides in the implied inequality

(19) $$kd > emk(h + d)$$

Canceling k, which is positive,

(20) $$d > em(h + d)$$

Adding the left-hand sides of (16) and (20), this sum exceeds the sum of the right-hand sides,

(21) $$h + d > b(1 - m)(h + d) + em(h + d)$$

Canceling $h + d$, which is positive,

(22) $$1 > b(1 - m) + em$$

Inequality (22) is a useful stability condition; it assures us that the denominator in the solution for Y must be positive (with e, m, and $1 - m$ positive) if the equation system is valid. We have not yet, however, established inequality (22), having only shown that it is an implication of the possibility of simultaneous downward adjustment of the variables. Again we must consider the possibility of oscillation, just as we did in the similar case in Chap. 7.

First we observe that if any of the three variables oscillates, they all do. d can turn down only while k is falling and can turn up only while k is rising. h can turn down only while d is falling and can turn up only while d is rising. Thus h can oscillate only when d and k oscillate. Furthermore, if k does oscillate h does. For if h moved steadily downward (upward), d could turn down (up) only while k is falling (rising) and for a time all three would be moving downward (upward) simultaneously. But it was shown in Chap. 7 that if the three variables once move in the same direction they continue to move in that one direction. Thus all three or none must oscillate. We shall concentrate on the behavior of h.

Let h_0 denote the value of h on some occasion when h is just turning down, i.e., a peak value of h. Then d must be moving downward, else $h + d$ could not have been moving downward to cause the downturn of h. k must then be moving upward if not all three move together in the same direction. The next peak value of h will be less than h_0 if inequality (22) holds, according to the following argument.

If the next peak value of h exceeds h_0, there must have been an intermediate point at which $h = h_0$ and h was rising, i.e.,

$$(23) \qquad h = h_0 < b(1 - m)(h_0 + d)$$

This implies that the value of d is greater than it was at the time of the previous peak value of h, that is,

$$(24) \qquad d > d_0$$

Since d was moving downward when h reached the earlier peak, it must have turned up in the interval; it cannot then have exceeded the greatest value of ek which occurred in the interval. Nor could k have exceeded the greatest value of $m(h + d)$ which occurred in the interval, since k could only rise so long as $m(h + d)$ exceeded k. Letting d' and k' denote the greatest values of d and k, respectively, which occurred during the interval, we have

$$(25) \qquad k' \leq m(h + d')$$

$$(26) \qquad d' \geq ek' \leq em(h + d')$$

$$(27) \qquad d' \leq \left(\frac{em}{1 - em} \right) h$$

$$(28) \qquad h < b(1 - m)(h + d')$$

$$h < b(1 - m) \left(1 + \frac{em}{1 - em} \right) h$$

$$1 < \frac{b(1 - m)}{1 - em}$$

Inequality (28) is an exact contradiction of (22). Thus, if (22) holds, the successive peak values of h are in *descending* order. The reader may restate the argument to show that if (22) does not hold, the successive trough values of h are in ascending order. [The case of $b(1 - m) + em$ equal to $+1$ must be interpreted in the light of Chap. 4; either there is no solution for the equations, or the solution is not unique.]

The entire argument may be put into terms of negative divergences from solution values by simply reversing some inequalities. The case of mixed divergences is more complicated. It is not presented here because the *necessity* of condition (22) is our principal conclusion; its *sufficiency* for stability may be worked out by the reader by treating the case of mixed divergences, some positive, some negative. (The case is not difficult, since initial mixed signs tend to give way to divergences of similar sign.)

The above analysis has rested on the limitation to positive values of e, m, and $1 - m$, as well as of b. Inequality (22) consequently implies that $b(1 - m)$ and em must each be less than $+1$. If we allow the value of e to become negative the possibility is suggested that $b(1 - m)$ may exceed $+1$ within the constraint imposed by (22). Let us consider this case.

First it must be noted that if $C + I + G$ adjusts very fast relative to the adjustment speed of M or E, stability will require that $b(1 - m)$ be less than $+1$. Otherwise it appears that $C + I + G$ will adjust upward for any positive values of h and d and the slowness of adjustment of d allows us to consider the value of d virtually constant. If, however, the adjustment speed of $C + I + G$ is not very great by comparison with that of M and E, the tendency for $C + I + G$ to rise will be offset by the tendency for d to become negative (with e negative and rising h) and the result may be stability. Regardless of the relative rates of adjustment, however, inequality (22) must hold for stability, for otherwise h would adjust forever upward from any initial set of positive divergences. This is seen to follow from the following considerations.

Let h, d, and k all be initially positive. With $b(1 - m)$ greater than $+1$, h will rise—away from its solution value—unless d becomes negative and $b(1 - m)(h + d)$ becomes less than h. Letting k' denote the minimum value ever reached by k, and d' the minimum value ever reached by d, up to the time when h begins to descend, the following inequalities necessarily hold when h turns toward its solution value:

$$(29) \qquad\qquad d' \geq ek'$$

$$(30) \qquad\qquad k' \geq m(h + d')$$

$$(31) \qquad\qquad h > b(1 - m)(h + d)$$

But these are precisely equivalent to the conditions (16), (17), and (18) from which inequality (22) has already been deduced.

In the event that m is negative, the same analysis applies, but the prospect for $b(1 - m)$ greater than $+1$ is enhanced for any given value of b. Inequality (22) is a necessary condition for stability; and if $C + I + G$ adjusts very rapidly relative to the adjustment speed of M or of E, $b(1 - m)$ must not exceed $+1$. If $C + I + G$ adjusts very slowly relative to the adjustment speeds of M and E, it is necessary that em be less than $+1$, otherwise we find the equations unstable for a constant value of $C + I + G$, and the value of the latter may be taken as virtually constant for purposes of stability analysis. [This condition is necessarily imposed by (22) alone, however, unless $b(1 - m)$ is considered capable of negative values.]

Shifts in the Import and Export Relationships

Having already derived the incremental ratios pertinent to variation in the parameter a of the consumption, investment, and government-expenditure equation, we have next to take up the case of variation in the parameters n and d of the import and export equations, that is, of a shift in the relationship of imports to expenditure or in the relationship of exports to imports.

We take up first the case of a shift in the export-import relationship, which we may interpret if we wish as a net addition to exports outside the relationship, *i.e.*, as a net addition to exports over and above the assumed relationship. Inspection of equation (4) shows that the effect of a change in d on the solution value of national income is identical with the effect of a change in the parameter a, and that the incremental ratio given in equation (5) applies to $\Delta Y/\Delta d$ as well as to $\Delta Y/\Delta a$. And it is natural that this should be so, for either Δd or Δa may be viewed as a net increase in expenditure superimposed on any relationship, and whether the goods purchased are utilized within or without the producing country the effect on national income or on total expenditure is the same.

So, as a matter of fact, is the effect on imports, since the change in imports depends, according to our import hypothesis, only on the total of $C, I, G,$ and E and not on the separate components of that total. (If we had distinguished different marginal ratios of M to $C, I, G,$ and E this statement would, of course, have to be modified.)

The total change in exports under the assumption of variation in d is given by

$$(32) \quad \Delta E = \Delta(d + eM) = \Delta d + e\,\Delta M = \Delta d + em\,\Delta(C + I + G + E)$$

$$= \Delta d \left[1 + \frac{em}{1 - b(1 - m) - em} \right] = \Delta d \left[\frac{1 - b(1 - m)}{D} \right]$$

if we take equation (6) as giving the increment in the sum of $C, I, G,$ and E. From this it follows that $\Delta E/\Delta d$ is positive except in the case of $b(1 - m)$ greater than $+1$. While we have seen that, if the export adjustment is rapid, $b(1 - m)$ may exceed 1, it is then necessary for stability that em be negative else $1 - b(1 - m) - em$ could not itself be positive. Thus exports will move opposite to the shift in the export relationship only if (a) the term $b(1 - m)$ is greater than $+1$, and (b) either imports vary inversely with expenditure or exports vary inversely with imports—either of which is generally considered "abnormal"—and (c) the export effect is not unduly delayed in occurring.

The effect on imports is given by

(33)
$$\Delta M = m \, \Delta(C + I + G + E)$$
$$= \left(\frac{m}{D}\right)\Delta d$$

if we again utilize equation (6) and the abbreviation D. Since we now have ΔY, ΔE, and ΔM we can obtain $\Delta(C + I + G)$ by subtraction as well as by application of the parameter b to ΔY;

(34)
$$\Delta(C + I + G) = \Delta Y - \Delta E + \Delta M$$

according to the national-income identity, so that

(35)
$$\Delta(C + I + G) = \left(\frac{1 - m}{D} - \frac{1 - b(1 - m)}{D} + \frac{m}{D}\right)\Delta d$$
$$= b\left(\frac{1 - m}{D}\right)\Delta d$$

as would be obtained by multiplying ΔY by the parameter b.

Comparison of ΔE and ΔM yields

(36)
$$\frac{\Delta E}{\Delta M} = \frac{1 - b(1 - m)}{m} \quad \text{or} \quad \Delta(E - M) = \left[\frac{(1 - b)(1 - m)}{D}\right]\Delta d$$

A rise in the value of d will therefore be accompanied by a rise in the export surplus, or fall in the import surplus, except in the case of b greater than 1 or in the case of m greater than 1. Note that this is different from the criterion for ΔE being negative; there the condition was that $b(1 - m)$ should exceed 1, here it is only that b should exceed 1. If m is a positive fraction, $1 - m$ is also a positive fraction, and b can exceed 1 without $b(1 - m)$ greater than 1. Thus the present criterion is less extreme in terms of the value of b.

The crucial significance of the value of b in regard to the behavior of the trade balance can also be seen from the following simple considerations: if, when Y rises, $C + I + G$ rises more (*i.e.*, if $b > 1$), then it must be that the rise in imports exceeds the rise in exports if all the relationships hold; for the rise in Y is equal to $\Delta(C + I + G) + \Delta E - \Delta M$, and if $\Delta(C + I + G)$ exceeds ΔY, ΔM must exceed ΔE. Any *tendency* for M to rise less than E would, in company with the large value of b, lead the variables away from their solution values, *i.e.*, would be dynamically incompatible with the satisfaction of the equations.

The other possibility, in order that ΔM might exceed ΔE when d increased, was that $1 - m$ should be negative. Although in this chapter we are not generally discussing values of m greater than 1, it is interesting to note what such a value would imply. Looking at equation (5), and knowing that the denominator must be positive if the equations hold, it appears that negative $1 - m$ means that national income *falls* if either a or d increases. This paradoxical result, since it is a consequence of m greater than 1, is only as paradoxical as a value of m in excess of 1. We shall continue, consequently, to classify as "peculiar" any value of m greater than 1 and defer its examination to a later chapter.

We next permit the parameter n to vary. Inspection of equation (4) indicates that

$$(37) \qquad \frac{\Delta Y}{\Delta n} = \frac{-(1 - e)}{D}$$

The interpretation of this ratio would seem to be as follows: the increase of imports by an amount Δn carries with it an increase in exports equal to $e \, \Delta n$ which is immediately attributable to Δn alone; thus $1 - e$ would be the *net* immediate impact on income, and dividing by D would apply the multiplier and give us the whole effect. The trouble with this interpretation is that the Δn represents an immediate impact on *income*, while the export effect, $e \, \Delta n$, is only an impact on expenditure and affects income only in reduced ratio since it entails further imports related to itself. This interpretation is, therefore, unclear and may contain an error. Let us try another approach.

If we concentrate on expenditure, $C + I + G + E$, rather than on income, the only effect of raising imports by Δn is to divert the impact from domestic income to abroad; instead of inducing $b \, \Delta n$ of additional $C + I + G$ expenditure it induces $e \, \Delta n$ of additional export expenditure; the expenditure multiplier then applies to this difference between $b \, \Delta n$ and $e \, \Delta n$. In other words we should expect total expenditure in the home country, $C + I + G + E$, to change by

$$(38) \qquad \frac{\Delta(C + I + G + E)}{\Delta n} = \frac{(e - b)}{D}$$

Associated with this change in expenditure would be a change in income given by

$$
\begin{aligned}
(39) \quad \Delta Y &= \Delta(C + I + G + E) - \Delta M \\
&= \Delta(C + I + G + E) - \Delta n - m \, \Delta(C + I + G + E) \\
&= (1 - m)\left(\frac{e - b}{D}\right)\Delta n - \Delta n \\
&= \left\{ \frac{(1 - m)(e - b) - [1 - b(1 - m) - em]}{D} \right\} \Delta n \\
&= \left[\frac{-(1 - e)}{D} \right]\Delta n
\end{aligned}
$$

If, therefore, we find that the change in total expenditure is as we have supposed it, we have an interpretation of our income effect in readily appreciable terms. Let us proceed, then, to the derivation of $\Delta(C + I + G)$, ΔE, and ΔM. Using equation (37) and the national-income identity, we have

(40)
$$\Delta Y - \Delta(C + I + G) = \Delta E - \Delta M$$

$$\left[\frac{-(1 - e)(1 - b)}{D}\right]\Delta n = (e - 1)\, \Delta M$$

since $\Delta E = e\, \Delta M$ and since $\Delta(C + I + G) = b\, \Delta Y$. Canceling, we have

(41)
$$\Delta M = \left(\frac{1 - b}{D}\right)\Delta n$$

(42)
$$\Delta E = \left[\frac{e(1 - b)}{D}\right]\Delta n$$

Combining these results we have, finally,

(43)
$$\Delta(C + I + G) + \Delta E = \left[\frac{-b(1 - e) + e(1 - b)}{D}\right]\Delta n$$

$$= \left[\frac{-(b - e)}{D}\right]\Delta n$$

as we earlier surmised. We also have $\Delta E/\Delta M = e$, as it must since no change has occurred in the export-import relationship. The trade balance moves one way or the other according as e is greater or less than 1. It also appears that the net over-all effect on imports is an increase for a positive Δn, if b is less than 1; if b exceeds 1 the net result of an upward shift in the import relationship will be a decrease in imports. In this case the adverse effect on total expenditure outweighs the upward shift in the import relationship in determining the final effect on M. Comparing (37) with (43) this point is seen clearly; if b exceeds 1, $b - e$ exceeds $1 - e$ and total expenditure, $C + I + G + E$, falls more than does national income, so that according to the national-income identity imports must also have fallen. And the case of $e > 1$, in which exports rise more than imports, is seen from (37) to involve a net rise in income since the numerator of (37) is positive with $e > 1$. (The implications of e greater than 1 were suggested by the last chapter; they will be explicitly treated in the next.)

We have still, however, to make intuitive sense out of equation (37). We have seen that equation (37) follows from an expenditure change which does make intuitive sense; but equation (37) itself is not what one would naturally have built up intuitively. The numerator cannot quite be identified. If the numerator is taken to display two parts, $-\Delta n$ and $+e\,\Delta n$, the first makes sense, for it represents a direct initial net impact on income. But $e\,\Delta n$ seems to be too crude a form of the export reflex, since $e\,\Delta n$ is an impact on expenditure, not on income, and is furthermore not the entire change in exports which can be directly associated with the rise in imports.

To understand the construction of equation (37) we must decompose the multiplier further. Let us therefore ignore for the moment the parameter b, that is, the relation of $C + I + G$ to Y. If there occurs any rise in C, I, or G, expenditure equal to Δa, what accompanying changes occur in E and M? Since $\Delta E = e\,\Delta M$, and $\Delta M = m(\Delta a + \Delta E)$, we have

$$(44) \qquad \Delta M = \left(\frac{m}{1 - em}\right)\Delta a$$

$$(45) \qquad \Delta E = \left(\frac{em}{1 - em}\right)\Delta a$$

$$(46) \qquad \Delta a + \Delta E = \left(1 + \frac{em}{1 - em}\right)\Delta a = \left(\frac{1}{1 - em}\right)\Delta a$$

Thus of the total change in expenditure $\Delta a + \Delta E$, a part equal to $em(\Delta a + \Delta E)$ represents ΔE and the remainder, equal to $(1 - em)(\Delta a + \Delta E)$, represents Δa. If, then, we confine our analysis to the change in $C + I + G$, we can convert our results to the change in $C + I + G + E$ by simply increasing the former in the ratio $1/(1 - em)$. And we can arrive at the change in income by reducing that total in the ratio m, so that $\Delta Y/\Delta(C + I + G + E) = 1 - m$ and $\Delta Y/\Delta(C + I + G) = (1 - m)/(1 - em)$.

This suggests that we may convert our multiplier, relating ΔY to Δa, to the following form:

$$(47) \qquad \frac{\Delta Y}{\Delta a} = \frac{(1 - m)/(1 - em)}{1 - b(1 - m)/(1 - em)}$$

where the numerator now relates to the whole rise in expenditure, $\Delta a + \Delta E$, which is immediately attributable to Δa, that is, without allowance for any induced rise in $C + I + G$. The denominator then allows for the entire rise in expenditure which is related to the induced rise in $C + I + G$, that is, for the induced rise in $C + I + G$ plus the rise in exports related not directly to Δa but to the further $\Delta(C + I + G)$ which accompanies Δa. The term $b(1 - m)/(1 - em)$ represents the marginal ratio of induced expenditure to total expenditure; for any rise in total expenditure raises income by $1 - m$ times this amount, inducing $b(1 - m)$ of additional

$C + I + G$ which is augmented in the ratio $1/(1 - em)$ to allow for the associated increment in exports.

As may quickly be tested, equation (47) is identical with the original multiplier, equation (5); the latter is obtained from the former by multiplying numerator and denominator by $1 - em$. Equation (47), then, is a valid form of the multiplier, and we may use it to explain the construction of equation (37). Dividing numerator and denominator of (37) by $1 - em$ we obtain, in the numerator,

$$(48) \quad \frac{-(1 - e)}{1 - em} = \frac{-(1 - e + em - em)}{1 - em} = \frac{-(1 - em) + e(1 - m)}{1 - em}$$

$$= -1 + e\left(\frac{1 - m}{1 - em}\right)$$

This numerator of the alternative multiplier form shows in more understandable form the distribution of the impact on income between the Δn reduction and the $e \Delta n$ returned exports. The $e \Delta n$ initial export effect is now augmented in the ratio $1/(1 - em)$, to allow for the entire export effect of Δn itself, and reduced in the ratio $(1 - m)$ to convert it from expenditure to income terms. The whole expression is now over a denominator which makes allowance for the induced changes in C, I, and G and for the induced change in exports associated with the induced changes in C, I, and G; the numerator allows for the change in exports directly attributable to the variation in the parameter n taken by itself.

Joint Shifts in Relationships

Although we have analyzed shifts in each of the three parameters, a, d, and n, we shall wish to analyze the effects of equal simultaneous changes in two parameters, or perhaps of equal simultaneous changes in all three. The purpose of such analysis would not be just to develop a complete catalogue of all conceivable parameter changes; the reason why we must consider the cases of certain simultaneous changes in two or more parameters is that certain changes in the behavior structure of the economy, even though they are singular rather than composite, must be represented in our analytical system as changes in two or more parameters.

Taking the case of the shift in the import relationship analyzed above, what sort of change in import behavior does it represent? Since there was no corresponding change in the (C,I,G) relationship it must have represented a change in the *distribution* of commodities, finished or raw materials, between domestic production and imports. In other words, it was a shift such that for any level of $C + I + G + E$ imports would be greater, domestic income less, than before the shift occurred. This is a very special sort of shift in import behavior; it is only one of several that we might wish to analyze.

Let us consider an alternative sort of change in import behavior, to see how it should be represented in our equation system. Suppose that the relationships shift in such fashion that, for any level of $C + I + G + E$, imports are greater than before the shift by the amount k, but that this extra import is a net addition to total expenditure, *i.e.*, it is expenditure over and above that represented by the $C + I + G$ equation. To fix ideas we may suppose that, over and above the investment accounted for in the $C + I + G$ equation, additional finished investment goods are to be imported at the rate of k per accounting period. What will be the effect on national income, on total domestic expenditure, on exports, and on imports? Our first task, the difficult one, is to phrase this hypothesis in terms of the parameters a, n, and d; the second task is to derive the increments in variables after we have decided on the appropriate parameter changes.

First, looking at the import equation, it appears that we must increase the parameter n by an amount $\Delta n = k$; for in addition to the ordinary imports accounted for in the equation $M = n + m(C + I + G + E)$, there will be the additional imports equal to k. Second, it appears that we should raise the value of the parameter a, also by an amount equal to $\Delta a = k$; for investment will be greater by k than is allowed for in the equation. It would appear, then, that this case is handled by supposing two simultaneous changes in n and a, equal to each other; and the effect on income, for example, would be equal to the sum of $\Delta Y/\Delta a$ and $\Delta Y/\Delta n$. The effect of such change on any of the other variables, E or M, could also be obtained by adding the incremental ratios to Δa and to Δn.

But there is an error in that treatment. To isolate the error, let us suppose that both b and e are equal to zero, *i.e.*, that the only dependent variable is imports. We should, under these hypotheses, have $\Delta M = \Delta n = \Delta a = k$ and $\Delta Y = 0$, for absolutely nothing would be affected except the magnitude of imports, and that only by the net addition represented by $\Delta n = k$. But if we add $\Delta M/\Delta a$ and $\Delta M/\Delta n$, putting $e = 0 = b$, we find that $\Delta M = (1 + m)k$, as is seen by putting denominators equal to $+1$ in equations (8) and (41) and dropping b from the sum of the numerators. The reason for this discrepancy is that, by adding k to both n and a, we have raised not only the imports corresponding to any given level of $C + I + G + E$, but we have also raised the latter by k, so that imports rise additionally by $m \Delta I = m \Delta(C + I + G + E) = mk$.

Now this result we probably do not want. We originally related M to I, as well as to C, G, and E, to suggest that any given level of investment entailed some level of imports of investment goods or of materials or services utilized in the production of investment goods. In other words, we supposed that any level of investment contained a certain distribution between domestic and imported goods, and between imported and domestically produced materials and services used in the production of investment goods. If, however, we superimpose on top of "normal" investment an arbitrary increment of imported investment goods, there seems to be no reason to suppose that imports rise additionally in conjunction therewith, for such rise as ordinarily occurs when investment rises is only designed to allow for the imported component of the increment in investment.

What we must do in order to remove this double counting of imports is to revise our import equation. Instead of writing $M = n + m(C + I + G + E)$ we must write it as $M = n + m(C + I + G + K - k)$ so that imports are related only to the "normal" production of $C, I, G,$ and E. That is to say, the variable I which appears in the import equation must be revised to read $I - k$ so that the special increment $\Delta I = k$ is not allowed to operate on imports, it being completely allowed for already in the enlargement of the parameter n. The net result of all this adjustment is to change the $C + I + G$ relationship from $a + bY$ to $a + bY + k$, and the import relationship from $n + m(C + I + G + E)$ to $n + k + m(C + I + G + E - k) = n + k(1 - m) + m(C + I + G + E)$.

Now we can solve for the effects on $Y, M, E,$ and $C + I + G$. We put $\Delta a = k, \Delta n = k(1 - m)$, and obtain, by combining equations (5) and (37), (8) and (41), etc.,

$$(49) \quad \Delta Y = \frac{(1 - m)\Delta a - (1 - e)\Delta n}{D} = \frac{(1 - m)k - (1 - e)(1 - m)k}{D}$$

$$= \left[\frac{e(1 - m)}{D}\right]k$$

$$(50) \quad \Delta M = \frac{m\,\Delta a + (1 - b)\Delta n}{D} = \frac{mk + (1 - b)(1 - m)k}{D}$$

$$= \left[\frac{1 - b(1 - m)}{D}\right]$$

etc.

We may finally suppose that the government undertakes certain expenditure for goods and services additional to those allowed for in $C + I + G$, in the amount h per accounting period, and that the expenditure is directed toward exclusively domestic production, i.e., domestically produced goods or services which involve the use of no imported goods or services. (Services may perhaps most plausibly be assumed to be "pure" of imports.) There are two parameter adjustments required in order to put this hypothesis into the analysis. The first is to raise the value of the parameter a by $\Delta a = h$; that is, raise $C + I + G$ from $a + bY$ to $a + bY + h$, the h representing the addition to the G component of $C + I + G$. The second is to isolate, in the import equation, this increment of G to which the marginal import ratio, $\dot{m}$, does not apply. That is, after G has been augmented by the increment h, the import equation must read $M = n + m(C + I + G - h + E) = n - mh + m(C + I + G + E)$.

Putting, therefore, $\Delta a = h$ and $\Delta n = -mh$, we have, from our previous equations,

$$(51) \quad \Delta Y = \frac{(1 - m)\Delta a - (1 - e)\Delta n}{D} = \frac{(1 - m)h + m(1 - e)h}{D}$$

$$= \left(\frac{1 - em}{D}\right) h \quad \text{or} \quad \left[1 + \frac{b(1 - m)}{D}\right] h$$

Similarly, we find that

$$(52) \quad \Delta(C + I + G) = \Delta a + b\,\Delta Y = \left[1 + \frac{b(1 - em)}{D}\right] h$$

$$= \left[\frac{1 + bm - em - bem}{D}\right] h$$

$$(53) \qquad\qquad\qquad \Delta M = \left(\frac{mb}{D}\right) h$$

$$(54) \qquad\qquad\qquad \Delta E = \left(\frac{emb}{D}\right) h$$

$$(55) \quad \Delta(C + I + G + E) = \left[\frac{1 + m(b - e)}{D}\right] h \quad \text{or} \quad \left(1 + \frac{b}{D}\right) h$$

The differences between the effects of an increment in G, represented by Δa, divided in "normal" fashion between domestic and imported goods and services, and an increment devoted exclusively to domestically produced goods and services, are apparent. Total income is greater in the latter case by $1/D$ times the difference between $1 - em$ and $1 - m$, or by $m(1 - e)/D$. This quantity is positive unless e exceeds $+1$. Total expenditure $C + I + G + E$ is greater by $m(b - e)/D$, which is positive unless e exceeds b. (This result is plausible intuitively, since the only effect on total expenditure of the diversion of the usual $m\,\Delta a$ to domestic income is to replace $em\,\Delta a$ of export expenditure with $bm\,\Delta a$ of domestic expenditure at an initial stage of the process, leaving the numerator of the expression greater by their difference.)

CHAPTER 15

INTERNATIONAL INCOME ANALYSIS—III

This chapter will take the third and final step toward the explicit analysis of two countries. In the first chapter of this part we considered the imports and exports of a single country, treating imports as a dependent, exports as an independent, variable. The existence of some second country was implicit in the definitions of imports and exports; but the second country was not only kept behind a screen through which only its international trade could be seen, it was not even allowed any economic behavior other than the passive purchase of an arbitrary quantity of "exports" from the first country, and the sale of the first country's "imports" in whatever quantity the first country's national-income and import behavior determined.

In the second chapter of this part we imputed to the second country a behavior structure which geared its own imports to its exports. Arguing from the analysis of Chap. 13 we might have supposed ourselves to have set up equations for the second country, solved them for imports in terms of exports, and so obtained the export-import equation $E = d + eM$. But we paid no attention to the effect of parameter changes in the first country on the national income of that second country; its economy remained screened, only its foreign trade being visible.

This chapter will remove the discrimination from our treatment of the two countries; each country will be treated just as explicitly as the other.* Our attention will be focused on the national income of one country no more than on the national income of the other, and all the conclusions will be reduced to terms of the elementary parameters of the basic behavior equations. We shall not, that is, use the equation $E = d + eM$; instead, we shall use postulated relationships between the second country's imports and its own C, I, G, and E, and between its own C, I, and G and its own national income. The equation previously used, $E = d + eM$, is thus a "partial solution" of the system which we can now dispense with since we shall obtain a complete solution for all the variables.

It could be argued that this step, solving explicitly for all variables of both countries, is unnecessary, that we have already derived all the elements we need to construct such a "complete solution" on the basis of the analysis of one country. We might, for example, return to Chap. 13

---

* For a very full treatment of this subject see J. E. Meade, "National Income, National Expenditure and the Balance of Payments," *Economic Journal*, vol. 58, pp. 483*ff.*

and appropriate equation (17), incrementally relating imports to exports for a given country, and replace the parameters with their equivalent Greek letters to indicate that they pertain to a second country; we could then rewrite equation (5) of Chap. 14, relating ΔY to Δa, as follows:

$$(1) \quad \frac{\Delta Y}{\Delta a} = \frac{1 - m}{1 - b(1 - m) - em} = \frac{1 - m}{1 - b(1 - m) - m\left[\dfrac{\mu}{1 - \beta(1 - \mu)}\right]}$$

in which the parameter e has been identified through the work of Chap. 13, equation (17), as an abbreviation for the bracketed part of the last term in the denominator. We should then have, assuming the argument to be correct, an expression for $\Delta Y/\Delta a$ in terms of the basic parameters of both countries. Then, if we let the letter X represent the national income of the second country, and let the parameter α be the counterpart in the second country to the parameter a, we could obtain the value of $\Delta X/\Delta \alpha$ by replacing b with β, m with μ, and vice versa in equation (1), by the same line of reasoning.

Next, when we wished to obtain the relation between the change in the parameter a relating to the first country, and the change in the national income of the second country, *i.e.*, the ratio $\Delta X/\Delta a$ (or $\Delta Y/\Delta \alpha$), we could go back to Chap. 13 and construct, on the basis of the multipliers derived there, an explicit equation relating not only the increment in M to the increment in E, but the whole of M to the whole of E; then we could see how the "constant" in that equation was affected by a change in the parameter a and express this result as a change in the parameter d. Having then identified both e and d in terms of the elementary parameters, we should be able to replace any multiplier of Chap. 14 with one stated in terms of b, β, m, and μ and without reliance on the short-cut parameters d and e.

This we could do; and, as a matter of fact, it would be a profitable exercise. But there are several advantages in beginning over again with elementary equations for each country and effecting a new solution. First, it is quicker, and more useful as a model for subsequent variation. Second, it illustrates a technique of solution which would become increasingly valuable as we added a third, a fourth, or more countries to the system. Third, it will give us an opportunity to revise our elementary equations, now that they are sufficiently familiar not to need their original simplicity, in the direction of greater detail, detail which will allow us to express hypotheses more efficiently in terms of parameter changes. Finally, it will help us isolate the crucial factors involved in the study of stability conditions.

The Equations and Their Solution

We shall continue in this chapter to keep the system of equations relatively simple; we shall not, for example, make allowance for taxes in the consumption equation.   It should be stressed, however, that at some cost in space and readability of equations we could readily make full allowance for any or all of the various relationships and separate variables heretofore treated throughout the book, and add any number of them to the system. Once the technique is recognized there is no limitation to the amount of detail that can be put into the equation system, save limitations of time, paper, and interest.   Variables and relationships in the present chapter will be limited to those necessary for the isolation of the special factors involved in the extension of analysis to more than one country; even so we shall have as many parameters as can conveniently be handled on these pages.

The two countries will be referred to as country Y and country X, and their national incomes denoted by the letters Y and X.   Other variables will be distinguished by subscripts to show the country to which they pertain, as in C_y and C_x for the consumption of countries Y and X, respectively.   We deal with a duplicate set of equations, each country displaying the same structure of behavior but with parameters assumed different in value.   The following equations describe the system:

$$(2) \qquad Y = C_y + I_y + G_y + E_y - M_y$$

$$(3) \qquad X = C_x + I_x + G_x + E_x - M_x$$

$$(4) \qquad C_y + I_y + G_y = a + bY$$

$$(5) \qquad C_x + I_x + G_x = \alpha + \beta X$$

$$(6) \qquad M_y = n + m(C_y + I_y + G_y + E_y - d)$$

$$(7) \qquad M_x = \nu + \mu(C_x + I_x + G_x + E_x - \delta)$$

$$(8) \qquad E_y = M_x$$

$$(9) \qquad E_x = M_y$$

We have eight variables, considering $(C + I + G)_y$ and $(C + I + G)_x$ to be single variables, and eight equations of which the first two and the last two are identities and the other four are relationships.

The only departure from previous usage involved in the above set of equations is the isolation of the new parameters d and δ.   The intention here is to identify some part of expenditure which is exclusively satisfied out of domestic resources, that is, some part to which there corresponds no importation of goods and services. The two parameters need not be taken to represent the entirety of such expenditure, but only some part which can be identified both as purely domestic and as independent, *i.e.*, not related to the values of any of the variables. The purpose is to allow later manipulation to observe the differential effects on national income of increases in expenditure of the sort which do, and of the sort which do not, involve imports.

Perhaps to clarify the concept we may suppose d and δ to represent government expenditure on certain services utilizing negligible amounts of imported materials or equipment. We may, moreover, suppose the initial values of d and δ to be zero; what matters is that we be able to insert positive values later in the analysis. Thus, even if their values be taken as "normally" equal to zero, the abstract parameters must be inserted at this stage of the analysis in order that their incidence in the solutions be clearly visible later.

Solution of the equations requires a good deal of paper work, and some of it will be left to the reader to complete. We shall make use of several abbreviatory parameters to outline the framework of the method. The first step is to combine equations (2), (4), and (6) to obtain an expression for Y in terms of E_y

$$(10) \qquad Y = (a + bY + E_y)(1 - m) - n + md$$

$$= \frac{a(1 - m) - n + md}{1 - b(1 - m)} + \frac{(1 - m)E_y}{1 - b(1 - m)}$$

$$= RA + R(1 - m)E_y$$

where R is introduced as an abbreviation for the reciprocal of $1 - b(1 - m)$, and A stands for the numerator of the first term. Next we obtain M_y from

$$(11) \qquad M_y = n + m(Y + M_y - d)$$

$$= \frac{n - md}{1 - m} + \left(\frac{m}{1 - m}\right)Y$$

$$= B + \bar{m}Y$$

where B is introduced to stand for the first term, and $\bar{m}$ is an abbreviation for $m/(1 - m)$.

Next we solve similarly for X and M_x. We need only to pretend to take this step, since the symmetry of the equations allows us to write down the expressions for X and M_x from those already obtained for Y and M_y, simply replacing b with β, m with μ, a with α, d with δ, n with ν, and vice versa. In this way we obtain

(12) $$X = R'A' + R'(1 - \mu)E_x$$

(13) $$M_x = B' + \bar\mu X$$

where R' and B' are the counterparts to R and B, i.e., the same as R and B except with Greek parameters exchanged for roman and vice versa.

Identifying E_y as M_x and E_x as M_y, we have

(14) $$Y = RA + R(1 - m)B' + R(1 - m)\bar\mu X$$

(15) $$X = R'A' + R'(1 - \mu)B + R'(1 - \mu)\bar m Y$$

Substituting (15) into (14) we obtain, finally,

(16) $$Y = \left(\frac{R}{1 - RR'm\mu}\right)[A + (1 - m)B' + (1 - m)\bar\mu R'A'$$
$$+ (1 - m)\bar\mu R'(1 - \bar\mu)B]$$

In the denominator of the first factor on the right-hand side of (16), $\bar m(1 - m)$ and $\bar\mu(1 - \mu)$ have been identified as m and μ.

The rest of the work must be left to the reader. What is required is to replace A, A', B, B', R, R', $\bar m$, and $\bar\mu$ by the original parameters which they replace, multiply out the expressions in parentheses, and combine terms to obtain, as the solution for Y,

(17) $$Y = \frac{a(1 - m) - (n - md)(1 - \mu R') + \alpha\mu(1 - m)R' + (\nu - \mu\delta)(1 - \mu R')\left(\frac{1 - m}{1 - \mu}\right)}{[1 - b(1 - m)] - \dfrac{m\mu}{[1 - \beta(1 - \mu)]}}$$

which yields at once the multiplier which we constructed in equation (1) of this chapter for variation in the parameter a. We have left in the numerator the abbreviation R' for convenience. We shall henceforth occasionally use R and R', and also the symbols D and D', where the latter stand for the reciprocals of R and R', that is, $D = 1 - b(1 - m)$; $D' = 1 - \beta(1 - \mu)$; and $R = 1/D$, $R' = 1/D'$.

An alternative form of the solution for Y is

(18) $$Y = \frac{a(1 - m)D' - (n - md)(D' - \mu) + \alpha\mu(1 - m) + (\nu - \mu\delta)(D' - \mu)\left(\frac{1 - m}{1 - \mu}\right)}{DD' - m\mu}$$

This form has the advantage of being symmetrical, in the denominator, as between D and D' and between m and μ. If we put the solution for X in the same form, the solutions for Y and X have identical denominators and comparison of incremental ratios will be facilitated. What we have done is to multiply numerator and denominator by D', the R' thus canceling out where it occurred, since $D'R' = 1$.*

The length of the numerator is, of course, a consequence of the complexity we put into the original equations. Each of the parameters a, α, n, ν, d, and δ must occur in the numerator, multiplied by some combination of m, μ, b, and β. When we derive incremental ratios, however, all but one or two terms will drop out.

We shall not take space to derive all the incremental ratios; they can be derived in straightforward fashion and their interpretations are already suggested by the work of the preceding chapter. The really interesting new problems of multiplier interpretation will be those that hinge on the permissibility of certain parameter values, the criteria for which must be developed through stability analysis. Those we shall defer until we have investigated the conditions for dynamic compatibility of equations later.

There are certain properties of the system, however, which it will be interesting to note. To these we turn.

Properties of the Solution

The first property to note about the general solution for Y or X of this chapter is its consistency or inconsistency with the results obtained through the less complete treatment of Chaps. 13 and 14. If we look at the solution for Y in Chap. 13 we find (equation 8)

$$(19) \qquad Y = \frac{(1 - m)a + (1 - m)E - n}{1 - b(1 - m)}$$

Neglecting for the moment the parameters d and δ, which have lately been inserted into the problem and are consequently not comparable with anything in Chap. 13, we may inquire whether the new solution (18) yields an identical value, supposing of course that parameter values are the same. We could check this consistency as follows: since the E in (19) is E_y, solve the new solutions of this chapter for $E_y = M_x$; substitute the expression obtained for E in (19), and then demonstrate by algebraic manipulation that the expressions are identical. This can also be done piecemeal, by demonstrating that all the incremental ratios, such as $\Delta Y/\Delta a$, are identical; for then the coefficients of all the parameters must be identical in the two expressions and the whole expressions therefore identical. We shall demonstrate the identity for one part of the problem, leaving it to the reader to deduce the equivalence of the other incremental ratios.

* It is suggested that the reader rewrite (18) in terms of X, *i.e.*, by interchanging Greek for roman and roman for Greek parameters, and replacing D with D' and vice versa. We shall refer to (18) as though it represented either Y or X.

We choose Δa as the denominator of the ratio we wish to test. In the full solution, equation (18), the incremental ratio $\Delta Y/\Delta a$, is equal to $HD'(1 - m)$, where H stands for the reciprocal of $DD' - mm$. From the alternative form, (19), we have $\Delta Y/\Delta a$ equal to $R(1 - m) + R(1 - m)\,\Delta E/\Delta a$. But $\Delta E/\Delta a$, or $\Delta M_x/\Delta a$ as we may write it, is equal to $[\mu/(1 - \mu)]\,\Delta X/\Delta a$, and $\Delta X/\Delta a$ would be, according to equation (18), equal to $Hm(1 - \mu)$. The condition for equivalence of the two expressions is thus:

$$(20) \qquad HD'(1 - m) = R(1 - m) + R(1 - m)m\mu H$$

If both sides are divided by $R(1 - m)H$, and then R replaced by $1/D$ and H by $1/(DD' - mm)$, the identity is evident. Thus $\Delta Y/\Delta a$ is the same according to either formula; the coefficients of a in the solution for each must then be the same. And so we could proceed for the rest of the parameters.

What, then, are the essential differences in result, if any? There are two differences between the results obtained in Chap. 13 and the results obtained in the present chapter; one is a difference in the amount of information obtained, the other is a difference in criteria for admissible values of parameters.

The difference in the amount of information contained in the two solutions may be expressed as follows. In Chap. 13, equation (8), we obtained the solution shown in (19) above. When, in Chap. 13, we investigated the effect on Y of a change in the parameter a, we obtained

$$(21) \qquad \frac{\Delta Y}{\Delta a} = \frac{1 - m}{1 - b(1 - m)}$$

Equation (21) is valid on the assumption of no related change in the value of E. The possibility of related variation in the value of E may be taken formally into account by deriving from equation (8) of Chap. 13 the full incremental equation

$$(22) \qquad \Delta Y = \left[\frac{1 - m}{1 - b(1 - m)}\right](\Delta a + \Delta E)$$

or, in either of two alternative ratio forms,

$$(23) \qquad \frac{\Delta Y}{\Delta a} = K\left(1 + \frac{\Delta E}{\Delta a}\right) = \frac{K}{1 - K(\Delta E/\Delta Y)}$$

where K stands for the bracketed factor in (22), that is, $K = (1 - m)/[1 - b(1 - m)]$.

Equations (22) and (23) allow for any change in the value of E associated with the changes in the values of any other variables; it is a purely formal allowance which is made, however, since there is no explicit indication as

to which other variable or variables E may be related to. Equations (23)
do move us one step toward analytical allowance for variation in E; they
provide a framework within which we may conveniently insert a parameter
describing such incremental ratio of E to a or of E to Y as we may postulate. If, *e.g.*, we wish to add the new relationship $E = p + qY$ to the
equation system, $q = \Delta E/\Delta Y$ may be inserted in the denominator of the
last ratio in (23). But if the new relationship to be postulated is between
E and, say, M, with incremental ratio $\Delta E/\Delta M = e$, equation (23) does
not provide such a framework. Equation (23) is valid, as may be checked
by derivation of $\Delta E/\Delta Y$ for a change in the value of a in the equation
systems of this or the preceding chapter, but it does not provide a particularly good insight into the effect on $\Delta Y/\Delta a$ of an additional relationship
between E and some other variable unless that other variable is Y itself.

The fuller treatment of Chaps. 14 and 15 fills the gap in equation (23)
by showing just how $\Delta E/\Delta a$ is related to the basic parameters which
describe expenditure behavior in the partner country. (The improvement
is, of course, purely formalistic if we know no more about those parameters
than we do about the behavior of E itself; but at least we have reduced the
ratio $\Delta E/\Delta a$ to more elementary terms which are comparable to the other
parameters of the system, and which may be more capable of observation.)

The other difference between the results of Chap. 13 and the results of
Chap. 14 or 15 has to do with the conditions for dynamic compatibility;
it, too, involves the question whether E is in reality independent. In
Chap. 13 we deduced that the dynamic compatibility of the equations was
conditional upon the value of $b(1 - m)$ not exceeding $+1$. This was the
correct criterion if E was really independent; but if E was not independent
the behavior of E in relation to other variables could affect the stability
of the system. A stability condition of Chap. 14 was that $b(1 - m) + em$
should not exceed $+1$; if e and m are of same sign, this is a more restrictive
condition. Thus the stability conditions, as well as the values of the
various multipliers, depend on the dependence or indepencence of E.
The stability conditions will be found to have been altered again, in an
interesting respect, in the present chapter.

To conclude this point we may summarize as follows: the multiplier
shown in (21) is correct, and its stability condition properly stated as
$b(1 - m) < +1$, only if E is actually independent; the multiplier shown
in (23) is formally correct regardless of the independence of E, since allowance has been made for related variation in E, but the stability condition
is correctly stated as $b(1 - m) < +1$ only if E actually is independent.

Another point of interest about the solutions of this chapter is that we
can now compare the changes in national incomes of the two countries,
the comparisons being expressed in terms of the parameters of the basic

relationships. Considering again the variation of the parameter a, which we may interpret as an independent addition to investment expenditure in country Y, we have the two income changes related as follows:

$$(24) \qquad \frac{\Delta X/\Delta a}{\Delta Y/\Delta a} = \left(\frac{m}{1-m}\right)\left(\frac{1-\mu}{D'}\right)$$

The relative size of ΔX, then, varies directly with m, indirectly with μ, and directly with $1/[1 - \beta(1 - \mu)]$, which is what its multiplier would be in the absence of export variation. These relations all appear reasonable. It should be noticed that, if the two countries display identical parameter values, that is, $m = \mu$ and $b = \beta$, equation (24) reduces to $m/D' = m/D$ which can exceed $+1$ only if both b and β exceed 1 or if both m and μ exceed 1; this, however, will later be shown to be inconsistent with stability. [$m > D$ implies $0 > (1 - b)(1 - m)$.]

Another interesting comparison is between $\Delta Y/\Delta \alpha$ and $\Delta Y/\Delta a$, that is, the effect on Y of an independent increment in expenditure abroad compared with that of an independent increment in expenditure at home. This ratio comes directly from the numerator of (18),

$$(25) \qquad \frac{\Delta Y/\Delta \alpha}{\Delta Y/\Delta a} = \frac{\mu(1-m)}{D'(1-m)} = \frac{\mu}{D'}$$

Notice that μ/D' is precisely the ratio of the amount by which X's imports would rise, if its exports were independent, to a rise in the value of α. The ratio is greater than 1 only if $\mu > D'$, or $(1 - \beta - \mu + \beta\mu) = (1 - \beta)(1 - \mu) < 0$. Aside from the possibility of μ exceeding 1, X would have to display a marginal ratio of expenditure to income greater than 1 in order that Y increase more with the incremental expenditure directed toward X. (As will be shown later, if $\mu > D'$ the counterpart condition cannot hold for the partner country, consistent with stability.)

It is worth noting, as a side light to equations (24) and (25), that the relative share of country Y may be greater with the increment of expenditure at home, while its absolute share may be greater with the increment abroad. This would be the case with

$$(26) \qquad \Delta Y/\Delta \alpha > \Delta Y/\Delta a > \Delta X/\Delta a$$

$$\mu(1-m) > D'(1-m) > m(1-\mu)$$

For this condition to hold, $\mu/(1 - \mu)$ must exceed $m/(1 - m)$, that is, $\mu > m$, so it cannot hold if the two countries display identical parameter values (as can be proved without the algebra, of course).

There are certain properties of the solutions of this chapter which we should normally anticipate; let us see whether they hold. First, suppose both countries' parameters were identical, $b = \beta$ and $m = \mu$; if we consider only the total income $Y + X$, it would seem that we could ignore imports and exports, on the analogy of income distribution within a single country, and the multiplier $\Delta(Y + X)/\Delta a$ ought to be equal to $1/(1 - b)$ where b is the common marginal ratio of expenditure to income. This property is quickly seen to be present, for, according to equation (18), if parameters are equal,

$$(27) \quad \Delta Y + \Delta X = [HD'(1 - m) + Hm(1 - \mu)]\Delta a$$
$$= H(D + m)(1 - m)\Delta a$$
$$= \left[\frac{(D + m)(1 - m)}{(D + m)(D - m)}\right]\Delta a = \left[\frac{(1 - m)}{(1 - b)(1 - m)}\right]\Delta a$$
$$= \left(\frac{1}{1 - b}\right)\Delta a$$

since $(D + m)(D - m) = DD - mm = 1/H$. Thus the whole structure degenerates into the simplest possible system upon removal of the essential distinctions between the two countries.

Again, considering only the sum of Y and X, it would seem that by analogy with problems in income distribution we should be able to write

$$(28) \qquad \frac{\Delta(Y + X)}{\Delta a} = \frac{1}{1 - bs - \beta\sigma}$$

where s and σ represent the marginal income shares of the two countries. This too may be checked; the relative income shares when a varies are given by $D'(1 - m)$ and $m(1 - \mu)$. Expressing each of these as ratios to their sum to obtain marginal income shares, we have

$$(29) \quad \frac{1}{1 - \dfrac{bD'(1 - m) + \beta m(1 - \mu)}{D'(1 - m) + m(1 - \mu)}}$$
$$= \frac{D'(1 - m) + m(1 - \mu)}{D'(1 - m)(1 - b) + m(1 - \mu)(1 - \beta)}$$
$$= \frac{D'(1 - m) + m(1 - \mu)}{D'(D - m) + m(D' - \mu)} = \frac{D'(1 - m) + m(1 - \mu)}{DD' - m\mu}$$

This is precisely what we deduce from (18) for the sum of $\Delta Y/\Delta a$ and $\Delta X/\Delta a$.

The same could be shown for variation in X and Y in connection with variation in any one of the other parameters; the particular relative marginal income shares, of course, differ in each case.

Conditions for Dynamic Compatibility of Equations

As in most of the cases studied throughout this book, the paradoxes and odd conclusions which may be reached in the present chapter are to be ruled out or explained on stability grounds, *i.e.*, ruled out on grounds that the parameter values necessary for the odd results are not consistent with dynamic compatibility of the relationships, or explained in terms of the perverse behavior which occurs when certain parts of an equation system which would be unstable in isolation are combined with other equations in such fashion that the combined system is stable. It is useful, therefore, to go as far as we can toward deriving the stability conditions for this chapter's equations.

Before getting involved in the stability analysis itself, it may be worthwhile to suggest where the difference will lie between the stability conditions relevant to the analysis of this chapter and those relevant to the preceding chapter in which the analysis had to do with the export-import equation $E = d + eM$. The crux of the difference is this: the equation $E = d + eM$ *may itself be unstable*, in which case the analysis of Chap. 14 is not valid, but the analysis of the present chapter may be, if parameter values are appropriate.

What would have been involved in the instability of the equation $E = d + eM$? First of all, the *interpretation* of instability of that equation would be that exports, if equal to $d + eM$, would tend to remain constant, but if not equal to $d + eM$ would adjust away from, rather than toward, $d + eM$. How could this sort of behavior arise? In Chap. 13 we saw that the solution of the equations relating to a single country, with exports treated as independent, was unstable if $1 - b(1 - m)$ was negative *i.e.*, if $b(1 - m)$ was greater than $+1$. If the solution is unstable, the relation between imports and exports, as well as the relation between national income and exports, is unstable, since the solution of the expenditure and import relationships gives them both in terms of an unstable relationship to E.

Thus an equation relating exports to imports, in which imports are the independent variable as far as that single relationship is concerned, is unstable if in the other country $\beta(1 - \mu)$ exceeds $+1$. Now in Chap. 14 we deduced the stability condition for country Y as $[1 - b(1 - m) - em] > 0$. In the present chapter we shall discover that *if* the parameter e comes from a relationship $E = d + eM$ which itself is unstable with M treated as independent, then it is *possible* for the two-country system to be stable even though $1 - b(1 - m) - em$ is negative. Or, since an unstable relationship between E and M (between, that is, E_y and M_y) follows from $1 - \beta(1 - \mu)$ being negative in the partner country, it will be found that *if* $1 - \beta(1 - \mu)$ is negative, certain parameter values allow the whole system to be stable and the denominators of (1) and (17) to be negative, so that such a multiplier as $\Delta Y/\Delta a$ may be negative.

In other words, if we look back at equation (12), we see that a step in the solution of equations in this chapter was the expression of each country's national income in terms of its own exports; then, relating each country's exports to the national income of the other country, we had Y related to X and X related to Y, two equations in X and Y which we solved to reach (18). If the first step yielded two equations (Y in terms of E_y and X in terms of E_x) one of which was an unstable relationship, the unstable one (corresponding to the solution in Chap. 13) is invalid taken by itself but may, when combined with the other one (*which must then be stable*, as will be seen below), yield a stable combined system.

Turning now to the actual stability analysis,* we shall again make certain assumptions to keep the number of adjusting variables manageably small. Before stating what these assumptions are we shall introduce some abbreviatory variables to facilitate exposition. The letter K will stand for the sum of $C_y + I_y + G_y$, while the letter K' will stand for $C_x + I_x + G_x$. The letter P will stand for $(C + I + G + E)_y$ or $K + E_y$ or $Y + M_y$; and the letter P' will stand for $(C + I + G + E)_x$ or $K' + E_x$ or $X + M_x$.

The first assumption is that the *use* of imported goods and services is instantaneously geared, according to the import relationship, to $C + I + G + E$, that is, to P (or P'). Thus any lag of imports behind the relationship is offset by accumulation or disaccumulation of inventory of imported goods, so that it is continuously true that

$$(30) \qquad\qquad Y = P(1 - m) - n$$

and similarly for X. Any lag in actual imports will be treated as a lag in the production of the export industries abroad.

The dynamic statement of the $C + I + G$ relationship for country Y is consequently

$$(31) \qquad \begin{cases} K \text{ adjusts toward } a + bY \\ \qquad\qquad \text{or} \\ K \text{ adjusts toward } a - bn + b(1 - m)P \end{cases}$$

We next introduce the symbol $\dot{K}$ to denote the absolute (not percentage) rate of adjustment of K over time. For example, if $K = 150$ and is increasing at a rate of 10 per month (or per year, whichever the accounting

<hr>

* For a different treatment of the stability problem, involving discrete rather than continuous adjustment, see L. A. Metzler, "Underemployment Equilibrium in International Trade," *Econometrica*, vol. 10, p. 97.

period is over which we measure our income variables), $\dot{K} = 10$. Although K and $\dot{K}$ may be measured in monthly or annual accounting terms, we allow them both continuous variation; $\dot{K}$ may equal 10 per month for less than a month, and then change to a different value, or it may be changing continuously, just as a car may travel (change its distance) at a rate of 40 miles per hour for less than an hour or may travel at continuously changing speed.

We now replace (31) with our specific adjustment equation,

$$(32) \qquad \dot{K} = r(a + bY - K) = r[(a - bn) + b(1 - m)P - K]$$

where r is the "relative rate of adjustment" over time of the variable K. We have, in equation (32), introduced a specific hypothesis about the pattern of adjustment of K; specifically we have supposed that the rate of change of K is proportional to the difference between the actual value of K and the value toward which it is currently adjusting. (We say "currently adjusting" because the value toward which it adjusts is also changing since P changes when K changes, unless E should happen to move in exactly the opposite direction at identical speed.) r is not, then, the relative rate at which K adjusts toward its solution value, $\bar{K}$, but the relative rate at which it adjusts toward the value on the right-hand side of the K equation.   By "relative rate" or "proportional rate" we mean the absolute rate of adjustment divided by the difference between the actual K and the equation value of K; *i.e.*,

$$(33) \qquad r = \frac{\dot{K}}{[(a - bn) + b(1 - m)P - K]}$$

It should be noticed that, since $\dot{K}$ is intended to be positive when K is below its equation value, and negative when K is above that value, r must be positive to express the meaning of our hypothesis.

The dynamic statement regarding export adjustment is

$$(34) \qquad E_y \text{ adjusts toward } \nu + \mu P'$$

That is to say, production of exports is taken to adjust toward the use of imports in the other country.   It should be noted that equation (34), in light of the identification of E_y with M_x, could as well be written

$$(35) \qquad M_x \text{ adjusts toward } \nu + \mu P'$$

We take (34) to be the fundamental form of this dynamic relationship because we shall assume that such lag as occurs in the behavior of imports and exports is a production lag in the exporting country.   Equation (34) is then replaced with the specific adjustment equation

$$(36) \qquad \dot{E}_y = r(\nu + \mu P' - E_y)$$

which embodies another assumption, namely that the relative rate of adjustment is the same in the export industries as in the industries producing for domestic markets. At substantial cost in simplicity we could remove this assumption, and give equation (36) an adjustment-rate parameter of its own different from r. It might be observed that we could, without spoiling equation (36), let it include allowance for both a lag on the side of importers and a lag on the side of the exporters; what is necessary for equation (36) is that the adjustment of E_y should be geared to $\nu + \mu P'$, that is, to the *use* of imports abroad, otherwise some simplifications to come could not be effected. Thus what is crucial to the set of equations being developed here is not that the lag occur exclusively in the export industries but that such lag as there is between the production of exports in one country and the use of those exports by the importing country should lead to an adjustment speed in the export industries which is proportional to the difference between the use and the production of the exports.

We wish now to put equations (32) and (36) together to obtain $\dot{P}$. To do this we identify

$$(37) \qquad\qquad \dot{P} = K + \dot{E}_y$$

on the grounds that the rate of increase of a sum is equal to the sum of the rates of increase of its separate parts. Substituting into (37) we obtain

$$(38) \qquad \dot{P} = r[(a - bn + \nu) + b(1 - m)P - P + \mu P']$$
$$= rG - rDP + r\mu P'$$

where G is introduced as an abbreviation for $a - bn + \nu$ and where D is used as before to stand for $1 - b(1 - m)$. (The lone P in the brackets of (38) is the sum of K and E_y which appears upon summation.)

By similar methods we obtain an equation giving the rate of adjustment of P', that is, of $(C + I + G + E)_x$, in terms of P' and P, namely,

$$(39) \qquad\qquad \dot{P}' = \rho G' - \rho D' P' + \rho m P$$

where ρ is the relative adjustment speed of K' and E_x, not necessarily equal to r, and where G' and D' denote the same as G and D but with roman and Greek parameters interchanged.

Let us take stock of what we have. We have one equation giving the rate of adjustment of P in terms of P and P', and another equation giving the rate of adjustment of P' in terms of P' and P. These rates of adjustment are given in terms of parameters all of which are based on the original parameters of the static equations except for r and ρ which are new and have no counterpart in the static analysis.

At this point we have two "simultaneous differential equations." If we solved them we should obtain, not particular values of P and P', but time patterns of P and P'; that is to say we should obtain equations giving P and P' in terms of the implicit variable, time. The paths of P and P' could then be traced out on a time chart and studied. We are not, however, interested in the precise paths followed by P and P', we wish only to know a single characteristic of those time patterns: do P and P' approach their solution values, $\overline{P}$ and $\overline{P}'$, which we obtained by solution of the original static equations? If they do, then we shall accept the results of the static analysis; if they do not, then the static results are largely irrelevant for they only show how the variables would behave if the equations held, *i.e.*, if P and P' tended to approximate their solution values.*

To answer this question we may call in a mathematician, and phrase for him a very general question. If there are any two variables whose rates of change are linearly related to the values of the variables themselves, do those variables approach certain fixed values over time? (If they approach any fixed values, those fixed values must be our solution values, since the rates of change are proportionate to differences between actual values and the values given by the equations, and if those differences are zero the equations must be satisfied, *i.e.*, the variables have their solution values.) The answer we get is that whether or not the two variables approach fixed values, or behave in some other fashion, depends on the parameters of those two linear relationships, that is to say, on the parameters of equations (37) and (38). Rephrasing the question we may ask for precisely what values of the parameters P and P' will approach their solution values, as contrasted with those parameter values which determine other forms of behavior.

If we were to ask such a question of a mathematician every time we set up an equation system for analysis, presenting all the parameters from the equation system to him for examination, we should be asking all too frequently for help. But if we phrase the question in very general form we may find a general answer which can be adapted to many of the particular equation systems which we wish to study. Let us set up the question in perfectly general form:

Let there be any two quantities, denoted by x and y, whose rates of change over time are denoted by $\dot{x}$ and $\dot{y}$, and whose rates of change are related to the values of the variables according to the two equations

$$(40) \qquad\qquad \dot{x} = d + px + sy$$

$$(41) \qquad\qquad \dot{y} = \delta + \pi y + \sigma x$$

---

* We shall ignore the possibility that P and P' approach their solution values but that their component parts, K and E_y and K' and E_x, fail to approach theirs. Note that such a case would require K and E_y to diverge by identical amounts in opposite directions from their respective solution values.

For what values of d, δ, p, π, s, and σ will x and y approach fixed values, and for what values of those parameters will they not? With an answer to this question we can then attach boundaries to the original parameters of our economics equation system. The parameter values which are consistent with stability of P and P' will be those which meet the criteria given in answer to the general question; for d, δ, p, π, s, and σ can then be identified with the parameters of equations (38) and (39) which can in turn be identified with a, α, b, β, m, and μ and the two adjustment-speed parameters, r and ρ.

Before giving the answer to this general mathematical question, let us notice a property of the equation system represented by (40) and (41). If x and y do approach fixed values, those values must satisfy

(42) $$d + px + sy = 0$$

(43) $$\delta + \pi y + \sigma x = 0$$

for if equations (42) and (43) did not hold, $\dot{x}$ and $\dot{y}$ would not be zero and x and y would not remain stationary. We could therefore solve equations (42) and (43) and from them deduce, by substitution of parameters, the solution values of P and P'. In other words, putting $\dot{P}$ and $\dot{P}'$ equal to zero in equations (38) and (39) and solving for P and P' is one way of solving our original equations for P and P'; this follows from the fact that the very conditions under which $\dot{P}$ and $\dot{P}'$ are zero are the conditions under which the original equations hold.

Now to the answer to our general question: the first part of the answer is that d and δ do not matter; only the coefficients of x and y are relevant to the stability of the equation system. We then have two conditions which those four parameters must meet in order that the solution be stable, $i.e.$, in order that $\dot{x}$ and $\dot{y}$ approach zero over time. They are

(44) $$p\pi - s\sigma > 0$$

(45) $$p + \pi < 0$$

To remember this pattern it helps to observe that p and π are the "direct" coefficients, s and σ the "cross" coefficients in equations (40) and (41). That is to say, p and π are the coefficients of y and x in the equations for their own rates of adjustment, while s and σ are the coefficients of y and x in each other's adjustment speed equation.

These, then, are the stability conditions for any two variables related as in (40) and (41).* To translate them into the terms of equations (38)

---

* By any two variables we mean that the stability conditions are as applicable to the case of two automobiles, where the speed of each car in any given direction is linearly related to the distance of each from certain base points, as they are to the

and (39) we rewrite them as

(46) $$(-rD)(-\rho D') - rm\rho\mu > 0$$

or

$$DD' - m\mu > 0$$

(47) $$(-rD) + (-\rho D') < 0$$

or

$$rD + \rho D' > 0$$

The first condition (46) involves the expression which we have often abbreviated as $1/H$; it appears in the denominator of every multiplier when we use the form of solution shown in equation (18). Thus H, or $1/H$, must be positive if our equations are to display dynamic stability, $i.e.$, if the relationships are to be dynamically compatible with each other.

The second condition may be interpreted as saying that a weighted average of D and D', that is, of $1 - b(1 - m)$ and $1 - \beta(1 - \mu)$, must be positive, where the weights are the relative adjustment speeds in the two countries. Since both r and ρ are taken to be positive, not both D and D' may be negative. Either one may be negative if the adjustment speed of the country to which it applies is sufficiently small.

It should be observed that the denominator of equation (1) may be negative and consistent with the above; $i.e$, for one of the two countries, speaking in terms of the preceding chapter, $1 - b(1 - m) - em$ may be negative, leading to a negative $\Delta Y/\Delta a$, etc. It may not, however, be negative for both of the countries. For $1 - b(1 - m) - em$ may also be written, by virtue of the work of this chapter, as

(48) $$D - \frac{m\mu}{D'} = \left(\frac{DD' - m\mu}{D'}\right)$$

which may be negative only if D' is negative, in which case according to (47) D must be positive and the other country's counterpart to (48), namely

(49) $$D' - \frac{m\mu}{D'} = \left(\frac{DD' - m\mu}{D}\right)$$

must then be positive, for both numerator and denominator must be positive if D' is negative.

Notice also that if D' is negative, the equation $E_y = d + eM_y$ is an

---

case of countries' national incomes. The two cars will approach the two fixed points indicated by the solution of equations (42) and (43) if the parameters in their speed relationships, equations (40) and (41), meet the conditions expressed in (44) and (45).

unstable equation with M_y considered the independent variable, for the partial solution for country X is, according to Chap. 13,

$$(50) \qquad\qquad X = \frac{\alpha(1 - \mu) + M_y}{D'}$$

which is an unstable solution with M_y considered independent; and the parameter e, equal to μ/D', is an "unstable" coefficient. But considered together the two countries' relationships may be stable.

Chapter 9 on income distribution presented an analogous case; either of the two income categories (such as profits and wages) might be associated with a marginal consumption-income ratio which, if typical of the other category as well, would be inconsistent with stability; their joint behavior pattern may be stable since it depends on the average of their marginal consumption-income ratios when weighted by their marginal income shares. Equations (28) and (29) of this chapter display the analogy; the weighted average of marginal expenditure-income relationships may be less than $+1$ although considered in isolation one country's marginal ratio, even after allowance for imports, exceeds $+1$.

But the income-distribution analogy must not be pushed too far. In the first place, whether income distribution is in accordance with the relative values of ΔY and ΔX associated with variation in the parameters (and these relative values are, of course, different for variation in the different parameters), as derived from the solutions for Y and X, may depend on the adjustment-speed parameters r and ρ. If either D or D' is negative only those values of r and ρ which make $rD + \rho D'$ positive will allow income to be distributed in accordance with the incremental ratios for ΔY and ΔX which we derive from those solutions, since the equations will only hold for those values of r and ρ.

In the second place—and this point has no explanation within the income-distribution analogy—it is possible that both b and β exceed $+1$ and yet the equations be dynamically consistent. The income-distribution analogy, in which stability requires that b and β when weighted by their respective marginal income shares average less than $+1$, would not seem to allow this event. Nevertheless it can be shown that not only *may* both b and β be greater than 1 but that, for certain values of m and μ, if either b or β exceeds 1, the other *must* also exceed 1, if the equations are to be stable.

The proof of the last point is simple. First it should be observed—and this observation is important aside from the particular point being proved here—that if either D or D' is negative, $-m\mu$ must be positive, that is, m and μ must be of opposite sign. This follows from the condition that $DD' - m\mu$ must be positive; and it implies that for one of the two countries imports must fall as total expenditure rises. Let us suppose that b exceeds $+1$, and that m is negative; then $b(1 - m) > b > 1$ and D is therefore negative. With D negative, $m\mu$ must be negative and since m is negative, μ is positive if the equations are stable.

Now rewrite $DD' - m\mu$ in the form

$$(51) \quad DD' - m\mu = (D - m)D' + m(D' - \mu)$$
$$= (1 - b)(1 - m)D' + m(1 - \beta)(1 - \mu) > 0$$

The first term after the equality sign is necessarily negative, since $b > 1$, $m < 0$, by our assumptions, and $D' > 0$ for stability. Stability also requires, then, that the second term be positive, since the whole expression must be positive; but since m is negative, either $1 - \beta$ or $1 - \mu$ must be negative. So, unless μ exceeds $+1$, β must exceed $+1$. And we have both b and β greater than $+1$, yet the equations are stable.

The problem of reconciling this result with the income-distribution analogy is solved by revising our original notion, based on the problem of Chap. 9, of marginal income shares. If we write a general multiplier as:

$$(52) \qquad \frac{\Delta Y + \Delta X}{\Delta a} = \frac{1}{1 - (bs + \beta\sigma)}$$

interpreting s and σ as marginal income shares, we can make this multiplier stable, with b and β both greater than 1, *if either s or σ is negative*. That is to say,

$$(53) \qquad bs + \beta\sigma < 1$$
$$bs + \beta(1 - s) < 1$$
$$s(b - \beta) < 1 - \beta$$

Since $1 - \beta$ is negative by hypothesis, either s or $b - \beta$ must be negative. If b exceeds β, s is negative and

$$(54) \qquad s < \frac{1 - \beta}{b - \beta} < 0$$

By the same reasoning, $\sigma(\beta - b)$ must be negative. Thus, if in both countries the marginal ratios represented by b and β exceed 1, the country with the greater marginal ratio, b or β, must incur a decrease in its national income when the joint income rises, and an increase when the joint income falls, if the equation system is to be stable. (The negative relation of Y or X to $Y + X$ is made possible by an inverse relation of M_y to Y or of M_x to X.)

It should be noticed that, in general, the absolute values of the marginal shares of Y and X in the total, $Y + X$, depend on which parameter changes to cause the change in the value of $Y + X$; but the opposition of the algebraic signs of ΔY and ΔX occurs whenever both b and β exceed $+1$ (and the equations are stable) regardless of which relationship it is that shifts. [Y and X may also, of course, move in opposite directions without b and β greater than 1; equation (24), for example, shows that negative m and positive D' make $\Delta Y/\Delta a$ of opposite sign to $\Delta X/\Delta a$.]

As a matter of fact, many of the apparent paradoxes to be obtained by deriving and comparing incremental ratios will be explained by the movement of one of the national incomes in a direction opposite to that in which our intuition expects it to go. This must not be taken to mean that *if* the two national incomes, X and Y, move oppositely to each other the equations are stable; it means only that for certain parameter values a necessary implication of stability is opposite variation in the two national incomes.

In other words, the system of relationships investigated in this chapter is sufficiently complex to allow certain extreme values to offset—in so far as stability is concerned—the extreme values of other parameters; and results are possible which contradict intuition. Undoubtedly many of the sets of parameter values consistent with peculiar or paradoxical results would be considered empirically unlikely. We must, however, understand their implications if we are not to be perplexed by apparent inconsistencies between our algebraic conclusions and our intuitive expectations.

Before turning to the actual study of some incremental ratios two qualifications are in order. First, the stability conditions presented above were derived under certain assumptions and have not necessarily any validity greater than that of the assumptions under which they were derived.* Second, the actual stability conditions for the general case contained in equations (40) and (41) have only been asserted, not proved. An outline of their actual derivation is presented in the Appendix.

The Rationale of Some Unusual Incremental Ratios

This section will look in some detail into a few of the incremental ratios that emerge when parameter values, though consistent with over-all stability for the equation system as a whole, are such that parts of the system considered in isolation from the rest would appear to be unstable. Specifically we shall suppose one of the expressions D or D' to be negative. It should be kept in mind throughout that with D or D' negative, over-all

---

* It should particularly be noted that we have so stated the hypothesis of adjustment behavior as to preclude "inventory instability." That is to say, we have adopted a dynamic hypothesis of production behavior such that no attempt is made to build up inventories which were drawn down when sales exceeded production, or to liquidate inventory accumulated when production exceeded sales. In Part IV we shall investigate the subject of inventory stability.

stability requires that m or μ be negative; and the empirical validity of such incremental ratios is no greater than the empirical validity of a negative value for m or μ, that is, of an inverse relation between imports and the sum of consumption, investment, exports, and government expenditure for goods and services.

Whatever the empirical application of the present case, it is useful to test on some system of equations the implications of "unusual" parameter values in order to become familiar with the interpretation of algebraic results. The present system offers an excellent opportunity, as will be seen below. This section may, if the reader finds the assumed parameter values implausible, be taken as an exercise in abstract stability analysis rather than as a study of international income behavior.

In what follows we shall impose one restriction on parameter values; the values of m and μ will be considered less than $+1$. This restriction is imposed solely to reduce the number of possible cases to be considered; it will be pointed out at the end of this chapter that the a priori plausibility of a value greater than $+1$ for m is much the same as that of a negative value of μ.

To begin, let us look again at the incremental ratios $\Delta Y/\Delta a = HD'(1-m)$ and $\Delta X/\Delta a = Hm(1-\mu)$. The former has the sign of D', the latter that of m, since we assume m and μ less than 1. With D' negative, either m or μ must be negative for stability, so we have two cases here to consider: $\Delta Y/\Delta a$ negative with $\Delta X/\Delta a$ positive, $\Delta Y/\Delta a$ negative with $\Delta X/\Delta a$ also negative. First suppose m positive, so that X rises with a rise in the value of a. In this case the immediate effect of a rise in a must be to raise the value of Y; as Y rises, M_y rises, since m is positive; since $M_y = E_x$ rises, X rises. But, since D' is negative, a higher value of X is consistent only with a lower value of E_x; the equations will hold only if E_x ultimately assumes a value below its original value. The rise in X is associated, via the negative value of μ, with falling $M_x = E_y$; and the fall in E_y must reverse the direction of change in Y, converting the initial rise into a downturn. Y must then go below its initial value in order that, with positive m, M_y may ultimately be less than before the change in the value of a. Thus it is the fall in Y, resulting from the fall in E_y consequent upon the rise in X, which eventually checks the otherwise unstable expansion of X. The net result is a higher value of X, a lower value of Y.

Next consider m negative with D' negative. If the equations hold, both Y and X fall with a rise in the value of a. The rationale is as follows: the initial rise in Y which accompanies the rise in a is associated with a fall in M_y, since m is negative; with the fall in $M_y = E_x$, X declines. Since D' is negative, a lower value of X is consistent only with a higher value of $E_x = M_y$, so that Y must fall in order that, with negative m, the value of

M_y may be higher than it was originally. It is the declining value of $M_x = E_y$, associated with the declining value of X, which pulls down the value of Y. In other words, the adverse effect of rising Y on X tends to be reciprocated by the adverse effect on Y's exports; and, since X is unstable considered in isolation, the latter effect must depress Y more than the rise in a raises it. Here we have a case in which, taking X and Y together, the multiplier is negative and valid. If this case be interpreted according to the "income-distribution" formulation of equation (28), it appears that the high value of β [which is necessary in order that $D' = 1 - \beta(1 - \mu)$ be negative with $1 - \mu$ a positive fraction] makes the denominator of (28) negative, yet the whole mechanism is stable.* (Notice that, in the present case, both Y and X would rise with a rise in the value of α as distinct from a rise in the value of a; considering the two countries together, an increase in the expenditure of the type represented by a or α leads to a rise in both incomes and therefore in the joint income, or to a fall in both and therefore in the joint income, depending on where its immediate impact is directed.)

In the event that D' is negative but both m and μ are positive, the system is unstable according to the criteria developed in the preceding section. The sequential rationale of the process is as follows: a rise in the value of a raises Y and consequently $M_y = E_x$; with higher E_x, X begins to rise. Since D' is negative, X can stop rising only with E_x lower than originally; but the rise in X tends only to raise, not lower, E_x, since M_x rises with X, Y rises with $M_x = E_y$, and $M_y = E_x$ rises with Y. Hence there is instability; once X begins rising, the mechanism keeps both X and Y rising, and the solution requires a lower value for Y.

Finally let us consider the case in which both D and D' are positive, but $m\mu$ exceeds DD'. This is a case of instability; but why is it that apparently large values of m and μ make the system unstable? Although we have seen that in stability analysis we cannot generally brush m and μ aside on the grounds that, between the two countries, imports and exports cancel out, nevertheless it is difficult to comprehend why especially large values of m and μ should lead to instability. The case is most easily explained when both m and μ are negative, yielding a positive product greater than the product of D and D'. The process is as follows: a rise in a initially raises Y; as Y rises, M_y falls and X tends to fall; as

---

* Intuitive comprehension of the adjustment mechanism is often helped by the elimination of certain parts. If the reader considers $b = 0$, and r very large relative to ρ, the present case becomes one in which Y may be taken to adjust instantaneously to the value of $(a + E_y)(1 - m) - n$. After this reduction of complexity the process may be traced through more easily, and the essential plausibility of the outcome more easily seen.

X falls, M_x rises, aggravating rather than checking the rise in Y. Thus, with the two countries' national incomes moving in opposite directions, the movement of each augments the movement of the other, and if m and μ are large enough the result is instability. The smaller are b and β, the larger must m and μ be to cause instability in this case.*

When both m and μ are positive there is a simpler algebraic reason to explain the instability, rather than a process to follow. For if DD' is less than $m\mu$, with D, D', m, and μ all positive, either b or β or both must be greater than $+1$ (with m and μ each less than $+1$).

(55) $$ m < 1 $$
$$ m(1 - b) < 1 - b \quad \text{(if } b \text{ is less than } +1) $$
$$ m < 1 - b(1 - m) = D $$

That is to say, with m less than $+1$, m is less than D if b is less than $+1$ (otherwise $1 - b$ is negative and the inequality is reversed). Since the same holds for μ and D', and since $m\mu$ cannot exceed DD' if m is less than D at the same time that μ is less than D', the instability follows from the fact that the parameters b and β are relatively large, one at least exceeding $+1$.

Let us turn next to the variations in Y and X associated with variation in the parameter n of Y's import relationship. If n increases, Y falls, according to the solution of the equations, unless $(D' - \mu) = (1 - \beta)(1 - \mu)$ is negative; and X rises unless $(D - m) = (1 - b)(1 - m)$ is negative. When b and β are both less than $+1$ (with m and μ still assumed less than $+1$) ΔX and Δn are of the same sign and opposite in sign to ΔY. There are, however, altogether four apparent possibilities to consider, namely, both ΔY and ΔX positive, both negative, or either of one sign and the other of the opposite. Can any be ruled out on stability grounds? Since we have already seen that either or both of b and β may exceed $+1$, none of the four combinations can be classed as inconsistent with stability.

The easiest of the four combinations of changes to rationalize, aside from the "normal" case of b and β both less than $+1$, are the two cases in which Y and X both rise or both fall. If both Y and X rise, with a rise in n, it is because country X undergoes rising income which can be checked only by $\Delta(E_x - M_x)$ becoming negative as it must if β is greater than $+1$. For with β greater than $+1$, $\Delta K'$ exceeds ΔX, which implies $\Delta(E_x - M_x)$ negative, that is, E_x rises less than or falls more than M_x. Since X will

---

* The instability in this case might best be described as instability in the *distribution* of the joint income between Y and X. Note that if we allow X to continue on downward to zero and stop there, Y will stop rising, since D is positive and Y is unstable only through the influence of its exports.

rise until $\Delta(E_x - M_x)$ is negative, it rises until $\Delta(E_y - M_y)$ is positive, which implies that the upward pull on Y represented by the rise in X and E_x outweighs the initial depression represented by the increase in the value of n.

If, on the other hand, both Y and X fall, it is for analogous considerations; b rather than β exceeds $+1$ in this case. Y starts falling with the rise in n, and the fall in Y can only be checked by a rise in $(E_y - M_y)$, that is, by a fall in $(E_x - M_x)$. Thus Y must fall, with b greater than $+1$, until Y's falling imports have outweighed, in country X, the initial stimulus represented by the increase in n.

Finally let us suppose both b and β greater than 1. According to the solutions for Y and X, Y rises and X falls in this case. That Y and X must move opposite to each other is seen from the following considerations. For an increase in Y, a value of b greater than $+1$ implies $\Delta K = b \, \Delta Y > \Delta Y = \Delta K + \Delta E_y - \Delta M_y$, or $\Delta(E_y - M_y) < 0$. By the same reasoning, for an increase in X, with β greater than $+1$, $\Delta(E_x - M_x) < 0$. But the latter is identical with $\Delta(M_y - E_y) < 0$ which contradicts the previous sentence. The same contradiction appears for decreases in both Y and X. Thus they must move in directions opposite to each other.

We next observe that with both b and β greater than $+1$, either m or μ must be negative. This follows from the fact that, with $1 - b$ and $1 - \beta$ negative, inequality (55) is reversed and we have $m > D$, $\mu > D'$. Consequently not both D and D' may be positive, else m and μ would be positive and $m\mu$ exceed DD', contradicting the stability conditions. Thus D or D' must be negative which implies either m or μ negative. Let it be D which is negative; then it is m, not μ, which is also negative, since $\mu > D' > 0$. Our rationale of the process is now as follows: the initial effect of an increase in n is a tendency for Y to fall and X to rise; the initial tendency for X to rise leads to a rise in $M_x = E_y$ which counteracts the initial tendency for Y to fall; Y then rises and must rise, since D is negative, until E_y is actually lower than originally. As Y rises, M_y falls (since m is negative) and the initial rise in X, which converted the fall in Y into a rise, now itself becomes converted into a decline; and with X falling, M_x falls and checks the rise in Y. It is important to observe that in this case, with D negative, Y's rate of adjustment, r, must not be very great relative to X's rate, ρ; otherwise Y will have fallen too far before the favorable reflex occurs on its exports, and the latter will be unable to convert Y's decline into the rise which leads to the solution value.

If we let it be D', rather than D, which is negative, then it is μ, not m, which is also negative. The sequence of reactions must then be: an initial . fall in Y which proceeds, with b greater than $+1$, so far that the induced fall in M_y outweighs the initial increment represented by Δn; since the result is a fall in E_x, X falls and continues falling until E_x rises. With μ negative, the fall in X does lead to a rise in E_x, since M_x rises, raising Y and raising in turn $M_y = E_x$. In this latter case it is ρ which must not be large relative to r, otherwise X will respond initially by rising with the increment in n and, with $\beta(1 - \mu)$ greater than $+1$, will have risen so far by the time the decline in Y makes itself felt that the latter will be relatively too small an effect to stop the growth of X. [The qualifications regarding r and ρ agree with inequality (47) that $rD + \rho D'$ must be positive.]

Many other "paradoxical" movements of the variables could be derived and rationalized in similar fashion. The pattern of interpretation would follow that of the foregoing paragraphs, and the reader may work out the remaining cases. The principal remaining types of variation to be investigated are simultaneous variation in a and d or α and δ, that is, an increment in the independent component of exclusively domestic expenditure, and simultaneous variation in a and n or α and ν, that is, independent increments in exclusively import demand.*

A few general observations which have been illustrated by the foregoing analysis can be made at this point. One is that for any country in which b exceeds $+1$, ΔK exceeds ΔY when ΔY is positive, $-\Delta K$ exceeds $-\Delta Y$ when ΔY is negative, and consequently ΔM_y exceeds ΔE_y when Y rises and $-\Delta M_y$ exceeds $-\Delta E_y$ when Y falls. If the equations are stable, then the other country's behavior must be such as to move the net foreign balance in the manner indicated. In other words, "partial instability" of the type represented by $b > 1$ requires that the net export balance, exports minus imports, move contrary to the direction of national income.

The second observation is that for any country in which $D = 1 - b(1 - m)$ is negative, exports (not the net export balance) must move contrary to the direction of the national income. For if $b(1 - m)$ is greater than $+1$, $\Delta K - \Delta M_y$ exceeds ΔY so that $\Delta K - \Delta M_y > \Delta K + \Delta E_y - \Delta M_y$ or $0 > \Delta E_y$.

Finally it should be observed that, if the whole system is stable, each of the multipliers derived in the two preceding chapters is valid, whether positive or negative, and indicates the size and direction of changes in the variables. These negative "partial multipliers" are the key to the paradoxical motions of the variables.

---

* For an interesting application of the analysis to a special problem, see L. A. Metzler, "The Transfer Problem Reconsidered," *Journal of Political Economy*, vol. 50, p. 397, reprinted in *Readings in the Theory of International Trade*, Philadelphia, 1949.

A Note on the Parameters m and μ

Throughout this chapter we have generally not considered values for m or μ as great as $+1$. This exclusion was for the purpose of keeping the number of possibilities treated in the text from being greater than it was. It was remarked earlier that the plausibility of a value greater than $+1$ for m is much the same as that of a negative value of μ; that remark will be explained here. First, however, we must dispose of one possible origin of a value greater than $+1$ for m.

If the value of imported goods and services going into the production of consumption, investment, exports, or goods and services bought by government were greater than the value of those final goods themselves, the parameter m would have a value greater than $+1$. If, for example, \$2 worth of imported goods was used in the production of \$1 worth of consumption goods the pertinent value of m would be 2. This possibility we reject because it conflicts with a hypothesis about price behavior, namely, that production at a loss is not the rule. If m is greater than $+1$, the explanation must be another.

The remaining possibility is that, as national income rises, the composition of goods and services produced undergoes change, i.e., consumers shift their purchases toward imported goods, or the character of investment shifts so that greater reliance is on imported goods and services going into investment. Thus, with respect to consumers, we might define as "luxuries" those goods of which relatively more are bought at higher levels of national income; then, if there is little domestic production of luxuries, the direction of consumption tends to shift toward imported goods and services as income rises. And it is possible that the absolute amount of shift exceeds the absolute value of the rise in national income.

A negative value of m would indicate the opposite. If domestic production is largely of luxuries (according to the definition of the word given above) and nonluxuries are purchased mainly abroad, a rise in national income tends to reduce the relative portion of imported consumption goods and services and may even reduce the absolute amount.

If the same commodities and services represent "luxuries" to the consumers of both countries, then when in one country m exceeds $+1$ it is because the other country is the producer of "luxuries"; and in the latter country the corresponding parameter, μ, should tend to be small or negative.

Imposing Outside Conditions on the Variables

This and the two preceding chapters have attended principally to the incremental derivations which may be performed. The type of analysis outlined in Chap. 10, however, may be applied to the subject of these chapters as well as to the subjects of other chapters. The usual qualification applies regarding the linearity of the relationships over the range of values investigated. Such questions may be investigated as what value of G or I will lead to $E_y = M_y$, what value of $(M_y - E_y)$ is associated with $Y = F$, where F is some particular value of the national income corresponding with, say, the "full employment" of the labor force, or what values of the parameters a and d (interpreted perhaps in terms of components of C and I and T_x) will lead to $Y = F$ at the same time as $E_y = M_y$, etc. In the present case conditions may be imposed on the values of parameters of both countries simultaneously, or on the joint national income, or on each of the separate national incomes simultaneously. The general method follows that outlined in Chap. 10 and requires no further development to be applicable to the subject of international-income analysis.

PART IV

CHAPTER 16

DYNAMICS—I

This chapter will deal with "dynamic" problems in national-income analysis.* It would be helpful to have at the outset a clear definition of "dynamic." But since the purpose of such a definition would be to characterize the types of problems to be undertaken in this chapter, and to isolate the essential difference between the problems of this chapter and those of the preceding chapters, it will serve a useful purpose to sketch briefly the types of problems we are about to study before attempting to summarize their characteristics in a definition, especially since some of the elements of the definition would be concepts not already familiar from the foregoing chapters.

To suggest what sort of problems we are about to look into, it may be remarked that "dynamic" problems are, for our purposes, those which in some essential way involve chronological sequence, or time. The systems of equations heretofore studied were—with the exception of the stability analyses which we labeled "dynamic" at the time—what we call "static" in that they did not essentially involve the element of time and there was no chronological sequence to the values of the variables. When we spoke of a "change" in the value of one variable being associated with a "change" in the value of another variable, the "changes" were essentially comparisons rather than the chronological supercession of one value by another. The "change" was the *difference* between two *alternative* values; or, if we really did intend to speak of changes over time, it was inconsequential which of the two values of a variable preceded the other in the course of time.

In "dynamics" the time element enters in an *essential* respect; the time element cannot be eliminated. It appears in the "solution" of the equations in that the solution gives us not a single set of values of the variables which satisfies the equations but time patterns of the variables which satisfy the equations. And it appears in the original relationships in such forms as the following:

Rate of change of dependent variable. One form of dynamic relationship—a form which has appeared occasionally in stability analysis in earlier chapters—is that between the rate of change of a variable and the values of other variables. Thus the rate of change of consumption expenditure may be related to the difference between actual consumption expenditure and

---

* An excellent discussion of the subject is to be found in P. A. Samuelson, "Dynamic Process Analysis," Chap. X of *A Survey of Contemporary Economics*, Philadelphia, 1948.

some function of disposable income; writing C for consumption, X for disposable income, and $\dot{C}$ for the rate of change of consumption, we may have $\dot{C} = R(a + bX - C)$ where $C = a + bX$ denotes the "normal" relationship of C to X, and R is the adjustment-rate parameter. If in numerical terms this dynamic relationship is $\dot{C} = 4(10 + 0.6X - C)$, values of 100 for C and 200 for X make $\dot{C} = 120$ to indicate that consumption is increasing at a rate of 120 per year, or 10 per month.* By the time C has increased to a value of 115, $\dot{C}$ should have declined to 60 per year or 5 per month, unless X has also changed; if X increases at the same rate as C, then when C has reached 115, X is at 215, and $\dot{C}$ equals 96 per year or 8 per month.

Rate of change of independent variable. Another form of dynamic relationship is that between the value of the dependent variable and the rate of change of another. If the absolute level of inventories tends to bear a fixed ratio to consumption sales, as in $I = kC$, where I denotes total inventories and k is the parameter of relationship, then that component of current investment which represents accumulation of inventory, denoted by $\dot{I}$, is proportional to the *rate of change* of C; that is, $\dot{I} = k\dot{C}$. If inventories tend to equal three months' sales, and if consumption be measured on an annual basis, k equals 0.25 to indicate that I tends to equal one quarter of the annual rate of consumption. If the annual rate of consumption sales increases at a rate of 10 per month, inventory accumulation must be at a rate of 2.5 per month to keep $I = 0.25C$. If consumption sales remain at a constant level, inventory accumulation is zero; if consumption sales increase or decrease, inventory is accumulated or disaccumulated at a rate equal to one quarter of the rate of change of the consumption level. (Notice that if consumption is measured at a monthly rate, then k equals 3 in the above example, and $\dot{I} = 3\dot{C}$.†)

Time lags. A relationship between two variables may become dynamic if the value of one at any given point in time is related to the value of the other at some previous point or points in time. If there is a lag in the production of consumption goods, production at one point in time (or during one interval of time) may tend to equal the sales of 1 month earlier

* The full statement would be that consumption increases at a rate of 120 per year per year or 10 per year per month, since consumption is measured as so much per year, *i.e.*, as an annual rate. The concept is similar to that of acceleration of an automobile: the speed of a car may increase at a rate of 10 miles per hour per minute which is equivalent to 600 miles per hour per hour.

† The rate of inventory accumulation is the same in either case. If consumption is measured at an annual rate we have consumption increasing at a rate of 10 per year per month; the same rate of increase of consumption, if measured at a monthly rate, is $10/12$ or 0.83 per month per month. Inventory accumulation is thus the same whether we compute it as 0.25 times 10 per month or 3 times 0.83 per month.

(or during the preceding month). Or consumption may tend to equal $a + bZ$, where Z is a weighted average of the current income and the income of the preceding year, quarter, or month. Or the rate of increase of productive capacity may tend to equal the rate of investment of n months earlier, where n months denotes the average period of time elapsing between the devotion of resources to capital-goods production and the availability of the finished capital goods for use.

Cumulative variables. If one of the variables of the system is the cumulative sum of previous values of another variable, the system may become dynamic. If, for example, we wish to consider consumption related both to the level of income and to the amount of total wealth, we may identify wealth—or a large part of total wealth—as equal to the sum of all investment to date; that is, we may identify investment as the rate of increase of productive assets. If the variable, investment, also appears in our analysis, we may have a dynamic system. If investment depends partly on the level of consumption, and consumption depends partly on the amount of total assets, we have the rate of change of productive assets partly related to the total value of productive assets.

The four preceding paragraphs have indicated four of the ways in which a system of equations may be dynamic; but the distinctions among the four are not essential. Whether the variable whose rate of change is involved in a relationship is the dependent or the independent variable has no particular effect on the method of solution or the nature of the solution. And the occurrence of a cumulative variable is just the other side of a rate of change, since it makes no difference whether we call investment the rate of change of productive assets or the latter the cumulative sum of past investment. And, finally, any rate of change may in a sense be considered a case of time lag, since a rate of change is essentially a comparison of values at two adjacent points in time.

It may be worth while to indicate a few cases of relationships which are not dynamic. A relation between the rate of change of consumption and the rate of change of income is not dynamic, since it follows necessarily from a static relation between C and Y. If $C = a + bY$, then any change in Y is accompanied by a change in C equal to $b \Delta Y$ and if we let ΔY be a change over time then $b \Delta Y$ is the change in C over time. This is a case in which the *statement* of the relationship may involve time, in the sense that rates of change over time are related to each other, but in which the time element is not essential and can be eliminated.

Again, whenever our analysis involves investment it involves the rate of change of productive assets, or of whatever we call the cumulative sum of investment; and whenever the analysis involves inventory accumulation as a part of investment it involves at the same time the rate of change of inventory. But unless the total of productive assets, or the total of in-ventories, enters essentially into the analysis the analysis may remain undynamic. Total population, or the rate of population growth, may be a determinant of investment or of consumption or of some other variable in the system; but the analysis becomes dynamic only if we have some relations such as between investment and total population, and between income and the birth rate. In that case both total population and the rate of population growth are essentially involved in the analysis, and the solution gives paths over time, rather than particular values, of the variables involved.

There are borderline cases between static analysis and dynamic analysis, but they need not concern us here. Our purpose is not to develop generally applicable definitions of "statics" and "dynamics," but rather only to distinguish between certain types of equation systems according to a significant characteristic. Our own definition wants, therefore, to hinge on the technique of mathematical treatment or the nature of the solution. We shall consequently use the term "dynamic" to refer to a system of equations whose solution gives, in terms of parameters, not particular values of the variables which satisfy the equations but paths over time of the variables which satisfy the equations. The principal purpose of this definition is only to point out that there are such systems of equations, and that they constitute the subject of this and the succeeding chapters.

The Technique of Analysis of Dynamic Systems

The mathematical formulation of the hypotheses into equations is substantially more difficult in the case of dynamic hypotheses than in the case of static hypotheses. In the case of static hypotheses we made the simplifying assumption that relationships were linear and, once we had chosen the variables to enter the relationship, there was nothing more difficult than the selection of convenient Greek or roman letters to construct the formula. In the present chapter we shall continue to restrict ourselves to linear relationships; but this restriction is no longer sufficient to determine their exact forms. There remain a great variety of forms to choose among.

For example, if there are involved two time lags in the system of equations, may we simplify the problem by assuming equal lags or must we distinguish two different critical intervals of time? If we are to relate consumption to current and past levels of income, may we take a simple weighted average of current income and income of one year before, or must we take a weighted average of the preceding dozen quarter years, with diminishing weights for earlier quarters? Must we consider all adjustments as smooth and continuous; or is it permissible to chop time into "periods" and assume all values constant within the period, or, alternatively, to focus attention solely on values at equidistant points of time and ignore values in between?

In general the problem we shall face is this: severely limiting assumptions must be made in order to keep the problem mathematically manageable, each piece of detail is included at high cost in simplicity; we must select only such detail as is absolutely essential to the economic problem at hand and be always on guard that the general character of the results is not too much a reflection of the particular *form* in which the problem has been set up. If, for example, we choose to cut time into finite successive "periods," and treat all values as constant within each period, we must try to eliminate from our conclusions any aspects which are solely due to the arbitrary way in which we have conceived time to pass.

Once the system has been "solved," we still have a complicated task of describing or interpreting the solution. The solution gives us a path of, say, income over time. The complete solution could only be fully described by the drafting of a chart or the compiling of a table of successive values to cover the entire range of time in which we may be interested. And then to investigate the effect of alternative parameter values on the solution path we should have to draw alternative charts or compile alternative tables corresponding to each different set of parameter values. We consequently simplify the interpretation of the solution by concentrating on certain significant characteristics of the time patterns of the variables. We ask simply: does income constantly increase, does it constantly decrease, does it fluctuate, does it increase without limit or toward some limiting value? If it fluctuates, do the waves increase in amplitude or damp down and converge on some fixed value? On which parameters does the rate of increase depend and how is it related to their values? In general the answer to each such question depends on parameter values; and we investigate the ranges of parameter values for which the national income does or does not approach some fixed value over time, or does or does not oscillate in a wavelike pattern, etc.

The general procedure in each case will be as follows. First, the various hypotheses must be expressed in the form of separate equations, some dynamic, some perhaps static. Second, these must be "solved" to yield an equation or equations relating the value of each important variable to the value of "time," *i.e.*, to the elapsed time from some base point in time. Sometimes this equation will be explicit, *i.e.*, a value for the variable can be computed for any given value of time; sometimes it will be implicit, in the sense that the "solution" gives the value at one point in time in terms of the value at some prior point in time, or gives the rate of change of a variable's value at any point in time in terms of the variable's value at that time; and by repeated application of the formula we can work our way toward the value at any desired point in time. (Usually there will be an arbitrary element involved, namely some base value; *i.e.*, the solution gives not a particular value for each point in time but a relationship between the values at any points in time and some "original" value at the base point.) Third, there is the analysis of the form of the time pattern contained in the solution, *i.e.*, the investigation of the answers to the questions outlined in the previous paragraph.

The One-period Lag

The first dynamic hypothesis we shall study is the case of a lagged relation between consumption and income. There are various forms this hypothesis may take; we shall begin with the simplest. We suppose time to be divided into "periods" of equal length, and ignore changes in the values of the variables within the period. We suppose consumption in any period to be related to the income of the preceding period; and for the time being we shall not inquire into the explanation of such a lag. We must date our variables, and shall do so by writing, for example, $C(t)$ to denote the consumption at some time, *i.e.*, during some period, and $C(t - 1)$ to denote the consumption during the preceding period, $C(t - 2)$ the consumption of the period before that, etc., and $C(t + 1)$ the consumption of the next period after period t. Similarly with $Y(t)$, $Y(t - 1)$, etc. Our hypothesis is then

$$(1) \qquad\qquad C(t) = a + bY(t - 1)$$

where t denotes *any* period of time and $t - 1$ the preceding period.* If the lag in the consumption-income relation were greater or less than one "period" we could simply redefine the period in terms of the length of the lag, and so obtain a one-period lag. What matters is that the lag be not so long that variation in the values of the variables within the period should be of major significance.

We shall identify only the consumption and the nonconsumption components of national income, writing

$$(2) \qquad\qquad Y(t) = C(t) + N(t)$$
$$Y(t - 1) = C(t - 1) + N(t - 1)$$
$$\text{etc.}$$

Let us next suppose N constant throughout all the periods and see what we get. Substituting (1) into (2) we obtain

---

* To say that we have "dated" our variables is not quite correct; more accurately we have "ordered" them chronologically. The base point from which we measure time is arbitrary.

(3) $Y(t) = N + a + bY(t - 1)$

$$= (N + a) + b[N + C(t - 1)]$$

$$= (N + a) + b[N + a + bY(t - 2)]$$

$$= (N + a)(1 + b) + b^2[N + a + bY(t - 3)]$$

$$= (N + a)(1 + b + b^2) + b^3Y(t - 3)$$

And so, by repeated application of the formula, we may obtain

(4) $Y(t) = (N + a)(1 + b + b^2 + b^3 + b^4 + \cdots + b^{t-1}) + b^tY(0)$

This gives us a general formula for computing the national income in any period t if we know the national income of some base period, period 0. We shall shortly put equation (4) into a more convenient form for such computation; for the time being let us see what general information we can obtain about the nature of the time pattern.

First let us ask whether there is some value of the national income such that, if it once occurs, it will repeat itself the following period. If there is such a value, and it occurs once, it will recur in all succeeding periods for the same reason that it occurred the first time. If there is such a value, let us call it $\bar{Y}$; it must satisfy the equation

(5) $\bar{Y} = a + b\bar{Y} + N$

$$= \frac{a + N}{1 - b}$$

This is the value which would satisfy static equations of the same parameters. Next let us inquire whether the national income, if it once has a value other than $\bar{Y}$, tends to approach $\bar{Y}$ or move away from it. If we compare two chronologically adjacent values of Y we find that

(6) $Y(t) - Y(t - 1) = [a + N + bY(t - 1)] - Y(t - 1)$

$$= (a + N) - (1 - b)Y(t - 1)$$

$$= (1 - b)\left[\frac{a + N}{1 - b} - Y(t - 1)\right]$$

$$= (1 - b)[\bar{Y} - Y(t - 1)]$$

Thus the difference between $Y(t)$ and $Y(t - 1)$ is equal to $1 - b$ times the difference between the actual value of $Y(t - 1)$ and the "equilibrium" value, $\bar{Y}$. If $1 - b$ is a positive fraction the change in the value of Y is in the direction of $\bar{Y}$ and the distance from Y to $\bar{Y}$ is reduced in the ratio b during each period. If $1 - b$ is negative, i.e., if b exceeds $+1$, the difference is of opposite sign and $Y(t)$ is farther from $\bar{Y}$ than was $Y(t - 1)$, farther in the ratio $1 - b$. Finally, if $1 - b$ is positive and greater than

+1, *i.e.*, if b is negative, the change is in the direction of $\bar{Y}$ but overshoots the distance; $Y(t)$ will be on the opposite side of $\bar{Y}$ and will be closer or farther according as $1 - b$ is less than or greater than $+2$, *i.e.*, according as $-b$ is greater or less than $+1$.

Equation (6) suggests a very convenient form in which the general formula for $Y(t)$ might be written. Since the difference between $\bar{Y}$ and $Y(t + 1)$ is b times the difference between $\bar{Y}$ and $Y(t)$, we should be able to express $Y(t)$ in terms of $\bar{Y}$ and some initial discrepancy, at time zero, between $\bar{Y}$ and $Y(0)$. This can in fact be readily developed from the first line of equation (3).

$$(7) \qquad Y(1) = a + N + bY(0)$$

$$\bar{Y} - Y(1) = \bar{Y} - a - N - bY(0)$$

$$= \frac{a + N}{1 - b} - (a + N) - bY(0)$$

$$= b[\bar{Y} - Y(0)]$$

Similarly,

$$(8) \qquad \bar{Y} - Y(2) = b[\bar{Y} - Y(1)] = b^2[\bar{Y} - Y(0)]$$

$$\bar{Y} - Y(\text{t}) = b^t[\bar{Y} - Y(0)]$$

Transposing, we have

$$(9) \qquad Y(t) = \bar{Y} - b^t[\bar{Y} - Y(0)]$$

which yields at once all the information about the path of Y over time. The difference between $Y(t)$ and $\bar{Y}$, for any value of t, is equal to b^t times the difference at time zero. If b is a positive fraction, this difference reduces in geometric ratio with the compounding of b; if b exceeds $+1$, the difference grows with the compounding of b; if b is negative, the difference changes sign between any two periods, and the absolute size of the difference is greater or less according as $-b$ is greater or less than $+1$.

Equation (4) can be converted to the same form by a process of algebraic summation which will be useful to have at hand. What we must do is find an equivalent form for the sum of $1 + b + b^2 + b^3 + \cdots$. Let S stand for the sum of these terms from 1 to b^{t-1}; write out this series and beneath it write out b times S by multiplying each term in S by b; bS is thus identical with S except for the absence of the initial $+1$ and the presence of a terminal b^t,

$$(10) \qquad S = 1 + b + b^2 + b^3 + \cdots + b^{t-1}$$

$$(11) \qquad bS = b + b^2 + b^3 + \cdots + b^{t-1} + b^t$$

If we subtract bS from S, all terms cancel out except the $+1$ and the $-b^t$, so that

(12) $S - bS = 1 - b^t$

$$S = \frac{1}{1 - b} - \frac{b^t}{1 - b}$$

Equation (4) can now be rewritten as

(13) $$Y(t) = \frac{N + a}{1 - b} - b^t \left[\frac{N + a}{1 - b} - Y(0) \right]$$

which is identical with (9).*

This about exhausts the simple case of the one-period consumption lag; it can be combined with other dynamic hypotheses to yield much more complicated patterns. Before leaving the present case several remarks are in order. First, if we consider the period very short, or the value of b quite small, any divergence between Y and $\bar{Y}$ is quickly narrowed down to what may be considered an insignificant difference. If changes in the value of N occur relatively slowly compared to the speed with which Y approaches $\bar{Y}$ we may, for many purposes, study the relation of $\bar{Y}$ to N and ignore the dynamic element of the hypothesis. This is, of course, what we did in the static analysis of the same problem in Chap. 3; and the present case may be considered a variant of the stability analysis applicable to Chap. 3.

Second, the possibility of alternation of Y about $\bar{Y}$ may be, in the present case, more a characteristic of the analytical technique than of the economic hypothesis. Since a negative relationship between consumption and income is seldom considered plausible, we shall not go into this possibility here; at a later point it will be shown for a similar case that *if* the lag is intended to represent an adjustment pattern of a variable certain types of alternation are inadmissible, since they contradict the intended behavior pattern and result only from the periodic treatment of time.

Third, we have not yet considered the case of variation in the value of N, having confined ourselves to the supposition that N is constant. If we revert to equations (1) and (2) and perform repeated substitutions, identifying each N according to the period to which it relates, we obtain

(14) $Y(t) = N(t) + a + b[N(t - 1) + a + bY(t - 2)]$

$\qquad = a + N(t) + b[a + N(t - 1)] + b^2[a + N(t - 2)] + \cdots$

$\qquad = \dfrac{a}{1 - b} + N(t) + bN(t - 1) + b^2 N(t - 2) + \cdots$

* Cf. P. A. Samuelson, "A Fundamental Multiplier Identity," *Econometrica*, vol. 11, p. 221.

Thus the value of $Y(t)$ is determined by all the values of N which have gone before; if b is a fraction, however, the farther in the past a particular value of N occurred, the smaller its weight in the value of $Y(t)$, since it is multiplied by b compounded to the number of periods elapsed since the occurrence of that value of N. In other words, $Y(t)$ is equal to $a/(1 - b)$ plus a weighted sum of all prior N's, the weights diminishing in geometrical ratio as they recede into the past.

There are two relatively easy questions we may ask about the effects of variation in the values of the N's. One is this: what difference would it have made to the value of $Y(t)$ if each foregoing value of N had been greater by the amount h? Raising the values of the N's to $N(t) + h, N(t - 1) + h$, $N(t - 2) + h$, etc., it can be seen that the effect is to raise the value of $Y(t)$ by an amount given by

$$(15) \qquad \Delta Y(t) = h + bh + b^2 h + b^3 h + \cdots$$

$$= h \left(\frac{1}{1 - b} - \frac{b^r}{1 - b} \right)$$

where r is the number of periods into the past to which we apply the increment h. If r is a large number and b is a fraction, we may take b^r as approximately zero and obtain $\Delta Y(t) = h/(1 - b)$ which is similar to the results of static analysis.

The other question is similar to the one just treated. If any particular N is increased by the amount h, what will be the sum of the effects on all subsequent Y's? Let it be $N(t)$ whose value is increased by the amount h. Then $Y(t)$ is greater by h, as is seen from equation (10); $Y(t + 1)$ is greater by bh, since a term in the formula for $Y(t + 1)$ is $bN(t)$; $Y(t + 2)$ is greater by $b^2 h$, since $N(t)$ appears in the formula for $Y(t + 2)$ with the coefficient b^2. And so on; the total for r successive periods of time will be

$$(16) \qquad \Delta \Sigma Y = h + bh + b^2 h + \cdots + b^{r-1} h$$

$$= \frac{h}{1 - b} - \frac{b^r h}{1 - b}$$

which approximates $h/(1 - b)$ as the number of periods taken into account increases, so long as b is less than 1.

Finally, let us suppose that N has been constant at a certain value for many periods up to $N(0)$, so that $Y(0)$ is approximately equal to $[a + N(0)]/(1 - b)$. Then let N in period $+1$ take a new value which it repeats during all periods up to and including period t. In that case we have, putting $Y(0)$ equal to $[a + N(0)]/(1 - b)$ in equation (9),

$$(17) \qquad Y(t) = \frac{a + N(1)}{1 - b} - b^t \left[\frac{N(1) - N(0)}{1 - b} \right]$$

There are many other ways in which a lagged consumption relationship may appear. One is to consider consumption related to an average of current and past income. Using the period concept of time, let us try a relationship of the form

$$(18) \qquad C(t) = a + b[pY(t) + qY(t - 1)]$$

where p and q are the weights used to form an average of income of the current period and of the next preceding period. We take $p + q$ to equal 1. Combining equation (18) with equation (2) we have

$$(19) \qquad Y(t) = a + bpY(t) + bqY(t - 1) + N(t)$$

$$= \frac{a + N(t) + bqY(t - 1)}{1 - bp}$$

$$= ka + kN(t) + kbqY(t - 1)$$

where k is introduced to stand for $1/(1 - bp)$. Dynamic stability would require bp less than $+1$, which it will be necessarily if b is less than 1, since p is not greater than 1 from $p + q = 1$. Writing $H = kbq$ to save space, repeated application of the substitution process yields

$$(20) \quad Y(t) = ka + kN(t) + kHa + kHN(t - 1) + kH^2a$$
$$+ kH^2N(t - 2) + \cdots$$

which gives us again $Y(t)$ in terms of all the preceding values of N. In equation (20) we have omitted a remainder term, which should appear as $H^rY(t - r)$, where r is the number of substitutions performed. If, however, H is less than $+1$, H^r approaches zero as more and more terms are taken, and we can ignore the remainder. Under what conditions will H be less than $+1$? The answer is that H will be less than 1 if b is less than 1, otherwise H exceeds 1 and the remainder term cannot be left out of equation (20). For, replacing H by kbq, and k by $1/(1 - bp)$, we have

$$(21) \qquad H = kbq = \frac{bq}{1 - bp} < 1$$

if and only if

$$(22) \qquad bq < 1 - b(1 - q) = 1 - b + bq$$

or

$$(23) \qquad b < 1$$

since $p = 1 - q$.

If, then, H is less than 1, i.e., if b is less than 1, we can use our general expression for the sum of a geometric series, developed in equations (10) through (12) above, and write

$$(24) \qquad Y(t) = \frac{k(a + N)}{1 - H}$$

for the case when N is constant. But $k/(1 - H)$ equals $1/(1 - b)$; for

$$(25) \qquad \frac{k}{1 - H} = \left(\frac{1}{1 - bp}\right)\left(\frac{1 - bp}{1 - bp - bq}\right) = \frac{1}{1 - b}$$

as is seen by writing out $1 - H$ and inverting, and identifying $p + q$ as equal to 1.

It is interesting to note that in the present case the relative influence of some particular value of N a given distance in the past is greater than in the previous case of lag. In the present case the influence of $N(t - r)$ is H times that of $N(t - r - 1)$ in the determination of the value of $Y(t)$; in the previous case the influence of $N(t - r)$ was b times that of $N(t - r - 1)$. And b is necessarily greater than H since $b/H = 1/kq = (1 - bp)/q = (1 - b + bq)/q$ which is greater than 1 if $1 - b$ exceeds $q(1 - b)$ which it must (with $b < 1$) for q is less than 1. At most q equals $+1$, in which case the two hypotheses are identical, for p must then be zero and $C(t) = a + bY(t - 1)$ as before.

Again we can consider the influence on $Y(t)$ of equal increments in all prior values of N; again we should find that if h is the increment in each N, $\Delta Y(t) = [1/(1 - b)]h$; and again the sum of all increments in subsequent Y's, corresponding to an increment h in any particular N, will equal $[1/(1 - b)]h$. These derivations are left to the reader.

Finally we may develop a consumption lag hypothesis through explicit consumption adjustment behavior. We postulate this fundamental dynamic consumption equation:

$$(26) \qquad C(t + 1) - C(t) = R[a + bY(t) - C(t)]$$

Calling $[a + bY(t)]$ the "normal" relationship value of $C(t)$ corresponding to $Y(t)$, equation (26) states that the change in the value of consumption, from one period to the next, is equal to R times the difference between actual and normal consumption during the period. It would be preferable in the present case to dispense with periods, and let the adjustment of consumption be continuous; we can do so with the same equation if we are willing to forego some accuracy. We shall let $C(t)$ refer not to consumption during a period, t, but at a point, t, in time. And $C(t + 1)$ is consumption at a subsequent point in time.

In this fashion we allow ourselves to think of the value of consumption as adjusting continuously, but we consider only values at successive points equally spaced in time. In other words, we analyze income on a snapshot basis.

The lost accuracy in our equation is this: we consider consumption to adjust, during the interval from time t to time $t + 1$, at a rate geared to the difference between normal and actual consumption at the point t. As a matter of fact, we should recognize that as C adjusts the value of Y changes; and therefore the adjustment rate of C changes during the period. But if we choose our intervals of time closely enough together, so that the change in the value of Y or of C between any two successive points in time is relatively small, equation (26) may serve as an algebraic approximation to what would otherwise involve us in the use of the calculus.

Substituting equation (2) into (26) we have

$$(27) \qquad C(t + 1) - C(t) = R[a + bN(t) + bC(t) - C(t)]$$

$$= R(1 - b)\left[\frac{a + bN(t)}{1 - b} - C(t)\right]$$

$$= R(1 - b)[\bar{C}(t) - C(t)]$$

where $\bar{C}(t)$ may be called the "current equilibrium value" of $C(t)$, namely the value such that if $C(t) = \bar{C}(t)$, then $C(t + 1)$ would be the same as $C(t)$. We use the word "current" because $N(t + 1)$ may differ from $N(t)$ and $\bar{C}(t + 1)$ accordingly differ from $\bar{C}(t)$. If, however, N remains constant for a succession of intervals of time, then $\bar{C}(t)$ may simply be written as $\bar{C}$ and it represents not only the value which, if it occurred at time t, would reoccur at $t + 1$, but the value toward which C approaches steadily if $R(1 - b)$ is a positive fraction, and toward which C approaches in alternation if $R(1 - b)$ is between $+1$ and $+2$. For in that case the same considerations apply to (27) as applied to equation (9).

If N is constant from time zero on, we may write the equation for $C(t)$ as

$$(28) \qquad C(t) = \bar{C} - [1 - R(1 - b)]^t[\bar{C} - C(0)]$$

since any initial difference between $\bar{C}$ and $C(0)$ reduces in the geometric ratio $[1 - R(1 - b)]$, per interval of time.

It follows from equation (2) that income is given by

$$(29) \qquad Y(t) = C(t) + N$$

$$= N + \frac{a + bN}{1 - b} - [1 - R(1 - b)]^t[\bar{C} - C(0)]$$

$$= \frac{a + N}{1 - b} - [1 - R(1 - b)]^t[\bar{C} - C(0)]$$

It would seem reasonable in the present case to rule out the possibility of $R(1 - b)$ exceeding $+1$ unless we wish to consider negative values of b. That is to say, we should consider R sufficiently small so that, if $1 - b$ is a positive fraction, $R(1 - b)$ is also a positive fraction, R not exceeding $+1$. The reason for this is that the length of our time interval is arbitrary; and the shorter the interval the smaller is the error involved in making consumption adjust at a fixed rate throughout the interval, rather than letting it adjust continuously toward the changing value of $a + bY$. At any rate, *if* we wish to use equation (26) as an approximation to continuous adjustment, we should not allow our intervals to be so long that consumption overshoots the mark and ends the interval on the opposite side of $a + bY$. We may always improve the accuracy, so to speak, of equation (26) by dividing the period into shorter periods. If we divide each period into n shorter periods, equation (28) becomes, for example,

$$(30) \qquad C(t) = \bar{C} - \left[1 - \frac{R}{n}(1 - b) \right]^{nt} [\bar{C} - C(0)]$$

This formula differs from that of equation (28) by "compounding" the adjustments more frequently, *i.e.*, by "revising" more frequently the value of $Y(t)$ in equation (26). The difference in the values obtained for $C(t)$ is analogous to the difference between compounding interest at 4 per cent per year, at 1 per cent per quarter, or at 0.33 per cent per month.

It should finally be observed that, if we should take the value of R at $+1$ in equation (26), that equation becomes identical with equation (1); if R equals $+1$ we may remove the brackets and cancel $C(t)$ from both sides obtaining $C(t + 1) = a + bY(t)$ which is identical with $C(t) = a + bY(t - 1)$. Thus one interpretation of equation (1) is that it represents the adjustment behavior of consumption toward its "normal" income relationship, with a particular value, namely $+1$, for the adjustment rate parameter R. The difficulty involved in using equation (1) for the investigation of adjustment behavior is that referred to a moment ago: we have used a time interval which is long relative to the adjustment speed of C, and the error of taking the adjustment rate as constant over the interval is correspondingly great. The discrepancy is analogous to this: the percentage error involved in compounding interest at 2 per cent per year rather than $\frac{1}{2}$ per cent per quarter is small compared with the percentage error involved in compounding interest at 100 per cent per year rather than at 25 per cent per quarter. In one case the annual growth is 2 per cent rather than 2.015 per cent; in the other case it is 100 per cent rather than 125 per cent.

The First-order Difference Equation

Time-lag equations of the sort studied in this chapter are often referred to as "difference equations" because they can be put into an alternative form relating the difference between two successive values of a variable

to the value at one of the two points in time. Equation (6) is in this
form; it relates $Y(t) - Y(t - 1)$ to the value of $Y(t - 1)$. In general
any equation relating the value of some variable, X, at time t, to its value
at time $t - 1$, can be put in this form,

$$(31) \qquad\qquad X(t) = A + BX(t - 1)$$

$$X(t) - X(t - 1) = A + (B - 1)X(t - 1)$$

Using $\Delta X(t)$ to denote the difference between $X(t + 1)$ and $X(t)$, and
using $\bar{X}$ to denote that value of X which will repeat itself, we have the
general form

$$(32) \qquad\qquad \Delta X(t) = (1 - B)[\bar{X} - X(t)]$$

CHAPTER 17

DYNAMICS—II

Problems of inventory adjustment illustrate many of the techniques used in dynamic analysis. This chapter will approach the inventory and production adjustment problem from several alternative directions, each approach illustrating a different formulation and a different form of "solution."

The analysis of inventory accumulation and the analysis of the adjustment of production are necessarily linked together, since any time lag between a change in sales and the corresponding adjustment in the rate of production involves a gain or loss of inventory equal to the cumulative difference between sales and production from the time the initial divergence occurs until the two have been brought into line.

The general structure of the problem is as follows. To each level of sales there corresponds some "normal" level of inventory; if inventory is "normal" in relation to sales, and if the level of sales is constant, inventory accumulation is zero. Any rise in the rate of sales entails an increase in the "normal" level of inventory; and if sales increase above some previous level, production must not only increase to match the higher rate of sales but must exceed sales over a period in order that inventory may be increased to its new "normal" level. Furthermore, any lag in the adjustment of the production rate behind the increase in the level of sales causes an actual loss of inventory during the period that sales exceed production; production must consequently exceed sales sufficiently not only to raise inventory to its new higher "normal" level but to recoup the inventory drain which occurred during the time that production lagged behind sales. If production can be adjusted almost instantaneously to sales the "recouping" may be nil; there is still, however, the need for production in excess of sales in order that inventory may be brought into its normal relation to the new level of sales.

The interest in the problem lies in the fact that sales may be in turn related to production, via a relation of consumption to income, so that the adjustment of production entails change in that very level of sales to which production is adjusting.

There are several parameters involved in the problem. First of all is the usual consumption-income relationship with the two parameters entailed by our restriction to straight-line relationships. Second is the parameter describing the normal relation of inventory to sales; for simplicity we take this relationship as one of proportionality, keeping its description limited thereby to a single parameter. Finally there is the set of parameters, at least two, describing the timing of the production response. We need one parameter to indicate the "normal" rate of inventory accumulation when actual inventory differs from "normal" inventory. For example, the normal rate of accumulation may be such as to bring actual inventory into line with its relationship to sales over a period of 1 month, or 3 months, or at a varying rate depending on the size of the discrepancy. For simplicity we shall assume that the absolute rate of inventory accumulation tends to be proportional to the discrepancy between actual inventory and the "normal" level corresponding to current sales. (This assumption amounts to the same thing as assuming that "normal" practice is to let any discrepancy between actual and normal inventory decrease in geometric ratio.) And we need another parameter to indicate the speed of adjustment of production toward its "normal" level, its normal level being a level such that it differs from sales by exactly the amount required to accumulate or disaccumulate inventory at the normal rate.

These hypotheses will become more clear as we set them out in algebraic form. But before writing them out as equations we must decide whether to deal with *continuous* variation or *periodic* variation. Each has its advantages. The assumption of continuous variation seems a more accurate description of actual economic processes; analysis of periodic variation possesses certain analytical advantages. Since the techniques in both cases are typical of many other problems of dynamic analysis, we shall take them both in turn. First we shall consider the case of continuous variation.

Continuous Treatment of the Inventory Problem

We distinguish between the rate of production of consumer goods and services and their rate of sale. Their difference represents the rate of inventory accumulation or disaccumulation. Letting I denote the *level* of inventory, and $\dot{I}$ the rate of change over time of that level (*i.e.*, the rate of inventory accumulation), we have the identity

$$(1) \qquad\qquad \dot{I} = P_c - S_c$$

where P_c and S_c denote, respectively, the rate of production and the rate of sale of consumer goods and services.

The national income can be represented in either of two forms, by virtue of (1),

$$(2) \qquad\qquad Y = P_c + N = S_c + \dot{I} + N$$

where N denotes the nonconsumption expenditure components of the national income—the net rate of private investment other than inventory accumulation plus the rate of government expenditure for goods and services plus the net export balance.

A relationship between consumption expenditure and national income is assumed to hold without appreciable time lag,

$$(3) \qquad\qquad S_c = a + bY$$

This relationship may be supposed to allow for the effects of taxation and transfer payments.

The second hypothesis is that the level of inventory tends to bear a certain "normal" relation to the rate of consumption sales; for simplicity we assume a "normal" relationship of proportionality,

$$(4) \qquad\qquad I' = kS_c$$

We denote by I' the normal level of inventory corresponding to any particular level of sales, to distinguish that normal level from the actual level, I. (We ignore in this analysis the inventory held in investment-goods industries.)

The third hypothesis is that the rate of production in consumer-goods industries tends to exceed or fall short of sales in a regular fashion designed to increase or decrease inventory toward its normal relation to sales,

$$
\begin{aligned}
(5) \qquad P_c' &= S_c + R(I' - I) \\
&= S_c + R(kS_c - I) \\
&= S_c(1 + Rk) - RI
\end{aligned}
$$

Equation (5), in which P_c' denotes the "normal" rate of production corresponding to any given rate of sales and level of inventory, makes the rate of inventory accumulation proportionate to the difference between actual and normal inventory, *i.e.*, to the total accumulation required to bring I into equality with kS_c, R being the parameter of proportionality. The alternative form of (5) is thus

$$(6) \qquad\qquad \dot{I}' = R(kS_c - I)$$

with $\dot{I}'$ denoting the "normal" rate of inventory accumulation corresponding to the actual values of kS_c and I.

The final hypothesis relates to the adjustment of production, P_c, toward its "normal" value, P_c'. When a change occurs in the rate of sales, production adjusts toward the value indicated by (5); but since any change in the rate of production constitutes a change in the level of income, it will itself further affect the rate of sales. The adjustment required, then, to bring P_c into equality with P_c', becomes apparent only as the adjustment proceeds, and the whole process of adjustment toward the (changing) value of P_c' takes time. Furthermore there may be some delay in the revision of production plans; sales records may become available only at intervals.

Thus an explicit hypothesis regarding the adjustment behavior of P_c is required; this we express in the form

$$(7) \qquad \dot{P}_c = r(P_c' - P_c)$$
$$= r[S_c + R(kS_c - I) - P_c]$$

It should be noted that equation (7) involves all three of the hypotheses regarding production and inventory; it contains the three parameters k, R, and r. The two preceding hypotheses, expressed in equations (4) and (5) or, alternatively, (4) and (6), serve the purpose only of leading up to the final equation (7) which expresses the entire relationship between the rate of production and the rate of sales and level of inventory. Thus the equation system which we use from here on is composed of the two identities, (1) and (2), and the two relationships, (3) and (7). We assume these four equations to hold at all times, while equations (4) and (5) or (6) only indicate the conditions necessary for $\dot{I} = 0$ or $\dot{P}_c = 0$, respectively.

Our aim will be to obtain two equations relating the rates of change of Y and I to the actual current values of Y and I. Those two equations will then be analyzed by the use of stability conditions developed in the Appendix. Once we have obtained two such equations it will be clear that the equation system set forth above is sufficient to determine the course over time of the values of all the variables once the initial values at any given point in time are known.

As a first step in the development of the desired two equations we observe that

$$(8) \qquad \dot{Y} = \dot{P}_c + \dot{N}$$

which follows from $Y = P_c + N$; the absolute rate of change of a sum is equal to the sum of the absolute rates of change of its parts. Holding N constant so that $\dot{N} = 0$, and substituting equations (2) and (3) into (7), we have

$$(9) \qquad \dot{Y} = \dot{P}_c = r(1 + Rk)(a + bY) - rRI - r(Y - N)$$
$$= A + BY + CI$$

where

$$(10) \qquad A = r[a(1 + Rk) + N]$$

$$(11) \qquad B = r[b(1 + Rk) - 1]$$

$$(12) \qquad C = -rR$$

Equation (9) is the first of the two equations we seek; the other, giving $\dot{I}$ in terms of Y and I, can be obtained by substitution as follows:

$$(13) \qquad \begin{aligned} \dot{I} &= P_c - S_c \\ &= Y - N - S_c \\ &= -(a + N) + (1 - b)Y \\ &= \mathbf{A} + \mathbf{C}Y \end{aligned}$$

where

$$(14) \qquad\qquad \mathbf{A} = -(a + N)$$

$$(15) \qquad\qquad \mathbf{C} = 1 - b$$

We shall consider equations (9) and (13) as the "solution"; further solution, to obtain explicit representations of Y and I in terms of t, will be left for the Appendix since something more than algebra is required. It will be necessary, in order to interpret the implications of equations (9) and (13), to draw on some outside information of a very general nature. Before asking the help, though, of a mathematician, let us see what general characteristics of the system and its solution we can develop without more mathematics than we already possess.

First let us be clear about what sort of questions we shall need answered regarding the system of variables and relationships before us. For one thing, we shall want to know whether there is an "equilibrium" set of values for all the variables, i.e., a set of values such that if the variables once have these values they tend to keep them in the absence of any outside disturbance. ("Outside disturbance" could take the form of a change in the value of N, a value we are for the present assuming constant, or a shift in the consumption sales parameter or in the inventory parameter, k.) Second, if there is such an equilibrium set of values, do the variables tend to approach those equilibrium values; i.e., assuming that the variables possess other values than their equilibrium values, do they in their courses over time approximate more and more closely the equilibrium values, so that if we allow a sufficient lapse of time the variables will remain, after that lapse of time, within any desired limits about their equilibrium values? (The length of time which must elapse, of course, would tend to depend on the limits we set.) Finally we may ask whether the direction of change of the variables is constant, or whether fluctuation may occur; and, if fluctuation occurs, do the waves damp down and converge on equilibrium values or do they grow greater and greater, or do they give way after a time to steady growth or decline?

First let us regard the equilibrium values: Since the entire system of relationships, in so far as Y and I are concerned, is contained in equations (9) and (13), i.e., since equations (9) and (13) completely describe the behavior of the variables I and Y, it is clear that equilibrium values are any values which make $\dot{Y}$ and $\dot{I}$ equal to zero. For if at any instant Y and I have values which cause $\dot{Y}$ and $\dot{I}$ to be zero, $\dot{Y}$ and $\dot{I}$ will be zero at all subsequent points in time; Y and I can change only if their values are different, and their values cannot be different if they do not change. Consequently, we may put $\dot{Y}$ and $\dot{I}$ equal to zero in equations (9) and (13) and solve the resulting equations for equilibrium values of Y and I.

$$(16) \qquad \dot{Y} = 0 = A + BY + CI$$
$$= r(1 + RK)(a + bY) - rRI - r(Y - N)$$

$$(17) \qquad \dot{I} = 0 = \mathbf{A} + \mathbf{C}Y$$
$$= -(a + N) + (1 - b)Y$$

Equation (17) by itself gives at once the equilibrium value of Y, namely,

$$(18) \qquad\qquad \bar{Y} = \frac{a + N}{1 - b}$$

which is certainly familiar in form. Next we solve (16) for I in terms of Y, and substitute for Y its value as given by (18); after canceling the r's,

$$(19) \qquad R\bar{I} = (1 + Rk)a + N + [(1 + Rk)b - 1]\frac{a + N}{1 - b}$$

$$I = k\left(\frac{a + bN}{1 - b}\right) = k\bar{S}_c$$

Using these expressions for $\bar{Y}$ and $\bar{I}$ we can rewrite equations (9) and (13) in terms of the differences, $Y - \bar{Y}$ and $I - \bar{I}$. As the reader may check by substitution and multiplying out, equations (9) and (13) can be converted to

$$(20) \qquad \dot{I} = (1 - b)(Y - \bar{Y}) = \mathbf{C}(Y - \bar{Y})$$
$$(21) \qquad \dot{Y} = -r[1 - b(1 + Rk)](Y - \bar{Y}) - rR(I - \bar{I})$$
$$= B(Y - \bar{Y}) + C(I - \bar{I})$$

From this conversion we may deduce that the patterns of behavior which may be displayed by I and Y over time do not depend on the values of the parameters A and $\mathbf{A}$, in equations (9) and (13), but only on the parameters B, C, and $\mathbf{C}$. For, given any two initial values of I and Y, they can be expressed as differences from $\bar{I}$ and $\bar{Y}$ and those differences put into equations (20) and (21). The entire courses over time of I and Y are then determined by the parameters we have called B, C, and $\mathbf{C}$ since to each value of I or Y there corresponds a particular rate of change over time, for each of the two variables, so that the values at the next instant of time are determined as are the rates of change at the next point in time, and so forth.

Looking into the composition of B, C, and $\mathbf{C}$ it appears that the patterns of behavior of I and Y are determined by the parameters b, k, r, and R. The equilibrium values do depend on the parameters A and $\mathbf{A}$; but whether the variables approach or do not approach those equilibrium values, and whether they fluctuate or move in constant directions, depend only on the values of b, k, r, and R. (Assuming, of course, that N remains constant; if the value of N changes, the equilibrium values change and the course over time of the variables is affected.)

We could proceed to deduce more information about the behavior of the variables over time. It will be useful, however, to draw at this stage on outside information to find out in general how the behavior of two variables over time, when those two variables are related in the general fashion of (9) and (13), is related to the parameter values. We can then manage to deduce some of the conclusions directly, without the outside information, the latter serving only to indicate the directions in which we should search for conclusions.

Let us pose, as we did in Chap. 15, this question: Suppose any two variables are related in the form

$$(22) \qquad\qquad \dot{X} = A + BX + CZ$$

$$(23) \qquad\qquad \dot{Z} = \mathbf{A} + \mathbf{B}Z + \mathbf{C}X$$

That is, suppose the rate of change of each variable is determined by the values of both variables. How does their behavior over time depend on the values of A, B, C, $\mathbf{A}$, $\mathbf{B}$, and $\mathbf{C}$? A partial answer was given in Chap. 15; in the present case we want to know more, in particular we want to know whether fluctuation, $i.e.$, wave motion, is a possible mode of behavior within the scope of this relationship.

We have phrased the question in very general form, putting in the term $\mathbf{B}Z$ even though there is no comparable term in equation (13), so that our answer may be applicable to the greatest number of different economic problems in which the present structure of behavior occurs. The general answer is as follows: there are four basic types of behavior which the variables may show; (a) they may increase or decrease indefinitely, at a rate approximating a compound-interest rate, toward no fixed limit, (b) they may increase or decrease toward a fixed limiting value, the distance between the variable's value and that limiting value decreasing at a rate approximating compound interest in reverse, $i.e.$, decreasing in geometric ratio, (c) they may oscillate about their equilibrium values in waves which increase in amplitude, the amplitude increasing at a rate approximating a compound-interest rate of growth, (4) they may oscillate about their equilibrium value in ever diminishing waves, converging on those equilibrium values, the amplitude of the waves diminishing at a rate approximating a geometric ratio.*

There are certain borderline cases. If all the variables should initially have their equilibrium values, they keep them indefinitely. If the parameters have certain borderline values the amplitude of oscillation may be constant, the variables progressing over time in regular waves.

In general, both variables must show the same type of behavior, although steady increase in one may be associated with steady decrease in the other. The exceptions require that some of the coefficients be zero, *i.e.*, that the relationship be essentially more simple than shown by the general form of (9) and (13).

Whether nonoscillatory behavior is an increase or a decrease depends on the initial values of the two variables.

The exact behavior over time depends on the initial values of I and Y; but the type of behavior does not.

Now for the criteria in terms of parameters. We shall refer to the equilibrium as "stable" or "unstable," according as the variables do or do not approach equilibrium over time. Stability of equilibrium requires

$$(24) \qquad\qquad B + \mathbf{B} < 0$$

$$(25) \qquad\qquad B\mathbf{B} - C\mathbf{C} > 0$$

and the variables will fluctuate if and only if

$$(26) \qquad\qquad 4(B\mathbf{B} - C\mathbf{C}) > (B + \mathbf{B})^2$$

Our next step, once we have these criteria, is to express them in terms of the particular parameters of the problem at hand, *i.e.*, in terms of b, k, R, and r. Referring back to equations (10) through (15) for the composition of the parameters A, B, C, $\mathbf{A}$, $\mathbf{B}$, $\mathbf{C}$, and noting that $\mathbf{B}$ is zero in our present problem, we have

$$(27) \qquad\qquad b(1 + Rk) < 1$$

$$(28) \qquad\qquad b < 1$$

as the two stability criteria. (We canceled out R and r for they are necessarily positive according to the way the problem was set up, and division by a positive quantity does not affect the direction of an inequality.) Inequality (28) can be dispensed with; since R and k are both positive, $1 +$

---

* The rate is not strictly described as a geometric ratio; it is a composite of two geometric ratios, *i.e.*, the difference between the actual value and the equilibrium value is the sum of two terms, each diminishing or growing in a (different) geometric ratio.

Rk is greater than 1 and if (27) holds, (28) necessarily holds. The single stability criterion is, consequently, that $b(1 + Rk)$ be less than $+1$.

Before inquiring into the implications of oscillation, let us see how we may interpret (27). Suppose that production could be adjusted instantaneously in accordance with equation (7), i.e., that the value of r is very great. In that case we may solve equations (2), (3), and (5) to obtain

$$(29) \qquad Y = \frac{a(1 + Rk) + N - RI}{1 - b(1 + Rk)}$$

In the very short run—and by "short run" we must mean relative to the value of R, for R determines the rate at which I is changing—we may take the value of I as constant. In that case we may derive three multipliers, relating to increments in a, in N, and in I. The denominator in each case is the quantity which, for stability, must be positive. Our stability criterion, then, is relevant to the determination of the algebraic signs of $\Delta Y/\Delta a$, $\Delta Y/\Delta N$, and $\Delta Y/\Delta I$. (There is no contradiction in taking I as constant and then investigating ΔI; ΔI, just like ΔN, refers in this statement to the difference between two alternative values at a given time.)

It is interesting at the same time to derive the values of $\Delta S_c/\Delta a$, $\Delta P_c/\Delta a$, etc., and by subtraction to arrive at $\Delta \dot{I}/\Delta a$, $\Delta \dot{I}/\Delta N$, or $\Delta \dot{I}/\Delta I$. In the case of change in the value of N we have the "current multipliers"

$$(30) \qquad \Delta S_c = b \, \Delta Y = \frac{b \, \Delta N}{1 - b(1 + Rk)}$$

$$(31) \qquad \Delta P_c = \Delta S_c(1 + Rk) = \frac{b(1 + Rk)\Delta N}{1 - b(1 + Rk)}$$

$$(32) \qquad \Delta \dot{I} = \Delta P_c - \Delta S_c = \frac{bRk \, \Delta N}{1 - b(1 + Rk)}$$

If, however, we take the longer run, and investigate the effect of a change, ΔN, on the equilibrium values of the variables, we must solve together equations (2), (3), and (6) with $\dot{I}$ put at zero in (6) since in the long run inventories are brought into normal alignment with sales, on the assumption of stability. These three equations together with $\dot{I} = 0$ yield the equilibrium value of Y already obtained. The pertinent multipliers, relating changes in Y, S_c, P_c, and $\dot{I}$ to ΔN, are $\Delta Y/\Delta N = 1/(1 - b)$; $\Delta S_c/\Delta N = b/(1 - b)$; $\Delta P_c/\Delta N = b/(1 - b)$; and $\Delta \dot{I}/\Delta N = 0$, for in the long run inventory accumulation is at a rate of zero for any value of N. In this case, however, we can apply a new incremental ratio, namely $\Delta I/\Delta N$ which according to equation (4) is necessarily equal to $k \, \Delta S_c/\Delta N$ or $kb/(1 - b)$.

These considerations suggest that we might call the two stability conditions the "short-run" and the "long-run" stability conditions. It happens in the present case that $(1 + Rk)b < 1$ implies $b < 1$, because we assumed both R and k positive. If, however, we had postulated a negative relation between inventories and sales, or if we postulate one now just to test the concepts, it appears that in the short-run equations (2), (3), and (5) will be dynamically compatible if $b(1 + Rk)$ is less than 1, while in the long-run equations (2), (3) and $\dot{I} = 0$ will be dynamically incompatible if b exceeds 1. Thus the relations

(33) $b > 1 > b(1 + Rk)$

which may hold if k is negative, would make the set of equations valid for the determination of Y in terms of N for a given value of I, but would lead to divergence of Y and I from their long-run equilibrium values, $\bar{I}$ and $\bar{Y}$.* If we operate on equation (6) this point becomes clear. Assuming $b(1 + Rk)$ less than 1, we have, according to equation (6),

(34) $\dot{I} = RkS_c - RI$

$$= \left[\frac{R}{1 - b(1 + Rk)} \right] (1 - b)(\bar{I} - I)$$

as may be seen by substituting equation (2) into (3), then (3) into (6), and using for $\bar{I}$ the expression already obtained in equation (19). Since R is positive, and since $1 - b(1 + Rk)$ is positive if equations (2), (3), and (5) are to hold, $1 - b$ must be positive if I is to increase when below $\bar{I}$, decrease when above it. If b exceeds 1, $1 - b$ is negative and the spread between I and its equilibrium value increases at a geometric rate equal to R times the ratio of $1 - b$ to $1 - b(1 + Rk)$. (Since $\bar{I}$ is constant, $I - \bar{I}$ changes over time at the same absolute rate as I.) Thus "long-run stability" of equilibrium requires $b < 1$, while "short-run stability" requires $b(1 + Rk) < 1$.

We next inquire into the condition for oscillation of Y and I over time. According to (26), oscillation will occur if

(35) $4[-(-rR)(1 - b)] > [1 - b(1 + Rk)]^2 r^2$

(since **B** is zero in the present set of equations). If the equations are stable, $1 - b(1 + Rk)$ is positive and, since r and R are necessarily positive, we may divide both sides by $Rr[1 - b(1 + Rk)]^2$ to obtain

(36) $\dfrac{4(1 - b)}{[1 - b(1 + Rk)]^2} > \dfrac{r}{R}$

---

* In other words, a static system composed of equations (2), (3), and (5) is stable and consequently a valid basis for analysis in the short run when I may be considered constant; a static system composed of (2), (3), and $\dot{I} = 0$ is unstable.

Supposing that the equations are stable, both sides of this inequality are positive. It follows that oscillation is the less likely, (a) the larger is r, (b) the smaller is R, (c) the smaller is k, and, if k is positive, (d) the smaller is b.*

The plausibility of this result may be made clear by the following considerations. First, a very large value of r relative to R is essentially the condition that for all practical purposes we may take equation (5) as giving P_c, setting aside equation (7). If, that is, production adjusts so rapidly toward the value shown in equation (5) that any change in the value of I during the interim can be ignored, the entire system reduces to the equations (2), (3), and (5) taken together which, as we have seen, involve the steady adjustment of I according to equation (34) and corresponding steady adjustment of Y, since Y is determined as in equation (29). Oscillation, then, may be said in this formulation of the inventory problem to be a result of the delay in adjustment of production.

Second, a large value of R tends to increase the likelihood of oscillation for two reasons. To make them both clear, let us consider for a moment what happens to production when, after a period during which all variables are close to their equilibrium values, the value of N increases, raising the equilibrium values and causing the variables to be immediately out of line with their equilibrium values. Production must rise, eventually, to the higher equilibrium level. If it rose steadily toward that level, never exceeding it, sales would never be less than production because sales exceed their original level by $b(\Delta N + \Delta P_c)$, and the new equilibrium level of P_c exceeds the old by $b\Delta N/(1 - b)$ as we saw earlier, and $b(\Delta N + \Delta P_c)$ is always greater than ΔP_c for values of ΔP_c less than $b\Delta N/(1 - b)$. Consequently there is no accumulation of inventory, and there is disaccumulation to the extent that P_c lagged behind S_c. If, then, k is positive, P_c must for some period of time exceed S_c; it must consequently exceed its new equilibrium.

If there is no oscillation, P_c recedes steadily from its peak toward the new equilibrium; oscillation occurs if inventory accumulation exceeds the amount required to bring it up to k times the new equilibrium level of sales; for in that case there must be a period of disaccumulation; and the consequent lowering of the rate of production is, of course, aggravated by the multiplier effect. If disaccumulation proceeds beyond the equilibrium level, production must swing upward and go above equilibrium, and so on.

Now it is clear that there are two factors which may keep production

---

* The statement regarding b is the only one which may not be evident from inspection. The reader can prove the statement by letting b increase to $b + h$ in the ratio on the left-hand side of (36) and proving that the new ratio exceeds the original. Multiplying out and regrouping he can obtain the statement that a known positive quantity exceeds zero which is certainly true.

from adjusting with sufficient alacrity. One is the height of the production peak above the new equilibrium, the other is the rate at which it must taper off in order not to accumulate excess inventory. The greater the rate of inventory accumulation, the speedier must be the decline of production toward its new equilibrium in order that accumulation of inventory not go beyond $k\bar{S}_c$, that is, beyond $\bar{I}$. And the greater the "current multiplier," the steeper must be this decline. The parameter R affects both of these factors. A large value of R, like a large value of k or of b, makes for a large value of the "current multiplier" [see equation (31)] both raising the numerator and lowering the denominator. It raises the numerator by raising the level of production corresponding to any *given* level of sales; and it lowers the denominator by raising the level of *sales* corresponding to any given rise in the value of N. The parameter R also represents the rate of inventory accumulation in the sense that, for any given value of the multiplier, the larger is R the greater is the rate of inventory accumulation. In other words, a large value of R both raises the height of the production peak and raises the absolute rate of inventory accumulation, in this manner entailing in both respects a steep decline of production toward its new equilibrium. Thus the greater the value of R, the greater is the likelihood of excess accumulation of inventory, followed by a swing below equilibrium to disaccumulate and, by repetition of the argument, followed again by a swing above, and so on.

The parameters b and k affect the likelihood of oscillation via their influence on the size of the multiplier; the larger b or k the higher is the initial peak of production; but a high value of $b(1 + Rk)$ on account of a large value of b does not to so great an extent as a large value of R entail a more rapid rate of inventory accumulation. (It does to some extent because of the multiplier effect on the level of sales and hence on inventory accumulation.) A large value of k indicates a high multiplier, and has consequently an effect similar to that of b; but since a large k indicates a large inventory requirement, it does not raise the rate of accumulation relative to requirements in the same manner as does a large R.

This completes our study of the "continuous-adjustment" case of the inventory problem; we turn next to its periodic treatment. Before doing so, however, several remarks are in order regarding the "time dimensions" of the variables.

Variables such as national income, consumption sales, production of consumption goods, etc., are considered to be rates per unit of time. Consumption of 150, for example, may be interpreted as consumption at a rate of 150 billion dollars per year; *i.e.*, as consumption at an "annual rate" of 150 billion dollars. We suppose the value of C to be continuously variable, so that we are not limited to consideration of values only for successive years. Thus consumption in July may be at an annual rate of 150 and in August may be at an annual rate of 160. July consumption would then be, in absolute terms, $^{150}/_{12}$, or 12.5, and in August consumption in absolute terms would be $^{160}/_{12}$, or 13.3. Furthermore the comparison of July with August could be stated as an increase in the annual rate of consumption at a rate of 10 per month, or as an increase in the annual rate of consumption at a rate of 120 per year. It would at the same time be an increase in the monthly rate of consumption of $^{10}/_{12} = 0.83$ per month or, if we wished to measure it so, an increase in the monthly rate of consumption at a rate of 10 per year. It is convenient but not necessary to measure the rate of change of a variable in terms of the same unit of time as we measure the variable itself, restricting ourselves to discussion of the annual rate of change of the annual rate of consumption, or the monthly rate of change of the monthly rate of consumption.

The value of total inventory, on the contrary, is not a measurement per unit of time; it is an absolute-value figure. The ratio of inventory to sales consequently depends on the time unit of measure of sales. If sales are at an annual rate of 120, and inventory is equal to 40, we have $I = S_c/3$; but if sales are measured on a monthly rate, the same sales are 10 per month and the ratio of inventory to sales is given by $I = 4S_c$. Thus the value of the parameter k is not invariant with respect to the time unit of measurement of variables.

The rate of inventory accumulation must be expressed on a per-unit-of-time basis; it is convenient but not necessary to express it in terms of the same time unit over which C, Y, etc. are measured. But if we do not measure it with respect to that same time unit, it is not true that $\dot{I} = P_c - S_c$; for if $P_c = 120$ and $S_c = 100$, measured at annual rates, the annual rate of inventory accumulation is 10, and the monthly rate would be 0.83 or $(P_c - S_c)/12$. Thus the formulation of equation (13) commits us to a unit of measure for inventory accumulation the same as for the measurement of C, Y, etc. If we had divided the right-hand side of equation (13) by, say, 12 to put it on a monthly rate basis, then we should have to divide the parameter R by 12 in equation (5) if the rate of accumulation is not to be altered by the shift in unit of measure. In like manner, equation (7) must be taken to express the rate of adjustment of the rate of production in annual terms if in equation (8) Y is to denote the annual rate of change of income. This is important because the stability criteria as presented in (27) and (28) would be altered if in (9) and (13) the measurements of $\dot{I}$ and $\dot{Y}$ were on different bases. If, for example, $\dot{I}$ were on a monthly basis while $\dot{Y}$ were on an annual basis, all the parameters in equation (13) should be multiplied by 12 before applying the stability conditions.

It becomes useful, consequently, to use a single unit of measure of time for all variables and for all rates of change. If the parameters a, b, and k relate to annual measures, then we must either measure all rates of change on an annual-rate basis, or adjust these three parameters accordingly. The adjustments would be as follows. For consumption,

$$C = a + bY$$

$$C/12 = a/12 + bY/12$$

or, using C' and Y' for monthly consumption and income,

$$C' = a/12 + bY'$$

Thus the parameter a must be divided by 12; the parameter b is kept unchanged.

For inventories, if S_c is to be converted from an annual to a monthly basis, and the value of I is not to be affected in equation (4), k must be multiplied by 12 so that, using S_c' for $S_c/12$, $I = k(^{12}\!/_{12})S_c = 12kS_c'$.

These and similar considerations will become even more important when we take up the case of period analysis, to which we turn now.

Periodic Treatment of the Inventory Problem*

The foregoing treatment of the accumulation of inventory and the adjustment of production considered production to adjust in continuous fashion toward the level dictated by sales in conjunction with the desired rate of inventory accumulation. In this section we shall consider production to adjust in discrete steps; the mathematical method to be followed differs substantially from that of the foregoing section, but the results of the analysis do not differ markedly. Since neither formulation can claim to be an exact replica of the economic system it attempts to represent, there is some advantage in putting the hypotheses into alternative forms to test, so to speak, the "invariance" of the conclusions with respect to the choice of formulation.

We assume in this section that production plans are made periodically, that production is at a constant rate during the interval between planning decisions. Periodically—and we shall assume periods of constant length— sales, production, and inventory are compared and production is adjusted to match expected sales plus or minus some intended rate of accumulation of inventory over the next ensuing period.

* For an extensive and very illustrative treatment of the inventory problem, see L. A. Metzler, "Nature and Stability of Inventory Cycles," *Review of Economic Statistics*, vol. 23, p. 113; "Factors Governing the Length of Inventory Cycles," *Review of Economic Statistics*, vol. 29, p. 1; and "Business Cycles and the Modern Theory of Employment," *American Economic Review*, vol. 36, p. 278.

We shall again assume a consumption-income relationship to operate without lag,

$$(37) \qquad\qquad S_c(t) = a + bY(t)$$

We again distinguish only three components of the national-income total, defined as before,

$$(38) \qquad\qquad Y(t) = P_c(t) + N(t) + i(t)$$

And the exact definition of $i(t)$, the rate of inventory accumulation, now that we are considering values of the variables at only separate points in time, is

$$(39) \qquad\qquad i(t) = I(t + 1) - I(t)$$

Equation (39) requires some explanation. Variables such as $Y(t)$, $C(t)$, $i(t)$, etc., are considered to have constant values during the period, *i.e.*, between the terminal points of the period; they are variables which are necessarily measured as rates over time. $I(t)$, on the other hand, is not a rate over time but a value at a fixed point in time; so long as $i(t)$ is not zero, the value of $I(t)$ changes during the period. Thus we must measure I not *over* a period of time but at the terminal points of a period. We consequently adopt the convention of measuring I at the *beginning* of the period to which t refers. (The value of t is thus taken to denote the period between two points in time, not one of the points.)

We require one more equation, expressing the behavior of production in terms of sales and inventory. Production of consumption goods is assumed to follow the relationship

$$(40) \qquad\qquad P_c(t) = S_c(t - 1) + R[kS_c(t - 1) - I(t)]$$

And the value of $i(t)$ is given by

$$(41) \qquad\qquad i(t) = P_c(t) - S_c(t)$$

Equation (40) contains in effect two different hypotheses. One is that sales during any given period are expected, at the beginning of that period when plans are made, to equal sales of the period before. The other is that producers consider "normal" inventory to equal k times sales, and that they attempt, during any given period, to reduce any difference between actual and normal inventory by R times that difference, so that $\bar{I} - I(t + 1)$ will be only $1 - R$ times as great as $\bar{I} - I(t)$. Both of these hypotheses deserve comment.

The first hypothesis contained in equation (40), namely that sales during the period to come are anticipated equal to sales of the period just closed, assumes that producers do not project trends. They may fail to project trends either because they do not believe in trends, *i.e.*, do not believe in the reliability of projections, or simply because it is easier to follow a rule of thumb and adjust inventory later than to bother with projections of sales. If the period is short, *i.e.*, if plans are readjusted frequently, a mistaken estimate of sales may be taken currently in the form of accumulation or disaccumulation of inventory and the difference made up out of later production for or use of inventory.   If, however, we wished to allow for projection of trends, we might replace the first term on the right-hand side of equation (40), that is, $S_c(t - 1)$, with a new term, "anticipated sales," denoted by $S_c'(t)$ with the equation of anticipation as follows:

$$(42) \qquad S_c'(t) = S_c(t - 1) + [S_c(t - 1) - S_c(t - 2)]$$
$$= S_c(t - 2) + 2\,\Delta S_c$$

where ΔS_c stands for the change in sales between the period just recorded and the immediately preceding period. Equation (42) would represent "linear" projection of sales; *i.e.*, it would express the hypothesis that producers expect, not that sales in the coming period will equal those of the period just past, but that sales are expected to rise over those of the period just past by the same amount as immediately past sales rose over sales of the prior period.   An alternative hypothesis of anticipation might be

$$(43) \qquad S_c'(t) = S_c(t - 1)[S_c(t - 1)/S_c(t - 2)]$$

Equation (43) would project not the absolute rate of sales increase but the relative rate, *i.e.*, the ratio of increase. We choose equation (40) because of its algebraic simplicity.

Just as in the preceding section, we adopt the hypothesis that the rate of inventory accumulation tends to be at a rate proportional to the total accumulation necessary to bring inventory into normal relation with sales. This particular formula for the behavior of I is chosen largely because of its mathematical tractability; it is workable in algebra. A principal characteristic of this formula is that it has inventory accumulation—if sales are constant—dwindling at a fixed proportional rate, approaching but never quite reaching zero. For most purposes it does no harm to suppose that our formula gives way, when inventory is about equal to kS_c, to a "straight-line" trend; *i.e.*, when $\overline{I} - I(t)$ is very small, i is kept equal to $R[\overline{I} - I(t)]$ for the next $1/R$ periods and the difference wiped out once for all, rather than reduced successively to $R[\overline{I} - I(t + 1)]$ etc. Or we may simply suppose that when $\overline{I} - I(t)$ is rather small, the difference is ignored. Thus the infinite diminution of the difference between actual and normal inventory need not be considered a "peculiarity" of the formula.

An alternative type of behavior with a good claim to validity might be this:

$$i(t) = R[kS_c - I(t)]$$
$$i(t + 1) = R[kS_c - I(t)]$$
$$\cdots\cdots\cdots\cdots\cdots\cdots\cdots\cdots\cdots\cdots\cdots$$
$$i(t + 1/R - 1) = R[kS_c - I(t)]$$
$$i(t + 1/R) = 0$$

That is, supposing S_c constant, any discrepancy between $\bar{I}$ and $I(t)$ is made up at a fixed rate over the next $1/R$ periods of time, beyond which i is zero. This is less plausible, however, when we consider that S_c is not necessarily constant; as long as S_c is changing, producers must change their production plans periodically, and it seems more plausible to assume that bygones are bygones and the current rate of inventory accumulation is always kept in line with the current discrepancy between I and kS_c. Otherwise the current rate of production is made to depend on certain facts of past history, such as the particular period in the past when sales changed. This dependence on the past may not be absurd, since it may lead to easier bookkeeping to lay out additive production plans, superimposing one change on top of another rather than taking new bearings on each planning occasion. Consequently, our choice of the form of equation (40) must be considered only one of several possible forms of the relationship, chosen for its simplicity under algebraic manipulation rather than because of its compelling plausibility.*

A remark is due on the value of R. We suppose that R must not be taken to exceed 1, for in that case producers would consciously have planned for excess inventory at the end of the period if they started out with deficiency, and vice versa.† The limiting case, then, is that of $R = 1$, in

* For reasons that are intuitively clear, certain forms of inventory behavior necessarily lead to oscillatory patterns of production. If production is raised and kept at a level such that it exceeds sales by a fixed amount, that difference being the inventory accumulation over a stretch of time, and production is then dropped toward the level of sales at the end of the period because the required deficiency of inventory has been made up, sales will fall according to $C = a + bY$ and so, consequently, will kS_c. Inventory will at once appear excessive, so that production must fall so far as to lie below the (lowered) level of sales until inventory has been brought into line with the lower level of sales, at which time the ensuing rise in production will again raise S_c, hence kS_c, and so entail a period of positive accumulation again, and so on indefinitely. (Stability of the pattern, *i.e.*, whether the waves damp down or grow, again depends on the same sort of parameter considerations as are now familiar.)

† On the other hand, projection of sales trends may lead to behavior similar to that implied by a value of R in excess of 1.

which the "accumulation period" is identical with the "planning period." Should we suppose these periods related to each other?

The length of the planning period probably wants to relate to the general behavior of sales. Producers review plans, we may suppose, at intervals not so great that sales variation of serious magnitude can be expected within the period. If fluctuations in sales have traditionally been sluggish, relatively infrequent reviews of plans are safe; if the sales market is volatile, producers may be obliged to review plans with great frequency. At the same time, there is probably a cost involved not only in making plans but in executing changes in the rate of production; sales trends expected shortly to reverse themselves may be ignored because of the cost of following them closely with quick changes in the level of production. Thus we may suppose that the length of the planning period varies inversely with the volatility of the sales market, and directly with the cost or trouble of reviewing plans and changing production rates.

The rate of accumulation of inventory may be supposed related to some extent to the volatility of sales markets; if long term changes in sales come quickly rather than gradually, quick inventory adjustment may appear advisable. On the production side, the rate of accumulation of inventory would seem to be related not so much to the cost or trouble of initiating changes in the production rate, but to the cost or trouble of making large changes. For example, suppose $S_c = 100$ per period, suppose $k = 2$ so that $\bar{I} = 200$. Now let sales rise to 120. The total required accumulation of inventory is 40, that is, $2(120 - 100)$. If this entire amount is accumulated in one period, production will have to rise from 100 to 160 in one period, and fall from 160 to 120 in the next.* If such large changes in the rate of production are difficult, costly, or impossible, then the rate of accumulation will have to be slower, e.g., 10 in the first period, so that P_c rises to 130 and tapers off to 120.

Thus there may be some relation, but not a very close one, between the rate of inventory accumulation and the length of the period; the relation is not so close that we can closely limit the value of R.

Finally we might remark on the value of k. If the variables Y, S_c, and P_c are measured on a monthly basis, and $k = 3$, then inventory tends to equal three months' sales. Suppose we lengthen the period, so that Y, S_c, and P_c are measured on a quarterly basis. What change must we make

---

* This, of course, is not a description of what would happen throughout the economy if the general level of sales rose; in that case a rise in production from 100 to 160 would lead to a further rise in sales. The arithmetic of this paragraph refers to the considerations pertinent to the reaction of a single firm. Note also that if it takes one period for the rise in sales to be noted, inventories will have fallen by 20 and the rate of production would have to be $120 + 20 + 2(120 - 100) = 180$.

in the value of k? According to the considerations of the previous section, it would appear that we must—if we wish to indicate the same inventory behavior—put the value of k at 1, so that inventory equals one quarter's sales as before. But there may be a relation between the value of k and the length of the planning period. It may be that one of the determinants of the size of "normal inventory" is the extent to which plans may go awry within a single period; inventory is the cushion between sales and production. If the planning period is lengthened, inventory requirements may be greater. Since there is perhaps some relation between the value of R and the length of the planning period, there may consequently be some relation between the values of R and k.* But it is not a close one, so far as these considerations show. We shall consequently place no restrictions on any of the parameters except—as noted above—that $R > 1$ is excluded.

We proceed now to a solution of the equations. The solution we are after will take the form of a relation between $P_c(t)$ and preceding values of P_c; we assume N constant again for simplicity.

The first step toward solution is to substitute equation (37) into equation (40), obtaining

$$
\begin{aligned}
(44) \quad P_c(t) &= [a + bY(t-1)][1 + Rk] - RI(t) \\
&= (a + bN)(1 + Rk) + bP_c(t-1)(1 + Rk) - RI(t) \\
&= A + BP_c(t-1) + CI(t)
\end{aligned}
$$

where

$$(45) \qquad\qquad\qquad A = (a + bN)(1 + Rk)$$

$$(46) \qquad\qquad\qquad B = b(1 + Rk)$$

$$(47) \qquad\qquad\qquad C = -R$$

We have, in equation (44), a linear relation between $P_c(t)$ and the current value of $I(t)$ (*i.e.*, the value at the beginning of the period) and the preceding value of P_c. Next we develop a relation between the value of $I(t)$ and the current or preceding values of $I(t)$ and $P_c(t)$. Substituting (41) this time into what we may call the definition of I in terms of i, we have

$$
\begin{aligned}
(48) \quad I(t) &= I(t-1) + i(t-1) = I(t-1) + P_c(t-1) - S_c(t-1) \\
&= I(t-1) - a - bN + (1-b)P_c(t-1) \\
&= \mathbf{A} + \mathbf{B}I(t-1) + \mathbf{C}P_c(t-1)
\end{aligned}
$$

* Notice that this argument holds only for changes in the length of a *planning* period, not for changes in the "accounting" period according to which our variables are measured. Converting from a monthly to a quarterly basis for the *measurement* of S_c, P_c, and Y involves just the straightforward conversion of the value of k.

where

(49) $$\mathbf{A} = -(a + bN)$$

(50) $$\mathbf{B} = 1$$

(51) $$\mathbf{C} = (1 - b)$$

Equations (44) and (48) give us I and P_c in terms of their own and each other's current or past values. We shall next arrange them so as to give P_c in terms of its own past values. To do this, we first substitute (48) into (44):

(52) $\quad P_c(t) = A + BP_c(t - 1) + CA + C\mathbf{B}I(t - 1) + C\mathbf{C}P_c(t - 1)$

Equation (46) gives $P_c(t)$ in terms of $I(t - 1)$ and $P_c(t - 1)$. We can eliminate $I(t - 1)$ if we are willing to insert into our equation the value of $P_c(t - 2)$. For if we subtract, from the right-hand side of equation (52), the equivalent of $\mathbf{B}P_c(t - 1)$, using equation (44) for the purpose, the terms in $I(t - 1)$ will cancel out,

(53) $\qquad \mathbf{B}P_c(t - 1) = A\mathbf{B} + \mathbf{B}\mathbf{B}P_c(t - 2) + C\mathbf{B}I(t - 1)$

Using equations (52) and (53) we have

(54) $\quad P_c(t) - \mathbf{B}P_c(t - 1)$

$$= [A(1 - \mathbf{B}) + CA] + (B + C\mathbf{C})P_c(t - 1) - \mathbf{B}\mathbf{B}P_c(t - 2)$$

Or, finally, noticing that $(1 - \mathbf{B}) = 0$ according to the present parameters,

(55) $\qquad P_c(t) = CA + (B + \mathbf{B} + C\mathbf{C})P_c(t - 1) - \mathbf{B}\mathbf{B}P_c(t - 2)$

This constitutes the "solution"; it is a formula giving the value of P_c during any period in terms of the values of P_c during the two preceding periods. We could similarly have eliminated P_c and obtained a solution for $I(t)$ in terms of $I(t - 1)$ and $I(t - 2)$.

Let us inquire first whether there is an equilibrium value for P_c. What do we mean by an equilibrium value? It cannot mean, as it did in the preceding chapter, a value such that if it occurs once it will repeat itself; for since any given value of P_c depends on both the two preceding values, the fact that it recurred once would not mean necessarily that it recurred again. It would consequently be of little interest. If, however, there is a value such that its occurrence twice consecutively implies its occurrence a third consecutive time, then we may state that its occurrence twice consecutively implies its indefinite repetition (so long as neither the parameters nor the given value of N change) since only the two preceding values are pertinent to the determination of P_c. If two occurrences give rise to a third, then the second and third give rise to a fourth, and so on indefinitely. We inquire, then, what value will occur a third consecutive time whenever it has occurred twice consecutively.

Such a value must satisfy the following equation; and any value of P_c which satisfies the equation is such a value.

$$(56) \qquad \overline{P}_c = C\mathbf{A} + (B + \mathbf{B} + C\mathbf{C} - B\mathbf{B})\overline{P}_c$$

$$= \frac{C\mathbf{A}}{1 - B - \mathbf{B} - C\mathbf{C} + B\mathbf{B}} = \frac{a + bN}{1 - b}$$

as is seen by substituting for A, B, etc. the parameters of the original equations. The equilibrium value of I is of course equal to $k\overline{P}_c = k\overline{S}_c = k(\overline{Y} - N)$, $\overline{Y}$ being given by substitution of $\overline{P}_c$ for P_c in equation (38), and i being put at zero to denote equilibrium of I.

A convenient representation of equation (55), now that we know the value of $\overline{P}_c$, is the following:

$$(57) \quad [\overline{P}_c - P_c(t)]$$
$$= (B + \mathbf{B} + C\mathbf{C})[\overline{P}_c - P_c(t - 1)] - B\mathbf{B}[\overline{P}_c - P_c(t - 2)]$$

as may be obtained by subtracting both sides of (55) from $\overline{P}_c$ and identifying $C\mathbf{A}$ as $(1 - B - \mathbf{B} - C\mathbf{C} + B\mathbf{B})\overline{P}_c$ by virtue of (56.) Substituting now the original parameter values we have

$$(58) \quad [\overline{P}_c - P_c(t)] = [1 + b(1 + Rk) - R(1 - b)][\overline{P}_c - P_c(t - 1)]$$
$$- b(1 + Rk)[\overline{P}_c - P_c(t - 2)]$$

With formula (58) or formula (55) (after substitution of original parameters) we could trace out the path over time of P_c, given any two initial consecutive values or—what is the same thing—given the distances of any two original values from the equilibrium value computed from (56). But generally we do not want to trace out the entire path over time, we want only to know some of the characteristics of that path. We again make the usual inquiries: does the path converge on equilibrium or does it diverge? Does it, in its convergence or divergence, oscillate about the equilibrium value, or does it move steadily upward or downward?

Again at this point we consult outside information, it being beyond the scope of this chapter to analyze in detail the "second-order difference equation" represented by (58). In the Appendix we shall outline the complete analysis. In this chapter we shall simply assert that if the current value of any variable, $X(t)$, is related to its two immediately preceding values by a linear relation of the form

$$(59) \qquad X(t) = p + qX(t - 1) - rX(t - 2)$$

where q and r are positive, the equilibrium represented by $X = p/(1 - q + r)$ is stable if and only if

(60) $$r < 1$$

(61) $$q - r < 1$$

The value of X will oscillate about that equilibrium value if and only if

(62) $$4r > q^2$$

Otherwise it will move continuously—after at most one change in direction*—toward or away from its equilibrium value.

In general there will be one change in direction in the path of Y in the stable, nonoscillatory case. A rise in the value of N or of a entails a rise in S_c which, because of the production lag, precedes the corresponding rise in P_c. There are also rises in the equilibrium levels of P_c, Y, and I. Thus P_c must not only approach a new higher level but must for some time exceed its new equilibrium level in order to exceed S_c for a sufficient time to permit accumulation of inventory to its new equilibrium level. Thus P_c rises above its new level, turns downward, and subsequently approaches $\overline{P}_c$ from above.

That the parameter p is not involved in the stability criteria was apparent already in the fact that equation (55) could be converted to equation (57), in which P_c is measured from $\overline{P}_c$ rather than from zero. In that form the "constant" in the original equation, comparable to p of equation (59), was absent; yet it is obvious that $P_c - \overline{P}_c$ is stable with respect to zero if and only if P_c is stable with respect to $\overline{P}_c$.

It may be noticed that if (62) holds, (61) holds necessarily, so that in the case of oscillation, (60) is the stability condition. This statement follows from the fact that if $q^2 < 4r$, it is also less than $(1 + r)^2$ since $[(1 + r)^2 - 4r] = [1 - 2r + r^2] = (1 - r)^2$ which, being a square, is necessarily positive except in the case of $r = 1$ when it is zero.

In terms of the original parameters, the stability conditions are

(63) $$r = B\mathbf{B} = b(1 + Rk) < 1$$

(64) $$q - r = (B + \mathbf{B} + C\mathbf{C} - B\mathbf{B}) = 1 - R(1 - b) < 1$$

With R and k positive, (63) requires $1 - b$ positive, so that (64) necessarily holds if (63) does in the case of the present parameters. The stability

---

* Let $X(t) = 1.0X(t - 1) - 0.2X(t - 2)$, and take 10, 20 as the two initial values for X. Subsequent values will be 18, 14, 10.4, 7.6, $\cdots$ toward zero. Again, let 100, 10 be the initial values; subsequent values will be -10, -12, -10, -7.6, -5.6, -4.1, ... toward zero. Thus there may be one reversal but from then on the course is monotonic, *i.e.*, always in the same direction.

condition is, then, identical in form with that of the preceding section where the condition was [cf. equation (27)] also that $b(1 + Rk)$ not exceed 1, although the interpretation of R differed somewhat in that analysis because of the continuous rather than periodic adjustment involved.

Let us next inspect the condition for oscillation or nonoscillation. In terms of original parameters, oscillation will occur if

$$(65) \qquad 4b(1 + Rk) > [1 + b(1 + Rk) - R(1 - b)]^2$$

This is a complicated expression; offhand its interpretation is not clear. It is not even immediately obvious whether parameter values consistent with stability necessarily imply oscillation or necessarily imply nonoscillation. Let us try to narrow down the problem.

First, suppose that R were zero. In that case there would in a sense be no "inventory problem"; production would always adjust toward sales, and inventory would simply accumulate or disaccumulate over any period during which sales and production differed, but there would be no control over inventory other than through an attempt perhaps to adjust production quickly and so to minimize changes in inventory. In that case we should expect no fluctuation, since fluctuation has been seen to be inherently an inventory problem. To check this statement let us try putting $R = 0$ in inequality (65). If we do the condition becomes

$$(66) \qquad 4b > (1 + b)^2 = 1 + 2b + b^2$$
$$0 > 1 - 2b + b^2 = (1 - b)^2$$

The inequality obviously cannot hold, for the square of any quantity is positive or, in the limiting case, zero. Thus there is no oscillation unless there is conscious inventory adjustment.

Next let us go to the other extreme. We earlier argued that the maximum sensible value which we might impute to R was the value 1. If we try $R = 1$ in (65) we obtain

$$(67) \qquad 4b(1 + k) > [b(2 + k)]^2$$

or

$$(68) \qquad b < \frac{4 + 4k}{4 + 4k + k^2}$$

It is still not immediately apparent whether this inequality holds. However, if the equations are stable, $b(1 + Rk)$ is less than $+1$; with R equal to 1, stability consequently requires $b(1 + k)$ less than $+1$. Since the largest value b may have, then, is the value $1/(1 + k)$, we may check whether this value is necessarily smaller than the right-hand side of (62);

writing down this inequality and cross multiplying to remove the fraction, we have

$$(69) \qquad\qquad 4 + 4k + k^2 < 4 + 8k + 4k^2$$

which obviously holds for any positive value of k. Thus we conclude that if R equals 1, *i.e.*, if there is an "inventory-accumulation" period equal to the "production-adjustment" period, stable behavior is necessarily oscillatory.

Knowing now that $b(1 + Rk)$ must be less than 1, we can state positively that the multipliers to be derived from equation (56) and similar equilibrium equations are positive, for with Rk positive, b must be less than 1 and the denominator of (56) positive. Writing $\bar{Y}$ for $N + \bar{P}_c$ and $\bar{I}$ for $k\bar{P}_c$ we have, from (56), $\Delta\bar{Y}/\Delta N = 1 + [b/(1 - b)] = 1/(1 - b)$; $\Delta\bar{P}_c/\Delta N = b/(1 - b)$; $\Delta\bar{I}/\Delta N = kb/(1 - b)$; and all three ratios are positive. If the value of N has been constant over a sufficient period of time to allow $Y(t)$, $P_c(t)$, and $I(t)$ to approach so closely to $\bar{Y}, \bar{P}_c$, and $\bar{I}$ that we may ignore the differences, and if the value of N then changes by the amount ΔN and retains the new value for a similarly long period of time, the differences between the original values of Y, P_c, and I and their values after they have approached the new equilibria are given by those ratios. Even if the value of N changes constantly, we may still say that $[a + bN(t)]/(1 - b)$ is the "current equilibrium value" of P_c, and similarly for Y and I, meaning thereby that they are the values which, in a current sense, the variables are "approaching."

As a special case let us consider $k = 0$. According to equation (40) above, a value of zero for the parameter k implies that a zero level of inventory is normal for any level of income. But the case of $k = 0$ may also be interpreted as the hypothesis that normal inventory is some constant level, not necessarily zero; that is, we may revise the implicit normal inventory equation corresponding to (40) so that it reads $I' = h + kS_c$ and put $k = 0$ so that $I' = h$. In that event, the criteria for stability and oscillation are the same as already derived, as the reader may verify. Thus $k = 0$ corresponds to the case of normal inventory invariant with respect to the level of sales or production.

Clearly, with $k = 0$, both the stability conditions reduce to the simple condition $b < 1$. The condition for oscillation becomes

$$(70) \qquad 4b > [(1 + b) - R(1 - b)]^2$$
$$4b > (1 + b)^2 - 2R(1 + b)(1 - b) + R^2(1 - b)^2$$

Since

$$(1 + b)^2 - 4b = 1 + 2b + b^2 - 4b = 1 - 2b + b^2 = (1 - b)^2$$

we can divide (70) by $(1 - b)^2$ to obtain

(71) $$0 > R^2 - 2R\left(\frac{1 + b}{1 - b}\right) + 1$$

To find the dividing line between values of R which imply oscillation and values of R which do not, we convert (71) to a statement of equality and solve for R in terms of b,*

(72) $$R = \frac{1 + b}{1 - b} \pm \sqrt{\left(\frac{1 + b}{1 - b}\right)^2 - 1}$$

There are two dividing lines, according as the plus or minus sign is imputed to the square root. However, since the value of R cannot reasonably be supposed greater than 1, and since $(1 + b)/(1 - b)$ is itself greater than $+1$ with $1 > b > 0$, only the negative value of the square root is applicable. (Note that the value under the radical is necessarily positive with $1 > b > 0$; there is no problem of how to interpret the square root of a negative value.) It is apparent that the value of R implied by the negative root is a positive fraction; it is not less than zero since the negative root must be less in absolute value than $(1 + b)/(1 - b)$, it being the square root of the square of $(1 + b)/(1 - b)$ reduced by 1; it cannot be as great as $+1$ for that would imply

(73) $$\frac{1 + b}{1 - b} - 1 \geq \sqrt{\left(\frac{1 + b}{1 - b}\right)^2 - 1}$$

$$\left(\frac{1 + b}{1 - b}\right)^2 - 2\left(\frac{1 + b}{1 - b}\right) + 1 \geq \left(\frac{1 + b}{1 - b}\right)^2 - 1$$

$$1 \geq \frac{1 + b}{1 - b}$$

which contradicts $0 < b < 1$. Thus, between the values $R = 0$ and $R = 1$ there is a critical value of R which divides stable oscillation from stable nonoscillation in the "constant normal inventory" case; it is clearly the range of values between zero and that critical value which corresponds to nonoscillation, since putting $R = 0$ in (71) contradicts the inequality while putting $R = +1$ satisfies the inequality. Thus small values of R determine—in the stable case with $k = 0$—nonoscillatory adjustment; large values of R (up to $R = 1$) determine oscillation.†

* This solution corresponds to the standard formula for solution of a quadratic equation, to be found in any algebra text; it is obtained by the process of "completing the square."

† If, for the sake of pure mathematics, we let the value of R rise above $+1$, we find a second critical value of R corresponding to the positive square root. For

values of R above that critical value there would be no oscillation according to the criterion (62) with $k = 0$. However, the conditions (60), (61), and (62) were developed only for the case of q and r positive in (59); with R greater then $(1 + b)/(1 - b)$, $q = [1 + b(1 + Rk) - R(1 - b)]$ is negative for $b < 1$ and $k = 0$; consequently condition (62) as it stands is not applicable to such parameter values. As a matter of fact, when R exceeds $(1 + b)/(1 - b)$ and k is zero, P_c alternates about $\bar{P}_c$ since inventory accumulation invariably overshoots the mark; we discarded values of R greater than $+1$ for precisely the reason that they implied such overshooting. On the other hand, with large enough values of k, such overshooting can give rise to unstable nonoscillatory adjustment, *i.e.*, growth or decline steadily away from equilibrium. These possibilities should not be entirely discarded since a more elaborate hypothesis of "sales projection"—as discussed in connection with equation (42) and (43)—could lead to results comparable to consistent overshooting. See in this connection Professor Lloyd Metzler's articles referred in the footnote on p. 243.

CHAPTER 18

DYNAMICS—III

This chapter will take up certain dynamic aspects of the investment-income relationship. We shall investigate two problems. The first will be the study of the dynamic implications of the static investment-income relationship already used occasionally throughout the book; the other will be the reformulation of the investment-income relationship in explicitly dynamic terms, namely, in the form usually referred to as the "acceleration principle."

Dynamic Implications of Investment

In the static analysis of the earlier chapters we treated parameters as "constants" except when deliberately making controlled changes in some of their values. At any rate they were considered to be independent of the values of the variables. This was natural in static analysis, for if the values of the parameters depend on the values of the variables, they should not be considered as parameters at all but rather as variables themselves. If, for example, the parameter a in the consumption-income equation varies with the value of Y, then we should write the equation $a = p + qY$, and combine it with $C = a + bY$ to obtain, as a partial solution of the equation system, $C = p + (q + b)Y = a' + b'Y$. Thus any dependence of the parameter values on the *current* values of the variables, *i.e.*, any simultaneous relationships between parameters and variables, should be separated out and treated as relationships between variables. We might be obliged, in treating our parameters as variables, to give up the useful idea that variables can generally be identified as "economic categories"; but that is what we should have to do unless we could also identify the parameter a as an economic category.

Consequently we may assume in static analysis that the parameters of the simultaneous equations are constants, else they would be singled out as variables and treated accordingly, their relationships to other variables being expressed in equations. There may, however, be another manner in which the parameter values are dependent on the values of the variables, a manner which does not affect the status of static analysis but which must be taken into consideration when the chronological relationships of variables are taken into account. It may be, in other words, that the parameter values change over time and that their *rates of change* are geared to the values of the variables. In this case we may still perform static analysis; but we must be ready to recognize that certain values of the parameters differ, at different points in time, in a manner which depends on the values taken by the variables. In the "short run" the parameters are constant.

By way of example, the birth rate may be supposed to depend in some fashion on the level of per capita income. And the level of income may be supposed, for purposes of illustration, to depend in some fashion on the size of the population in the sense that the value of some parameter in the system—in the consumption equation, the tax equation, or the investment equation—reflects among other things the size of the total population. In that event, the value of the parameter which is affected by the size of the population changes over time in a manner depending, since it depends on the birth rate, on the level of income over that period of time. If, however, our static analysis is concerned with short periods of time the population may be taken as constant; however great the birth rate, we may take a "short run" so short that the population is virtually constant during the interval of the short run. And we may still discuss, through our static analysis, the implications of *alternative* values of the parameters including alternative sizes of total population.

Now there is one economic variable excluded from our static analysis whose rate of change is necessarily related to the values of one of the variables, namely the total stock of accumulated capital goods. For investment, a variable never absent from our system and whose value is never taken to be necessarily zero, can be identified as the rate of change over time of that stock of capital equipment, or at least of some part of the total stock. Similarly there is the economic variable, total wealth, or a variant of it, total private wealth, which is necessarily changing over time in a manner determined by the values of the variables, since its rate of growth is given (according to certain definitions which are generally appropriate to our analysis) by the difference between national income and consumption or, in the case of private wealth, by the difference between disposable income and consumption. ("Private wealth" denotes here the difference between total wealth and that part of total wealth represented by the net assets of some or all government bodies.)

If, then, we suppose that the rate of investment, the rate of consumption, the rate of taxation, or any of the other variables of the system are influenced by these aggregates of assets, the structure of the consumption, investment, or taxation equation is to be considered as changing over time in a manner partly determined by the rate of investment, the level of income, the rate of consumption, etc. It is the purpose of the present section to investigate the implications of the identification of I, $Y - C$, or $Y - T_x - C$ with the rates of change of certain stocks of assets.

First let us look at the consumption equation, ordinarily represented by

$C = a + bY$ or by $C = a + bX$ where X denotes disposable income. Let us now suppose that, when wealth is taken into account, the equation is to be written as

$$(1) \qquad\qquad C = a + bY + pA$$

where A (for "assets") denotes total wealth. We take both b and p to be positive; consumption varies directly not only with the level of income but also with the amount of total wealth. The argument would be that the rate of consumption is limited to some extent by the desire to save, *i.e.*, to accumulate wealth; and the greater the amount of wealth the less the desire to accumulate and hence the greater the freedom to consume. (If the reader prefers psychological arguments to the effect that greater wealth leads to a greater pressure to save—*for any given level of income*— he may interpret p as negative; no damage is done thereby to the analysis which follows.) Since assets can grow only with the passage of time— outside of gifts from abroad or damage due to the elements—we may take A as constant at any point in time and substitute $a' = a + pA$ in the equation and eliminate A for static analysis.

Next let us look at the investment equation. Instead of relating investment linearly only to income let us also relate it to the level of total capital goods, denoted by A',

$$(2) \qquad\qquad I = u + vY - wA'$$

where we suppose v and w positive. The incremental relation of I to A' is supposed negative on the grounds that the necessity to construct productive equipment is the less, the greater the stock of such equipment already in possession. Again, for static analysis, we may consider A' as fixed in value since it, too, can change only with the passage of time except for certain occurrences such as gifts or damage due to the elements. (We need not, of course, eliminate A' and A from static analysis by suppressing their identities; if we wish to investigate the relative effects of their alternative values on the values of the other variables we should keep, for example, $a + pA$ in equation (1) rather than condense it into a'.)

The dynamic element comes in at the next step, the identification of A and of A'. We define A' so that

$$(3) \qquad\qquad I = \dot{A}'$$

That is, A' represents the cumulative sum of investment to date, and investment is the rate of change of A'. For simplicity of analysis we shall tentatively define A according to

$$(4) \qquad \dot{A} = (Y - T_x) - C = I + (G - T_x) + (E - M)$$

where E and M denote exports and imports respectively, and G denotes government expenditure for goods and services. Thus A represents only "private wealth," which we assume the pertinent variable for the personal-consumption equation. To simplify the analysis we shall assume that $G - T_x$ and $E - M$ are not large relative to I, or, conversely, that some part of $G - T_x$ or $E - M$ belongs in the rate of change of A, so that for practical purposes we can identify A with A' and rewrite equations (1) and (2) with only A and not A'. (So long as their rates of change are identical we may do this; if A and A' differ by some fixed amount—some "initial" discrepancy related, perhaps, to the monetary stock—we can make allowance for this discrepancy in either of the parameters a or u.)

Solving the static equations, and using for the purpose only $Y = C + I$, we have

$$(5) \qquad Y = \frac{(a + u) + (p - w)A}{1 - b - v} = H + KA$$

In passing we may note the formula for the multiplier relating ΔY to ΔA; it is $(p - w)$ times the multiplier relating to either a or u. A change in the value of A has the effect of raising a by $p\,\Delta A$ and of lowering u by $w\,\Delta A$. Stability of the static equations requires $b + v < 1$ for reasons made clear earlier.

We now investigate the patterns of Y, A, and I over time. In particular we inquire whether there is an equilibrium value for A, for Y, for I, and, if so, whether it represents a stable equilibrium in the sense that from any initial set of values the variables approach their equilibrium values. Clearly equilibrium occurs only when $I = 0$, for otherwise the value of A would be changing, which contradicts the notion of equilibrium. Similarly it is clear that $I = 0$ implies $\dot{Y} = 0$, etc., for according to (5) the value of Y will change only if that of A changes (aside from any shifts in parameter values).

Similarly, if the value of A tends to approach its equilibrium value, that of Y also tends to approach its equilibrium value, from the same or from the opposite direction—i.e., from above or below—according as $p - w$ is positive or negative. An adequate analysis then of this equilibrium question will involve checking the tendency of I to approach zero. Substituting the solution value of Y, using the summary parameters H and K, of equation (5) into equation (2),

$$(6) \qquad I = \dot{A} = u + vH + (vK - w)A$$

Putting $\dot{A} = 0$ yields the equilibrium value

$$(7) \qquad \bar{A} = \frac{-(u + vH)}{vK - w}$$

Equation (6) may now be rewritten in terms of $\bar{A}$,

$$(8) \qquad \dot{A} = (vK - w)(A - \bar{A})$$

The rate of change of A is proportional to the difference between A and $\bar{A}$. Stability requires that when A exceeds $\bar{A}$ (*i.e.*, when $A - \bar{A}$ is positive) A should decrease, and vice versa. Stability requires, then, that $vK - w$ be negative. In order that $\bar{A}$ have a positive value—and a negative value would make sense only with difficulty—$u + vH$ must be positive. [If the value of $\bar{A}$ is negative, we may suppose this to indicate that the value of A goes to zero and, since it cannot go below zero, stays there. It could not rise for, from any positive value, it would decrease according to (8) if the equations are stable.]

In terms of original parameters, the stability condition is that

$$(9) \qquad \frac{v(p - w)}{1 - b - v} - w < 0$$

which may be rewritten, after separating terms in w and canceling the denominator which is known to be positive,

$$(10) \qquad vp < w(1 - b)$$

or

$$\frac{v}{w} < \frac{1 - b}{p}$$

or

$$\frac{v}{1 - b} < \frac{w}{p}$$

Identifying these parameters in terms of incremental ratios out of equations (1) and (2) we may state the stability condition as follows: the ratio of the income effect on investment to the asset effect on investment must be less than the ratio of the income effect on saving to the asset effect on saving; or that the ratio of the income effect on investment to the income effect on saving must be less than the ratio of the asset effect on investment to the asset effect on saving. (The asset effect on investment is a negative effect, as it is on saving.)*

It should be observed that the condition for stability of long-run equilibrium is only the condition that, in the static equations, $\Delta I/\Delta A$ should be negative. For, substituting in the investment equation (2) the solution for Y in terms of A [equation (5)] we have

---

* The reference to "saving" follows from the identification of the current rate of saving as $Y - C = Y - a - sY - pA = -a + (1 - b)Y - pA$

(11) $$\Delta I = v\,\Delta Y - w\,\Delta A$$

$$= v\left(\frac{p-w}{1-b-v}\right)\Delta A - w\,\Delta A$$

The stability condition for long-run equilibrium is or is not met according as $\Delta I/\Delta A$ is negative or positive in (11). It may also be observed that if $p - w$ is negative the long-run equilibrium is necessarily stable, always assuming that equation (5) represents a stable solution. For $1 - b - v$ is positive if equation (5) is to hold; and since v and w are taken to be positive, $\Delta I/\Delta A$ is necessarily negative if w exceeds p. This is the case, as is seen directly from (5), in which $\Delta Y/\Delta A$ is negative; a higher value of A reduces investment more than it raises consumption and the net effect on income is depressing. In that case ΔI is negative both directly because of the higher value of A and indirectly because of the induced lower value of Y. As a special case of negative $p - w$ we may deduce that if there is no asset effect on consumption, $i.e.$, if p is zero, the long-run equilibrium is necessarily stable if the short-run solution is stable.

It may be observed that, in the case of long-run stable equilibrium, Y does not necessarily approach $\bar{Y}$ from the same direction as that from which A approaches $\bar{A}$. If $p - w$ is negative, $i.e.$, if the level of assets has a greater effect on the rate of investment than on the rate of consumption (the "effect" measured in terms of a given level of income), Y is below $\bar{Y}$ when A is above $\bar{A}$ and vice versa, so that when A rises toward $\bar{A}$, Y descends toward $\bar{Y}$. If $p - w$ is positive, $\Delta Y/\Delta A$ is positive and both Y and A ascend or descend toward their respective equilibrium values. It also follows that the rate of investment rises toward zero or falls toward zero according as A falls or rises toward $\bar{A}$, since I must be positive if A rises, negative if A falls, and in either case I approaches zero as A approaches any fixed value.

Just as in equation (8) $\dot{A}$ was expressed in terms of $A - \bar{A}$, so may we also express all variables in terms of differences from long-run equilibrium values. If the reader does so he will find that the relative rates of change of all these differences over time are equal. That is to say, using $\mathbf{Y}$, $\mathbf{I}$, and $\mathbf{A}$ to denote $Y - \bar{Y}$, $I - \bar{I}$, and $A - \bar{A}$, we have

(12) $$\frac{\dot{\mathbf{A}}}{\mathbf{A}} = \frac{\dot{\mathbf{Y}}}{\mathbf{Y}} = \frac{\dot{\mathbf{I}}}{\mathbf{I}} = v\left(\frac{p-w}{1-b-v}\right) - w$$

It is interesting to note from this that the rate of investment grows or declines at the same relative rate as does the value of total assets. Thus if the rate of investment (measured, say, as an annual rate) is equal to 5 per cent of total assets, then the rate of increase of the rate of investment is also (measured on an annual basis) 5 per cent of current investment. This follows from the fact that if $\mathbf{I} = k\mathbf{A}$, $\dot{\mathbf{I}} = k\dot{\mathbf{A}} = k\mathbf{I}$.

In the event that long-run equilibrium is unstable, equations (12) give us the relative rate of continuous growth (or decline) of the values of the variables, when the variables are measured as differences from their (unstable) equilibrium values. (Note that a positive relative rate implies an increasing distance from the zero point, *i.e.*, from the equilibrium value; a negative relative rate means a decreasing difference.)

The Acceleration Principle

The "acceleration principle" is the name ordinarily given to a relationship between the rate of investment and the change in the level of national income.* The rationale of such a relationship is that to each level of national income there corresponds an appropriate stock of productive assets, that a change over time in the level of income entails a corresponding change in the appropriate stock of productive assets, and that the rate of investment—being itself the rate of change over time of the stock of assets— consequently reflects the difference between the actual and the appropriate sizes of the stock of assets. If the level of income remains constant over a sufficient period of time, assets will accumulate via the rate of investment toward their normal or appropriate relationship to income and, as assets approach that normal value, investment will taper off and disappear, or taper off to some value reflecting that part of investment not subject to interpretation according to the principle of acceleration.

Assuming, then, that assets once bear their "normal" relation to national income, any change in the level of income will induce a rate of investment geared not to the absolute level of income but to the difference between the original and the new levels, since it is that difference which determines the required accumulation of assets. While, at any given point in time, investment is thus geared to the level of income—in the sense that alternative levels of income entail different rates of investment— nevertheless, in a more fundamental sense, it is a comparison of current with past income which determines the rate of investment. And a general formula relating the rate of investment to the current level of income cannot describe the relationship; any particular formula valid at any particular time requires, as a parameter of the equation, the actual stock of assets and consequently, assuming that stock geared to the prior level of income, the prior level of income.

Thus the relationship expressed by the principle of acceleration is inherently a dynamic relationship, for the investment equation expresses a relationship between the rate of change of assets and the actual values of income and assets.

* Cf. J. M. Clark, "Business Acceleration and the Law of Demand: a Technical Factor in Economic Cycles," *Journal of Political Economy*, vol. 25, p. 217, reprinted in *Readings in Business Cycle Theory*, Philadelphia, 1944.

We may build up our investment equation as follows. First we postulate the asset-income relationship toward the satisfaction of which investment is oriented. For this relationship we write

$$(13) \qquad\qquad A' = h + kY$$

where we use A' rather than A in order to allow expressly that the value of A may differ from its "normal" or "appropriate" value. Next we suppose investment geared to the difference between actual assets, A, and that value which would be normal at the current level of income,

$$(14) \qquad\qquad I = R(A' - A)$$

This formula assumes, for algebraic simplicity, that the rate of investment is proportionate to the difference between actual and normal assets—normal always being understood, it must be emphasized, in relation to the *current* level of income. If, now, we combine equations (13) and (14) we obtain

$$(15) \qquad\qquad I = Rh + RkY - RA$$

What we obtain is a formula identical in structure with that already analyzed, namely a linear relation between the rate of investment and the values of income and total assets. All we have to do is write $w = R$, $u = Rh$, and $v = Rk$ to obtain equation (2) of the present chapter.

Thus, so far as this formulation is concerned, we have already analyzed the implications of the acceleration principle. If we wish to analyze it in the absence of the asset-consumption effect, we have only to put the parameter p equal to zero in equation (1) and everywhere else it occurs and we have behind us the analysis of the problem of acceleration.

Now, however, that we have identified the origin, or a possible origin, of the type of relationship expressed earlier by equation (2), we may go on to build up more complex behavior equations, utilizing the argument of this section and equations (13) and (14) for the purpose. In particular we may investigate the implications of a lag in the response of investment.

Let us postulate that investment requires planning, and that plans require time to be set into operation, so that the rate of investment fails to be continuously geared to the difference $A' - A$ in the manner expressed by (14). The rate of investment is taken to adjust always toward its "normal" rate, as given by (14), although at any moment it may be greater or less than $R(A' - A)$, time being required to raise or lower the rate of construction of productive facilities. We shall consequently revise equation (14) to read

$$(16) \qquad\qquad I' = R(A' - A)$$

where I' now represents the "normal" rate of investment appropriate to any discrepancy between A and A', but where we expressly allow the actual rate of investment, I, to differ from the normal rate, I'. The actual rate of investment then follows a relationship of the form

(17) $$\dot{I} = r(I' - I)$$

Thus the rate of investment adjusts over time toward I' at a rate proportionate to the difference between I and I'. Again we choose a fixed proportionate rate of adjustment for purposes of algebraic convenience. It must still be recognized—even though it does not appear explicitly in equation (17) as written—that A' and I' depend on the current level of income; the most interesting part of the problem arises from the fact that one additive component of the national income is the rate of investment, I.

For convenience we shall assume again that the national income can be represented by the simple identity

(18) $$Y = C + I$$

where C may be interpreted to include consumption, government expenditure, and even the net balance of exports over imports, it being assumed that a sufficient representation of the behavior of all those income components is

(19) $$C = a + bY + pA$$

That is, government expenditure, etc., is taken to be either constant or else determined solely by the current values of Y and A; and we do not concern ourselves with the separate values of the components of C.

We assume (19) to hold without lag; the problem could be complicated by assuming for C a rate of adjustment toward its equation value similar to the rate of adjustment of I. Since the essence of the problem is to be an investment lag, we shall leave out any hypothesis of consumption lag.

We require one more concept before putting our equations together, namely the identity of $\dot{I}$ in terms of A. It should be noted that $\dot{I}$ stands in the same relation to I that $\dot{A}$ does to A, also that I is $\dot{A}$. Thus $\dot{I}$ is the rate of change over time of the rate of change of A over time. We might express this by putting another dot over $\dot{A}$; this we shall do by writing*

* The relationship of $\ddot{A}$ to $\dot{A}$ and A may be made more clear by an analogy which uses the concept of "acceleration" in its more familiar context. Writing D for the distance of a car from its starting point, the car's speed may be denoted by $\dot{D}$, the rate of change over time of the car's distance. The car's rate of acceleration is the rate of change of its speed; using S for speed we have acceleration given by $\dot{S}$. Since, however, $S = \dot{D}$ we have $\dot{S} = \ddot{D}$. We must be careful to measure $\dot{S}$ and $\dot{D}$ in terms of the same time unit, else a correction is necessary. If speed is measured in miles per hour, and acceleration is measured as the change in miles per hour per second, $\dot{S}$ will equal 3,600 times $\ddot{D}$. In the text it is assumed that adjustment rate parameters are all expressed in terms of the basic accounting period over which Y, C, and I are measured.

(20) $$\dot{I} = \ddot{A}$$

Substituting (19) into (18) yields, as a "current" solution for Y in terms of I and A,

(21) $$Y = \frac{a + I + pA}{1 - b}$$

Equation (21) represents a "partial" solution, even in the static sense, for the value of I is left undetermined. Next we substitute (21) into (13) obtaining an expression for A' in terms of I and A; this expression for A' is inserted in (16) to obtain I' in terms of I and A; and finally this in turn is inserted into (17) to obtain

(22) $\dot{I} = \ddot{A} = r[R(h + kY - A) - I]$

$$= rR\left(h + \frac{ka}{1-b}\right) + r\left(\frac{Rk}{1-b} - 1\right)\dot{A} + rR\left(\frac{kp}{1-b} - 1\right)A$$

$$= \alpha + \beta\dot{A} + \gamma A$$

Thus we obtain, finally, a linear relationship between the values of A, $\dot{A}$, and $\ddot{A}$. What we have is called a "second-order differential equation"; its interpretation will depend, in the present chapter, on outside information. The Appendix will outline its explicit analysis; for the present we shall again pose a general question of the sort posed in the previous chapter: if there is any variable whose rate of change behaves in the general manner expressed by equation (22), how does the path of that variable over time depend on the values of the three parameters α, β, and γ? The answer is that the possible paths over time are those described in the preceding chapter; the conditions for stable equilibrium are*

---

* Although no general proof of these conditions is offered in the present chapter, the following considerations may *suggest their plausibility*. Let us concentrate on the case of steady approach to equilibrium without oscillation. We suppose that A exceeds $\bar{A}$ and is returning to $\bar{A}$, coming continuously closer and closer to $\bar{A}$. It follows that $\dot{A}$ must be negative; it further follows that $\dot{A}$ must be *increasing* as A decreases, *i.e.*, $\dot{A}$ is negative and approaching zero. (If it does not approach zero, A will cross $\bar{A}$ when it reaches that value.) Thus with positive A, negative $\dot{A}$, $\ddot{A}$ must be positive. According to equation (22) either γ is positive or β is negative, then, for stable, nonoscillatory equilibrium; for if γ were negative *and* β were positive both $\beta\dot{A}$ and γA would be negative and the value of $\ddot{A}$ could not be positive. We shall now show that γ must be negative, consequently that β must also be negative.

Suppose that the variable A is initially in equilibrium, that is, $A = \bar{A}, \dot{A} = \ddot{A} = 0$. Now let the value of A arbitrarily increase. If A is ever to return to $\bar{A}$, $\dot{A}$ must become negative; since $\dot{A}$ is initially zero it must sometime decrease. Therefore $\ddot{A}$ must sometime become negative, to indicate decreasing $\dot{A}$. If γ equals zero, no change occurs anywhere and we have "neutral" equilibrium; no tendency for $\ddot{A}$ to

(23) $$\beta < 0$$

(24) $$\gamma < 0$$

And the path will oscillate about the equilibrium value if

(25) $$\beta^2 < -4\gamma$$

The equilibrium value is obviously given by

(26) $$\bar{A} = -\frac{\alpha}{\gamma}$$

since it must be a value, satisfying equation (22), such that both $\dot{A}$ and $\ddot{A}$ are zero. It may be noted that if condition (25) is met, *i.e.*, if the path is oscillatory, γ must be negative (since β^2 is necessarily positive whatever the value of β) and the oscillations converge on $-\alpha/\gamma$ or swing wider and wider about that value according as β is negative or positive.

Conditions (23), (24), and (25) apply to any variable whose rate of change behaves in the manner expressed by (22). To apply these criteria to the particular problem before us we translate them into terms of the original parameters, obtaining as the stability conditions

(27) $$Rk < 1 - b$$

(28) $$kp < 1 - b$$

The condition for oscillatory behavior is

(29) $$r\left(\frac{Rk}{1-b} - 1\right)^2 < 4R\left(1 - \frac{kp}{1-b}\right)$$

[Since r and R are assumed to be positive they have been partly canceled out of (27) and (28) without changing the direction of inequality.]

---

change from zero, hence no tendency for $\dot{A}$ to change from zero, hence no tendency for A to move again one way or the other. Thus γ must be positive or negative. If γ is positive, $\ddot{A}$ increases and the value of $\dot{A}$ becomes positive so that A moves upward, away from equilibrium. $\dot{A}$ cannot ever become negative—as it must if A is to move toward equilibrium—because if it ever did become zero, on its way toward a negative value, $\ddot{A}$ would become at once positive according to (22) and so $\dot{A}$ would again become positive. Thus A cannot move toward equilibrium unless $\dot{A}$ becomes negative at some point, and $\dot{A}$ cannot become negative until $\ddot{A}$ has become negative, which it cannot if γ is positive. Thus stability without oscillation requires γ negative. Since we have seen that either β must be negative or γ positive, and since γ is necessarily negative according to this paragraph, β must be negative. Thus we have the conditions of (23) and (24) for this one stable case.

The equilibrium value of A is

$$(30) \qquad \bar{A} = -\frac{\alpha}{\gamma} = \frac{ka + h(1 - b)}{1 - b - kp}$$

And the value of $\bar{Y}$ may be obtained from either (13) or (21), putting $A' = A$ and $I = 0$,

$$(31) \qquad \bar{Y} = \frac{\bar{A} - h}{k} = \frac{a + p\bar{A}}{1 - b} = \frac{a + ph}{1 - b - kp}$$

We observe at once that the denominator of $\bar{A}$ or $\bar{Y}$ is positive if the equilibrium is stable. We may consequently derive incremental ratios such as $\Delta\bar{Y}/\Delta a$, $\Delta\bar{A}/\Delta a$, etc., of unequivocal sign, since the denominator is positive, since $1 - b$ is necessarily positive also if k is positive, and since we may certainly take k to be positive. The sign of $\Delta\bar{A}/\Delta h$ is similarly positive; that of $\Delta\bar{Y}/\Delta h$ has the sign of p.

We may, in the interpretation of the stability conditions, relate each of the two conditions to a stability concept. First let us eliminate the time lag in the adjustment of I; i.e., let us consider r very great and replace equations (16) and (17) with equation (14). This step reduces the system to that analyzed in the previous section. Putting A equal to some fixed value yields a static solution whose stability condition may be found to be identical with (27), the denominator of the static solution for Y in that case being $1 - b - Rk$. Thus condition (27) is akin to "short-run" stability, i.e., to the dynamic compatibility of the static equations in the absence of the investment lag.

Still using (14) in place of (16) and (17), i.e., still working with the reduced system of the preceding section, we can identify condition (28) as the condition for "long-run" stability of equilibrium, where long-run equilibrium refers of course to $\dot{A} = \dot{Y} = 0$. For if the parameters of (15) be used in place of those of equation (2), condition (9) becomes

$$(32) \qquad \frac{v(p - w)}{1 - b - v} - w = \frac{Rk(p - R)}{1 - b - Rk} - R < 0$$

which reduces to $kp < 1 - b$.

Thus the two stability conditions are identical with those of the preceding section in which investment was assumed to satisfy (14) without lag. One is the condition of short-run stability of the static equations, the other is the condition of long-run approach toward fixed values of the variables, in the absence of investment lag.

Since instantaneous satisfaction of equation (14) makes the present system identical with the one already analyzed, and since by taking the value of r large enough we may make the investment lag as small as we please, it follows that we can guarantee the absence of oscillation by taking the value of r great enough, for oscillation was not a possible pattern in the reduced system of equations. Looking at (29) we see that this deduction is consistent with the stated condition for oscillation: r multiplies a squared quantity, therefore a positive quantity, on the left-hand side, and does not occur on the right; we can make the left-hand side as great as we please by taking r large enough, thereby violating the condition for oscillation.

It also follows that if kp exceeds $1 - b$, and the latter is positive, the path is steadily away from equilibrium rather than oscillatory, for the right-hand side of (29) is then negative while the left-hand side is necessarily positive and the condition for oscillation cannot possibly be met.

If, however, the system is stable, we can guarantee oscillation by taking R large enough; on the left-hand side as we raise the value of R the value of the squared quantity approaches zero, on the right-hand side a positive quantity increases, and we can consequently make the left-hand side smaller than the right by taking R large enough. In fact, if kp is less than $1 - b$, we may take R so small as to guarantee stability without oscillation, then raise R to yield stability with oscillation, and finally raise R again to make the system unstable and oscillatory. For at $R = 0$, (27) is met and (29) violated; at $R = (1 - b)/k$ the system becomes unstable and (29) is met; for some value of R in between the system is stable but (29) can be met.

If we put $k = 0$, so that assets and investment become independent of the level of income, the stability condition is simply that $1 - b$ be positive. In that case there is oscillation or not according as r is less than or greater than $4R$. By taking k large enough we can make the system unstable. If R is greater than p, the left side of (29) can be made smaller than the right without violating the stability condition and we can have stable oscillation whatever the value of r. If R is less than p the right-hand side of (29) can be made less than the left without violating the stability condition and we can consequently have stable nonoscillation whatever the value of r, by choosing an appropriate value of k. (In either of these cases we may think of putting k equal to $(1 - b)/R$ or $(1 - b)/p$ and then decreasing it by a very small amount to meet the stability condition.)

Before leaving the continuous-adjustment case there are two matters of interpretation yet to be considered. The first involves the comparison of R and p. We have already seen that equation (14) is conceptually identical with equation (2), *i.e.*, that either involves a linear relation of I with Y and A. We may similarly throw equation (1) into the general form of (14). For let us suppose that to each level of income there corresponds some "equilibrium" level of assets from the consumption-saving point of view; that is, *to each level of income* there corresponds some quantity of wealth which would determine a zero rate of saving. Let us denote this level of assets by A'', and relate it to income by

$$(33) \qquad\qquad A'' = m + nY$$

We now define the rate of saving, S, as $Y - C$, and postulate as our consumption-income equation

$$(34) \qquad\qquad S = Y - C = p(A'' - A)$$

From (33) and (34) we obtain

$$(35) \qquad\qquad C = -pm + (1 - pn)Y + pA$$

By letting $a = -pm$ and $b = (1 - pn)$ we have from (35) our original consumption equation (1) in terms of Y and A. The stability conditions are, in terms of the parameters of (35),

$$(36) \qquad\qquad Rk < pn$$

$$(37) \qquad\qquad k < n$$

In the lagless system, i.e., using (14) rather than the adjustment rate equation for investment, the short-run stability condition is $pn > Rk$ for dynamic compatibility of the static equations, and the long-run equilibrium is stable if $n > k$.

The second point of interpretation has to do with the relation of the analysis of this chapter to that of the preceding chapter. There is substantial similarity between the "acceleration-principle" formulation of this chapter and the inventory-adjustment problem treated in Chap. 17. Essentially there was postulated in each case a relation of assets to income or to a component of income, and investment was considered to adjust toward a value which was geared to the discrepancy between actual total assets and the "equilibrium" value of assets corresponding to current income. The results of the two analyses differ slightly; their similarity is apparent by even casual inspection of, e.g., the stability conditions. In the present chapter one stability condition, (27), was that $1 - b - Rk$ should be positive; in Chap. 17 the comparable stability condition [equation (19) of that chapter] was that $1 - b - bRk$ should be positive. The similarity is apparent.

It may be well to note, consequently, how the one problem differs from the other. First, the present chapter relates total assets to national income; in Chap. 14 total assets (which in that case were composed exclusively of inventory) were related only to the value of consumption. Second, in the present chapter the value of I adjusts toward I' at a rate proportional to $I' - I$; in the preceding chapter it was not the value of $\dot{I}$ but the value of P_c which adjusted at a rate proportional to the difference between actual P_c and the normal rate of P_c. There is this difference: when P_c adjusted, so did S_c, and the actual rate of change of $\dot{I}$ was less than that of P_c, so that $\dot{I}$ adjusted at a slower rate than P_c, slower by an amount depending on the parameter b, since the rate of change of S_c was involved at the same time. These differences account for the lack of identity in the results. Nevertheless, both may be considered cases of the "acceleration principle"; indeed, the term is used with respect to the inventory component of assets as well as with respect to the durable component.

Before closing the chapter there are two extensions of the analysis which may be outlined. One is the treatment of the discrete adjustment case, utilizing an investment equation of the form

$$(38) \qquad I(t) = I(t - 1) + r[I'(t - 1) - I(t - 1)]$$

$$= (1 - r)I(t - 1) + rR[A'(t - 1) - A(t - 1)]$$

$$= (1 - r)I(t - 1) + rRkY(t - 1) - rRA(t - 1)$$

Putting $Y(t - 1)$ equal to $[a + bY(t - 1) + pA(t - 1) + I(t - 1)]$ in equation (38) then yields an equation relating $Y(t)$ to $Y(t - 1)$ and $Y(t - 2)$ or, alternatively, relating $A(t)$ to $A(t - 1)$ and $A(t - 2)$. These could then be analyzed by the method developed in Chap. 17; the general stability conditions and conditions for oscillation given in that chapter can be applied to the parameters of these equations.

Another extension of the present analysis would make it even closer to the inventory analysis. This extension involves the inclusion of a "depreciation" equation. The investment equations used in this chapter relate to *net* investment, *i.e.*, gross investment minus the depreciation of assets. The definition of A as the cumulative sum of past investment, *i.e.*, the identity $I = \dot{A}$, makes necessary the identification of investment as a net concept. There are perhaps two reasons why gross investment might be a more useful concept to utilize in the present analysis. One would be an empirical reason; we may wish to restrict the size of a negative value for I, not considering economically meaningful any negative value of gross investment, thus not considering sensible any negative value of net investment greater than the value of depreciation.

The other reason for using gross investment in the analysis would be to allow a relation between depreciation and the values of the other variables, in particular to relate depreciation to the value of national income to suggest that the *use* of assets in production influences the rate of depreciation. If we wished to remodel the analysis along these lines we should interpret I as gross investment, let D denote depreciation, and define $\dot{A}$ as

$$(39) \qquad\qquad \dot{A} = I - D$$

We should then insert the relation

(40) $$D = e + dY$$

and revise the national-income identity to read

(41) $$Y = C + I - D$$

We now interpret equation (17) to relate to gross investment; the rate of change of net investment now depends on what happens to depreciation and that in turn depends on what happens to income as investment changes. The general conclusions can be deduced in the fashion already familiar; the most interesting point about this depreciation case is that, if investment is slow to adjust, a rise in the level of income may cause a diminution of assets via depreciation before investment responds, and the possibility of oscillation is enhanced.

One final point: In the inventory case the combination of our equations led to a solution composed of two equations, one relating $\dot{Y}$ to A and Y, the other relating $\dot{A}$ to Y (using $\dot{A}$ in place of the letter I used there). In the present chapter we obtained a single equation relating $\ddot{A}$ to $\dot{A}$ and A. This difference in the form of our solution is not essential, and does not signify any difference in the structure of the problem. That either system has the same structure as the other may be demonstrated by the following manipulations. Let there be two equations such as the following:

(42) $$\dot{X} = \mathbf{A} + \mathbf{B}X + \mathbf{C}Y$$

(43) $$\dot{Y} = \text{a} + \text{b}Y + \text{c}X$$

From these we may derive an equation relating $\ddot{X}$ to $\dot{X}$ and X and one relating $\ddot{Y}$ to $\dot{Y}$ and Y. For from (42), for example,

(44) $$\ddot{X} = \mathbf{B}\dot{X} + \mathbf{C}\dot{Y}$$

which follows from the fact that over any period of time,

$$\Delta \dot{X} = \mathbf{B}\,\Delta X + \mathbf{C}\,\Delta Y$$

if equation (42) is satisfied. Substituting (43) into (44) we have

(45) $$\ddot{X} = \mathbf{B}\dot{X} + \mathbf{C}\text{a} + \mathbf{C}\text{b}Y + \mathbf{C}\text{c}X$$

To eliminate the term in Y we may multiply equation (42) by b and subtract from both sides

(46) $$\ddot{X} - \text{b}\dot{X} = (\mathbf{B}\dot{X} + \mathbf{C}\text{a} + \mathbf{C}\text{b}Y + \mathbf{C}\text{c}X) - (\text{b}\mathbf{A} + \text{b}\mathbf{B}X + \text{b}\mathbf{C}Y)$$

and finally, canceling out the term in Y,

(47) $$\ddot{X} = (\mathbf{C}\text{a} - \text{b}\mathbf{A}) + (\mathbf{B} + \text{b})\dot{X} + [\mathbf{C}\text{c} - \mathbf{B}\text{b}]X$$

The same may be done for $\ddot{Y}$; the resulting equation in terms of $\dot{Y}$ and Y will be found to have the same coefficients, $\mathbf{B} + \text{B}$ and $\mathbf{C}\text{c} - \mathbf{B}\text{b}$, as is evident from the symmetry of those coefficients.*

The Appendix will present the outline of the mathematical analysis of equations of the form of (47) and their stability conditions.†

* If the reader looks again at inequalities (16), (17), and (18) of the preceding chapter, he will see that the conditions for stability and the condition for oscillation are, in view of (47) of this chapter, consistent with inequalities (23), (24), and (25) of the present chapter.

† In connection with this chapter the following articles will be found especially interesting: P. A. Samuelson, "Interaction between the Multiplier Analysis and the Principle of Acceleration," *Review of Economic Statistics*, vol. 21, p. 75, reprinted in *Readings in Business Cycle Theory*, p. 261, Philadelphia, 1944; R. M. Goodwin, "Secular and Cyclical Aspects of the Multiplier and the Accelerator," Chap. V of *Income, Employment and Public Policy, Essays in Honor of Alvin H. Hansen*, p. 108, New York, 1948; E. D. Domar, "Expansion and Employment," *American Economic Review*, vol. 37, p. 34, and "The 'Burden of the Debt' and the National Income," *American Economic Review*, vol. 34, p. 798.

APPENDIX

DERIVATION OF STABILITY CONDITIONS

In Chaps. 15, 17, and 18 conditions for the stability of certain general types of dynamic equation systems were asserted but not demonstrated.* This Appendix will outline the derivation of those stability conditions.

There are two cases to be considered, the case of "continuous variation" of the variables, and the case of "discrete" or "periodic" variation. The analyses of the two cases are analogous. The continuous case requires some use of the calculus—specifically it requires recognition of the derivative of an "exponential" or "logarithmic" function; the periodic case requires, for the outline which will be given here, no mathematics additional to what has been required throughout this book. We shall consequently deal first with the periodic case in order that the general nature of the analysis of the continuous case may be clear even though the derivation of the required derivative will not be demonstrated.

Periodic Case

The periodic case may appear in two forms, either as a simple second-order linear difference equation

$$(1) \qquad Y(t) = AY(t - 1) + BY(t - 2) + C$$

or as two simultaneous first-order difference equations in the form

$$(2) \qquad Y(t) = aY(t - 1) + bX(t - 1) + c$$

$$(3) \qquad X(t) = \alpha X(t - 1) + \beta Y(t - 1) + \gamma$$

The second form may be converted to the first, so that a single analysis is sufficient for both cases.†

* Chapter 15, equations (39) through (44) and related discussion; Chap. 17, equations (22) through (26) and equations (59) through (62), and related discussion; Chap. 18, equations (30) through (33) and related discussion.

† Only "second-order" difference equations will be analyzed in this Appendix, the second order being the highest order required for the stability conditions asserted in Chaps. 15, 17, and 18. More elaborate hypotheses can give rise to difference equations of the third or higher orders; they would be analyzed by the same *method* as is developed in this Appendix. They are more difficult to analyze because they involve, as will be apparent by comparison with the analysis of the second-order equation, analysis of the values of the roots of cubic equations (for the third-order difference equation, *i.e.*, the equation involving four consecutive periods of, or points in, time) or equations of higher order. The same applies to the differential equations, *i.e.*, those in which rates of change are treated as continuous rather than periodic.

Let us first convert equations (2) and (3) to the general form of equation (1). To do this we first rewrite (3) in the equivalent form

(4) $$X(t - 1) = \alpha X(t - 2) + \beta Y(t - 2) + \gamma$$

Next we substitute this expression for $X(t - 1)$ in (2), and beneath it we write the value of $\alpha Y(t - 1)$,

(5) $$Y(t) = aY(t - 1) + b\alpha X(t - 2) + b\beta Y(t - 2) + b\gamma + c$$

(6) $$\alpha Y(t - 1) = \alpha b X(t - 2) + \alpha a Y(t - 2) + \alpha c$$

Subtracting (6) from (5) we have

(7) $$Y(t) - \alpha Y(t - 1) = aY(t - 1) + (b\beta - a\alpha)Y(t - 2) + [b\gamma + c(1 - \alpha)]$$

Transposing (7),

(8) $$Y(t) = (a + \alpha)Y(t - 1) + (b\beta - a\alpha)Y(t - 2) + [b\gamma + c(1 - \alpha)]$$

Thus equations (2) and (3) have been converted to the form of equation (1), with the following relationships among the parameters:

(9) $$A = a + \alpha$$

(10) $$B = (b\beta - a\alpha)$$

(11) $$C = b\gamma + c(1 - \alpha)$$

Second, let us eliminate the "constant," C. If X and Y are stable about their equilibrium values, the deviations of X and Y from their equilibrium values are stable about zero; and if X and Y oscillate about their equilibrium values, the deviations of X and Y from their equilibrium values oscillate about zero. Thus the conclusions reached concerning $Y - \bar{Y}$ and $X - \bar{X}$ can be generalized to X and Y; analysis of the deviations $X - \bar{X}$ and $Y - \bar{Y}$ allows us to dispense with the constant in the equation.

The equilibrium value of Y is the value such that, occurring twice, it occurs a third time (and consequently a fourth, a fifth, etc.). It is therefore a value satisfying

(12) $$Y = AY + BY + C$$

$$= \frac{C}{1 - A - B} = \bar{Y}$$

Rewriting (1),

(13) $$Y - \bar{Y} = A[Y(t - 1) - \bar{Y}]$$
$$+ B[Y(t - 2) - \bar{Y}] + C + A\bar{Y} + B\bar{Y} - \bar{Y}$$

But

(14) $\quad C + A\bar{Y}_{\cdot} + B\bar{Y} = C + (A + B)\left(\dfrac{C}{1 - A - B}\right) = \dfrac{C}{1 - A - B} = \bar{Y}$

Writing, then, y for $Y - \bar{Y}$,

(15) $\qquad\qquad y(t) = Ay(t - 1) + By(t - 2)$

Thus the stability and oscillation of (1) or of (2) and (3) depend on the stability and oscillation of (15) with suitable allowance for the parameter relationships (9) through (11).

Third, we observe that the course of Y (or y) over time is unique once two initial values are given; that is, for any particular values of $y(t - 2)$ and $y(t - 1)$ there is a corresponding unique value to be computed for $y(t)$; and to the given value of $y(t - 1)$ and the unique value computed for $y(t)$ there corresponds a single value of $y(t + 1)$ satisfying the relationship (15), etc. Thus if we can find any formula for y in terms of t which satisfies the general relationship expressed in (15), and can fit that formula in unique fashion to any particular values chosen for $y(t - 1)$ and $y(t - 2)$, we have *the* explicit formula for Y in terms of t.

To find such a formula we *suppose* it to be capable of representation in the form

(16) $\qquad\qquad y(t) = R^t$

where R is a new parameter. This formula yields a geometrical progression for the values of y, *i.e.*, it is of the "compound-interest" type. If R were equal to 2 it would yield values of 1, 2, 4, 8 . . . for y from time zero; if R were equal to $\frac{2}{3}$ it would yield successive values of 1, $\frac{2}{3}$, $\frac{4}{9}$, $\frac{16}{81}$, . . . from time zero on.

Substituting (16) into (15), and transposing,

(17) $\qquad\qquad R^t - AR^{t-1} - BR^{t-2} = 0$

Dividing through by R^{t-2},

(18) $\qquad\qquad . \ R^2 - AR - B = 0$

Solving this quadratic equation for R in terms of A and B,*

(19) $\qquad\qquad R = \dfrac{A}{2} \pm \sqrt{\dfrac{A^2}{4} + B}$

There are thus two values of R which satisfy the relationship, one corre-

---

* This solution for R follows the general solution of a quadratic equation which may be found in any algebra text.

sponding to the plus sign and one corresponding to the minus sign before the radical. Let us denote the two roots of (18) by r and ρ,

$$(20) \qquad r = \frac{A}{2} + \sqrt{\frac{A^2}{4} + B}$$

$$(21) \qquad \rho = \frac{A}{2} - \sqrt{\frac{A^2}{4} + B}$$

In view of the manner of their derivation, it is clear that either $y = r^t$ or $y = \rho^t$ satisfies (15), *i.e.*,

$$(22) \qquad r^t = Ar^{t-1} + Br^{t-2}$$

and similarly for ρ^t*.

It also follows that any weighted sum of r^t and ρ^t satisfies (15) for if (22) holds for both r^t and ρ^t then, for any values of p and q,

$$(23) \qquad pr^t + q\rho^t = Apr^{t-1} + Aq\rho^{t-1} + Bpr^{t-2} + Bq\rho^{t-2}$$
$$= (Apr^{t-1} + Bpr^{t-2}) + (Aq\rho^{t-1} + Bq\rho^{t-2})$$

Equation (23) is identical with the equation obtained by adding left sides and right sides of the two equations, in r and ρ, represented by (22).

Now it is clear that the values of r and ρ depend only on the values of the parameters A and B. They are independent of the particular values of $y(t-1)$ and $y(t-2)$ since they satisfy (15) for any values of $y(t)$, $y(t-1)$, and $y(t-2)$; that is, any weighted sum of r^t and p^t satisfies the general equation (15) with parameters A and B. We have yet, however, to "fit" the weighted sum of r^t and ρ^t to the particular values of $y(t-1)$ and $\dot{y}(t-2)$. We have two arbitrary parameters in (23), p and q; we have two conditions to impose on the weighted sum, namely that it "fit" the two initial values $y(t-2)$ and $y(t-1)$. With two equations and two "variables" we can solve for p and q in terms of $y(t-2)$ and $y(t-1)$, just as already we have solved for r and ρ in terms of A and B. The two equations may be written as

$$(24) \qquad pr^{t-2} + q\rho^{t-2} = y(t-2)$$

$$(25) \qquad pr^{t-1} + q\rho^{t-1} = y(t-1)$$

If we are willing to start counting time from the point at which $y = y(t-2)$ these last two equations may be simplified for computational convenience as

---

* The reader may divide (22) by r^{t-2}, obtaining $r^2 = Ar + B$, and substitute for r the expression given in (20) to check this statement.

(26) $$pr^0 + q\rho^0 = p + q = y(0)$$

(27) $$pr^1 + q\rho^1 = pr + q\rho = y(1)$$

Solving (26) and (27) simultaneously for p and q in terms of r, ρ, $y(0)$, and $y(1)$,

(28)
$$p = \frac{y(1) - q\rho}{r}$$

$$= \frac{y(1) - \rho[y(0) - p]}{r}$$

$$= \frac{y(1) - \rho y(0)}{r - \rho}$$

The value of q is obtained by subtracting this value of p from $y(0)$ according to (26).

Thus we have

(29)
$$y(2) = pr^2 + q\rho^2$$
$$y(3) = pr^3 + q\rho^3$$
$$\cdot \quad \cdot \quad \cdot \quad \cdot \quad \cdot \quad \cdot$$
$$y(t) = pr^t + q\rho^t$$

where the values of r and ρ depend in the manner shown by (20) and (21) on the particular values of the *parameters* A and B, and the values of p and q depend, in the manner shown by (28) and its analogue in terms of q, on the two successive values of y which we choose to specify. We cannot specify more than two values of y since only by coincidence could, for example, $pr^2 + q\rho^2 = k$ where k is some arbitrary value for $y(2)$; and we must specify two if the course of y is to be unique, else we cannot determine the values of p and q.*

Before deriving stability conditions for (29) an important qualification must be made: the above results are without meaning for us if $(A^2/4) + B$ is negative, *i.e.*, if B is negative and $-B$ is greater than $A^2/4$. In that case the value under the radical sign in (20) and (21) is negative and since,

---

* Actually the two specified values of y need not be successive. Equation (27) could be replaced with $pr^6 + q\rho^6 = y(6)$; solution of (26) and (27) for p and q would then be substantially more difficult but logically just as valid. We may as well, however, think of the two arbitrary values as successive since, as of any given point in time, all previous values are history and the latest two values are available; also because we may suppose parameters to have shifted in the past so that the relationships whose stability is under investigation really depend on the two values relevant to the determination of the "next" one in equation (1).

according to the ordinary rules of multiplication, the square of any positive or negative value is positive, there is no square root of a negative value, *i.e.*, no value such that its square is the negative value under the radical. We must make separate provision later for the case of $A^2/4 < -B$.

We now proceed to the stability of the dynamic equation (29). Stability requires that, as the value of t increases, the successive values of y ultimately approach zero. Since r^t is the value of r compounded t times, r^t increases in geometric ratio with t if r exceeds $+1$, diminishes in geometric progression toward zero if r is a positive fraction, remains constant if $r = +1$. If r is negative, alternate values of r^t are of opposite sign since r^t is positive for even values of t (it is then the square of $r^{t/2}$) and negative for odd values of t (it is then r times the square of $r^{(t-1)/2}$) and the alternate values increase in absolute value if $-r$ exceeds $+1$, decrease if r is between zero and -1, are constant if $r = -1$. If r is zero, $pr^t = 0$ for all values of t. Whether pr^t grows or diminishes, whether it oscillates or not, is independent of the value of p; the sign of p determines the algebraic sign of pr^t, but the value of p does not affect the stability of pr^t.

Stability then requires that neither r nor ρ be of absolute value as great as 1. For if, say, r were a fraction while ρ were greater than $+1$ or less than -1, the first term of $pr^t + q\rho^t$ would disappear as t increased and the continuous increase of $q\rho^t$ would make their sum increase forever. Neither may consequently be as great as $+1$ or as small as -1. (If the larger equals $+1$ or -1, y does not diverge further and further but neither does it approach closer to equilibrium.)

First let us suppose A positive. In that case the absolute value of r is greater than that of ρ, since r is the sum, ρ the difference, between two positive terms. It is thus both necessary and sufficient that r, which is positive, be less than $+1$.

(30)
$$r = \frac{A}{2} + \sqrt{\frac{A^2}{4} + B} < +1$$

$$\frac{A^2}{4} + B < \left(1 - \frac{A}{2}\right)^2 = 1 - A + \frac{A^2}{4}$$

$$+ B < 1 - A$$

$$A + B < 1$$

Squaring $1 - (A/2)$ leaves the inequality valid, since $1 - (A/2)$ is necessarily positive. If it were not, $A/2$ would exceed $+1$ and r would consequently exceed $+1$; so if the stability condition is met the operations performed in (30) are valid. We have thus derived as a stability condition that $A + B$ be less than $+1$. The second condition referred to in Chap. 15 is that the value of B should be between $+1$ and -1. If B is negative, $-B$ cannot be as great as $+1$, else it would make $(A^2/4) + B$ negative; and we are *assuming* $(A^2/4) + B$ positive. If B is positive, it cannot be as great as $+1$, else $A + B$ would be greater than $+1$ (still supposing A positive) and could not meet condition (30). Thus *if A is positive*, then $A + B < +1$ and $-1 < B < +1$ for the case of $(A^2/4) + B$ positive.

If A is negative, then the absolute value of ρ is greater than that of r; and the necessary and sufficient condition is that

$$(31) \qquad \rho = \frac{A}{2} - \sqrt{\frac{A^2}{4} + B} > -1$$

Writing A' for $-A$, so that A' is positive, (31) can be rewritten as

$$(32) \qquad \frac{A'}{2} + \sqrt{\frac{A^2}{4} + B} < +1$$

Inequality (32) is identical with (30) except that the negative of A is involved; the conditions for stability derived from (30) apply here to A' and B,

$$(33) \qquad A' + B = B - A < +1; \qquad -1 < B < +1$$

Thus whether A is positive or negative, B must have an absolute value less than 1 for stability, and $A + B$ must be less than $+1$ if A is positive, $-A + B$ must be less than $+1$ if A is negative. Note that A cannot be as great as $+2$ when positive, nor can $-A$ be as great as $+2$ when A is negative. Thus always $-2 < A < +2$, $-1 < B < +1$, and $A + B$ or $-A + B$ is less than 1 according as A is positive or negative. These conditions, which correspond to those asserted in Chap. 17, apply to the case of positive $(A^2/4) + B$.

In the event that $(A^2/4) + B$ is negative (in which case B is necessarily negative, it should be noted), we define the new variable, Θ, as the angle, the cosine of which is equal to $A/(2\sqrt{-B})$, and the sine of which is, accordingly, equal to the square root of $1 + (A^2/4B)$.* That is,

$$(34) \qquad \Theta = \text{arc cos}\left(\frac{A}{2\sqrt{-B}}\right) = \text{arc sin}\sqrt{1 + \frac{A^2}{4B}}$$

We shall demonstrate next that equation (15) is satisfied by the following formula for the value of y in terms of t:

$$(35) \qquad y(t) = (\sqrt{-B})^t[p(\cos t\Theta) + q(\sin t\Theta)]$$

---

* Note that $A^2/4B$ is necessarily a negative fraction in the case under study, and that $A/(2\sqrt{-B})$ is a positive or negative fraction. It should be recalled that, for any angle, Θ, $(\sin \Theta)^2 + (\cos \Theta)^2 = +1$.

Let us consider the three points in time represented by $t = 0$, $t = 1$, and $t = 2$. At time zero the value of $t\Theta$ is zero; since the cosine of zero equals $+1$ and the sine of zero equals zero, and since $(\sqrt{-B})^0 = 1$, we have

(36) $$y(0) = p$$

At time $t = 1$ the value of $t\Theta$ is equal to Θ and

(37) $$y(1) = \sqrt{-B}\left(\frac{pA}{2\sqrt{-B}} + q\sqrt{1 + \frac{A^2}{4B}}\right)$$

Finally, at time $t = 2$ the value of $t\Theta$ is equal to 2Θ and the value of $y(2)$ is given by*

(38) $$y(2) = -B[p(\cos\Theta)^2 - p(\sin\Theta)^2 + 2q(\cos\Theta)(\sin\Theta)]$$

$$= -B\left[p\left(\frac{A^2}{-4B}\right) - p\left(1 + \frac{A^2}{4B}\right) + \left(\frac{qA}{\sqrt{-B}}\right)\sqrt{1 + \frac{A^2}{4B}}\right]$$

The values of $y(0)$, $y(1)$, and $y(2)$ given by equations (36), (37), and (38) satisfy the relationship $y(2) = Ay(1) + By(0)$, as may be verified by multiplying $y(1)$ by A, $y(0)$ by B, and comparing their sum with $y(2)$, observing that $-B/\sqrt{-B} = \sqrt{-B}$. The reader may next perform similar operations to convince himself that

(39) $$(\sqrt{-B})^{t+2}\{p[\cos(t+2)\Theta] + q[\sin(t+2)\Theta]\}$$

$$= A(\sqrt{-B})^{t+1}\{p[\cos(t+1)\Theta] + q[\sin(t+1)\Theta]\}$$

$$+ B(\sqrt{-B})^t\{p[\cos\Theta] + q[\sin\Theta]\}$$

The paper work is rather extensive and will not be shown here. The first step is to divide through by $(\sqrt{-B})^t$, leaving, as coefficients before the brackets, $(\sqrt{-B})^2$, $A\sqrt{-B}$, and $+B$. Then $\cos(t+2)\Theta$ is identified as $(\cos t\Theta)(\cos 2\Theta) - (\sin t\Theta)(\sin 2\Theta)$, and $\sin(t+2)\Theta$ as $(\cos t\Theta)(\sin 2\Theta) + (\cos 2\Theta)(\sin t\Theta)$; and similarly for $\cos(t+1)\Theta$, etc. Cos 2Θ and sin 2Θ are then identified, as before, as $(\cos\Theta)^2 - (\sin\Theta)^2$ and $2(\cos\Theta)(\sin\Theta)$. Finally $\cos\Theta$ is replaced by $A/2(\sqrt{-B})$ and $\sin\Theta$ by $\sqrt{1 + (A^2/4B)}$. The equality is then apparent.

Thus we have, in equation (35), a trigonometric formula for y in terms of t, involving the two parameters A and B (since Θ involves only A and B), which satisfies the general equation (15) when $A^2 + 4B$ is negative. We

---

* This follows from the rules for obtaining the sine or cosine of the sum of two angles, $\cos(a+b) = (\cos a)(\cos b) - (\sin a)(\sin b)$; $\sin(a+b) = (\cos a)(\sin b) + (\sin a)(\cos b)$. In the particular case of (38), $t\theta = 2\theta = (\theta + \theta)$, hence the expression inside the brackets of (38).

have yet to fit this general formula to the two specific initial values chosen for $y(t - 1)$ and $y(t - 2)$. Clearly the two arbitrary parameters p and q allow us to fit the formula to the two initial values; and, in fact, equations (36) and (37) do fit the values of p and q to those of $y(0)$ and $y(1)$.

Again we may argue that the equation obtained by putting $\theta = \text{arc}$ $\cos A/(2\sqrt{-B})$, $p = y(0)$, and q equal to the value for which (37) may be solved after putting $p = y(0)$, is the unique formula. Stability then depends on the value of B alone; the trigonometric function in brackets is a weighted sum of p and q with weights which never exceed the limits $+1$ and -1, since the sine or cosine of no angle lies outside these limits. Thus the controlling factor is the coefficient $(\sqrt{-B})^{t}$, which grows indefinitely or declines to zero according as $\sqrt{-B}$ is greater or less than 1, which it is according as $-B$ is greater or less than 1. Thus the negative value of B must not be absolutely as large as 1. This is the sole stability condition in the oscillatory case; it is identical with one of the stability conditions for the nonoscillatory case, namely that $-1 < B < +1$. The other stability condition for the nonoscillatory case holds automatically in the oscillatory case if B is less than $+1$, since *negative* $A^2 + 4B$ then implies $A + B < 1$ for positive A; $-A + B < 1$ for negative A.

The last point is proved as follows:

$$(40) \qquad A + B \geqslant 1$$

$$A \geqslant 1 - B$$

$$A^2 \geqslant 1 - 2B + B^2 = (1 + 2B + B^2) - 4B$$

$$= (1 + B)^2 - 4B \geqslant -4B$$

since $(1 + B)^2$ is positive (or zero) for any value of B. Thus we may still assert that, if the equations are stable, $A + B < 1$ (or $-A + B < 1$) and $-1 < B < +1$; if either of these conditions fails to hold, the equations are unstable.

We have referred to the case of $A^2 + 4B < 0$ as the "oscillatory" case. The value of y in that case is zero whenever $p(\cos t\theta) = -q(\sin t\theta)$, that is, when $\tan t\theta = -p/q$, or when $t = [\text{arc tan } (-p/q)]/\theta$. During each period that $t\theta$ increases by 360 degrees (or 2π radians) the value of $p(\cos t\theta) + q(\sin t\theta)$ goes through a fixed pattern, and any value of $p(\cos t\theta) + q(\sin t\theta)$ repeats itself after a period of time equal to $\Delta t = 360°/\theta$ (or $2\pi/\theta$ when measured in radians).

(In order that y actually equal zero whenever $\tan t\theta = -p/q$, we should have to treat y as varying continuously during periods, rather than as fixed over the intervals between integral values of t. Then y would equal zero twice in each interval of $\Delta t = 2\pi/\theta$.)

Before leaving this analysis of the second-order difference equation there is one further point to clear up. In the event that $A^2 + 4B = 0$, we have the particular case of $r = \rho = A/2$, without oscillation, as is seen by referring to (20) and (21). In that case we cannot fit the formula $pr^t + q\rho^t$ to two arbitrary values of $y(0)$ and $y(1)$, since $pr^t + q\rho^t = (p + q)r^t = sr^t$ where $s = p + q$ is a single parameter. Having only one parameter to fit, we cannot satisfy two separate conditions by the choice of its value. In that case, however, we can put $y(t) = pr^t + qtr^t$ to obtain a formula which does contain two arbitrary parameters and which satisfies (15). The values of p and q can then be so chosen as to meet the two conditions.*

Both terms of this formula are stable if $r = A/2$ is less than 1 in absolute value; otherwise, they are unstable. In this case the same two stability conditions derived above remain valid, however, since $B = -A^2/4$ is necessarily a negative fraction if $r = A/2$ is a positive or negative fraction; and since $A + B = A - (A^2/4)$ is equal to $1 - [(A - 2)^2/4] < 1$ (where A stands for $-A$ in case A is negative).

It will be noticed that, in the oscillatory case, we did not specify whether the positive or the negative square root of $-B$ was to be employed. It does not matter; as the reader will see if he follows the suggested proof of the formula, radical signs always occur in pairs, as products or quotients, so that the choice is immaterial as long as we are careful to choose consistently either positive or negative values for all square roots.

Continuous Case

We turn next to the case of continuous adjustment of the variables X and Y. As shown already in Chap. 18 [equations (42) to (47)] the case of two simultaneous first-order linear differential equations can be converted to that of a single second-order linear differential equation of the form

(1′) $$\ddot{Y} = A\dot{Y} + BY + C$$

The constant in (1′) can be eliminated by the expression of Y in terms of its deviation from $\bar{Y}$, the equilibrium value of Y. Since the rate of change over time of the difference between the value of Y and any fixed value is equal to the rate of change of Y itself; and since the equilibrium value of Y, denoted by $\bar{Y}$, is equal to $-C/B$ (that being the value of Y consistent with $\dot{Y} = 0$ for which $\ddot{Y} = 0$); we have

(2′) $$\ddot{y} = A\dot{y} + By$$

* $q(t + 2)r^{t+2} = Aq(t + 1)r^{t+1} + Bqtr^t$. Divide through by r^t to obtain $qtr^2 + 2qr^2 = Aqtr + Aqr + Bqt$. Since $r^2 = Ar + B$, $qtr^2 = Aqtr + Bqt$ and the equation becomes $2qr^2 = Aqr$ or $2r = A$ which is already satisfied by the derivation of r.

where the final term $B(-C/B) + C$ is identified as equal to zero. Thus the stability of (2′) is a sufficient subject for the investigation of the stability of any relationships giving rise to a second-order linear differential equation in one variable. [Note, however, that the coefficients of any two simultaneous first-order equations must be converted into terms of A and B in the manner shown in Chap. 18, equations (42), (43), and (47).]

We *suppose* y capable of representation in terms of t in the form

(3′) $$y = Ke^{Rt}$$

Differentiating y twice with respect to t,

(4′) $$\dot{y} = RKe^{Rt}$$

(5′) $$\ddot{y} = R^2Ke^{Rt}$$

Substituting these values in (2′),

(6′) $$R^2Ke^{Rt} = ARKe^{Rt} + BKe^{Rt}$$

Division by Ke^{Rt} and transposition yields

(7′) $$R^2 - AR - B = 0$$

with the two roots

(8′)
$$\begin{cases} r = \dfrac{A}{2} + \sqrt{\dfrac{A^2}{4} + B} \\ \rho = \dfrac{A}{2} - \sqrt{\dfrac{A^2}{4} + B} \end{cases}$$

Again we have a weighted sum: either r or ρ will satisfy (2′) and so, consequently, will a weighted sum with any weights; we consequently write the general formula for y (which is meaningful only if $A^2 + 4B \geqslant 0$),

(9′) $$y = pe^{rt} + qe^{\rho t}$$

The reader may differentiate this expression to demonstrate that it satisfies the condition (2′).

Again, then, we have two free parameters in the general formula, so that the particular values of p and q may be chosen to make (9′) fit any two (simultaneous) initial values of y and $\dot{y}$. If we let $t = 0$ at the initial values of y and $\dot{y}$, we have

(10′) $$y(0) = p + q$$

(11′) $$\dot{y}(0) = rp + \rho q$$

From (10′) and (11′) it is an easy step to the determination of the values of p and q which fit the initial values of y and $\dot{y}$.

Stability of equation (9′) requires that both terms approach zero as t increases; e^{rt} or $e^{\rho t}$ will either increase continuously with t (if r or ρ is positive) or decrease continuously (if r or ρ is negative). Both must tend toward zero if the deviation of Y from $\bar{Y}$ is to approach zero. Thus stability requires r and ρ both negative. Since ρ is less than r (having the minus sign in front of the radical) it is necessary and sufficient that r be negative. Since the second term in r is positive, A must be negative. We have, then,

(12′)
$$r = \frac{A}{2} + \sqrt{\frac{A^2}{4} + B} < 0$$

$$\frac{A^2}{4} + B < \frac{A^2}{4}$$

$$B < 0$$

Thus A and B must both be negative if the deviation of Y from $\bar{Y}$ is to approach zero. (The squaring of $-A/2$ on the right-hand side of the second line of (12′) is valid since $-A/2$ is positive with A negative.)

Next we consider the case of $(A^2/4) + B < 0$, in which case r and ρ have no meaningful interpretations. In this case we can satisfy equation (2′) with the formula

(13′)
$$y = e^{At/2}[p(\cos t\Theta) + q(\sin t\Theta)]$$

where

(14′)
$$\Theta = \sqrt{-\frac{A^2}{4} - B}$$

That this formula satisfies (2′) may be seen from differentiation with respect to t,

(15′)
$$\dot{y} = \left(\frac{A}{2}\right)y + e^{At/2}[\Theta q(\cos t\Theta) - \Theta p(\sin t\Theta)]$$

(16′)
$$\ddot{y} = \left(\frac{A}{2}\right)\dot{y} + e^{At/2}[-\Theta^2 q(\sin t\Theta) - \Theta^2 p(\cos t\Theta)]$$

$$+ \left(\frac{A}{2}\right)e^{At/2}[\Theta q(\cos t\Theta) - \Theta p(\sin t\Theta)]$$

$$= \left(\frac{A}{2}\right)\dot{y} - \Theta^2 y + \left(\frac{A}{2}\right)\left[\dot{y} - \left(\frac{A}{2}\right)y\right]$$

$$= A\dot{y} + By$$

after replacing Θ with its value as given by (14′).

Again we can fit the formula (13′) to any particular initial pair of values for y and $\dot{y}$ through choice of the values of p and q.

Stability in this case depends solely on whether the exponent of e in (13′) is negative; if A is negative, that exponent is negative and the exponential factor of the formula goes to zero with the increase in t; if A is positive the exponential factor increases without bound as t increases. The trigonometric factor represents a fixed pattern of oscillation about zero, and causes the value of y to oscillate about zero, the amplitude increasing with time if A is positive, decreasing with time if A is negative. The "period" of oscillation is given by $\Delta t = 360/\Theta$ or $2\pi/\Theta$ according as the angle is measured in degrees or radians. Thus the period is proportionate to the value of $A^2 + 4B$.

Note that in the oscillatory case it is still true that A and B are both negative if the equilibrium is stable, since $A^2 + 4B$ is negative only when B is negative. Thus the general conditions remain: the equilibrium value of y implicit in equation (2′) is stable if and only if A and B are both negative.

INDEX